Market Risk Analysis
Volume I

Quantitative Methods in Finance

Market Risk Analysis
Volume I

Quantitative Methods in Finance

Carol Alexander

John Wiley & Sons, Ltd

Published in 2008 by   John Wiley & Sons Ltd, The Atrium, Southern Gate, Chichester,
                            West Sussex PO19 8SQ, England

                            Telephone   (+44) 1243 779777

Email (for orders and customer service enquiries): cs-books@wiley.co.uk
Visit our Home Page on www.wiley.com

Other Wiley Editorial Offices

John Wiley & Sons Inc., 111 River Street, Hoboken, NJ 07030, USA

Jossey-Bass, 989 Market Street, San Francisco, CA 94103-1741, USA

Wiley-VCH Verlag GmbH, Boschstr. 12, D-69469 Weinheim, Germany

John Wiley & Sons Australia Ltd, 42 McDougall Street, Milton, Queensland 4064, Australia

John Wiley & Sons (Asia) Pte Ltd, 2 Clementi Loop #02-01, Jin Xing Distripark, Singapore 129809

John Wiley & Sons Canada Ltd, 6045 Freemont Blvd, Mississauga, Ontario, Canada L5R 4J3

Wiley also publishes its books in a variety of electronic formats. Some content that appears in print may not be
available in electronic books.

British Library Cataloguing in Publication Data

A catalogue record for this book is available from the British Library

ISBN 978-0-470-99800-7 (HB)

Typeset in 10/12pt Times by Integra Software Services Pvt. Ltd, Pondicherry, India
Printed and bound in Great Britain by Antony Rowe Ltd, Chippenham, Wiltshire

SKY10091245_111824

To Walter Ledermann

Contents

List of Figures

List of Tables

List of Examples

Foreword

How many children dream of one day becoming risk managers? I very much doubt little Carol Jenkins, as she was called then, did. She dreamt about being a wild white horse, or a mermaid swimming with dolphins, as any normal little girl does. As I start crunching into two kilos of Toblerone that Carol Alexander-Pézier gave me for Valentine's day (perhaps to coax me into writing this foreword), I see the distinctive silhouette of the Matterhorn on the yellow package and I am reminded of my own dreams of climbing mountains and travelling to distant planets. Yes, adventure and danger! That is the stuff of happiness, especially when you daydream as a child with a warm cup of cocoa in your hands.

As we grow up, dreams lose their naivety but not necessarily their power. Knowledge makes us discover new possibilities and raises new questions. We grow to understand better the consequences of our actions, yet the world remains full of surprises. We taste the sweetness of success and the bitterness of failure. We grow to be responsible members of society and to care for the welfare of others. We discover purpose, confidence and a role to fulfil; but we also find that we continuously have to deal with risks.

Leafing through the hundreds of pages of this four-volume series you will discover one of the goals that Carol gave herself in life: to set the standards for a new profession, that of market risk manager, and to provide the means of achieving those standards. Why is market risk management so important? Because in our modern economies, market prices balance the supply and demand of most goods and services that fulfil our needs and desires. We can hardly take a decision, such as buying a house or saving for a later day, without taking some market risks. Financial firms, be they in banking, insurance or asset management, manage these risks on a grand scale. Capital markets and derivative products offer endless ways to transfer these risks among economic agents.

But should market risk management be regarded as a professional activity? Sampling the material in these four volumes will convince you, if need be, of the vast amount of knowledge and skills required. A good market risk manager should master the basics of calculus, linear algebra, probability – including stochastic calculus – statistics and econometrics. He should be an astute student of the markets, familiar with the vast array of modern financial instruments and market mechanisms, and of the econometric properties of prices and returns in these markets. If he works in the financial industry, he should also be well versed in regulations and understand how they affect his firm. That sets the academic syllabus for the profession.

Carol takes the reader step by step through all these topics, from basic definitions and principles to advanced problems and solution methods. She uses a clear language, realistic illustrations with recent market data, consistent notation throughout all chapters, and provides a huge range of worked-out exercises on Excel spreadsheets, some of which demonstrate analytical tools only available in the best commercial software packages. Many chapters on advanced subjects such as GARCH models, copulas, quantile regressions, portfolio theory, options and volatility surfaces are as informative as and easier to understand than entire books devoted to these subjects. Indeed, this is the first series of books entirely dedicated to the discipline of market risk analysis written by one person, and a very good teacher at that.

A profession, however, is more than an academic discipline; it is an activity that fulfils some societal needs, that provides solutions in the face of evolving challenges, that calls for a special code of conduct; it is something one can aspire to. Does market risk management face such challenges? Can it achieve significant economic benefits?

As market economies grow, more ordinary people of all ages with different needs and risk appetites have financial assets to manage and borrowings to control. What kind of mortgages should they take? What provisions should they make for their pensions? The range of investment products offered to them has widened far beyond the traditional cash, bond and equity classes to include actively managed funds (traditional or hedge funds), private equity, real estate investment trusts, structured products and derivative products facilitating the trading of more exotic risks – commodities, credit risks, volatilities and correlations, weather, carbon emissions, etc. – and offering markedly different return characteristics from those of traditional asset classes. Managing personal finances is largely about managing market risks. How well educated are we to do that?

Corporates have also become more exposed to market risks. Beyond the traditional exposure to interest rate fluctuations, most corporates are now exposed to foreign exchange risks and commodity risks because of globalization. A company may produce and sell exclusively in its domestic market and yet be exposed to currency fluctuations because of foreign competition. Risks that can be hedged effectively by shareholders, if they wish, do not have to be hedged in-house. But hedging some risks in-house may bring benefits (e.g. reduction of tax burden, smoothing of returns, easier planning) that are not directly attainable by the shareholder.

Financial firms, of course, should be the experts at managing market risks; it is their métier. Indeed, over the last generation, there has been a marked increase in the size of market risks handled by banks in comparison to a reduction in the size of their credit risks. Since the 1980s, banks have provided products (e.g. interest rate swaps, currency protection, index linked loans, capital guaranteed investments) to facilitate the risk management of their customers. They have also built up arbitrage and proprietary trading books to profit from perceived market anomalies and take advantage of their market views. More recently, banks have started to manage credit risks actively by transferring them to the capital markets instead of warehousing them. Bonds are replacing loans, mortgages and other loans are securitized, and many of the remaining credit risks can now be covered with credit default swaps. Thus credit risks are being converted into market risks.

The rapid development of capital markets and, in particular, of derivative products bears witness to these changes. At the time of writing this foreword, the total notional size of all derivative products exceeds $500 trillion whereas, in rough figures, the bond and money markets stand at about $80 trillion, the equity markets half that and loans half that again. Credit derivatives by themselves are climbing through the $30 trillion mark. These derivative markets are zero-sum games; they are all about market risk management – hedging, arbitrage and speculation.

This does not mean, however, that all market risk management problems have been resolved. We may have developed the means and the techniques, but we do not necessarily understand how to address the problems. Regulators and other experts setting standards and policies are particularly concerned with several fundamental issues. To name a few:

1. How do we decide what market risks should be assessed and over what time horizons? For example, should the loan books of banks or long-term liabilities of pension funds be marked to market, or should we not be concerned with pricing things that will not be traded in the near future? We think there is no general answer to this question about the most appropriate description of risks. The descriptions must be adapted to specific management problems.
2. In what contexts should market risks be assessed? Thus, what is more risky, fixed or floating rate financing? Answers to such questions are often dictated by accounting standards or other conventions that must be followed and therefore take on economic significance. But the adequacy of standards must be regularly reassessed. To wit, the development of International Accounting Standards favouring mark-to-market and hedge accounting where possible (whereby offsetting risks can be reported together).
3. To what extent should risk assessments be 'objective'? Modern regulations of financial firms (Basel II Amendment, 1996) have been a major driver in the development of risk assessment methods. Regulators naturally want a 'level playing field' and objective rules. This reinforces a natural tendency to assess risks purely on the basis of statistical evidence and to neglect personal, forward-looking views. Thus one speaks too often about risk 'measurements' as if risks were physical objects instead of risk 'assessments' indicating that risks are potentialities that can only be guessed by making a number of assumptions (i.e. by using models). Regulators try to compensate for this tendency by asking risk managers to draw scenarios and to stress-test their models.

There are many other fundamental issues to be debated, such as the natural tendency to focus on micro risk management – because it is easy – rather than to integrate all significant risks and to consider their global effect – because that is more difficult. In particular, the assessment and control of systemic risks by supervisory authorities is still in its infancy. But I would like to conclude by calling attention to a particular danger faced by a nascent market risk management profession, that of separating risks from returns and focusing on downside-risk limits.

It is central to the ethics of risk managers to be independent and to act with integrity. Thus risk managers should not be under the direct control of line managers of profit centres and they should be well remunerated independently of company results. But in some firms this is also understood as denying risk managers access to profit information. I remember a risk commission that had to approve or reject projects but, for internal political reasons, could not have any information about their expected profitability. For decades, credit officers in most banks operated under such constraints: they were supposed to accept or reject deals a priori, without knowledge of their pricing. Times have changed. We understand now, at least in principle, that the essence of risk management is not simply to reduce or control risks but to achieve an optimal balance between risks and returns.

Yet, whether for organizational reasons or out of ignorance, risk management is often confined to setting and enforcing risk limits. Most firms, especially financial firms, claim to have well-thought-out risk management policies, but few actually state trade-offs between risks and returns. Attention to risk limits may be unwittingly reinforced by regulators. Of course it is not the role of the supervisory authorities to suggest risk–return trade-offs; so supervisors impose risk limits, such as value at risk relative to capital, to ensure safety and fair competition in the financial industry. But a regulatory limit implies severe penalties if breached, and thus a probabilistic constraint acquires an economic value. Banks must therefore pay attention to the uncertainty in their value-at-risk estimates. The effect would be rather perverse if banks ended up paying more attention to the probability of a probability than to their entire return distribution.

With *Market Risk Analysis* readers will learn to understand these long-term problems in a realistic context. Carol is an academic with a strong applied interest. She has helped to design the curriculum for the Professional Risk Managers' International Association (PRMIA) qualifications, to set the standards for their professional qualifications, and she maintains numerous contacts with the financial industry through consulting and seminars. In *Market Risk Analysis* theoretical developments may be more rigorous and reach a more advanced level than in many other books, but they always lead to practical applications with numerous examples in interactive Excel spreadsheets. For example, unlike 90% of the finance literature on hedging that is of no use to practitioners, if not misleading at times, her concise expositions on this subject give solutions to real problems.

In summary, if there is any good reason for not treating market risk management as a separate discipline, it is that market risk management should be the business of *all* decision makers involved in finance, with primary responsibilities on the shoulders of the most senior managers and board members. However, there is so much to be learnt and so much to be further researched on this subject that it is proper for professional people to specialize in it. These four volumes will fulfil most of their needs. They only have to remember that, to be effective, they have to be good communicators and ensure that their assessments are properly integrated in their firm's decision-making process.

Jacques Pézier

Preface to Volume I

Financial risk management is a new quantitative discipline. Its development began during the 1970s, spurred on by the first Basel Accord, between the G10 countries, which covered the regulation of banking risk. Over the past 30 years banks have begun to understand the risks they take, and substantial progress has been made, particularly in the area of market risks. Here the availability of market data and the incentive to reduce regulatory capital charges through proper assessment of risks has provided a catalyst to the development of market risk management software. Nowadays this software is used not only by banks, but also by asset managers, hedge funds, insurance firms and corporate treasurers.

Understanding market risk is the first step towards managing market risk. Yet, despite the progress that has been made over the last 30 years, there is still a long way to go before even the major banks and other large financial institutions will really know their risks. At the time of writing there is a substantial barrier to progress in the profession, which is the refusal by many to acknowledge just how mathematical a subject risk management really is.

Asset management is an older discipline than financial risk management, yet it remains at a less advanced stage of quantitative development. Unfortunately the terms 'equity analyst', 'bond analyst' and more generally 'financial analyst' are something of a misnomer, since little analysis in the mathematical sense is required for these roles. I discovered this to my cost when I took a position as a 'bond analyst' after completing a postdoctoral fellowship in algebraic number theory.

One reason for the lack of rigorous quantitative analysis amongst asset managers is that, traditionally, managers were restricted to investing in cash equities or bonds, which are relatively simple to analyse compared with swaps, options and other derivatives. Also regulators have set few barriers to entry. Almost anyone can set up an asset management company or hedge fund, irrespective of their quantitative background, and risk-based capital requirements are not imposed. Instead the risks are borne by the investors, not the asset manager or hedge fund.

The duty of the fund manager is to be able to describe the risks to their investors accurately. Fund managers have been sued for not doing this properly. But a legal threat has less impact on good practice than the global regulatory rules that are imposed on banks, and this is why risk management in banking has developed faster than it has in asset management. Still, there is a very long way to go in both professions before a firm could claim that it has achieved 'best practice' in market risk assessment, despite the claims that are currently made.

At the time of writing there is a huge demand for properly qualified financial risk managers and asset managers, and this book represents the first step towards such qualification. With this book readers will master the basics of the mathematical subjects that lay the foundations for financial risk management and asset management. Readers will fall into two categories. The first category contains those who have been working in the financial profession, during which time they will have gained some knowledge of markets and instruments. But they will not progress to risk management, except at a very superficial level, unless they understand the topics in this book. The second category contains those readers with a grounding in mathematics, such as a university degree in a quantitative discipline. Readers will be introduced to financial concepts through mathematical applications, so they will be able to identify which parts of mathematics are relevant to solving problems in finance, as well as learning the basics of financial analysis (in the mathematical sense) and how to apply their skills to particular problems in financial risk management and asset management.

AIMS AND SCOPE

This book is designed as a text for university and professional courses in quantitative finance. It is ideal for readers with university degree in a quantitative discipline, but the level should also be accessible to intelligent and motivated students with an understanding of mathematics at the high school level. No prior knowledge of finance is necessary. For ease of exposition the emphasis is on understanding ideas rather than on mathematical rigour, although the latter has not been sacrificed as it is in some other introductory level texts. Illustrative examples are provided immediately after the introduction of each new concept in order to make the exposition accessible to a wide audience.

Some other books with similar titles are available. These tend to fall into one of two main categories:

- Those aimed at 'quants' whose job it is to price and hedge derivative products. These books, which include the collection by Paul Wilmott (2006, 2007), focus on continuous time finance, and on stochastic calculus and partial differential equations in particular. They are usually written at a higher mathematical level than the present text but have fewer numerical and empirical examples.
- Those which focus on discrete time mathematics, including statistics, linear algebra and linear regression. Among these books are Watsham and Parramore (1996) and Teall and Hasan (2002), which are written at a lower mathematical level and are less comprehensive than the present text.

Continuous time finance and discrete time finance are subjects that have evolved separately, even though they approach similar problems. As a result two different types of notation are used for the same object and the same model is expressed in two different ways. One of the features that makes this book so different from many others is that I focus on *both* continuous and discrete time finance, and explain how the two areas meet.

Although the four volumes of *Market Risk Analysis* are very much interlinked, each book is self-contained. This book could easily be adopted as a stand-alone course text in quantitative finance or quantitative risk management, leaving more advanced students to follow up cross references to later volumes only if they wish. The other volumes in *Market Risk Analysis* are:

Volume II: *Practical Financial Econometrics*

Volume III: *Pricing, Hedging and Trading Financial Instruments*

Volume IV: *Value at Risk Models*.

OUTLINE OF VOLUME I

This volume contains sufficient material for a two-semester course that focuses on basic mathematics for finance or financial risk management. Because finance is the study of the behaviour of agents operating in financial markets, it has a lot in common with economics. This is a so-called 'soft science' because it attempts to model the behaviour of human beings. Human behaviour is relatively unpredictable compared with repetitive physical phenomena. Hence the mathematical foundations of economic and econometric models, such as *utility theory* and *regression analysis*, form part of the essential mathematical toolkit for the financial analyst or market risk manager. Also, since the prices of liquid financial instruments are determined by demand and supply, they do not obey precise rules of behaviour with established analytic solutions. As a result we must often have recourse to *numerical methods* to resolve financial problems. Of course, to understand these subjects fully we must first introduce readers to the elementary concepts in the four core mathematics subjects of calculus, linear algebra, probability and statistics. Besides, these subjects have far-reaching applications to finance in their own right, as we shall see.

The introduction to Chapter 1, *Basic Calculus for Finance*, defines some fundamental financial terminology. Then the chapter describes the mathematics of graphs and equations, functions of one and of several variables, differentiation, optimization and integration. We use these concepts to define the return on a portfolio, in both discrete and continuous time, discrete and continuous compounding of the return on an investment, geometric Brownian motion and the 'Greeks' of an option. The last section focuses on Taylor expansion, since this is used so widely in continuous time finance and all three subsequent volumes of *Market Risk Analysis* will make extensive use of this technique. The examples given here are the delta–gamma–vega approximation to the change in an option price and the duration–convexity approximation to the change in a bond price, when their underlying risk factors change.

Chapter 2, *Essential Linear Algebra for Finance*, focuses on the applications of matrix algebra to modelling linear portfolios. Starting from the basic algebra of vectors, matrices, determinants and quadratic forms, we then focus on the properties of covariance and correlation matrices, and their eigenvectors and eigenvalues in particular, since these lay the foundations for principal component analysis (PCA). PCA is very widely used, mainly in discrete time finance, and particularly to orthogonalize and reduce the dimensions of the risk factor space for interest rate sensitive instruments and options portfolios. A case study in this chapter applies PCA to European equity indices, and several more case studies are given in subsequent volumes of *Market Risk Analysis*. A very good free downloadable Excel add-in has been used for these case studies and examples. Further details are given in the chapter.

Chapter 3, *Probability and Statistics*, covers the probabilistic and statistical models that we use to analyse the evolution of financial asset prices or interest rates. Starting from the basic concepts of a random variable, a probability distribution, quantiles and population and sample moments, we then provide a catalogue of probability distributions. We describe the theoretical properties of each distribution and give examples of practical applications to finance. Stable distributions and kernel estimates are also covered, because they have broad applications to financial risk management. The sections on statistical inference and maximum likelihood lay the foundations for Chapter 4. Finally, we focus on the continuous time and discrete time statistical models for the evolution of financial asset prices and returns, which are further developed in Volume III.

Much of the material in Volume II rests on the *Introduction to Linear Regression* given in Chapter 4. Here we start from the basic, simple linear model, showing how to estimate and draw inferences on the parameters, and explaining the standard diagnostic tests for a regression model. We explain how to detect autocorrelation and heteroscedasticity in the error process, and the causes and consequences of this. Then we use matrix notation to present the general multivariate linear regression model and show how to estimate such a model using both the Excel data analysis tools and the matrix operations in Excel. The chapter concludes with a long survey of applications of regression to finance and risk management, which includes many references to later volumes of *Market Risk Analysis* where the applied regression models are implemented and discussed in finer detail.

Chapter 5 covers *Numerical Methods in Finance*. Iterative methods form the basis for numerical optimization, which has a huge range of applications to finance from finding optimal portfolios to estimating parameters of GARCH models. Extrapolation and interpolation techniques such as cubic splines are illustrated by fitting currency option smiles and yield curves. Binomial lattices are applied to price European and American options consistently with the Black–Scholes–Merton model, and Monte Carlo simulation is applied to simulate correlated geometric Brownian motions, amongst other illustrative examples. As usual, all of these are contained in an Excel workbook for the chapter on the website, more specific details of which are given below.

The presentation in Chapter 6, *Introduction to Portfolio Theory*, follows the chronological development of the subject, beginning with decision theory and utility functions, which were pioneered by Von Neumann and Morgenstern (1947). We describe some standard utility functions that display different risk aversion characteristics and show how an investor's utility determines his optimal portfolio. Then we solve the portfolio allocation decision for a risk averse investor, following and then generalizing the classical problem of portfolio selection that was introduced by Markowitz (1959). This lays the foundation for our review of the theory of asset pricing, and our critique of the many risk adjusted performance metrics that are commonly used by asset managers.

ABOUT THE WEBSITE

My golden rule of teaching has always been to provide copious examples, and whenever possible to illustrate every formula by replicating it in an Excel spreadsheet. Virtually all the concepts in this book are illustrated using numerical and empirical examples, and the Excel workbooks for each chapter may be found on the accompanying website. Simply search for the book on wiley.com and select 'Related Resources' to access the material.

Within these spreadsheets readers may change any parameters of the problem (the parameters are indicated in *red*) and see the new solution (the output is indicated in *blue*). Rather than using VBA code, which will be obscure to many readers, I have encoded the formulae directly into the spreadsheet. Thus the reader need only click on a cell to read the formula. Whenever a data analysis tool such as regression or a numerical tool such as Solver is used, clear instructions are given in the text, and/or using comments and screenshots in the spreadsheet. Hence the spreadsheets are designed to offer tutors the possibility to set, as exercises for their courses, an unlimited number of variations on the examples in the text.

Several case studies, based on complete and up-to-date financial data, and all graphs and tables in the text are also contained in the Excel workbooks on the website. The case study data can be used by tutors or researchers since they were obtained from free internet sources, and references for updating the data are provided. Also the graphs and tables can be modified if required, and copied and pasted as enhanced metafiles into lecture notes based on this book.

ACKNOWLEDGEMENTS

During many years of teaching mathematics at the introductory level I believe I have learned how to communicate the important concepts clearly and without stressing students with unnecessary details. I have benefited from teaching undergraduate students at the University of Sussex from the mid-1980s to the mid-1990s and, for the past 10 years, from teaching master's courses in market risk, volatility analysis and quantitative methods at the ICMA Centre at the University of Reading. The last of these, the core course in quantitative finance, is quite challenging since we often have around 200 students on different master's degrees with very diverse backgrounds. The student feedback has been invaluable, and has helped me develop a skill that I have tried to exercise in writing this book. That is, to communicate worthwhile and interesting information to two very different types of students simultaneously. This way, the book has been aimed at those with a quantitative background but little knowledge of finance *and* those with some understanding of finance but few mathematical skills.

I would also like to acknowledge my PhD student Joydeep Lahiri for his excellent computational assistance and many staff at Wiley, Chichester. These include Sam Whittaker, Editorial Director in Business Publishing, for her unerring faith in my judgement when one book turned into four, and for her patience when other work commitments hampered my progress on the books; the terrific work of Viv Wickham, Project Editor, and her team; and of Caitlin Cornish, Louise Holden and Aimee Dibbens on the editorial and marketing side.

Thanks to my copy editor, Richard Leigh, for using his extraordinary combination of mathematical and linguistic knowledge during his extremely careful copy-editing. With Richard's help my last text book (Alexander, 2001) was virtually error-free.

Many thanks to my dear husband, Professor Jacques Pézier, whose insightful suggestions and comments on the last chapter were invaluable. Any remaining errors are, naturally, his fault. I am indebted to Professor Walter Ledermann for his meticulous proof-reading of the early chapters, during which he spotted many errors. Walter was the supervisor of my PhD and since then he has been a much-valued friend and co-author. I hold him responsible for my (very happy) career in mathematics. Finally, sincere thanks to my new friends Ronnie Barnes and Philippe Derome, for being enthusiastic enough about these books to alert me to the errors and typos in the first printing. Due to their careful and insightful reading I trust that very few errors remain – but, if they do, it is (of course) my sole responsibility.

Basic Calculus for Finance

I.1.1 INTRODUCTION

This chapter introduces the functions that are commonly used in finance and discusses their properties and applications. For instance, the *exponential function* is used to discount forward prices to their present value and the inverse of the exponential function, the natural *logarithmic function* or 'log' for short, is used to compute returns in continuous time. We shall encounter numerous other financial applications of these functions in the subsequent volumes. For instance, the fair price of a *futures* contract is an exponential function of an interest rate multiplied by the spot price of the underlying asset. A standard futures contract is a contract to buy or sell a *tradable asset* at some specified time in the future at a price that is agreed today. The four main types of tradable assets are stocks, bonds, commodities and currencies.

The futures price is a linear function of the underlying asset price. That is, if we draw the graph of the futures price against the price of the underlying we obtain a straight line. But *non-linear functions*, which have graphs that are not straight lines, are also used in every branch of finance. For instance, the price of a bond is a non-linear function of its yield. A *bond* is a financial asset that periodically pays the bearer a fixed *coupon* and is redeemed at maturity at *par* value (usually 100). The *yield* (also called *yield to maturity*) on a bond is the fixed rate of interest that, if used to discount the payments (i.e. the *cash flow*) to their present value, makes the net present value of the cash flow equal to the price of the bond.

Functions of several variables are also very common in finance. A typical example of a function of several variables in finance is the price of an *option*. An option is the right to buy or sell an underlying asset on (or before) a certain time in the future at a price that is fixed today. An option to buy is called a *call option* and an option to sell is called a *put option*. The difference between a futures contract and an option is that the holder of a futures contract is bound to buy or sell at the agreed price, but the holder of the option has the right to buy or sell the asset if he chooses. That is, the holder has the 'option' of exercising their right or not.[1] Early exercise of the option is not possible with a *European option*, but an *American option* or a *Bermudan option* may be exercised before the expiry of the contract. Americans can be exercised at any time and Bermudans can be exercised on selected dates.

After an informal description of the concepts of continuous and differentiable functions we focus on standard techniques for differentiation and integration. Differentiation is a core concept, and in finance the derivatives of a function are commonly referred to as *sensitivities* rather than 'derivatives'.[2] This is because the term *derivative* when used in a financial

---

[1] Hence buying options is not nearly as risky as selling (or *writing*) options.

[2] Derivatives of a function are not *always* called sensitivities in finance. For instance in Chapter I.6 we introduce *utility functions*, which are used to assess the optimal trade-off between risk and return. The first and second derivatives of an investor's utility function tell us whether the investor is risk averse, risk loving or risk neutral.

context refers to a financial instrument that is a contract on a contract, such as a futures contract on an interest rate, or an option on an interest rate swap.[3]

We shall employ numerous sensitivities throughout these volumes. For instance, the first order yield sensitivity of a bond is called the *modified duration*. This is the first partial derivative of the bond price with respect to the yield, expressed as a percentage of the price; and the second order yield sensitivity of a bond is called the *convexity*. This is the second derivative of the bond price with respect to its yield, again expressed as a percentage of the price.

The first and second derivatives of a function of several variables are especially important in finance. To give only one of many practical examples where market practitioners use derivatives (in the mathematical sense) in their everyday work, consider the role of the *market makers* who operate in exchanges by buying and selling assets and derivatives. Market makers make money from the *bid–ask spread* because their *bid price* (the price they will buy at) is lower than their *ask price* (the price they will sell at, also called the *offer price*). Market makers take their profits from the spread that they earn, not from taking risks. In fact they will *hedge* their risks almost completely by forming a *risk free portfolio*.[4] The *hedge ratios* determine the quantities of the underlying, and of other options on the same underlying, to buy or sell to make a risk free portfolio. And hedge ratios for options are found by taking the first and second partial derivatives of the option price.

The pricing of financial derivatives is based on a *no arbitrage* argument. No arbitrage means that we cannot make an instantaneous profit from an investment that has no uncertainty. An investment with no uncertainty about the outcome is called a *risk free investment*. With a risk free investment it is impossible to make a 'quick turn' or an instantaneous profit. However, profits will be made over a period of time. In fact no arbitrage implies that all risk free investments must earn the same rate of return, which we call the *risk free return*.

To price an option we apply a no arbitrage argument to derive a *partial differential equation* that is satisfied by the option price. In some special circumstances we can solve this equation to obtain a formula for the option price. A famous example of this is the *Black–Scholes–Merton formula* for the price of a standard European option.[5] The model price of an option depends on two main variables: the current price of the underlying asset and its *volatility*. Volatility represents the uncertainty surrounding the expected price of the underlying at the time when the option expires. A standard European call or put, which is often termed a *plain vanilla option*, only has value because of volatility. Otherwise we would trade the corresponding futures contract because futures are much cheaper to trade than the corresponding options. In other words, the bid–ask spread on futures is much smaller than the bid–ask spread on options.

Taylor expansions are used to approximate values of non-linear differentiable functions in terms of only the first few derivatives of the function. Common financial applications include the *duration–convexity approximation* to the change in value of a bond and the *delta–gamma approximation* to the change in value of an options portfolio. We also use Taylor expansion to simplify numerous expressions, from the adjustment of Black–Scholes–Merton options

---

[3] *Financial instrument* is a very general term that includes tradable assets, interest rates, credit spreads and all derivatives.
[4] A *portfolio* is a collection of financial instruments, i.e. a collection of assets, or of positions on interest rates or of derivative contracts.
[5] Liquid options are not actually priced using this formula: the prices of all liquid assets are determined by market makers responding to demand and supply.

prices to account for uncertainty in volatility to the stochastic differential equations that we use for modelling continuous time price processes.

Integration is the opposite process to differentiation. In other words, if f is the derivative of another function F we can obtain F by integrating f. Integration is essential for understanding the relationship between continuous probability distributions and their *density functions*, if they exist. Differentiating a probability distribution gives the density function, and integrating the density function gives the distribution function.

This chapter also introduces the reader to the basic analytical tools used in portfolio mathematics. Here we provide formal definitions of the *return* and the *profit and loss* on a single investment and on a portfolio of investments in both discrete and continuous time. The *portfolio weights* are the proportions of the total capital invested in each instrument. If the weight is positive we have a *long position* on the instrument (e.g. we have bought an asset) and if it is negative we have a *short position* on the instrument (e.g. we have 'short sold' an asset or written an option). We take care to distinguish between portfolios that have constant holdings in each asset and those that are rebalanced continually so that portfolio weights are kept constant. The latter is unrealistic in practice, but a constant weights assumption allows one to represent the return on a linear portfolio as a weighted sum of the returns on its constituent assets. This result forms the basis of portfolio theory, and will be used extensively in Chapter I.6.

Another application of differentiation is to the *optimal allocation* problem for an investor who faces certain constraints, such as no short sales and/or at least 30% of his funds must be invested in US equities. The investor's problem is to choose his portfolio weights to optimize his objective whilst respecting his constraints. This falls into the class of constrained optimization problems, problems that are solved using differentiation.

Risk is the uncertainty about an expected value, and a *risk-averse investor* wants to achieve the maximum possible return with the minimum possible risk. Standard measures of portfolio risk are the *variance* of a portfolio and its square root which is called the *portfolio volatility*.[6] The portfolio variance is a quadratic function of the portfolio weights. By differentiating the variance function and imposing any constraints we can solve the optimal allocation problem and find the *minimum variance portfolio*.

Very little prior knowledge of mathematics is required to understand this chapter, although the reader must be well motivated and keen to learn. It is entirely self-contained and all but the most trivial of the examples are contained in the accompanying Excel spreadsheet. Recall that in all the spreadsheets readers may change the values of inputs (marked in red) to compute a new output (in blue).

I.1.2 FUNCTIONS AND GRAPHS, EQUATIONS AND ROOTS

The value of a function of a single variable is written $f(x)$, where f is the *function* and x is the *variable*. We assume that both x and $f(x)$ are real numbers and that for each value of x there is only one value $f(x)$. Technically speaking this makes f a 'single real-valued function of a single real variable', but we shall try to avoid such technical vocabulary where possible. Basically, it means that we can draw a *graph* of the function, with the values x along the horizontal axis and the corresponding values $f(x)$ along the vertical axis, and that this graph

---

[6] Volatility is the annualized standard deviation, i.e. the standard deviation expressed as a percentage per annum.

has no 'loops'. Setting the value of a function $f(x)$ equal to 0 gives the values of x where the function crosses or touches the x-axis. These values of x satisfy the equation $f(x) = 0$ and any values of x for which this equation holds are called the *roots* of the equation.

I.1.2.1 Linear and Quadratic Functions

A *linear function* is one whose graph is a straight line. For instance, the function $f(x) = 3x + 2$ is linear because its graph is a straight line, shown in Figure I.1.1. A linear function defines a linear equation, i.e. $3x + 2 = 0$ in this example. This has a root when $x = -2/3$. Readers may use the spreadsheet to graph other linear functions by changing the value of the coefficients a and b in the function $f(x) = ax + b$.

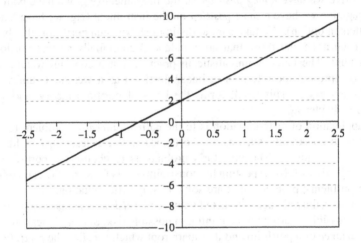

Figure I.1.1 A linear function

By contrast, the function $f(x) = 4x^2 + 3x + 2$ shown in Figure I.1.2 defines an equation with no real roots because the function value never crosses the x-axis. The graph of a general *quadratic function* $f(x) = ax^2 + bx + c$ has a '∩' or '∪' shape that is called a *parabola*:

- If the coefficient $a > 0$ then it has a ∪ shape, and if $a < 0$ then it has a ∩ shape. The size of a determines the steepness of the curve.
- The coefficient b determines its horizontal location: for $b > 0$ the graph is shifted to the left of the vertical axis at $x = 0$, otherwise it is shifted to the right. The size of b determines the extent of the shift.
- The coefficient c determines its vertical location: the greater the value of c the higher the graph is on the vertical scale.

Readers may play with the values of a, b and c in the spreadsheet for Figure I.1.2 to see the effect they have on the graph. At any point that the graph crosses or touches the x-axis we have a real root of the quadratic equation $f(x) = 0$.

A well-known formula gives the *roots of a quadratic equation* $ax^2 + bx + c = 0$ where a, b and c are real numbers. This is:

$$x = \frac{-b \pm \sqrt{b^2 - 4ac}}{2a}.$$

(I.1.1)

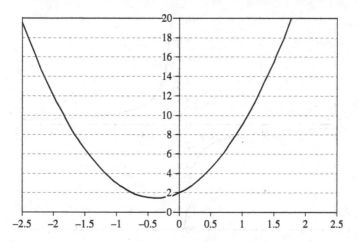

Figure I.1.2   The quadratic function $f(x) = 4x^2 + 3x + 2$

The term inside the square root, $b^2 - 4ac$, is called the *discriminant* of the equation. If the discriminant is negative, i.e. $b^2 < 4ac$, the quadratic equation has no real roots: the roots are a pair of complex numbers.[7] But if $b^2 > 4ac$ there are two distinct real roots, given by taking first '+' and then '−' in (I.1.1). If $b^2 = 4ac$ the equation has two identical roots.

EXAMPLE I.1.1: ROOTS OF A QUADRATIC EQUATION

Find the roots of $x^2 - 3x + 2 = 0$.

SOLUTION   We can use formula (I.1.1), or simply note that the function can be factorized as

$$x^2 - 3x + 2 = (x - 1)(x - 2),$$

and this immediately gives the two roots $x = 1$ and $x = 2$. Readers can use the spreadsheet for this example to find the roots of other quadratic equations, if they exist in the real numbers.

I.1.2.2   Continuous and Differentiable Real-Valued Functions

Loosely speaking, if the graph of a function $f(x)$ has no jumps then $f(x)$ is *continuous function*. A *discontinuity* is a jump in value. For instance the *reciprocal function*,

$$f(x) = x^{-1}, \text{ also written } f(x) = \frac{1}{x},$$

has a graph that has a shape called a *hyperbola*. It has a discontinuity at the point $x = 0$, where its value jumps from $-\infty$ to $+\infty$, as shown in Figure I.1.3. But the reciprocal function is continuous at all other points.

Loosely speaking, if the graph of a continuous function $f(x)$ has no corners then $f(x)$ is a *differentiable function*. If a function is not differentiable it can still be continuous, but if it is not continuous it cannot be differentiable. A differentiable function has a unique *tangent*

---

[7] The *square root function* $\sqrt{x}$ or $x^{1/2}$ is only a real number if $x \geq 0$. If $x < 0$ then $\sqrt{x} = i\sqrt{-x}$, where $i = \sqrt{-1}$ is an *imaginary* or *complex* number.

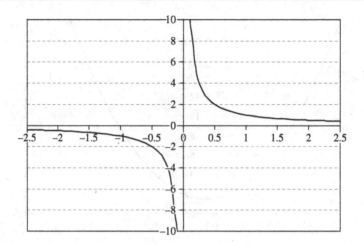

Figure I.1.3   The reciprocal function

line. That is, f is differentiable at x if we can draw only one straight line that touches the graph at x.

Functions often have points at which they are not continuous, or at least not differentiable. Examples in finance include:

- **The pay-off to a simple call option**. This is the function $\max(S - K, 0)$, also written $(S - K)^{+}$, where S is the variable and K is a constant, called the strike of the option. The graph of this function is shown in Figure III.3.1 and it is clearly not differentiable at the point $S = K$.
- **Other option pay-offs**. Likewise, the pay-off to a simple put option is not differentiable at the point $S = K$; more complex options, such as barrier options may have other points where the pay-off is not differentiable.
- **The indicator function**. This is given by

$$1_{\{\text{condition}\}} = \begin{cases} 1 \text{ if the condition is met,} \\ 0 \text{ otherwise.} \end{cases} \qquad (\text{I.1.2})$$

For instance, $1_{\{x>0\}}$ is 0 for non-positive x and 1 for positive x. There is a discontinuity at $x = 0$, so the function cannot be differentiable there.

- **The absolute value function**. This is written $|x|$ and is equal to x if x is positive, $-x$ if x is negative and 0 if $x = 0$. Clearly there is a corner at $x = 0$, so $|x|$ is not differentiable there.

I.1.2.3   Inverse Functions

The inverse function of any real-valued function $f(x)$ is *not* its reciprocal value at any value of x:[8]

$$f^{-1}(x) \neq \frac{1}{f(x)}.$$

---

[8] The reciprocal of a real number a is $1/a$, also written a^{-1}.

Instead

$$f^{-1}(x) = g(x) \Leftrightarrow f(g(x)) = x.$$

That is, we obtain the inverse of a function by reflecting the function in the 45% line, as shown in Figure I.1.4.

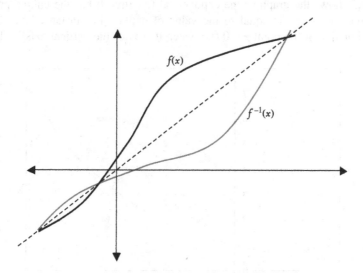

Figure I.1.4   The inverse of a function

I.1.2.4   The Exponential Function

An *irrational number* is a real number that has a decimal expansion that continues indefinitely without ever repeating itself, i.e. without ending up in a cycle, and most irrational numbers are transcendental numbers.[9] Even though there are infinitely many transcendental numbers we only know a handful of them. The ancient Greeks were the first to discover a transcendental number $\pi = 3.14159\ldots$. The next transcendental number was discovered only many centuries later. This is the number $e = 2.7182818285\ldots$.

Just as π is a real number between 3 and 4, e is simply a (very special) real number between 2 and 3. Mathematicians arrived at e by computing the limit

$$e = \lim_{n \to \infty} \left(1 + \frac{1}{n} \right)^n. \tag{I.1.3}$$

---

[9] According to Professor Walter Ledermann: Every *periodic* decimal expansion, that is, an expansion of the form $N.a_1 a_2 \ldots a_n (b_1 b_2 \ldots b_s)(b_1 b_2 \ldots b_s)$ is equal to a *rational* number m/n where m and n are integers and $n \neq 0$. Conversely, every rational number has a periodic decimal expansion. Hence a real number is irrational if and only if its decimal expansion is non-periodic. For example the expansion $\sqrt{2} = 1.414213562\ldots$ is non-periodic. There are two types of irrational number. A solution of a polynomial equation

$$a_0 x^n + a_1 x^{n-1} + \ldots + a_{n-1} x + a_n = 0 \ (a_0 \neq 0)$$

with integral coefficients a_i is called an *algebraic number*. For example $\sqrt{2}$ is an algebraic number because it is a solution of the equation $x^2 - 2 = 0$. An irrational number which is not the solution of any polynomial equation with integral coefficients is called a *transcendental number*. It is obviously very difficult to prove that a particular number is transcendental because all such polynomials would have to be considered.

We can consider the functions 2^x and 3^x where x is any real number, so we can also consider e^x. This is called the exponential function and it is also denoted $\exp(x)$:

$$e^x = \exp(x) = \lim_{n \to \infty}\left(1 + \frac{x}{n}\right)^n. \qquad (I.1.4)$$

Thus $\exp(1) = e$ and $\exp(0) = 1$. Indeed, any number raised to the power zero is 1.

Figure I.1.5 shows the graph of the exponential function. It has the unique property that at every point x its slope is equal to the value of $\exp(x)$. For instance, the slope of the exponential function at the point $x = 0$ (i.e. when it crosses the vertical axis) is 1.

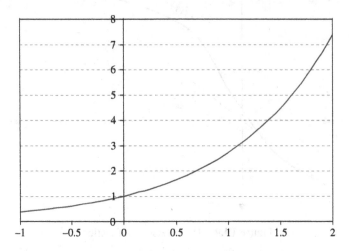

Figure I.1.5 The exponential function

Since e is a real number, $\exp(x)$ obeys the usual *laws of indices* such as[10]

$$\exp(x + y) = \exp(x)\exp(y), \qquad (I.1.5)$$

$$\exp(x - y) = \frac{\exp(x)}{\exp(y)}. \qquad (I.1.6)$$

The exponential function may be represented as a *power series*, viz.,

$$\exp(x) = 1 + x + \frac{x^2}{2} + \frac{x^3}{3!} + \frac{x^4}{4!} + \ldots, \qquad (I.1.7)$$

where $n!$ denotes the *factorial function*:

$$n! = n \times (n - 1) \times (n - 2) \times \ldots \times 3 \times 2 \times 1,$$
$$0! = 1. \qquad (I.1.8)$$

Power series expansions are useful for approximating the value of a function when x is not too large. Thus

$$e = \exp(1) \approx 1 + 1 + \frac{1}{2} + \frac{1}{6} + \frac{1}{24} = 2.708$$

---

[10] For any real numbers a, b and c we have $a^b a^c = a^{b+c}$.

and, for instance,

$$7.389 = \exp(2) \approx 1 + 2 + 2 + \frac{4}{3} + \frac{2}{3} + \frac{4}{15} = 7.267.$$

I.1.2.5 The Natural Logarithm

The inverse of the exponential function is the natural logarithm function, abbreviated in the text to 'log' and in symbols to 'ln'. This function is illustrated in Figure I.1.6. It is only defined for a positive real number x.[11]

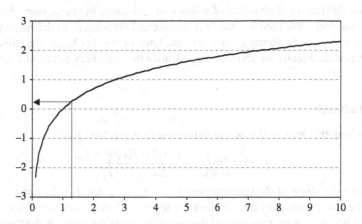

Figure I.1.6 The natural logarithmic function

Notice that $\ln 1 = 0$, and $\ln x < 0$ for $0 < x < 1$. The dotted arrow on the graph shows that the natural logarithm function is approximately linear in the region of $x = 1$. That is,

$$\ln(1 + x) \approx x \text{ when } x \text{ is small.} \tag{I.1.9}$$

More generally, we have the following *power series expansion* for the log function:

$$\ln(1 + x) = x - \frac{x^2}{2} + \frac{x^3}{3} - \frac{x^4}{4} + \ldots \text{ provided} - 1 < x. \tag{I.1.10}$$

The logarithm function is useful for a number of reasons. One property that is important because it often makes calculations easier is that the log of a product is the sum of the logs:

$$\ln(xy) = \ln(x) + \ln(y). \tag{I.1.11}$$

Also,

$$\ln(x^{-1}) = -\ln(x). \tag{I.1.12}$$

Putting these together gives

$$\ln\left(\frac{x}{y}\right) = \ln(x) - \ln(y). \tag{I.1.13}$$

---

[11] This is not strictly true, since we can extend the definition beyond positive real numbers into complex numbers by writing, for negative real x, $\ln(x) = \ln(-x \exp(\pi i)) = \ln(-x) + \pi i$, where the imaginary number i is the square root of -1. You do not need to worry about this for the purposes of the present volumes.

I.1.3   DIFFERENTIATION AND INTEGRATION

The *first derivative* of a function at the point x is the slope of the tangent line at x. All linear functions have a constant derivative because the tangent at every point is the line itself. For instance, the linear function $f(x) = 3x + 2$ shown in Figure I.1.1 has first derivative 3. But non-linear functions have derivatives whose value depends on the point x at which it is measured. For instance, the quadratic function $f(x) = 2x^2 + 4x + 1$ has a first derivative that is increasing with x. It has value 0 at the point $x = -1$, a positive value when $x > -1$, and a negative value when $x < -1$.

This section defines the derivatives of a function and states the basic rules that we use to differentiate functions. We then use the first and second derivatives to define properties that are shared by many of the functions that we use later in this book, i.e. the monotonic and convexity properties. Finally we show how to identify the stationary points of a differentiable function.

I.1.3.1   Definitions

Technically speaking, we can define the derivative of a function f as:

$$f'(x) = \lim_{\Delta x \downarrow 0} \left(\frac{f(x + \Delta x) - f(x)}{\Delta x} \right).$$ (I.1.14)

That is, we take the slope of the chord between two points a distance Δx apart and see what happens as the two points get closer and closer together. When they touch, so the distance between them becomes zero, the slope of the chord becomes the slope of the tangent, i.e. the derivative.

This is illustrated in Figure I.1.7. The graph of the function is shown by the black curve. The chord from P to Q is the dark grey line. By definition of the slope of a line (i.e. the vertical height divided by the horizontal distance), the slope of the chord is:

$$\frac{f(x + \Delta x) - f(x)}{\Delta x}.$$

The tangent line is drawn in light grey and its slope is the derivative $f'(x)$, by definition. Now we let the increment in x, i.e. Δx, get smaller. Then the point Q moves closer to P and

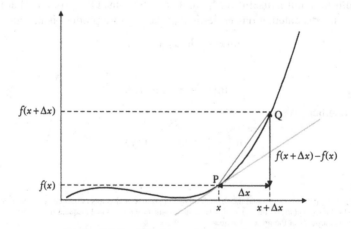

Figure I.1.7   Definition of the first derivative

the slope of the chord gets closer to the slope of the tangent, i.e. the derivative. In the limit, when $\Delta x = 0$, the points P and Q coincide and the slope of the chord, i.e. the right-hand side of (I.1.14), is equal to the slope of the tangent, i.e. the left-hand side of (I.1.14).

Notation and Terminology

- The *second derivative* is the derivative of the derivative, given by

$$f''(x) = \lim_{\Delta x \downarrow 0}\left[\left(\frac{f'(x+\Delta x) - f'(x)}{\Delta x}\right)\right], \tag{I.1.15}$$

  and higher derivatives are defined analogously. If we differentiate the function m times, we denote the mth derivative by $f^{(m)}(x)$.

- We can use the alternative notation $\dfrac{df}{dx}$ for the first derivative $f'(x)$, and more generally the notation $\dfrac{d^m f}{dx^m}$ also stands for the mth derivative.

- Associated with the definition of derivative is the *differential operator d*. The *differential* or *total derivative* of a function $f(x)$ is given by:

$$df(x) = f'(x)\, dx. \tag{I.1.16}$$

The differential operator is used, for instance, in Section I.1.4.5 below to describe the dynamics of financial asset returns in continuous time.

I.1.3.2 Rules for Differentiation

A number of simple rules for differentiation may be proved using the methodology depicted in Figure I.1.7 to calculate the derivatives of certain functions from first principles. These are summarized as follows:

1. **Power**. The derivative of ax^n is nax^{n-1} for any constant a and any (positive or negative) real number n: in other words,

$$\frac{d}{dx}(ax^n) = nax^{n-1}.$$

2. **Exponential**. The derivative of $\exp(x)$ is $\exp(x)$: in other words,

$$\frac{d}{dx}(e^x) = e^x.$$

3. **Logarithm**. The derivative of $\ln x$ is x^{-1}: in other words,

$$\frac{d}{dx}(\ln x) = \frac{1}{x}.$$

4. **Chain rule**. The derivative of a function of another function $f(g(x))$ is the product of the two derivatives, i.e.

$$\frac{d}{dx}f(g(x)) = f'(g(x))g'(x).$$

5. **Sum**. The derivative of a sum is the sum of the derivatives, i.e.

$$\frac{d}{dx}(f(x) + g(x)) = f'(x) + g'(x)$$

6. **Product**. For the derivative of $f(x)g(x)$:

$$\frac{d}{dx}(f(x)g(x)) = f'(x)g(x) + g'(x)f(x)$$

7. **Quotient.** The derivative of the reciprocal of $f(x)$:

$$\frac{d}{dx}\left(\frac{1}{f(x)}\right) = -\frac{f'(x)}{f(x)^2}.$$

More generally, the derivative of a quotient of functions is:

$$\frac{d}{dx}\left(\frac{g(x)}{f(x)}\right) = \frac{f'(x)g(x) - g'(x)f(x)}{f(x)^2}.$$

These rules allow the derivatives of certain functions to be easily computed. For instance, we can use rule 1 to find successive derivatives of $f(x) = x^4$, that is:

$$f'(x) = 4x^3, f''(x) = 12x^2, f'''(x) = f^{(3)}(x) = 24x, f^{(4)}(x) = 24 \text{ and } f^{(5)}(x) = 0,$$

Similarly, rules 1 and 5 together show that the first derivative of $f(x) = 2x^2 + 4x + 1$ is $4x + 4$.[12]

EXAMPLE I.1.2: CALCULATING DERIVATIVES

Find the first derivative of the functions whose graphs are shown in Figure I.1.8, viz.

(a) $x^3 - 7x^2 + 14x - 8$

(b) $10 - 0.5x^2 + \sqrt{\ln(1 + x^2)} - \dfrac{4\ln(x)}{\exp(x)}$

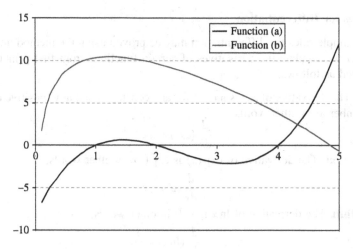

Figure I.1.8 Two functions

SOLUTION

(a) This function is a cubic polynomial, and its graph crosses the x-axis at the points $x = 1$, $x = 2$ and $x = 4$. We know this because the function may also be written

$$f(x) = x^3 - 7x^2 + 14x - 8 = (x - 1)(x - 2)(x - 4).$$

---

[12] So the first derivative is zero when $x = -1$.

By the summation rule (5) we just differentiate each term in $x^3 - 7x^2 + 14x - 8$ separately using rule 1, and then sum the results:

$$\frac{d}{dx}\left(x^3 - 7x^2 + 14x - 8\right) = 3x^2 - 14x + 14.$$

(b) We again differentiate term by term, and the first two terms are easy:

$$\frac{d}{dx}\left(10 - 0.5x^2\right) = -x.$$

For the next term use the chain rule (4):

$$\frac{d}{dx}\left(\sqrt{\ln\left(1+x^2\right)}\right) = \frac{d}{dx}\left(\ln\left(1+x^2\right)\right)^{1/2} = \frac{1}{2}\left(\ln\left(1+x^2\right)\right)^{-1/2} \times \frac{d}{dx}\left(\ln\left(1+x^2\right)\right).$$

Then by the chain rule again and rule 3 for the derivative of the log,

$$\frac{d}{dx}\left(\ln\left(1+x^2\right)\right) = 2x\left(1+x^2\right)^{-1}.$$

Hence

$$\frac{d}{dx}\left(\sqrt{\ln\left(1+x^2\right)}\right) = x\left(\ln\left(1+x^2\right)\right)^{-1/2}\left(1+x^2\right)^{-1}.$$

For the last term we use the quotient rule (7) and rules 2 and 3 for the derivatives of the exponential and log functions:

$$\frac{d}{dx}\left(\frac{-4\ln x}{\exp(x)}\right) = 4\frac{\ln x\exp(x) - \exp(x)x^{-1}}{\exp(x)^2} = 4\frac{\ln x - x^{-1}}{\exp(x)}.$$

Finally, summing these derivatives give the result:

$$\frac{d}{dx}\left(10 - 0.5x^2 + \sqrt{\ln\left(1+x^2\right)} - \frac{4\ln(x)}{\exp(x)}\right) = -x + x\left(\ln\left(1+x^2\right)\right)^{-1/2}\left(1+x^2\right)^{-1}$$

$$+ 4\frac{\ln x - x^{-1}}{\exp(x)}.$$

Of course, this example is not a standard function. It has merely been provided for readers to practice using the rules for differentiation.

I.1.3.3 Monotonic, Concave and Convex Functions

A differentiable function is *strictly monotonic increasing* if $f'(x) > 0$ for all x. That is, the function always increases in value as x increases. Similarly, we say that f is *strictly monotonic decreasing* if $f'(x) < 0$ for all x. Sometimes we drop the 'strictly', in which case we allow the function to be flat at some points, i.e. to have zero derivative for some x. *Concavity* and *convexity* are related to the second derivative, $f''(x)$:

$$f \text{ is strictly concave if } f''(x) < 0 \text{ and strictly convex if } f''(x) > 0. \tag{I.1.17}$$

We drop the 'strictly' if the inequalities are not strict inequalities. Hence:

$$f \text{ is concave if } f''(x) \leq 0 \text{ and convex if } f''(x) \geq 0. \tag{I.1.18}$$

For instance, the logarithmic function is a strictly monotonic increasing concave function and the exponential function is a strictly monotonic increasing convex function. Other functions may be concave on some ranges of x and convex on other ranges of x. Any point at which a function changes from being concave to convex, or from convex to concave, is called a *point of inflexion*. At a point of inflexion $f''(x) = 0$. For instance, the cubic polynomial function (a) shown in Figure I.1.8 is concave for $x < 7/3$ and convex for $x > 7/3$. We find this inflexion point 7/3 by setting $f''(x) = 0$, i.e. $6x - 14 = 0$.

If a function is strictly concave then the value of the function at any two points x_1 and x_2 is greater than the corresponding weighted average of the function's values. In other words, the graph of a function that is strictly concave (convex) in the range $[x_1, x_2]$ always lies above (below) the chord joining two points $f(x_1)$ and $f(x_2)$. For instance, the function (b) in Figure I.1.8 is strictly concave. Formally, f is strictly concave if and only if

$$f(px_1 + (1-p)x_2) > pf(x_1) + (1-p)f(x_2) \text{ for every } p \in [0, 1].$$ (I.1.19)

Likewise, if a function is strictly convex then

$$f(px_1 + (1-p)x_2) < pf(x_1) + (1-p)f(x_2) \text{ for every } p \in [0, 1].$$ (I.1.20)

We shall encounter many examples of concave and convex functions in this book. For instance, the price of a bond is a convex monotonic decreasing function of its yield. For this reason we call the second derivative of the bond price with respect to its yield the convexity of the bond; and the Black–Scholes–Merton price of an in-the-money or an out-of-the money option is a convex monotonic increasing function of the implied volatility.

I.1.3.4 Stationary Points and Optimization

When $f'(x) = 0$, x is called a *stationary point* of f. Thus the tangent to the function is horizontal at a stationary point. For instance, the cubic polynomial function (a) in Figure I.1.8 has two stationary points, found by solving

$$\frac{d}{dx}(x^3 - 7x^2 + 14x - 8) = 3x^2 - 14x + 14 = 0.$$

Using (I.1.1) gives the stationary points $x = 1.451$ and $x = 3.215$, and we can see from the figure that the tangent is indeed horizontal at these two points.

A function f has a *local maximum* at a stationary point x if $f''(x) < 0$ and a *local minimum* if $f''(x) > 0$. For instance, the cubic polynomial function (a) in Figure I.1.8 has second derivative $6x - 14$, which is negative at $x = 1.451$ and positive at $x = 3.215$. Hence the function has a local maximum at $x = 1.451$ and a local minimum at $x = 3.215$. A stationary point that is neither a local maximum nor a local minimum is called a *saddle point*.

EXAMPLE I.1.3: IDENTIFYING STATIONARY POINTS

Find the stationary point of the function $f(x) = x^2 \ln x$, $x > 0$, and identify whether it is a maximum, minimum or saddle point.

SOLUTION   We have

$$f'(x) = 2x \ln x + x,$$

$$f''(x) = 2 \ln x + 3.$$

Hence a stationary point in the region $x > 0$ is the point x where $2x \ln x + x = 0$. That is, $\ln x = -\frac{1}{2}$ so $x = \exp(-\frac{1}{2}) = 0.6065$. At this point $f''(x) = 2$ so it is a local minimum.

If, as well as $f'(x) = 0$, we have $f''(x) = 0$ then the point *could* be neither a maximum nor a minimum but a point of inflexion at which $f'(x)$ also happens to be 0. But the point might also be a maximum, or a minimum. The only way we can tell which type of point it is, to find the value of the derivative either side of x. If the derivative is positive (negative) just below x and negative (positive) just above x, then x is a maximum (minimum). If the derivative has the same sign just above and just below x, then x is a saddle point.

I.1.3.5   Integration

The integral of a function is the area between the curve and the x-axis. If the area is above the axis it is positive and if it is below the axis it is negative. When we place limits on the integral sign then the area is calculated between these limits, as depicted in Figure I.1.9. We call this the *definite integral* because the result is a number, as opposed to *indefinite integral*, which is a function.

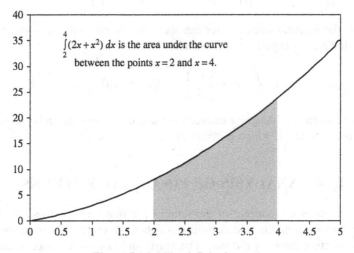

Figure I.1.9   The definite integral

Integration is the opposite process to differentiation:

$$\text{if } f(x) = F'(x) \text{ then } F(x) = \int f(x)\, dx.$$

Rules for integration are the opposite of the rules for differentiation. For instance,[13]

$$\int x^{-1} dx = \ln x + c \text{ and } \int x\, dx = \tfrac{1}{2}x^2 + c,$$

where c is an arbitrary constant. Therefore if we know the rules for differentiation, we can find the integral of a function.

For the definite integral we write

$$\int_a^b f(x)\, dx,$$

---

[13] The indefinite integral is determined only up to an additive constant because $f(x) = F'(x) \Rightarrow f(x) = (F(x) + c)'$.

where a is the lower limit and b is the upper limit of the range over which the area is calculated. Then, if $f(x) = \int f(x)dx$ we calculate the area as:

$$\int_a^b f(x)\, dx = F(b) - F(a). \tag{I.1.21}$$

EXAMPLE I.1.4: A DEFINITE INTEGRAL

Find the area under the curve defined by the function $f(x) = 2x + x^2$ between the points $x = 2$ and $x = 4$ as depicted in Figure I.1.9.

SOLUTION   We have

$$\int_2^4 (2x + x^2)\, dx = \left[x^2 + \frac{x^3}{3} \right]_2^4 = \left(4^2 + \frac{4^3}{3} \right) - \left(2^2 + \frac{2^3}{3} \right) = 12 + \frac{56}{3} = 30.67.$$

In this example the function value always lies above the x-axis so the area was positive. But an area below the axis is negative. For instance,

$$\int_{-1}^1 x\, dx = \left[\frac{x^2}{2} \right]_{-1}^1 = {}^1\!/_2 - {}^1\!/_2 = 0$$

because the area under the line $y = x$ between -1 and 0 is below the axis and equal in size to the area between 0 and 1, which is above the axis.

I.1.4   ANALYSIS OF FINANCIAL RETURNS

This section introduces the concept of the return on a financial asset and the return on a portfolio. We provide notation and definitions in both discrete and continuous time and explain the connection between the two. The *profit and loss* on an asset is the change in price of an asset over a period of time. It is henceforth usually abbreviated to P&L.[14] When the price of the asset or the value of the portfolio is always positive we may also define the *percentage return* as the change in price divided by the current price. We shall see that over short time periods the percentage return may be well approximated by the *log return*.

I.1.4.1   Discrete and Continuous Time Notation

It is usually easier to derive theoretical pricing models for bonds and derivatives assuming that interest rates and the prices of assets can be measured in continuous time, and assuming we know the value of an instrument at any point in time. But in reality we only accrue interest over discrete time intervals and we only observe prices at discrete points in time.

The definition of a return requires the distinction between discrete and continuous time modelling. This is a source of confusion for many students. The continuous and discrete time approaches to financial models were developed independently, and as a result different

---

[14] The P&L on an asset is the change in value, and this should be distinguished from the change in an interest rate. The latter corresponds to the percentage return on a bond and does *not* represent a profit and loss.

notations are often used for the same thing, or one notation can mean two different things depending on whether the analysis is in discrete or continuous time.

In continuous time we often use $S(t)$ to denote the value of an investment, e.g. the price of a single asset or the value of a portfolio at time t. But in discrete time the notations P_t or p_t are standard. In each case we mean that the asset price or portfolio value is a function of time. And in both cases it is common to drop the time dependence notation, i.e. denote the price or value by S or P depending on whether time is continuous or discrete; their implicit dependence on time is assumed, because the price or value at time t is a random variable.

The use of the Δ notation in discrete and continuous time must also be distinguished. In discrete time it denotes the *first difference operator*, i.e. the difference between two consecutive values, but in continuous time it is used to denote an *increment* in a variable; that is, a small change in the value of a variable. That is, in continuous time ΔX denotes an increment in a random variable X, which is not necessarily linked to a change happening over time. However, Δt is a small amount of time.[15]

We also distinguish between whether one is looking forward or backward in time. Hence the change in price is denoted

$$\Delta P_t = P_t - P_{t-1} \tag{I.1.22}$$

when looking backward, but

$$\Delta P_t = P_{t+1} - P_t \tag{I.1.23}$$

when looking forward.

I.1.4.2 Portfolio Holdings and Portfolio Weights

Consider a simple portfolio with positions on k assets and denote the ith asset price at time t by p_{it}. At time 0 a certain amount is invested in each of these assets, so that the portfolio contains a unit amount n_i of asset i, for $i = 1, 2, \ldots, k$. The set $\{n_1, n_2, \ldots, n_k\}$ is called the vector of *portfolio holdings* at time 0. If we *rebalance* the portfolio at some point in time the holdings in certain assets may change, but without rebalancing the portfolio holdings will be constant over time.

In a *long portfolio* all the holdings are positive; in a *short portfolio* all the holdings are negative; and a portfolio with some negative and some positive holdings is a *long-short portfolio*. Negative holdings may be achieved by either taking a short position in a futures or forward contract or by making a *short sale*. The latter requires using the *repo market* to borrow a security that you do not own, with an agreement to return this security at a later date.[16]

Suppose there is no rebalancing over time, and that there are no dividends if the asset is an equity and no coupons if the asset is a bond. Then at any time $t > 0$, the *value of the portfolio* is the sum of the product of asset prices and holdings,

$$P_t = \sum_{i=1}^{k} n_i p_{it}. \tag{I.1.24}$$

This is positive for a long portfolio, negative for a short portfolio and it may be positive, negative or zero for a long-short portfolio.

---

[15] We should mention that the reason why we do not use capital letters to denote the 'Greeks' of option portfolios in this book is to avoid confusion between the option 'delta' and these other usages of the Δ notation.
[16] A *security* is a tradable financial claim that is usually listed on an exchange, such as a stock or a bond.

The proportion of capital invested in a certain asset i at time t is called the *portfolio weight* on this asset. The portfolio weight on asset i is

$$w_{it} = \frac{n_i p_{it}}{P_t}. \tag{I.1.25}$$

This is positive for a long portfolio, negative for a short portfolio and it may be positive, negative or zero for a long-short portfolio. For a *self-financing portfolio* the sum of the weights is 0 and in a *fully-funded* portfolio the sum of the weights is 1.

When the portfolio's holding in each asset remains constant, i.e. there is *no rebalancing* over time, the proportion of capital invested in each asset changes whenever the price of one of the assets changes. Hence, the portfolio weights change over time unless the portfolio is continually rebalanced whenever an asset price moves to keep the weights constant. The following example illustrates:

EXAMPLE I.1.5: PORTFOLIO WEIGHTS

Suppose we invest in two assets whose dollar prices at the beginning of four consecutive years are as shown in Table I.1.1. At the beginning of 2003 we buy 600 units of asset 1 and 200 units of asset 2. Find the portfolio weights and the portfolio value over the rest of the period when the portfolio is not rebalanced.

Table I.1.1   Asset prices

Year	Price of asset 1	Price of asset 2
2003	100	200
2004	125	500
2005	80	250
2006	120	400

SOLUTION   In 2003 the portfolio value is $600 \times 100 + 200 \times 200 = \$100,000$ and the weight on asset 1 is $60,000/100,000 = 0.6$, so the weight on asset 2 is 0.4. In 2004 the portfolio value is $600 \times 125 + 200 \times 500 = \$175,000$ and the weight on asset 1 is $75,000/175,000 = 0.429$, so the weight on asset 2 is 0.571. Continuing in this way, the results for all four years are shown in Table I.1.2.

Table I.1.2   Portfolio weights and portfolio value

Year	Price 1	Price 2	Weight 1	Weight 2	Value 1	Value 2	Portfolio Value
2003	100	200	0.600	0.400	60,000	40,000	100,000
2004	125	500	0.429	0.571	75,000	100,000	175,000
2005	80	250	0.490	0.510	48,000	50,000	98,000
2006	120	400	0.474	0.526	72,000	80,000	152,000

The above example shows that if the portfolio is not rebalanced then the portfolio weights will change when the prices of the assets change. That is, constant holdings imply variable weights and constant weights imply variable holdings over time.

I.1.4.3 Profit and Loss

Discrete Time

Consider first the discrete time case, letting P_t denote the value of a portfolio at time t. In a long-short portfolio this can be positive, negative or indeed zero, as we have seen above. The *profit and loss* is the change in the value of the portfolio between two consecutive times. Thus the P&L at time t is either (I.1.22) or (I.1.23) depending on whether we are looking backward or forward in time. Here the subscript t denotes the price at that time and Δ denotes either the:

- *backward difference operator*, in (I.1.22), for instance when we are dealing with historical data; or the
- *forward difference operator*, in (I.1.23), for instance when we are making forecasts of what could happen in the future.

Continuous Time

The forward-looking P&L over a very small 'infinitesimal' time interval of length Δt is $S(t + \Delta t) - S(t)$ and the backward looking P&L is $S(t) - S(t - \Delta t)$. But by definition of the derivative,

$$\lim_{\Delta t \downarrow 0} \left[\frac{S(t + \Delta t) - S(t)}{\Delta t} \right] = \lim_{\Delta t \downarrow 0} \left[\frac{S(t) - S(t + \Delta t)}{\Delta t} \right] = \frac{dS(t)}{dt}. \tag{I.1.26}$$

In other words, we can use the differential, $dS(t)$ to denote the P&L in continuous time.

Note that P&L is measured in *value terms*, i.e. in the same units as the investment. For instance, if the investment is in a hedge fund with a net asset value measured in US dollars then the P&L is also measured in US dollars. This can sometimes present a problem because if prices have been trending then a P&L of $1 million today has a different economic significance than a P&L of $1 million some years ago. For this reason we often prefer to analyse returns, if possible.

I.1.4.4 Percentage and Log Returns

Discrete Time

We shall phrase our discussion in terms of backward-looking returns but the main results are the same for forward-looking returns. Suppose that:

- the portfolio value P_t is always positive;
- there are no interim payments such as dividends on stocks or coupons on bonds.[17]

Then the one-period percentage return on the investment is

$$R_t = \frac{P_t - P_{t-1}}{P_{t-1}} = \frac{\Delta P_t}{P_{t-1}}. \tag{I.1.27}$$

Whereas the P&L is measured in value terms, the percentage return (often called just the *return*) is a relative change in value, and it is normally quoted as a percentage.

---

[17] If a dividend or coupon is received between time t and time $t + 1$ then this, and any interest accruing on this, should be added to the numerator. For commodities the carry cost can be treated like a negative dividend or coupon. See Section III.2.3.6 for further details on carry costs.

But what is the return if the value of the investment is negative or zero? If the investment *always* has a negative value, for instance when one goes short every asset, then (I.1.27) still gives a meaningful definition. But it is very difficult to define a return on an investment in a long-short portfolio, although the P&L *is* well defined for any type of portfolio. A return must be defined as the P&L relative to some price level. We cannot take the current price because this could be zero! And if it is small but not zero the return can be enormous. For this reason we often analyse long-short portfolios by their P&L rather than by their returns.

If it is absolutely essential to work with returns then some convention must be agreed. For instance we might assume that the P&L is measured relative to the *size* of investment that is necessary to make the trade. If the value can be either positive or negative and we really have to define a return, provided that the price is never zero we could define a one-period return as

$$R_t = \frac{\Delta P_t}{|P_{t-1}|}. \tag{I.1.28}$$

EXAMPLE I.1.6: RETURNS ON A LONG-SHORT PORTFOLIO

A British bank sells short £2 million of US dollar currency and purchases sterling. The trade was made when the exchange rate was 1.65 US dollars per British pound. Later, when the bank closes out the position, the exchange rate has moved to 1.75. What is (a) the P&L (measured in £s since this is from the British bank's perspective) and (b) the corresponding return? You may assume, for simplicity, that interest rates are zero on both sides of the Atlantic.[18]

SOLUTION   When the trade is made the bank has a long position of £2 million in sterling and a short position of $2 \times 1.65 = \$3.3$ million in US dollars. The position has a net value of zero, but the size of the investment is £2 million. When the position is closed the exchange rate has changed to 1.75 US dollars per British pound. So we only need to use

$$\frac{3,300,000}{1.75} = £1,885,714$$

to close the position. Hence the bank has made a profit of $£2,000,000 - £1,885,714 = £114,286$. If this is measured relative to the initial size of the investment, the return is

$$\frac{114,286}{2,000,000} = 5.7143\%.$$

This example calculates the return over only one period. When there are many periods we may still use the same convention, i.e. that the return on a long-short portfolio is the P&L divided by the investment required to take the position. This investment would be the *initial* outlay of funds (i.e. £2 million in the above example) which is fixed over time, plus the funding costs of this outlay, which will change over time.

---

[18] Hence there is zero interest on the sterling position and the US dollar forward rates are equal to the spot exchange rates used in the question. In reality, we would need to include changes in interest rates to define the total return.

Continuous Time

If the value of a portfolio is strictly positive then the forward-looking percentage return over a time interval of length Δt is

$$R(t) = \frac{(S(t+\Delta t) - S(t))}{S(t)}.$$

Note that

$$1 + R(t) = \frac{S(t+\Delta t)}{S(t)}.$$

If the increment Δt is a very small interval of time then the percentage return is small. Now recall the property (I.1.9) that

$$\ln(1+x) \approx x \quad \text{if } x \text{ is small.}$$

Hence, for small Δt,

$$R(t) \approx \ln(1 + R(t));$$

in other words,

$$R(t) \approx \ln S(t+\Delta t) - \ln S(t).$$

So over small time periods the percentage return is very close to the *log return*. By (I.1.16) we know that, in the limit as the time increment tends to zero, the log return is given by the differential of the log price, $d \ln S(t)$. Hence the log return is the *increment in the log price of the asset*.

I.1.4.5   Geometric Brownian Motion

We use the differential operator to describe the evolution of prices of financial assets or interest rates in continuous time. Let $S(t)$ denote the price of an asset at some future time t, assuming the current time is $t = 0$. Consider the price $S(t)$ at $t > 0$. If there were no uncertainty about this price we might assume that its growth rate is constant. The growth rate is the *proportional* change per unit of time. So if the growth rate is a constant μ, we can write

$$\frac{dS(t)}{dt} = \mu S(t). \tag{I.1.29}$$

Now by the chain rule,

$$\frac{d \ln S(t)}{dt} = \frac{d \ln S(t)}{dS(t)} \frac{dS(t)}{dt} = S(t)^{-1} \frac{dS(t)}{dt}.$$

Thus an equivalent form of (I.1.29) is

$$\frac{d \ln S(t)}{dt} = \mu. \tag{I.1.30}$$

Integrating (I.1.30) gives the solution

$$S(t) = S(0) \exp(\mu t). \tag{I.1.31}$$

Hence, the asset price path would be an exponential if there were no uncertainty about the future price.

However, there *is* uncertainty about the price of the asset in the future, and to model this we add a *stochastic differential* term $dW(t)$ to (I.1.29) or to (I.1.30). The process $W(t)$ is called a *Wiener process*, also called a *Brownian motion*. It is a continuous process that has independent increments $dW(t)$ and each *increment* has a normal distribution with mean 0 and variance dt.[19] On adding uncertainty to the exponential price path (I.1.31) the price process (I.1.29) becomes

$$\frac{dS(t)}{S(t)} = \mu\, dt + \sigma dW(t). \tag{I.1.32}$$

This is an example of a *diffusion process*. Since the left-hand side has the proportional change in the price at time t, rather than the absolute change, we call (I.1.32) *geometric Brownian motion*. If the left-hand side variable were $dS(t)$ instead, the process would be called *arithmetic Brownian motion*. The *diffusion coefficient* is the coefficient of $dW(t)$, which is a constant σ in the case of geometric Brownian motion. This constant is called the *volatility* of the process. By definition $dW(t)$ has a normal distribution with mean 0 and variance dt, so $dS(t)/S(t)$ has a normal distribution with mean μdt and variance $\sigma^2 dt$.[20]

I.1.4.6   Discrete and Continuous Compounding in Discrete Time

Another way of expressing the return (I.1.27) is:

$$1 + R_t = \frac{P_t}{P_{t-1}}. \tag{I.1.33}$$

On the left-hand side we have the *discrete compounding factor*, so called because the above is also equivalent to

$$P_t = (1 + R_t)\, P_{t-1}. \tag{I.1.34}$$

For example, if $P_0 = 100$ and $P_1 = 105$ then by (I.1.33) $R_1 = 5\%$ and (I.1.34) becomes $105 = 1.05 \times 100$.

Alternatively, using Δ to denote the *forward* difference operator, the one-period *forward-looking* return is

$$R_t = \frac{P_{t+1} - P_t}{P_t} = \frac{\Delta P_t}{P_t}, \tag{I.1.35}$$

and turning this equation around now gives

$$P_{t+1} = (1 + R_t)\, P_t. \tag{I.1.36}$$

Definition (I.1.34) applies when returns are discretely compounded, but under continuous compounding we use *log returns*. The one-period historical log return is defined as

$$r_t = \ln\left(\frac{P_t}{P_{t-1}}\right) = \ln P_t - \ln P_{t-1} = \Delta \ln P_t. \tag{I.1.37}$$

Another way of expressing (I.1.37) is:

$$\exp(r_t) = \frac{P_t}{P_{t-1}}. \tag{I.1.38}$$

---

[19] See Section I.3.3.4 for an introduction to the normal distribution.
[20] See Section I.3.7 for further details on stochastic processes in discrete and continuous time.

On the left-hand side we have the *continuous compounding factor*, so called because the above is also equivalent to

$$P_t = \exp(r_t) P_{t-1}. \tag{I.1.39}$$

For example, if $P_0 = 100$ and $P_1 = 105$ then by (I.1.37) $r_1 = \ln(1.05) = 4.879\%$ and (I.1.39) becomes:

$$105 = \exp(0.04879) \times 100 = 1.05 \times 100.$$

Our numerical examples above have shown that for the same prices at the beginning and the end of the period the continuously compounded return (i.e. the log return) is *less* than the discretely compounded return. Other examples of discrete and continuous compounding are given in Section III.1.2.

I.1.4.7 Period Log Returns in Discrete Time

Using (I.1.9) we can write the log return over one period as

$$\ln\left(\frac{P_t}{P_{t-1}}\right) = \ln\left(\frac{P_t - P_{t-1}}{P_{t-1}} + 1\right) \approx \frac{P_t - P_{t-1}}{P_{t-1}}. \tag{I.1.40}$$

Similarly, the forward-looking one-period log return is

$$r_t = \ln\left(\frac{P_{t+1}}{P_t}\right) = \ln P_{t+1} - \ln P_t = \Delta \ln P_t \tag{I.1.41}$$

and

$$\ln\left(\frac{P_{t+1}}{P_t}\right) \approx \frac{P_{t+1} - P_t}{P_t}. \tag{I.1.42}$$

So the log return is approximately equal to the return but, as shown in Section I.1.4.4, the approximation is good *only* when the return is small. It is often used in practice to measure returns at the daily frequency.

In market risk analysis we often need to predict risk over several forward-looking periods such as 1 day, 10 days or more. The forward-looking *h-period return* is

$$R_{ht} = \frac{P_{t+h} - P_t}{P_t} = \frac{\Delta_h P_t}{P_t},$$

where Δ_h denotes the h-period forward difference operator. The *h-period log return* is

$$r_{ht} = \ln\left(\frac{P_{t+h}}{P_t}\right) = \ln P_{t+h} - \ln P_t = \Delta_h \ln P_t.$$

Note that

$$\ln P_{t+h} - \ln P_t = \ln P_{t+h} + \left[-\ln P_{t+h-1} + \ln P_{t+h-1}\right] + \left[-\ln P_{t+h-2} + \ln P_{t+h-2}\right] + \ldots +$$
$$\left[-\ln P_{t+1} + \ln P_{t+1}\right] - \ln P_t$$
$$= \left[\ln P_{t+h} - \ln P_{t+h-1}\right] + \left[\ln P_{t+h-1} - \ln P_{t+h-2}\right] + \ldots + \left[\ln P_{t+1} - \ln P_t\right].$$

That is,

$$r_{ht} = \sum_{i=0}^{h-1} r_{t+i}, \tag{I.1.43}$$

or equivalently,

$$\Delta_h \ln P_t = \sum_{i=0}^{h-1} \Delta \ln P_{t+i}.$$

Hence the h-period log return is the sum of h consecutive one-period log returns. This property makes log returns very easy to analyse and it is one of the main reasons we prefer to work with log returns whenever possible.

When analysing historical time series data we often convert the historical prices into a return series. If the data are sampled at a monthly frequency, the one-period return is a monthly return; similarly, weekly data give weekly returns, when measured over one time period, and daily data give daily returns. We can also create weekly or monthly log returns from daily log returns, using a result similar to (I.1.43), viz.

$$r_{ht} = \sum_{i=1}^{h} r_{t-i}, \tag{I.1.44}$$

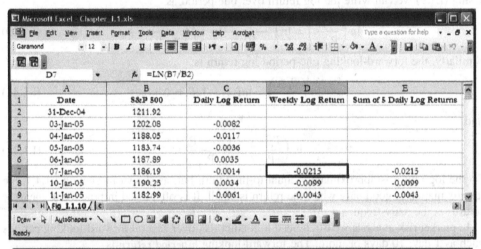

Figure I.1.10 The h-period log return is the sum of h consecutive one-period log returns

or equivalently, $\Delta_h \ln P_t = \sum_{i=1}^{h} \Delta \ln P_{t-i}$. For instance, the Excel spreadsheet for Figure I.1.10 takes daily data on the S&P 500 index from 31 December 2004 to 30 December 2005 and computes the 5-day log return by (a) taking the difference of the log prices 5 days apart and (b) summing five daily log returns. The answers are the same.

I.1.4.8   Return on a Linear Portfolio

We now prove one of the most fundamental relationships in portfolio mathematics: that the percentage return on a long-only portfolio may be written as a weighted sum of the asset returns, with weights given by the portfolio's weights at the *beginning* of the period.

To prove this, we denote the one-period percentage return on the portfolio from time 0 to time 1 by

$$R = \frac{P_1 - P_0}{P_0}.$$

Suppose there are k assets in the portfolio. Then, by definition,

$$1 + R = \frac{P_1}{P_0} = \frac{\sum_{i=1}^{k} n_i p_{i1}}{P_0} = \sum_{i=1}^{k} \frac{n_i p_{i0}}{P_0} \frac{p_{i1}}{p_{i0}}.$$

In other words, letting R_i denote the one-period return on asset i and w_i denote the portfolio weight on asset i at the beginning of the period, we have

$$1 + R = \sum_{i=1}^{k} w_i (1 + R_i) = \sum_{i=1}^{k} w_i + \sum_{i=1}^{k} w_i R_i = 1 + \sum_{i=1}^{k} w_i R_i.$$

Hence,

$$R = \sum_{i=1}^{k} w_i R_i. \tag{I.1.45}$$

I.1.4.9   Sources of Returns

Since (I.1.45) defines the portfolio as a linear function of the returns on its constituent assets we call such a portfolio a *linear portfolio*. The relationship (I.1.45) shows that the return, and therefore also the risk, of the portfolio may be attributed to two sources:

- changes in the prices of the individual assets;
- changes in portfolio weights.

The following example illustrates the effect of these two sources of risk and return. In the first case the portfolio return is due to both changes in asset prices and portfolio weights, but in the second case the portfolio returns only comes from changes in asset prices because we rebalance the portfolio continually so that its weights are held constant.

EXAMPLE I.1.7: PORTFOLIO RETURNS

Continuing Example I.1.5, find the portfolio's annual returns under the assumption that:

(i) portfolio holdings are held constant, i.e. there is no rebalancing; and
(ii) portfolio weights are held constant, i.e. the portfolio is rebalanced every quarter so that 60% of the portfolio's value is invested in asset 1 and 40% is invested in asset 2.

SOLUTION

(i) The values of the constant holdings portfolio in each year are given in the solution to Example I.1.5. The returns are summarized as follows:

$$2003\text{--}2004 : 75/100 = 75\%,$$

$$2004\text{--}2005 : -77/175 = -44\%,$$

$$2005\text{--}2006 : 54/98 = 55.1\%.$$

(ii) For the constant weights portfolio we use (I.1.45) to find the portfolio return as the weighted sum of the individual asset returns. The returns are different from those obtained in part (i). For comparison with Table I.1.2 we compute the portfolio value using (I.1.36) and the beginning-of-year holdings in each asset that keep the weights constant. The results are summarized in Table I.1.3.

Table I.1.3   Portfolio returns

Year	Price 1	Price 2	Return 1	Return 2	Portfolio return	Portfolio value	Holding 1	Holding 2
2003	100	200				100,000	600	200
2004	125	500	25%	150%	75%	175,000	840	140
2005	80	250	−36%	−50%	−41.6%	102,200	767	164
2006	120	400	50%	60%	54%	157,388	787	157

In practice neither portfolio weights nor portfolio holdings remain constant. To rebalance a portfolio continually so that the portfolio weights are the same at the beginning of every day or at the beginning of every week is difficult, if not impossible. Even at the monthly frequency where constant weights rebalancing may be feasible, it would incur very high transactions costs. Of course portfolios are rebalanced. The holdings do change over time, but this is normally in accordance with the manager's expectations of risk and return.

However, in theoretical models of portfolio risk and return it greatly simplifies the analysis to make the constant weights assumption. It can also make sense. Ex post, risk and return can be calculated using the actual historical data on asset values and holdings. For ex post analysis a constant weights assumption is not necessary, but it is sometimes made for simplification. But when we are forecasting risk and return we want to capture the risk and returns arising from the risks and returns of the assets, not from portfolio rebalancing. So for ex ante analysis it is standard to keep portfolio weights constant. This way, the risk and return on the current portfolio can be forecast using changes in asset returns as the *only* influence on portfolio value changes.

I.1.5   FUNCTIONS OF SEVERAL VARIABLES

A function $f(x, y)$ of two variables x and y has a three-dimensional graph, such as that shown in Figure I.1.11 below. We can think of it like a landscape, with a mountaintop at a local maximum and a valley at a local minimum. More generally, a real-valued function of

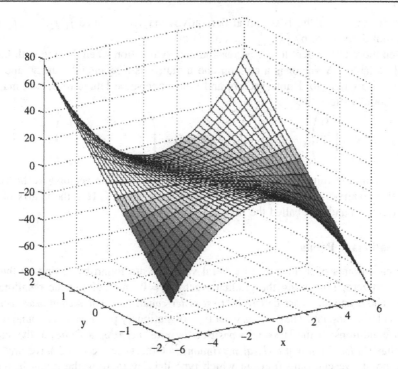

Figure I.1.11   Graph of the function in Example I.1.8

several real variables $f(x_1, \ldots, x_n)$ is an object in $(n+1)$-dimensional space. This section introduces the two types of derivatives of functions of several variables, partial derivatives and total derivatives. We characterize the stationary points of a function of several variables and show how to optimize such a function.

I.1.5.1   Partial Derivatives: Function of Two Variables

The first partial derivative gives the slope of the tangent to the curve that is found by cutting through the graph of the function, holding one of the variables constant, so that we cut through the graph in a direction parallel to one axis. The partial derivative with respect to x is obtained by holding y constant and differentiating with respect to x, and we denote this by either f_x or $\frac{\partial f}{\partial x}$. Similarly, f_y or $\frac{\partial f}{\partial y}$ is obtained by holding x constant and differentiating with respect to y.

The second partial derivatives are obtained by partial differentiation of the first partial derivatives. There are three of them:

$$f_{xx}, f_{xy} \text{ and } f_{yy}, \text{ also denoted } \frac{\partial^2 f}{\partial x^2}, \frac{\partial^2 f}{\partial x \partial y} \text{ and } \frac{\partial^2 f}{\partial y^2}.$$

Note that it does not matter in which order we differentiate the cross derivative, the result is the same: $f_{xy} = f_{yx}$.

I.1.5.2   Partial Derivatives: Function of Several Variables

Partial derivatives of a function of more than two variables are defined analogously. Sometimes we use number subscripts rather than letters to denote the derivatives. Hence for a function $f(x_1, \ldots, x_n)$ the first partial derivatives may be denoted $f_1, f_2, \ldots, f_n$ and the second partial derivatives by $f_{11}, f_{12}, \ldots$ and so on.

It is often more convenient to use *vector* and *matrix* notation when dealing with functions of several variables. A vector is a column and a matrix is a rectangular array, and we use bold lower-case letters to denote vectors and bold upper-case letters to denote matrices.[21] Hence we could write

$$\mathbf{x} = \begin{pmatrix} x_1 \\ \vdots \\ x_n \end{pmatrix}, \quad \mathbf{g} = \begin{pmatrix} f_1 \\ \vdots \\ f_n \end{pmatrix}, \quad \text{and} \quad \mathbf{H} = \begin{pmatrix} f_{11} & \cdots & f_{1n} \\ \vdots & \ddots & \vdots \\ f_{n1} & \cdots & f_{nn} \end{pmatrix},$$

so we may write the function $f(x_1, \ldots, x_n)$ as $f(\mathbf{x})$ for short. The vector $\mathbf{g}$ is the vector of first partial derivatives of f and is called the *gradient vector* of f. $\mathbf{H}$ is the matrix of second partial derivatives and it is called the *Hessian matrix* of f.

I.1.5.3 Stationary Points

The stationary points of a function of several variables are found by setting all the partial derivatives to zero, i.e. setting the gradient vector $\mathbf{g} = \mathbf{0}$, and solving the resulting set of equations. These equations are called the *first order conditions*. The *second order conditions* are to do with the Hessian. They tell us what type of stationary point we have found using the first order conditions: If the Hessian is *positive definite* (*negative definite*) at the stationary point we have a *local minimum* (*local maximum*).[22] Otherwise we could have any type of stationary point: we can only find out which type it is by plotting the graph in the small region around the point. Note that functions of two or more variables can take quite complex shapes. We have local maxima and minima, but we also have *saddle points* which are a maximum in the direction of some variables and a minimum in the direction of others.

EXAMPLE I.1.8: STATIONARY POINTS OF A FUNCTION OF TWO VARIABLES

Find the stationary points, if any, of the function $f(x, y) = x^2 y - 2x - 4y$.

SOLUTION   Taking the first and second partial derivatives gives the gradient vector and Hessian matrix:

$$\mathbf{g} = \begin{pmatrix} 2xy - 2 \\ x^2 - 4 \end{pmatrix}, \quad \mathbf{H} = \begin{pmatrix} 2y & 2x \\ 2x & 0 \end{pmatrix}.$$

Setting $\mathbf{g} = \mathbf{0}$, for the stationary points, gives two equations:

$$xy = 1 \quad \text{and} \quad x^2 = 4.$$

The second equation gives $x = \pm 2$ and using the first equation gives two stationary points:

$$(2, 0.5) \quad \text{and} \quad (-2, -0.5).$$

The Hessian matrix at each point is:

$$\begin{pmatrix} 1 & 4 \\ 4 & 0 \end{pmatrix} \quad \text{and} \quad \begin{pmatrix} -1 & -4 \\ -4 & 0 \end{pmatrix}.$$

---

[21] See Section I.2.1 for an introduction to vectors and matrices.
[22] See Section I.2.4 for the definitions of positive and negative definite matrices and for methods for discerning whether a given matrix is positive or negative definite.

Neither matrix is positive definite or negative definite. They are not even semi-definite. So we need to consider the function itself to find out what type of stationary points we have found.

Since $x^2 = 4$ at the stationary points we have $f(x, y) = -2x$ so the function has the value 4 for all y when $x = -2$, or the value -4 for all y when $x = 2$. Thus in the y direction we have neither a maximum nor a minimum: the function is just a horizontal line at this point. In the x direction we have a minimum at the point $(2, 0.5)$ and a maximum at the point $(-2, -0.5)$, as can be seen from Figure I.1.11.

I.1.5.4 Optimization

An *unconstrained optimization* problem is to find the global maximum or minimum of a function of several variables. It is written

$$\max_{\mathbf{x}} f(\mathbf{x}), \tag{I.1.46}$$

which is shorthand for 'find the value of $\mathbf{x}$ for which $f(\mathbf{x})$ takes its maximum value'.[23] In this context the function $f(\mathbf{x})$ is called the *objective function*, because it is the object of the maximization. A common example of unconstrained optimization in finance is the maximization of a likelihood function, used to estimate the parameters of a distribution of asset prices or asset returns.[24]

We know from Section I.1.5.3 that (I.1.46) is solved by setting the gradient vector to zero, giving n equations in n unknowns, which we hope can be solved to find the local stationary points. Then examining the Hessian matrix for positive definiteness, or evaluating the function at and around these points, will tell us whether a given stationary point is a local maximum, a local minimum or neither. Once we have found all possible local maxima and minima, the global maximum (if it exists) is the one of the local maxima where the function takes the highest value and the global minimum (if it exists) is the one of the local minima where the function takes the lowest value.

More generally, a *constrained optimization* problem takes the form

$$\max_{\mathbf{x}} f(\mathbf{x}) \quad \text{such that} \quad \mathbf{h}(\mathbf{x}) \le \mathbf{0}, \tag{I.1.47}$$

where $\mathbf{h}(\mathbf{x}) \le \mathbf{0}$ is a set of linear or non-linear equality or inequality constraints on $\mathbf{x}$. Examples of constrained optimization in finance include the traditional portfolio allocation problem, i.e. how to allocate funds to different types of investments when the investor has constraints such as *no short sales* and/or at least 50% of his capital must be in UK bonds.

To find a constrained optimum we must introduce new variables, which are called *Lagrange multipliers* and denoted $\boldsymbol{\lambda} = (\lambda_1, \ldots, \lambda_k)$, where k is the number of constraints on the objective. Then we augment the objective function by subtracting the product of the Lagrange multipliers and their constraints, thus forming the *Lagrangian function*. Next we solve (I.1.47) by maximizing the Lagrangian, i.e. we maximize

$$L(x_1, \ldots, x_n; \lambda_1, \ldots, \lambda_k) = f(x_1, \ldots, x_n) - \sum_{i=1}^{k} \lambda_i h_i(x_1, \ldots, x_n) \tag{I.1.48}$$

---

[23] Note that finding a minimum of $f(\mathbf{x})$ is equivalent to finding a maximum of $-f(\mathbf{x})$, so it is without loss of generality that we have used the maximum here.

[24] Maximum likelihood estimation is introduced in Section I.3.6.

or, in matrix notation,

$$L(\mathbf{x}, \boldsymbol{\lambda}) = f(\mathbf{x}) - \boldsymbol{\lambda}.\mathbf{h}(\mathbf{x}).$$

Now the first order conditions are obtained by setting all partial derivatives of the Lagrangian to zero, including the partial derivatives with respect to the Lagrange multipliers. Of course, taking the partial derivatives with respect to the Lagrange multipliers just returns us to the conditions $\mathbf{h}(\mathbf{x}) = \mathbf{0}$. So if the original constraints have any inequalities then we need to introduce another set of conditions, called the *Kuhn–Tucker conditions*, which are added to the first order conditions as we identify the stationary points.

The second order conditions for maximizing or minimizing (I.1.48) are on the Hessian of second partial derivatives of the Lagrangian. If this is positive definite then we have a minimum and if this is negative definite then we have a maximum. If the Hessian is neither then we have to explore the *constrained* function's values in the region of the stationary point.

EXAMPLE I.1.9: CONSTRAINED OPTIMIZATION[25]

Find the optimal values of x and y for the problem

$$\max_{x,y} \; x^2 + xy - y^2 \quad \text{such that} \quad x + y = 4.$$

SOLUTION The Lagrangian is

$$L(x, y, \lambda) = x^2 + xy - y^2 - \lambda\,(x + y - 4),$$

and differentiating this gives the first order conditions:

$$2x + y = \lambda,$$

$$x - 2y = \lambda,$$

$$x + y = 4.$$

Their solution is

$$x = 6, \; y = -2, \; \lambda = 10,$$

so the stationary point is at $(6, -2)$ at which point $x^2 + xy - y^2 = 20$. The Hessian matrix is

$$\begin{pmatrix} 2 & 1 & -1 \\ 1 & -2 & -1 \\ -1 & -1 & 0 \end{pmatrix}.$$

In this case we can tell at a glance that this matrix is neither positive nor negative definite. Positive definite matrices must have positive diagonal elements, and negative definite matrices must have negative diagonal elements.[26] Since the diagonal elements are 2, -2 and 0, the Hessian is neither positive nor negative definite. Thus the point could be a maximum, a minimum or a saddle. We can only tell which type of point it is by examining the values of the constrained function in the region of the stationary point. The constrained function

---

[25]This problem is easily treated by elementary methods, since we may substitute $y = 4 - x$ into the objective function and thence maximize a function of a single variable. However, we want to illustrate the use of the Lagrangian function to solve constrained optimization problems, so we shall find the solution the long way in this example.

[26] See Section I.2.4.

is obtained by substituting in the constraint to the objective function. In this case the constrained function is $-x^2 + 12x - 16$ and it can easily be seen that when x is a little more or less than 6, the function has a value less than 20. Hence the point $(6, -2)$ is a constrained maximum.

I.1.5.5 Total Derivatives

The partial derivative examines what happens to the function when only one variable changes and the others are held fixed. The total derivative examines what happens to the function when all the variables change at once. We express this in terms of the differential operator, defined analogously to (I.1.16). For instance, consider a function of two variables. The *total differential* gives the *incremental change* in the function when each variable changes by a small amount. So if dx and dy are the increments in x and y, the total differential is defined as

$$df(x, y) = f(x + dx, y + dy) - f(x, y),$$ (I.1.49)

and the first order approximation to the total derivative is

$$df = f_x dx + f_y dy.$$ (I.1.50)

The extension to functions of more than two variables is obvious.

EXAMPLE I.1.10: TOTAL DERIVATIVE OF A FUNCTION OF THREE VARIABLES

Find an expression for the total derivative of the function

$$f(x, y, z) = x^2 y + 2xyz - z^3$$

and write down the total derivative at the point $(x, y, z) = (1, -1, 0)$.

SOLUTION

$$f_x = 2xy + 2yz, \quad f_y = x^2 + 2xz, \quad f_z = 2xy - 3z^2,$$

Hence

$$df = (2xy + 2yz)\, dx + (x^2 + 2xz)\, dy + (2xy - 3z^2)\, dz.$$

At the point $(x, y, z) = (1, -1, 0)$,

$$df = -2dx + dy - 2dz.$$

I.1.6 TAYLOR EXPANSION

This section introduces a mathematical technique that is very commonly applied to analyse the risk and return of portfolios whose value function is a non-linear function of the underlying asset prices (or, if the portfolio contains bonds, a non-linear function of interest rates). Taylor expansion techniques also provide useful approximations to the values of many theoretical functions, such as variance. For this reason the Taylor expansion technique will be relied on extensively throughout all four volumes.

I.1.6.1 Definition and Examples

Let $f(x)$ be a non-linear function with derivatives up to the nth order. We denote by $f'(x)$ the first derivative of f with respect to x and by $f''(x), f'''(x), \ldots, f^{(n)}(x)$ the second, third and higher order derivatives of f, assuming these exist. A *Taylor approximation* of $f(x)$ about a particular point x_0 gives a polynomial approximation to $f(x)$ in the region of x_0.

The nth order Taylor approximation of $f(x)$ about x_0 is

$$f(x) \approx f(x_0) + (x - x_0)f'(x_0) + \frac{(x - x_0)^2}{2!}f''(x_0) + \ldots + \frac{(x - x_0)^n}{n!}f^{(n)}(x_0), \qquad \text{(I.1.51)}$$

where $f^{(n)}(x_0)$ is shorthand for $f^{(n)}(x)\big|_{x=x_0}$. That is, we first take the derivative of the function to obtain another function of x, and then put in the value $x = x_0$. The expansion (I.1.51) gives an nth order approximation to the function that is valid only in a small region around $x = x_0$, that is, it is a *local approximation*.

This may look rather daunting at first, but a simple example of its application should clarify the idea. In the following we find a cubic polynomial to a function, which is a reasonably good approximation for values of x not too far from $x = 1$, by taking a third order Taylor expansion.

EXAMPLE I.1.11: TAYLOR APPROXIMATION

Find a third order Taylor approximation to the function

$$f(x) = x^3 - 2\ln x$$

about the point $x = 1$.

SOLUTION

$$f(1) = 1,$$
$$f'(x) = 3x^2 - 2x^{-1} \Rightarrow f'(1) = 1,$$
$$f''(x) = 6x + 2x^{-2} \Rightarrow f''(1) = 8,$$
$$f'''(x) = 6 - 4x^{-3} \Rightarrow f'''(1) = 2.$$

Hence the third order Taylor expansion about $x = 1$ is

$$f(x) \approx 1 + (x - 1) + 4(x - 1)^2 + \frac{(x - 1)^3}{3},$$

which simplifies to the cubic polynomial

$$f(x) \approx \frac{x^3}{3} + 3x^2 - 6x + \frac{11}{3}.$$

For values of x that are very close to $x = 1$ this approximation is fairly accurate. For example, if $x = 1.02$ then the actual value of $f(x)$ is 1.021603 and the value of $f(x)$ approximated by the above cubic is 1.021597. But for values of x that are not very close to $x = 1$ this approximation is not accurate. For example, if $x = 1.5$ then the actual value of $f(x)$ is 2.564 but the value of $f(x)$ approximated by the above cubic is 2.458.

Again consider the nth order Taylor expansion (I.1.51) of an n times differentiable function $f(x)$ about a fixed point x_0, but now let us write x in place of x_0 and $x + \Delta x$ in place of x. This way we obtain the nth order Taylor approximation to the *change* in the function's value when x changes by a small amount Δx as

$$f(x + \Delta x) - f(x) \approx f'(x)\Delta x + \frac{1}{2!}f''(x)(\Delta x)^2 + \ldots + \frac{f^{(n)}}{n!}(\Delta x)^n. \qquad (I.1.52)$$

The form (I.1.52) is very commonly used in finance, as we shall see throughout the course of this text. But before providing a simple example of its application we must digress to introduce some financial terminology.

I.1.6.2   Risk Factors and their Sensitivities

A typical portfolio contains hundreds of positions on different risky assets, including stocks, bonds or commodities. To model the risk and return on a large portfolio we map the portfolio to its *risk factors*.[27] The risk factors include the prices of broad market indices, or futures on these indices, foreign exchange rates (for international portfolios) and zero coupon market interest rates of different maturities in the domestic currency and in each foreign currency to which the portfolio is exposed. We call a portfolio *linear* or *non-linear* depending on whether its price is a linear or a non-linear function of its risk factors. The standard example of a non-linear portfolio is one that contains options. Each option price is a non-linear function of the underlying asset price and the underlying asset volatility.

The *risk factor sensitivity* of an asset, or a portfolio of assets, measures the change in its price when a risk factor changes, holding all other risk factors constant. Risk factor sensitivities are given special names depending on the asset class. For instance, in a stock portfolio the risk factor sensitivities are called *factor betas*. The *market beta* of a stock portfolio measures the portfolio's price sensitivity to movements in the broad market index risk factor.

The measurement of market risk requires large portfolios to be 'mapped' to their risk factors. This consists of identifying the risk factors and then measuring the portfolio's sensitivity to each of these risk factors. For instance, in Chapter II.1 we introduce the *factor model* representation of a stock portfolio and show how regression is used to estimate the factor betas. But in a non-linear portfolio the mapping is based on Taylor expansion and the risk factor sensitivities are calculated using analytic formulae or using simple numerical differentiation.

I.1.6.3   Some Financial Applications of Taylor Expansion

For the moment let us regard the underlying asset price S as the only risk factor of an option, and so we denote its price by $g(S)$. We define the option *delta* and *gamma* as the first and second derivatives, $\delta = g'(S)$ and $\gamma = g''(S)$.[28] Taking $n = 2$ in (I.1.52), we obtain

---

[27] The mapping methodology depends on the type of assets in the portfolio, and is described in detail in Chapter III.5.
[28] In general the *delta* and the *gamma* are the first and second order price sensitivities of an option or of an options portfolio. They are calculated by taking the first and second partial derivative of the option price with respect to the price of the underlying. They measure the change in portfolio value for small changes in the underlying price. See Section III.3.4 for further details.

the following approximation to the change in the option price when there is a small change of an amount ΔS in S:

$$g(S + \Delta S) - g(S) \approx \delta \Delta S + \frac{1}{2}\gamma(\Delta S)^2. \tag{I.1.53}$$

The approximation (I.1.53) is called a *delta–gamma approximation*. It shows, amongst other things, that portfolios with positive gamma have less price risk than linear portfolios and that those with negative gamma have more price risk than linear portfolios. To see why, suppose we have a linear portfolio with $\delta = 0.5$. If the underlying price increases by €1 then the portfolio price will increase by €0.50 and if the underlying price decreases by €1 then the portfolio price will decrease by €0.50. Now consider two options, Option A has $\delta = 0.5$ and $\gamma = 0.1$ and option B has $\delta = 0.5$ and $\gamma = -0.1$. If the underlying price increases by €1 then option A price increases by €0.55 but option B price only increases by €0.45; and if the underlying price decreases by €1 then option A price decreases by €0.45 but option B price decreases by €0.55. Hence option A is preferable to the linear position but option B is not. In general, positive gamma reduces risk but negative gamma increases risk.

In Chapter III.1 we shall also use a second order Taylor approximation for the P&L of a bond portfolio: this is called the *duration–convexity approximation*. The duration is the coefficient on the linear term in the expansion and the convexity is the coefficient on the quadratic term. These coefficients are called the *interest rate sensitivities* of the portfolio. They are found by differentiating the portfolio price with respect to its yield.

I.1.6.4 Multivariate Taylor Expansion

In this subsection we consider Taylor approximations to the change in the value of a function of several variables, using a function of two variables $f(x, y)$ for illustration. The second order Taylor approximation to the change in the function's value when both x and y change by small amounts Δx and Δy is

$$f(x + \Delta x, y + \Delta y) - f(x, y) \approx f_x \Delta x + f_y \Delta y + \frac{1}{2}\left[f_{xx}(\Delta x)^2 + f_{yy}(\Delta y)^2 + 2f_{xy}\Delta x \Delta y\right],$$

$$\tag{I.1.54}$$

where we use subscripts to denote partial derivatives, as defined in Section I.1.5.1.

Higher order multivariate Taylor expansions are obtained using higher partial derivatives, for instance the multivariate Taylor approximation to the third order in x and the first order in y is, ignoring the cross derivatives,

$$f(x + \Delta x, y + \Delta y) - f(x, y) \approx f_x \Delta x + f_y \Delta y + \frac{1}{2}f_{xx}(\Delta x)^2 + \frac{1}{3!}f_{xxx}(\Delta x)^3. \tag{I.1.55}$$

In Chapter III.5 we shall use multivariate Taylor expansions to approximate the P&L of an options portfolio. For instance, the *delta–gamma–vega approximation* for a single option is based on a Taylor approximation of a function of two variables, i.e. the underlying asset price and its volatility, with a second order approximation to price changes and first order approximation to volatility changes, again ignoring the cross derivatives. In addition to delta and gamma, this 'Greeks' approximation uses the *vega* of an option. The option vega is the sensitivity of an option price to volatility, i.e. it measures the change in the option price for small changes in the underlying volatility. It is calculated as the first partial derivative of the option price with respect to the volatility.

I.1.7 SUMMARY AND CONCLUSIONS

The *natural log function* is a strictly concave monotonic increasing function that is defined only for positive values of x and takes the value 0 when $x = 1$. The *exponential function* is a strictly convex monotonic increasing function whose value is always positive[29] and takes the value 1 when $x = 0$. They are inverse functions, that is

$$\ln(\exp(x)) = x \text{ and } \exp(\ln(x)) = x.$$

The exponential translates sums to products but the log function translates products to sums, which is often more useful. We usually prefer to use log usually returns rather than ordinary returns, because they are additive.

Loosely speaking, *continuous functions* have no jumps and *differentiable* functions have no corners. *Strictly monotonic functions* either always increase or always decrease, and their curvature determines their *concavity* or *convexity*. We have introduced the *derivative* of a function as the slope of the tangent line and the *integral* of a function as the area under the graph. Integration is the opposite of differentiation. Both the exponential and the natural log function are continuous and differentiable. Since the slope of the exponential function is equal to the value of exponential function at that point, the derivative of $\exp(x)$ is $\exp(x)$. However, the exponential is the only function that has this special property; in general we find derivatives using certain rules that can be derived from first principles.

Higher derivatives are derivatives of derivatives. Provided a function is sufficiently smooth we can find second, third, fourth, ... derivatives by successive differentiation. But if we hit a corner or a jump, no derivative exists at that point. *Stationary points* occur when the first derivative is zero, i.e. the tangent line is flat. These points can be *maxima, minima* or *points of inflexion*. We can usually find which type of point it is by examining the sign of the second derivative. Finding a stationary point is more generally known as an *optimization problem*.

Simple *portfolios* can be characterized by their positions in financial assets as: long-only, when portfolio weights are positive; short-only, when portfolio weights are negative; or long-short, when weights can be positive or negative. We are usually interested in the return on an investment portfolio, but in the case of a long-short portfolio, which may of course have a value of 0, this is difficult to define, so we usually work with the *profit and loss* instead, which can always be defined. Returns and P&L can be defined in both discrete and continuous time. In discrete time we distinguish between *discrete compounding* and *continuous compounding* of returns. The continuously compounded return is called the *log return* and in discrete time the log return is approximately equal to the return over very short time intervals. Profit and loss, returns and log returns can be forward-looking, as when we try to forecast their risk, or backward looking, as when we analyse historical data.

Functions of one or more variables are very common in financial analysis. For instance, the price of a portfolio may be approximated by a simple function of several risk factors. Common risk factors include equity indices, exchange rates and interest rates and, for options portfolios, volatility. The *partial derivatives* of the portfolio price with respect to the risk factors are called the risk factor sensitivities of the portfolio. A portfolio is classified as linear or non-linear according to whether it is a linear or a non-linear function of its risk

---

[29] Again (as for the natural logarithm function–see note 11) this is not strictly true.

factors. A typical example of a linear portfolio is a portfolio of cash positions on stocks, or a portfolio of futures contracts on equity indices. But as soon as we introduce options the portfolio becomes a non-linear function of its risk factors.

Taylor expansions have numerous applications to simplify complex functions in finance, such as the price of a portfolio of options or bonds. The coefficient of x^n in the Taylor expansion is given by the nth derivative, evaluated at the current value of x, and divided by $n!$. A Taylor approximation is only a *local approximation* to the change in the function's value, i.e. it is only a good approximation for *small* increments. The more terms used in the expansion the more accurate the approximation.

I.2
Essential Linear Algebra for Finance

I.2.1 INTRODUCTION

This chapter aims to equip readers with the tools of matrix algebra that are applied in finance. Starting with basic definitions and notation, we provide a detailed understanding of matrix algebra and its important financial applications. An understanding of matrix algebra is necessary for modelling all types of portfolios. Matrices are used to represent the risk and return on a linear portfolio as a function of the portfolio weights and the returns and covariances of the risk factor returns. Examples include *bond portfolios*, whose value is expressed as a discounted cash flow with market interest rates as risk factors, and *stock portfolios*, where returns are represented by linear factor models. Matrices are used to represent the formulae for parameter estimates in any multiple linear regressions and to approximate the returns or changes in price of non-linear portfolios that have several risk factors.

Without the use of matrices the analysis becomes extremely cumbersome. For instance, it is easy to use matrices to solve a set of simultaneous equations in many variables, such as the linear equations that arise when a trader hedges an options portfolio against changes in its risk factors. The *covariance matrix* and the *Cholesky decomposition* of this matrix lie at the heart of financial analysis: they are used to simulate correlated returns and to measure portfolio risk. In highly correlated systems, such as returns on futures contracts on the same underlying but with different expiry date, we use the *eigenvalues* and *eigenvectors* of a matrix to identify the most important sources of variability in the system. Eigenvalues and eigenvectors are also used to ensure that a covariance matrix is *positive definite*, so that every portfolio containing these assets is guaranteed to have positive variance.

The outline of this chapter is as follows: Section I.2.2 defines and illustrates the fundamental concepts in matrix algebra that are used in portfolio analysis. Starting from the basic laws of matrix algebra (i.e. addition, multiplication and inversion of matrices), we represent a set of linear equations in matrix form. This will be used extensively in linear regression models. And the solution of a set of linear equations is used to calculate the gamma and vega hedges for an options portfolio in Section III.3.4. The section ends by introducing *quadratic forms*. These are used to represent the variance of a linear portfolio, as we shall see in Section I.2.4.

Section I.2.3 introduces the eigenvalues and eigenvectors of a square matrix and explores their properties. We show how to compute eigenvalues and eigenvectors and we implement the method in Excel. Section I.2.4 begins by defining the return and the risk of a linear portfolio in matrix notation. Then we introduce the covariance matrix of asset returns and explain why this matrix lies at the heart of portfolio risk analysis. We show how a portfolio's covariance matrix is related to the volatilities and correlations of the constituent asset (or risk factor) returns, and explain why it must always be positive definite. As well as defining the concept of 'definiteness' for square matrices, we use our knowledge of eigenvalues and eigenvectors to test whether a given matrix is positive definite.

Different types of matrix decomposition are described in Section I.2.5. The Cholesky decomposition of a positive definite matrix is used to simulate returns on correlated assets in Section I.5.7.4. This is a fundamental tool for Monte Carlo value-at-risk models, as we shall see in Volume IV.

The eigenvectors of a covariance or correlation matrix of a set of returns can be used to form new variables, which are called the *principal components*. Principal component analysis (PCA) is introduced in Section I.2.6. We end this chapter with a case study that examines the historical behaviour of major European equity indices and shows how their returns can be modelled using PCA.

We shall be applying PCA quite frequently throughout the later volumes of this book. It is an extremely useful tool for modelling the risk of all types of portfolios, particularly fixed income portfolios and portfolios with positions in many futures of different maturities. Readers are recommended to try to fully understand the Excel spreadsheet for the case study, which computes the principal components with the aid of an Excel add-in freeware program.

I.2.2 MATRIX ALGEBRA AND ITS MATHEMATICAL APPLICATIONS

This section and Section I.2.3 are similar to an 'Algebra 101' course. No finance or risk management will be covered until Section I.2.4. The aim of these two preliminary sections is for the reader to become properly acquainted with the language and methods of linear algebra.

I.2.2.1 Basic Terminology

A *matrix* is a rectangular array of objects. For our purposes these objects will be *real numbers*. A non-technical definition of the set of real numbers is a continuum of numbers between plus infinity and minus infinity that can be represented on a line. We denote the set of real numbers by the symbol $\Re$. A real $m \times n$ matrix is an array of real numbers with m rows and n columns. For instance,

$$\begin{pmatrix} -1 & -0.5 & 3 \\ 0.4 & 0 & 2 \end{pmatrix}$$

is a 2×3 matrix. We use bold upper-case letters such as $\mathbf{A}$ or $\mathbf{V}$ to denote matrices, hence we may write

$$\mathbf{A} = \begin{pmatrix} -1 & -0.5 & 3 \\ 0.4 & 0 & 2 \end{pmatrix}$$

If $m = n$ the matrix is called a *square matrix*.

The *matrix transpose*, denoted using the symbol "'" just interchanges the rows and the columns.[1] Hence,

$$\mathbf{A}' = \begin{pmatrix} -1 & 0.4 \\ -0.5 & 0 \\ 3 & 2 \end{pmatrix}.$$

If $\mathbf{A}$ is square and also $\mathbf{A} = \mathbf{A}'$ then $\mathbf{A}$ is called a *symmetric matrix*.

---

[1] Note that some texts use the notation $^\mathrm{T}$ for the transpose of a vector or matrix.

A real *vector* is a row or a column of real numbers. The transpose of a row vector is a column vector. We use bold lower-case letters such as $\mathbf{x}$ or $\mathbf{w}$ to denote vectors. In this text when we write a vector as $\mathbf{x}$ it will always be taken to be a column vector.

The set of all vectors $\mathbf{x} = (x_1, \ldots, x_n)'$ with $x_i \in \Re$ for each $i = 1, \ldots, n$ is called n-dimensional *Cartesian space* and it is denoted by $\Re^n$. For instance, when $n = 2$ we have the *Cartesian plane* and a two-dimensional vectors of the form

$$\mathbf{x} = \begin{pmatrix} x_1 \\ x_2 \end{pmatrix}, \text{ or equivalently } \mathbf{x} = (x_1, x_2)',$$

represents a point in the plane.

I.2.2.2 Laws of Matrix Algebra

The first law of matrix algebra is that matrices of the *same dimension* can be added element by element. Thus

$$\begin{pmatrix} 1 & 2 \\ 3 & 4 \end{pmatrix} + \begin{pmatrix} 5 & 6 \\ 7 & 8 \end{pmatrix} = \begin{pmatrix} 6 & 8 \\ 10 & 12 \end{pmatrix}.$$

Similarly they can be subtracted, element by element. If they do not have the same dimension they cannot be added or subtracted. The *zero matrix* has zero in every element; it is denoted $\mathbf{0}$. Clearly $\mathbf{A} + \mathbf{0} = \mathbf{A}$ for any matrix $\mathbf{A}$ and $\mathbf{A} + (-\mathbf{A}) = \mathbf{0}$, where $\mathbf{0}$ must be of the same dimension as $\mathbf{A}$.

There are several products associated with matrices:

- A matrix $\mathbf{A}$ is multiplied by a scalar x by multiplying each element of $\mathbf{A}$ by x;[2] this simple *scalar product* is denoted $x\mathbf{A}$. For instance,

$$2 \begin{pmatrix} 0 & 1 \\ -1 & 2 \end{pmatrix} = \begin{pmatrix} 0 & 2 \\ -2 & 4 \end{pmatrix}.$$

- The *dot product* of two non-zero vectors is the sum of the element-by-element products.[3] It is only defined for two vectors of the same dimension. For instance:

$$\begin{pmatrix} 1 \\ 2 \\ 3 \end{pmatrix} \cdot \begin{pmatrix} -1 \\ 1 \\ 2 \end{pmatrix} = (1 \times -1) + (2 \times 1) + (3 \times 2) = 7.$$

When the dot product of two non-zero vectors is 0, the vectors are called *orthogonal*, which means that the angle between the two vectors when represented geometrically in $\Re^n$ is 90°.

- The *matrix product* of two matrices only exists if the number of rows in the second matrix is equal to the number of columns in the first matrix. Thus we can only find the matrix product $\mathbf{AB}$ if $\mathbf{A}$ is $m \times n$ and $\mathbf{B}$ is $n \times k$. Then the dimension of the product will be $m \times k$. The element in the ith row and jth column of $\mathbf{AB}$ is found by taking the ith row of $\mathbf{A}$ and the jth column of $\mathbf{B}$ and finding the dot product, i.e. the sum of the products of the elements.

---

[2] For our purposes, since we only consider matrices of real numbers, a *scalar* is just another name for a real number.
[3] This is denoted SUMPRODUCT in Excel.

For instance, to find the element in the second row and the third column of the product we take the second row of A and the third column of B and find the dot product of the two vectors. So in the product:

$$\begin{pmatrix} 0 & 1 & -1 \\ 1 & 2 & 0 \end{pmatrix} \begin{pmatrix} 1 & 0 & 2 & 1 \\ 0 & 0 & 1 & -1 \\ 2 & -1 & 0 & 2 \end{pmatrix} = \begin{pmatrix} * & * & * & * \\ * & * & 4 & * \end{pmatrix},$$

the number 4 is found as $1 \times 2 + 2 \times 1 + 0 \times 0 = 4$. The other elements in the product, marked with * above, are calculated using the same rule. It is very easy to multiply matrices in Excel, as the following example shows:

EXAMPLE I.2.1: FINDING A MATRIX PRODUCT USING EXCEL

Use Excel to show that

$$\begin{pmatrix} 0 & 1 & -1 \\ 1 & 2 & 0 \end{pmatrix} \begin{pmatrix} 1 & 0 & 2 & 1 \\ 0 & 0 & 1 & -1 \\ 2 & -1 & 0 & 2 \end{pmatrix} = \begin{pmatrix} -2 & 1 & 1 & -3 \\ 1 & 0 & 4 & -1 \end{pmatrix},$$

SOLUTION   Excel calculates this product as follows:

- Highlight a 2×4 array of blank cells.
- Click on the formula bar and type in = MMULT(array1,array2) where array1 contains the cell references for the first matrix and array2 contains the cell references for the second matrix.
- Press Control and Shift and, holding down both of these keys, press Enter.

There are other laws of matrix algebra.[4] Perhaps the most important of these is that matrices are non-commutative. That is, it *matters in which order we do the multiplication.* Formally, if A and B are two square matrices of the same dimension, so that you can find both AB and BA, then $AB \neq BA$ in general. Only some matrices, called *commutative matrices,* have the property that $AB = BA$. A *diagonal matrix* is a square matrix with all non-diagonal elements being zero. Clearly diagonal matrices are commutative.

Another useful law of matrix algebra is that the transpose of a product of two matrices is the product of the transposes in *reverse* order:

$$(AB)' = B'A'. \tag{I.2.1}$$

A similar change of ordering is necessary when we take the *inverse* of a product of two square matrices – see below.

I.2.2.3 Singular Matrices

The *unit* or *identity* matrix I is a special square matrix with 1s along the main diagonal and 0s everywhere else. For instance, the 4×4 identity matrix is

$$I = \begin{pmatrix} 1 & 0 & 0 & 0 \\ 0 & 1 & 0 & 0 \\ 0 & 0 & 1 & 0 \\ 0 & 0 & 0 & 1 \end{pmatrix}$$

---

[4] See http://en.wikipedia.org for more information. For instance, the *associative law* is $(AB)C = A(BC)$. Thus, to multiply three matrices together, we can do the products in either order, provided we do not change the order of the matrices in the product.

It acts like the number 1 in ordinary algebra, i.e. $\mathbf{AI} = \mathbf{A}$ and $\mathbf{IA} = \mathbf{A}$.

The *inverse* of a square matrix $\mathbf{A}$ is denoted by $\mathbf{A}^{-1}$. It has the property that $\mathbf{AA}^{-1} = \mathbf{A}^{-1}\mathbf{A} = \mathbf{I}$, where $\mathbf{I}$ is the $n \times n$ identity matrix. Thus all matrices commute with their inverse. And if $\mathbf{A}$ and $\mathbf{B}$ are both square matrices of the same dimension then

$$(\mathbf{AB})^{-1} = \mathbf{B}^{-1}\mathbf{A}^{-1}. \tag{I.2.2}$$

But not all square matrices have an inverse. A matrix that has an inverse is called a *non-singular matrix*; otherwise it is called a *singular matrix*. A singular matrix has at least one row (or column) that is a weighted sum of some other rows (or columns). That is, there is a linear relationship between the rows (or columns) and for this reason the rows (or columns) are called *linearly dependent*.

I.2.2.4 Determinants

Given any 2×2 square matrix $\begin{pmatrix} a & b \\ c & d \end{pmatrix}$ the quantity $ad - bc$ is called the *determinant* of the matrix. It is denoted $\det(\mathbf{A})$ or $|\mathbf{A}|$. Thus the determinant of a 2×2 matrix is

$$\det \begin{pmatrix} a & b \\ c & d \end{pmatrix} = \begin{vmatrix} a & b \\ c & d \end{vmatrix} = ad - bc.$$

For instance,

$$\begin{vmatrix} 1 & 2 \\ 3 & 4 \end{vmatrix} = -2.$$

The determinant of a 3×3 matrix is given by

$$\begin{vmatrix} a_{11} & a_{12} & a_{13} \\ a_{21} & a_{22} & a_{23} \\ a_{31} & a_{32} & a_{33} \end{vmatrix} = a_{11} \begin{vmatrix} a_{22} & a_{23} \\ a_{32} & a_{33} \end{vmatrix} - a_{12} \begin{vmatrix} a_{21} & a_{23} \\ a_{31} & a_{33} \end{vmatrix} + a_{13} \begin{vmatrix} a_{21} & a_{22} \\ a_{31} & a_{32} \end{vmatrix},$$

and as the dimension increases we calculate the determinant in a similar recursive fashion.

In general, taking the first row and writing the determinant as a sum of lower order determinants gives the determinant. In fact, we do not need to expand the determinant using the first row as we have done above – it makes sense to expand by any row (or column) with plenty of zeros if possible.

If the determinant of an $n \times n$ matrix $\mathbf{A}$ is expanded relative to the ith row then

$$\det(\mathbf{A}) = a_{i1}C_{i1} + \ldots + a_{in}C_{in}, \tag{I.2.3}$$

where C_{ij} is the determinant obtained from $\det(\mathbf{A})$ by deleting the ith row and the jth column from $\mathbf{A}$ and affixing the *position sign* $(-1)^{i+j}$ to it. Analogous expansions exist relative to any particular column, thus:

$$\det(\mathbf{A}) = a_{1j}C_{1j} + \ldots + a_{nj}C_{nj}. \tag{I.2.4}$$

Let M_{ij} be the determinant obtained by deleting the ith row and the jth column from $\mathbf{A}$. Then

$$C_{ij} = (-1)^{i+j} M_{ij}. \tag{I.2.5}$$

M_{ij} is called the i,jth *minor* and C_{ij} is called the i,jth *cofactor* of $\mathbf{A}$. When $i = j$ they are called *principal minors* and *principal cofactors*, respectively.

EXAMPLE I.2.2: CALCULATING A 4×4 DETERMINANT

Calculate the determinant of

$$A = \begin{pmatrix} 1 & 2 & 1 & 0 \\ 0 & 1 & -1 & 2 \\ 1 & 0 & 0 & 1 \\ 2 & 2 & 1 & 1 \end{pmatrix}.$$

SOLUTION   Expanding by the third row gives

$$\begin{vmatrix} 1 & 2 & 1 & 0 \\ 0 & 1 & -1 & 2 \\ 1 & 0 & 0 & 1 \\ 2 & 2 & 1 & 1 \end{vmatrix} = \begin{vmatrix} 2 & 1 & 0 \\ 1 & -1 & 2 \\ 2 & 1 & 1 \end{vmatrix} - \begin{vmatrix} 1 & 2 & 1 \\ 0 & 1 & -1 \\ 2 & 2 & 1 \end{vmatrix} = 2 \begin{vmatrix} -1 & 2 \\ 1 & 1 \end{vmatrix} - \begin{vmatrix} 1 & 2 \\ 2 & 1 \end{vmatrix} - \begin{vmatrix} 1 & -1 \\ 2 & 1 \end{vmatrix}$$

$$-2 \begin{vmatrix} 2 & 1 \\ 1 & -1 \end{vmatrix} = -6 + 3 - 3 + 6 = 0.$$

A matrix that has a zero determinant, as in Example I.2.2, must be a singular matrix. Indeed in this example the sum of the first and third rows is equal to the fourth row, so the rows are linearly dependent.

The determinant is zero if and only if the matrix is singular, which means it has no inverse. Put another way, if the determinant is non-zero we can find a unique inverse matrix, and conversely, if the matrix has a unique inverse it must be non-singular, i.e. it will have a non-zero determinant. In summary, the following statements are *equivalent*:

- A matrix is non-singular.
- The determinant is non-zero.
- The matrix has a unique inverse.

Put another way:

- A square matrix has an inverse (i.e. it is non-singular) if and only if its determinant is non-zero.
- When a square matrix A is singular the determinant of A is zero, it has no inverse A^{-1} and the columns of A are linearly dependent, i.e. there is some weighted sum, or linear combination of the column vectors that is the zero vector. Similarly, the rows of A will also be linearly dependent.

Other properties of determinants are:

$$|A'| = |A| \qquad \text{for any square matrix } A,$$

$$|A^{-1}| = |A|^{-1} \qquad \text{for any invertible matrix } A,$$

$$|A| = 0 \qquad \text{for a singular (non invertible) matrix } A,$$

$$|cA| = c^n |A| \qquad \text{for a constant } c \text{ and an } n \times n \text{ matrix } A,$$

$$|AB| = |A| |B| \qquad \text{if } A \text{ and } B \text{ are both } n \times n.$$

It can be shown that the determinant of a square matrix is the product of all its eigenvalues (see Section I.2.3). Hence a square matrix is singular if and only if it has at least one zero eigenvalue.

A square matrix $\mathbf{A}$ is *diagonalizable* if there exists another matrix $\mathbf{P}$ such that

$$\mathbf{P}^{-1}\mathbf{A}\mathbf{P}=\mathbf{D}, \tag{I.2.6}$$

where $\mathbf{D}$ is a diagonal matrix. If $\mathbf{A}$ is diagonalizable then the number of non-zero eigenvalues is called the *rank* of $\mathbf{A}$ and the number of zero eigenvalues of $\mathbf{A}$ is called the *nullity* of $\mathbf{A}$. Thus the rank and nullity sum to n. But this definition will not suffice if $\mathbf{A}$ is not diagonalizable. For example, all eigenvalues of the matrix

$$\mathbf{A}=\begin{pmatrix} 0 & 1 & 0 \\ 0 & 0 & 1 \\ 0 & 0 & 0 \end{pmatrix}$$

are zero, but $\mathbf{A}$ has rank 2 (and therefore, nullity 1). In general, the rank of $\mathbf{A}$ is the number of linearly independent rows of $\mathbf{A}$ (and the nullity is the number of linearly dependent rows). It can be shown that the rank is also equal to the number of linearly independent columns (and the nullity is the number of linearly dependent columns).

I.2.2.5 Matrix Inversion

If the determinant of a matrix is non-zero then the following formula can be used to find the inverse of the matrix:

$$\mathbf{A}^{-1} = \frac{1}{|\mathbf{A}|}\left(C_{ij}\right)' = \frac{1}{|\mathbf{A}|}\left(C_{ji}\right) = \frac{1}{|\mathbf{A}|}\begin{pmatrix} C_{11} & C_{21} & \cdots & C_{n1} \\ C_{12} & \ddots & & C_{n2} \\ \vdots & & \ddots & \vdots \\ C_{1n} & \cdots & \cdots & C_{nn} \end{pmatrix}, \tag{I.2.7}$$

where C_{ij} is the i,jth cofactor defined above.

In the special case of $n=2$, the formula for the inverse is simple:

$$\begin{pmatrix} a & b \\ c & d \end{pmatrix}^{-1} = \frac{1}{ad-bc}\begin{pmatrix} d & -b \\ -c & a \end{pmatrix}. \tag{I.2.8}$$

For instance,

$$\begin{pmatrix} 1 & 2 \\ 3 & 4 \end{pmatrix}^{-1} = \frac{1}{-2}\begin{pmatrix} 4 & -2 \\ -3 & 1 \end{pmatrix} = \begin{pmatrix} -2 & 1 \\ 1.5 & -0.5 \end{pmatrix},$$

and we can check this as follows:

$$\begin{pmatrix} 1 & 2 \\ 3 & 4 \end{pmatrix}\begin{pmatrix} -2 & 1 \\ 1.5 & -0.5 \end{pmatrix} = \begin{pmatrix} -2+3 & 1-1 \\ -6+6 & 3-2 \end{pmatrix} = \begin{pmatrix} 1 & 0 \\ 0 & 1 \end{pmatrix}.$$

It is easy to find the determinant and inverse of a square matrix using Excel, as the following example shows:

EXAMPLE I.2.3: FINDING THE DETERMINANT AND THE INVERSE MATRIX USING EXCEL

Use Excel to find the determinant and the inverse, if it exists, of the matrix

$$\mathbf{A}=\begin{pmatrix} 1 & -2 & 3 \\ 2 & 4 & 0 \\ 0 & 2 & -1 \end{pmatrix}.$$

SOLUTION   We use the function MDETERM(array) where array contains the cell references for the matrix, as in the spreadsheet for this example. The result is $|A| = 4$. Since this is non-zero we can find the inverse as follows:

- Highlight a 3×3 array of blank cells;
- Click on the formula bar and type in = MINVERSE(array);
- Press Control and Shift and, holding down both of these keys, press Enter.

The result is:

$$A^{-1} = \begin{pmatrix} -1 & 1 & -3 \\ 0.5 & -0.25 & 1.5 \\ 1 & -0.5 & 2 \end{pmatrix}.$$

I.2.2.6   Solution of Simultaneous Linear Equations

Simultaneous linear equations must be solved in hedging problems, e.g. to find gamma neutral and/or vega neutral portfolios (see Section III.3.4). They are also used to find the eigenvector of a matrix, as in Example I.2.11 below.

An example of a simultaneous system of linear equations is

$$x - 2y + 3z = 1$$

$$2x + 4y = 3 \tag{I.2.9}$$

$$2y - z = 0.$$

Here we have three equations in three unknowns. It is not always possible to find a unique solution to such a system. However, in this example we can find a single point (x, y, z) that satisfies all three equations at the same time. From the third equation we know that $z = 2y$. So we can rewrite the first two equations as:

$$x + 4y = 1$$

$$2x + 4y = 3. \tag{I.2.10}$$

Taking the first equation from the second equation gives $x = 2$. Hence

$$2 + 4y = 1, \quad y = -0.25, \quad z = -0.5,$$

and the unique solution is

$$(x, y, z) = (2, -0.25, -0.5). \tag{I.2.11}$$

This is all very well when we have only three variables but what if we had ten variables? It would be rather laborious to calculate the solution, and how do we know that a unique solution exists? It is much better to represent the system in matrix form as

$$Ax = b, \tag{I.2.12}$$

where A is the matrix of coefficients, x is the vector of variables and b is the vector of constants. For instance, in the system (I.2.9) we have

$$A = \begin{pmatrix} 1 & -2 & 3 \\ 2 & 4 & 0 \\ 0 & 2 & -1 \end{pmatrix}, \quad x = \begin{pmatrix} x \\ y \\ z \end{pmatrix} \text{ and } b = \begin{pmatrix} 1 \\ 3 \\ 0 \end{pmatrix}.$$

There is a unique solution to (I.2.12) if and only if A is a square non-singular matrix, i.e. if its inverse A^{-1} exists. To see this, pre-multiply (I.2.12) by A^{-1} to obtain

$$x = A^{-1}b. \tag{I.2.13}$$

EXAMPLE I.2.4: SOLVING A SYSTEM OF SIMULTANEOUS LINEAR EQUATIONS IN EXCEL

Find the solution to (I.2.9) using Excel.

SOLUTION   We have

$$A = \begin{pmatrix} 1 & -2 & 3 \\ 2 & 4 & 0 \\ 0 & 2 & -1 \end{pmatrix}, \quad x = \begin{pmatrix} x \\ y \\ z \end{pmatrix} \text{ and } b = \begin{pmatrix} 1 \\ 3 \\ 0 \end{pmatrix}$$

and we know from Example I.2.3 that

$$A^{-1}b = \begin{pmatrix} -1 & 1 & -3 \\ 0.5 & -0.25 & 1.5 \\ 1 & -0.5 & 2 \end{pmatrix} \begin{pmatrix} 1 \\ 3 \\ 0 \end{pmatrix}.$$

Using the MMULT command gives the result (I.2.11).

I.2.2.7   Quadratic Forms

If A is a square matrix of dimension n (i.e. there are n rows and n columns) and x is an n-dimensional vector, then the expression $x'Ax$ is called a *quadratic form*. For instance, if

$$x = \begin{pmatrix} -1 \\ 1 \end{pmatrix} \text{ and } A = \begin{pmatrix} 1 & 2 \\ 3 & 4 \end{pmatrix}$$

then

$$x'Ax = \begin{pmatrix} -1 & 1 \end{pmatrix} \begin{pmatrix} 1 & 2 \\ 3 & 4 \end{pmatrix} \begin{pmatrix} -1 \\ 1 \end{pmatrix} = \begin{pmatrix} 2 & 2 \end{pmatrix} \begin{pmatrix} -1 \\ 1 \end{pmatrix} = 0.$$

The result is a single number (i.e. a *scalar*), not a matrix.

EXAMPLE I.2.5: A QUADRATIC FORM IN EXCEL

Find the value of the quadratic form $x'Ax$ when A is as in Examples I.2.3 and I.2.4 and

(a) $x = (0.5, 0.3, 0.2)'$
(b) $x = (1, 0, -1)'$

SOLUTION   Use the command MMULT(MMULT(TRANSPOSE(array1), array2), array1) in Excel. We obtain the results

$$x'Ax = 0.99 \quad \text{when } x = (0.5, 0.3, 0.2)'$$

and

$$x'Ax = -3 \quad \text{when } x = (1, 0, -1)'.$$

Given any square matrix A and an arbitrary vector x then every term in $x'Ax$ has *order* 2 in the x variables, and this is why we call $x'Ax$ a quadratic form. To see this consider

$$\begin{pmatrix} x_1 & x_2 \end{pmatrix} \begin{pmatrix} 1 & 2 \\ 3 & 4 \end{pmatrix} \begin{pmatrix} x_1 \\ x_2 \end{pmatrix} = x_1^2 + 5x_1x_2 + 4x_2^2$$

and, for a general 2×2 matrix,

$$\begin{pmatrix} x_1 & x_2 \end{pmatrix} \begin{pmatrix} a_{11} & a_{12} \\ a_{21} & a_{22} \end{pmatrix} \begin{pmatrix} x_1 \\ x_2 \end{pmatrix} = a_{11}x_1^2 + (a_{12} + a_{21})x_1x_2 + a_{22}x_2^2.$$

When the matrix has an arbitrary dimension n then the quadratic form will have many terms, but they will all be of order 2. That is, the terms will be in x_i^2 and in $x_i x_j$. The coefficients of these terms are derived from the elements of the matrix.

When writing a quadratic form as $\mathbf{x}'\mathbf{A}\mathbf{x}$ it is customary to assume that $\mathbf{A}$ is not only square but also symmetric. There is no loss of generality in making this assumption. To see why, note that $(\mathbf{x}'\mathbf{A}\mathbf{x})' = \mathbf{x}'\mathbf{A}'\mathbf{x} = \mathbf{x}'\mathbf{A}\mathbf{x}$, since $\mathbf{x}'\mathbf{A}\mathbf{x}$ is a scalar. Therefore

$$\mathbf{x}'\mathbf{A}\mathbf{x} = \frac{1}{2}\mathbf{x}'(\mathbf{A} + \mathbf{A}')\mathbf{x} = \mathbf{x}'\mathbf{B}\mathbf{x},$$

where $\mathbf{B}$ is symmetric. For instance,

$$\mathbf{A} = \begin{pmatrix} 1 & 2 \\ 3 & 4 \end{pmatrix} \Rightarrow \mathbf{B} = \begin{pmatrix} 1 & 2.5 \\ 2.5 & 4 \end{pmatrix}$$

so

$$\begin{pmatrix} x_1 & x_2 \end{pmatrix} \begin{pmatrix} 1 & 2 \\ 3 & 4 \end{pmatrix} \begin{pmatrix} x_1 \\ x_2 \end{pmatrix} = \begin{pmatrix} x_1 & x_2 \end{pmatrix} \begin{pmatrix} 1 & 2.5 \\ 2.5 & 4 \end{pmatrix} \begin{pmatrix} x_1 \\ x_2 \end{pmatrix} = x_1^2 + 5x_1 x_2 + 4x_2^2.$$

I.2.2.8   Definite Matrices

In the previous example the value of the quadratic form could be zero, positive or negative, depending on the vector $\mathbf{x}$. In fact there are many real matrices $\mathbf{A}$ for which the quadratic form $\mathbf{x}'\mathbf{A}\mathbf{x}$ can be zero, positive or negative, depending on the values in $\mathbf{x}$. But a *positive definite* matrix is a square matrix $\mathbf{A}$ that has the property that $\mathbf{x}'\mathbf{A}\mathbf{x}$ is *always* positive, whatever the values in the vector $\mathbf{x}$, except when they are all zero.

EXAMPLE I.2.6: POSITIVE DEFINITENESS

Is the matrix $\mathbf{A} = \begin{pmatrix} 1 & 3 \\ 3 & 4 \end{pmatrix}$ positive definite?

SOLUTION   Since $\mathbf{x}'\mathbf{A}\mathbf{x} = x_1^2 + 6x_1 x_2 + 4x_2^2$, it is possible for this expression to become negative when x_2 is positive and x_1 is negative. Indeed, if $x_1 = -x_2$ then $\mathbf{x}'\mathbf{A}\mathbf{x} = -x_1^2 < 0$. We have found a whole plane of vectors, of the form $(x, -x)$ for any real number x, for which the value of the quadratic form is negative. Hence, the answer is no.

Consider again the matrix

$$\mathbf{A} = \begin{pmatrix} 1 & -2 & 3 \\ 2 & 4 & 0 \\ 0 & 2 & -1 \end{pmatrix}.$$

We have:

$$\begin{aligned}
\mathbf{x}'\mathbf{A}\mathbf{x} &= 1 \text{ if } \mathbf{x} = (1\ 0\ 0)', \\
\mathbf{x}'\mathbf{A}\mathbf{x} &= 4 \text{ if } \mathbf{x} = (0\ 1\ 0)', \\
\mathbf{x}'\mathbf{A}\mathbf{x} &= -1 \text{ if } \mathbf{x} = (0\ 0\ 1)'.
\end{aligned}$$

So we know that the matrix above is not positive definite.

These special *unit vectors* pick out the diagonal elements of $\mathbf{A}$ when we take the quadratic form. So we can use a unit vector in the quadratic form and the result will be a diagonal element. Hence, a positive definite matrix must always have positive diagonal elements.

A *negative definite* matrix is a square matrix $\mathbf{A}$ having the property that $\mathbf{x}'\mathbf{A}\mathbf{x}$ is always negative, for every non-zero vector $\mathbf{x}$. So, we also know that the matrix above is not negative definite because negative definite matrices must always have negative diagonal elements.

A positive definite matrix must have positive elements on the main diagonal, but this in itself does not mean that the matrix is necessarily positive definite, unless the matrix is a diagonal matrix. Similarly, a negative definite matrix must have negative elements along the main diagonal, but this condition is only necessary and not sufficient for negative definiteness in non-diagonal matrices.

Sometimes we relax the above definitions a little, defining a *positive semi-definite* matrix as one where $x'Ax$ is positive *or zero* for any x, and a *negative semi-definite* matrix as one where $x'Ax$ is negative *or zero* for any x. Formally, a square matrix A is:

- positive definite if all quadratic forms $x'Ax > 0$ for every non-zero vector x;
- positive semi-definite if all quadratic forms $x'Ax \geq 0$ for every vector x;
- negative definite if all quadratic forms $x'Ax < 0$ for every non-zero vector x;
- negative semi-definite if all quadratic forms $x'Ax \leq 0$ for every vector x.

We can use determinants to test whether a matrix is positive definite:[5]

- A symmetric matrix is positive definite if and only if all its principal minors have positive determinant.
- A symmetric matrix is positive semi-definite if all its principal minors have positive or zero determinant.
- A symmetric matrix is negative definite if and only if the determinants of the principal minors are non-zero and alternate in signs as $\{-, +, -, +, \ldots\}$.
- A symmetric matrix is negative semi-definite if the determinants of the principal minors alternate in signs as $\{\leq 0, \geq 0, \leq 0, \geq 0, \ldots\}$.

EXAMPLE I.2.7: DETERMINANT TEST FOR POSITIVE DEFINITENESS

Is the following matrix positive definite?

$$A = \begin{pmatrix} 1 & 1 & 2 \\ 1 & 5 & -4 \\ -2 & -4 & 6 \end{pmatrix}.$$

SOLUTION In order to apply the test we must replace the matrix A by its symmetric equivalent in the quadratic form. That is, we do the test on the matrix

$$B = \frac{1}{2}(A + A') = \begin{pmatrix} 1 & 1 & 0 \\ 1 & 5 & -4 \\ 0 & -4 & 6 \end{pmatrix}.$$

Now we examine the principal minors of B, i.e. the determinants of the cofactors where the index of the column that is deleted is the same as the index of the row that is deleted. The principal minors of order 1 are the diagonal elements and these are all positive. The principal minors of order 2 are

$$M_{11} = \begin{vmatrix} 5 & -4 \\ -4 & 6 \end{vmatrix} = 14, \quad M_{22} = \begin{vmatrix} 1 & 0 \\ 0 & 6 \end{vmatrix} = 6, \quad M_{33} = \begin{vmatrix} 1 & 1 \\ 1 & 5 \end{vmatrix} = 4,$$

and these are all positive. The principal minor of order 3 is the determinant of B, which is 8. Since all the principal minors are positive, B is positive definite. Hence, we conclude that $x'Ax$ is always positive, for every non-zero vector x. That is, A is positive definite.

---

[5] This assumes that the matrix in the quadratic form is symmetric, because in order to prove the test we must know that the eigenvalues are real.

I.2.3   EIGENVECTORS AND EIGENVALUES

Every square matrix has the same number of eigenvalues as its dimension. Thus a 2×2 matrix has two eigenvalues. The eigenvalues are scalars but they need not be real numbers (they can be complex) and they need not be distinct (the eigenvalues could be identical). To each distinct eigenvalue there belongs an infinite set of eigenvectors.

This section starts by describing how matrices correspond to a linear transformation and then introduces eigenvectors as those vectors that are (almost) invariant under the linear transformation defined by the matrix. To be more precise, an eigenvector is a vector that is expanded or contracted, but *not* rotated, by the matrix transformation. The eigenvalue is the scaling constant by which the eigenvector is expanded or contracted. So it is only when the eigenvalue is 1 that an eigenvector is exactly invariant under the matrix transformation.

Once the concepts of eigenvalues and eigenvectors are understood, we explore their properties, focusing on those of *real symmetric matrices* because most of the matrices used in finance are real symmetric matrices.

I.2.3.1   Matrices as Linear Transformations

Consider the product $\mathbf{Ax}$ where $\mathbf{x}$ is an n-dimensional vector and $\mathbf{A}$ is an $m \times n$ matrix. The product is an m-dimensional vector. For instance,

$$\begin{pmatrix} 1 & 0 & -1 \\ 0 & 1 & 2 \end{pmatrix} \begin{pmatrix} 1 \\ 2 \\ 3 \end{pmatrix} = \begin{pmatrix} -2 \\ 8 \end{pmatrix}.$$

Hence an $m \times n$ matrix transforms an n-dimensional vector into an m-dimensional vector. For this reason we call a matrix a *linear transformation* and the study of the properties of matrices is called *linear algebra*. A 2×2 matrix can be considered as a transformation of the plane. One such transformation is shown in Figure I.2.1.

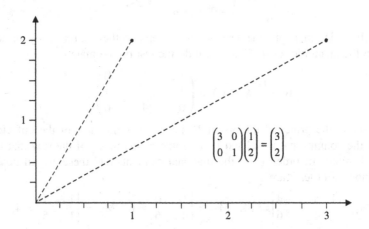

$$\begin{pmatrix} 3 & 0 \\ 0 & 1 \end{pmatrix} \begin{pmatrix} 1 \\ 2 \end{pmatrix} = \begin{pmatrix} 3 \\ 2 \end{pmatrix}$$

Figure I.2.1   A matrix is a linear transformation

In the following we shall always be dealing with square matrices of dimension n and we shall be considering their properties as linear transformations on n-dimensional space.

Where does the matrix

$$A = \begin{pmatrix} 1 & 2 \\ 2 & 4 \end{pmatrix}$$

send the vector

$$x = \begin{pmatrix} 2 \\ 1 \end{pmatrix}?$$

The answer, which is illustrated in Figure I.2.2, is

$$Ax = \begin{pmatrix} 4 \\ 8 \end{pmatrix}.$$

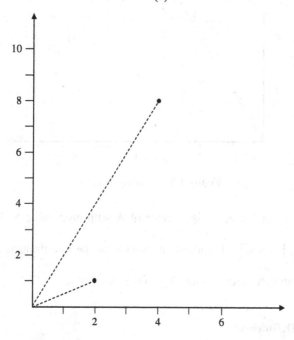

Figure I.2.2   A vector that is not an eigenvector

Note that $\begin{pmatrix} 2 \\ 1 \end{pmatrix}$ and $\begin{pmatrix} 4 \\ 8 \end{pmatrix}$ do not lie on the same line, in other words there is no constant λ such that

$$\begin{pmatrix} 2 \\ 1 \end{pmatrix} = \lambda \times \begin{pmatrix} 4 \\ 8 \end{pmatrix}.$$

As a result, we know that $\begin{pmatrix} 2 \\ 1 \end{pmatrix}$ cannot be an 'eigenvector' of A. However, let us consider the vector $\begin{pmatrix} 1 \\ 2 \end{pmatrix}$ instead of $\begin{pmatrix} 2 \\ 1 \end{pmatrix}$:

$$\begin{pmatrix} 1 & 2 \\ 2 & 4 \end{pmatrix} \begin{pmatrix} 1 \\ 2 \end{pmatrix} = \begin{pmatrix} 5 \\ 10 \end{pmatrix} = 5 \times \begin{pmatrix} 1 \\ 2 \end{pmatrix}.$$

This tells us that $\begin{pmatrix} 1 \\ 2 \end{pmatrix}$ *is* an eigenvector of A, with corresponding eigenvalue 5 as illustrated in Figure I.2.3.

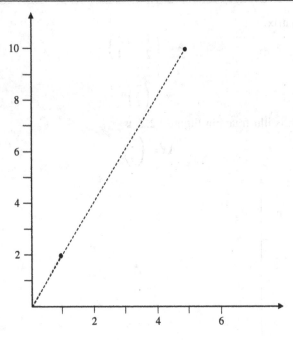

Figure I.2.3   An eigenvector

Note that $\begin{pmatrix}1\\2\end{pmatrix}$ is not the only eigenvector of **A** with eigenvalue 5. The matrix **A** also

sends $\begin{pmatrix}2\\4\end{pmatrix}$ to $\begin{pmatrix}10\\20\end{pmatrix}=5\times\begin{pmatrix}2\\4\end{pmatrix}$. Indeed any vector on the line through the origin and the

point $\begin{pmatrix}1\\2\end{pmatrix}$ is also an eigenvector belonging to the eigenvalue 5.

I.2.3.2   Formal Definitions

The general definition of an eigenvector **w** of a square matrix **A** is any vector **w** such that

$$\mathbf{Aw}=\lambda\mathbf{w} \qquad (I.2.14)$$

for some constant λ. In other words, eigenvectors are those vectors that are translated by the matrix to another vector on the same line through the origin. This λ is called the *eigenvalue* belong to the *eigenvector* **w**.

For instance, the matrix

$$\mathbf{A}=\begin{pmatrix}1&2\\2&1\end{pmatrix} \text{ has eigenvectors } \begin{pmatrix}1\\1\end{pmatrix} \text{ and } \begin{pmatrix}1\\-1\end{pmatrix},$$

with eigenvalues 3 and -1 respectively, because

$$\begin{pmatrix}1&2\\2&1\end{pmatrix}\begin{pmatrix}1\\1\end{pmatrix}=3\begin{pmatrix}1\\1\end{pmatrix} \text{ and } \begin{pmatrix}1&2\\2&1\end{pmatrix}\begin{pmatrix}1\\-1\end{pmatrix}=\begin{pmatrix}-1\\1\end{pmatrix}=-1\begin{pmatrix}1\\-1\end{pmatrix}.$$

That is, **A** transforms each eigenvector to another vector that is just a multiple of the eigenvector. Put another way, **Ax** lies on the same line through the origin as **x**.

However, we know from the above that the eigenvector corresponding to a given eigen-value is not unique. A square matrix $\mathbf{A}$ of dimension m has exactly m eigenvalues. Some of them may be zero, or repeated. Each eigenvalue has infinitely many eigenvectors. Any two eigenvectors belonging to the same eigenvalue lie on the same line through the origin. That is, they are linearly dependent. For instance, if $(1, 2)'$ is an eigenvector for a certain eigenvalue then so also are $(2, 4)'$ and $(\frac{1}{2}, 1')$ and $(-1, -2)'$ and $(20, 40)'$ and so on. That is, if $\mathbf{w}$ is an eigenvector of $\mathbf{A}$ then so is $k\mathbf{w}$, for any real number k. There is only a unique *line* in two-dimensional space or, more generally a unique *plane* in n-dimensional space that is invariant under the matrix transformation.

We usually take a representative *normalized eigenvector*. For instance, we may consider only eigenvectors $\mathbf{w}$ that have unit *distance from the origin*, which is measured by the square root of the sum of the squared elements of $\mathbf{w}$. In other words a representative normalized eigenvector $\mathbf{x} = (x_1, \ldots, x_n)'$ is taken so that

$$\left(x_1^2 + \ldots + x_n^2\right)^{1/2} = 1.$$

Even then there are still two possible eigenvectors for each eigenvalue, because if $\mathbf{w}$ is a normalized eigenvector with eigenvalue λ then so is $-\mathbf{w}$.

I.2.3.3 The Characteristic Equation

The eigenvalues are found by solving the characteristic equation for the matrix. Let us rewrite the definition (I.2.14) as

$$(\mathbf{A} - \lambda\mathbf{I})\mathbf{w} = \mathbf{0}.$$

Any non-zero solution $\mathbf{w}$ of this equation is an eigenvector of $\mathbf{A}$. But a non-zero solution for $\mathbf{w}$ exists only if the matrix $(\mathbf{A} - \lambda\mathbf{I})$ cannot be inverted, i.e. if det $(\mathbf{A} - \lambda\mathbf{I}) = 0$. The equation

$$\det(\mathbf{A} - \lambda\mathbf{I}) = 0 \qquad\qquad (I.2.15)$$

is called the *characteristic equation* of $\mathbf{A}$. When $\mathbf{A}$ is an $m \times m$ matrix it has m solutions for λ and these are the eigenvalues of $\mathbf{A}$. When $\mathbf{A}$ is real and symmetric, as it will always be in our case, the characteristic equation will have real roots. Hence, the eigenvalues will not be complex numbers. Having found the eigenvalues, it is simple to calculate the eigenvectors, as the following example shows.

EXAMPLE I.2.8: FINDING EIGENVALUES AND EIGENVECTORS

Find the eigenvalues and eigenvectors of the matrix

$$\mathbf{A} = \begin{pmatrix} 2 & -1 \\ -2 & 3 \end{pmatrix}.$$

SOLUTION   The characteristic equation is

$$\begin{vmatrix} 2 - \lambda & -1 \\ -2 & 3 - \lambda \end{vmatrix} = 0.$$

In other words, the characteristic equation is

$$(2 - \lambda)(3 - \lambda) - 2 = 0, \quad \text{i.e. } \lambda^2 - 5\lambda + 4 = 0.$$

The roots of this quadratic equation are $\lambda = 1$ and $\lambda = 4$, so these are the eigenvalues of $\mathbf{A}$. Now the eigenvectors are found by solving:

$$\begin{pmatrix} 2 & -1 \\ -2 & 3 \end{pmatrix} \begin{pmatrix} w_1 \\ w_2 \end{pmatrix} = \begin{pmatrix} w_1 \\ w_2 \end{pmatrix} \quad \text{and} \quad \begin{pmatrix} 2 & -1 \\ -2 & 3 \end{pmatrix} \begin{pmatrix} w_1 \\ w_2 \end{pmatrix} = 4 \begin{pmatrix} w_1 \\ w_2 \end{pmatrix}.$$

The first set of linear equations has the solution $w_1 = w_2 = 1$ giving an eigenvector $(1, 1)'$ for the eigenvalue 1. The second set of linear equations has the solution $w_1 = 1$, $w_2 = -2$ giving an eigenvector $(1, -2)'$ for the eigenvalue 4.

However, neither of these is normalized to have unit length. The normalized eigenvectors (with a positive first coordinate) are

$$\left(\frac{1}{\sqrt{2}}, \frac{1}{\sqrt{2}} \right)' \quad \text{and} \quad \left(\frac{1}{\sqrt{5}}, \frac{-2}{\sqrt{5}} \right)'.$$

I.2.3.4 Eigenvalues and Eigenvectors of a 2 × 2 Correlation Matrix

For any real number r,

$$\begin{pmatrix} 1 & r \\ r & 1 \end{pmatrix} \begin{pmatrix} 1 \\ 1 \end{pmatrix} = (1+r) \begin{pmatrix} 1 \\ 1 \end{pmatrix} \quad \text{and} \quad \begin{pmatrix} 1 & r \\ r & 1 \end{pmatrix} \begin{pmatrix} 1 \\ -1 \end{pmatrix} = (1-r) \begin{pmatrix} 1 \\ -1 \end{pmatrix}. \tag{I.2.16}$$

In particular, the eigenvalues of a 2 × 2 correlation matrix with correlation r are:

$$1 + r, \quad \text{with normalized eigenvector} \quad \left(\frac{1}{\sqrt{2}}, \frac{1}{\sqrt{2}} \right)';$$

$$1 - r, \quad \text{with normalized eigenvector} \quad \left(\frac{1}{\sqrt{2}}, -\frac{1}{\sqrt{2}} \right)'.$$

I.2.3.5 Properties of Eigenvalues and Eigenvectors

Not all eigenvalues are distinct, or different from zero. For instance, the matrix

$$\mathbf{A} = \begin{pmatrix} 1 & 2 \\ 2 & 4 \end{pmatrix}$$

has two distinct eigenvalues: 5 (as shown above) and 0. An eigenvector belonging to the zero eigenvalue is $(-2, 1)'$. Two things should be noticed here:

- Any two eigenvectors corresponding to the different eigenvalues are *perpendicular* in the two-dimensional plane. This is because $\mathbf{A}$ is symmetric.
- The matrix $\mathbf{A}$ above has a zero determinant (i.e. $1 \times 4 - 2 \times 2 = 0$) and this is why it has a zero eigenvalue.

For any symmetric matrix, any two eigenvectors belonging to the different eigenvalues must be *orthogonal*. That is, their dot product is 0. In two dimensions, this means that the eigenvectors of a symmetric matrix are perpendicular.

Thus if $\mathbf{A}$ is an $n \times n$ symmetric matrix with eigenvectors $\mathbf{w}_1$ and $\mathbf{w}_2$ corresponding to distinct eigenvalues of $\mathbf{A}$, then

$$\mathbf{w}_1.\mathbf{w}_2 = \mathbf{w}_1'\mathbf{w}_2 = 0. \tag{I.2.17}$$

From this property we know, for instance, that if $(1, 2)'$ is an eigenvector of a 2 × 2 symmetric matrix then the eigenvectors belonging to the other eigenvalue lie on the line through $(2, -1)'$. Similarly, if we know two eigenvectors for a symmetric 3 × 3 matrix the orthogonality condition (I.2.17) helps us to find the other eigenvector. In general, if we know

$n - 1$ eigenvectors of an $n \times n$ symmetric matrix we can find the last eigenvector using the orthogonality condition.

EXAMPLE I.2.9: FINDING EIGENVECTORS

Suppose that $(1, \, -1, \, 2)'$ and $(1, \, 1, \, 0)'$ are distinct eigenvectors of a symmetric matrix. Find an eigenvector belonging to the third eigenvalue.

SOLUTION   The eigenvectors $(w_1, w_2, w_3)'$ corresponding to the other two eigenvalues must have a dot product with $(1, \, -1, \, 2)'$ that is equal to zero, i.e. $w_1 - w_2 + 2w_3 = 0$. Similarly, it must have a dot product with $(1, \, 1, \, 0)'$ that is equal to zero, i.e. $w_1 + w_2 = 0$. Hence any vector such that $w_1 = -w_2 = -w_3$ will do. For instance, $(1, \, -1, \, -1)'$ is a possible eigenvector belonging to the third eigenvalue.

Denote the matrix of eigenvectors by $\mathbf{W}$. That is, each column of $\mathbf{W}$ is an eigenvector of $\mathbf{A}$. When the eigenvectors are normalized to have unit length the eigenvectors are called *orthonormal vectors* and the matrix of eigenvectors is called an *orthogonal matrix*, or an *orthonormal matrix* (unfortunately there is no universal terminology for this property). The important point is that when $\mathbf{A}$ is symmetric then $\mathbf{W}$ is an orthogonal matrix, i.e. a matrix having the property that its inverse is equal to its transpose:

$$\mathbf{W}^{-1} = \mathbf{W}'. \tag{I.2.18}$$

Hence it is very easy to find the inverse of an orthogonal matrix.

I.2.3.6   Using Excel to Find Eigenvalues and Eigenvectors

Up to now we have managed to solve for the eigenvector and eigenvalues of small matrices using some basic algebra. In reality, we shall need to find the eigenvalues and eigenvectors for covariance and/or correlation matrices that have quite high dimensions. This is not an easy task: many methods have been developed and the best method to choose depends on the size and the properties of the matrix concerned.

For symmetric matrices, such as covariance and correlation matrices, the mathematician Carl Gustav Jacobi (1804–1851) developed a relatively simple algorithm. *Jacobi's algorithm* relies on the spectral decomposition (see Section I.2.5.1) by translating the matrix into an equivalent diagonal matrix and reading off the eigenvalues as the diagonal elements of this matrix. Then the eigenvectors are the columns of the transformation matrix. A more powerful algorithm suitable for finding eigenvalues and eigenvectors of non-symmetric matrices is a modified *power iteration*.[6]

Finally, it is worth mentioning that Googling 'eigenvector excel' should bring up (freeware) *Excel add-ins* for finding eigenvalues and eigenvectors of real covariance and correlation matrices. One such add-in, developed by Leonardo Volpi of the Foxes team, Italy, has plenty of matrix functions including eigenvector and eigenvalue routines, Cholesky decomposition, covariance and correlation and so forth. It has been used for the examples in this book where Excel cannot perform the exercise without an add-in.[7]

---

[6] For more details on this and other eigenvalue algorithms, see http://en.wikipedia.org/wiki/Eigenvalue_algorithm.
[7] This add-in should be loaded just like any other Excel add-in: under 'Tools' select 'Add-Ins' and then browse to locate the add-in as you have placed it on your machine. Having added this in once, you should not need to do so again.

EXAMPLE I.2.10: USING AN EXCEL ADD-IN TO FIND EIGENVECTORS AND EIGENVALUES

Find the eigenvalues and eigenvectors of the correlation matrix

$$C = \begin{pmatrix} 1 & 0.5 & 0.2 \\ 0.5 & 1 & 0.3 \\ 0.2 & 0.3 & 1 \end{pmatrix}.$$

SOLUTION   The power iteration method has been used for this example. It gives the eigen-values 1.6839, 0.8289 and 0.4872 in decreasing order of magnitude. We use the array command

$$MEigenvalpow(array)$$

and enter it just like any of the other Excel array functions (i.e. by highlighting an array of the appropriate size, typing in the formula bar and holding down Control and Shift before pressing Enter). A similar command,

$$MEigenvecpow(array),$$

gives the three eigenvectors, but these are not normalized. The orthogonal matrix of eigen-vectors is found, after normalization, to be

$$W = \begin{pmatrix} 0.6076 & 0.4559 & 0.6504 \\ 0.6466 & 0.1917 & -0.7384 \\ 0.4613 & -0.8691 & 0.1783 \end{pmatrix}.$$

Note that you can change the correlations in the spreadsheet and see the eigenvectors and eigenvalues change also.

I.2.3.7   Eigenvalue Test for Definiteness

The following conditions are equivalent:[8]

- A symmetric matrix A is positive definite.
- The quadratic form $x'Ax$ is positive for every vector $x \neq 0$.
- All eigenvalues of A are positive.

Also, the following conditions are equivalent:

- A symmetric matrix A is positive semi-definite.
- The quadratic form $x'Ax \geq 0$ for every vector x.
- All eigenvalues of A are non-negative.

In the above we can substitute 'negative' for 'positive'. Thus to test that a given matrix is positive or negative (semi-)definite we only need to find its eigenvalues. A square matrix is positive definite if and only if all its eigenvalues are positive. If some of the eigenvalues are zero but the rest are positive, it is positive semi-definite. Similarly, a square matrix is negative definite if and only if all its eigenvalues are negative. If some of the eigenvalues are zero but the rest are negative, it is negative semi-definite.

---

[8] That is, one condition holds if and only if the other conditions also hold.

I.2.4   APPLICATIONS TO LINEAR PORTFOLIOS

To measure the market risk of a large portfolio it should first be mapped to its risk factors[9]. The portfolio mapping depends on the type of assets in the portfolio. It is different for equity portfolios compared with bond portfolios, and quite different again for portfolios containing options. In Volume III we shall cover portfolio mapping separately for each asset class.

A *linear portfolio* is one whose return may be represented as a linear function of its underlying risk factor returns. Portfolios with only cash, futures or forward positions are linear. But options portfolios are non-linear. Bond portfolios are also non-linear functions of interest rates; however, we shall see in Chapter III.1 that the cash flow representation of a bond (or a loan, or indeed any interest rate sensitive portfolio) can be regarded as a linear function of interest rates. The non-linear relationship between prices and interest rates is captured in the risk factor sensitivities.

As we have not yet dealt with the intricacies of portfolio mapping we shall here only consider linear portfolios that are small enough to be represented at the asset level. Then, for the portfolio to be linear, its return must be a linear combination (i.e. a weighted sum) of the returns on its constituent assets. In this case it is convenient to represent the portfolio's risk and return in matrix form. The remainder of this section shows how this is done.

I.2.4.1   Covariance and Correlation Matrices

The *covariance matrix* is a square, symmetric matrix of variance and covariances of an $m \times 1$ vector of m returns, where the variances of the returns are displayed along the diagonal and their covariances are displayed in the other elements.[10] We write

$$
\mathbf{V} = \begin{pmatrix}
\sigma_1^2 & \sigma_{12} & \cdots & \cdots & \sigma_{1m} \\
\sigma_{21} & \sigma_2^2 & \cdots & \cdots & \sigma_{2m} \\
\sigma_{31} & \sigma_{32} & \sigma_3^2 & \cdots & \sigma_{3m} \\
\cdots & \cdots & \cdots & \cdots & \cdots \\
\sigma_{m1} & \cdots & \cdots & \cdots & \sigma_m^2
\end{pmatrix}. \tag{I.2.19}
$$

We use the notation $\mathbf{V}$ for an arbitrary covariance matrix of returns, and in particular when the returns are on individual assets. The notation $\mathbf{\Omega}$ is reserved for a covariance matrix of risk factor returns as used, for instance, in Chapters II.1, IV.2.

Since

$$
\begin{pmatrix}
\sigma_1^2 & \sigma_{12} & \cdots & \cdots & \sigma_{1m} \\
\sigma_{21} & \sigma_2^2 & \cdots & \cdots & \sigma_{2m} \\
\sigma_{31} & \sigma_{32} & \sigma_3^2 & \cdots & \sigma_{3m} \\
\cdots & \cdots & \cdots & \cdots & \cdots \\
\sigma_{m1} & \cdots & \cdots & \cdots & \sigma_m^2
\end{pmatrix} = \begin{pmatrix}
\sigma_1^2 & \varrho_{12}\sigma_1\sigma_2 & \cdots & \cdots & \varrho_{1m}\sigma_1\sigma_m \\
\varrho_{21}\sigma_2\sigma_1 & \sigma_2^2 & \cdots & \cdots & \varrho_{2m}\sigma_2\sigma_m \\
\varrho_{31}\sigma_3\sigma_1 & \varrho_{32}\sigma_3\sigma_2 & \sigma_3^2 & \cdots & \varrho_{3m}\sigma_3\sigma_m \\
\cdots & \cdots & \cdots & \cdots & \cdots \\
\varrho_{m1}\sigma_m\sigma_1 & \cdots & \cdots & \cdots & \sigma_m^2
\end{pmatrix},
$$

any covariance matrix can also be expressed as

$$
\mathbf{V} = \mathbf{DCD} \tag{I.2.20}
$$

---

[9] Only in this way we can attribute risk to different sources.
[10] The variance, standard deviation, covariance and correlation operators are introduced formally in the next chapter, in Sections I.3.2 and I.3.4.

where $\mathbf{D}$ is a *diagonal matrix* of returns standard deviations and $\mathbf{C}$ is the returns *correlation matrix*. That is,

$$\begin{pmatrix} \sigma_1^2 & \sigma_{12} & . . & \sigma_{1m} \\ \sigma_{12} & \sigma_2^2 & . . & \sigma_{2m} \\ . & . & . & . & . \\ . & . & . & . & . \\ \sigma_{1m} & \sigma_{2m} & . . & \sigma_m^2 \end{pmatrix} = \begin{pmatrix} \sigma_1 & 0 & . . & 0 \\ 0 & \sigma_2 & 0 . & 0 \\ 0 & 0 & . . & \\ . & . & . . & 0 \\ 0 & , . & . 0 & \sigma_m \end{pmatrix} \begin{pmatrix} 1 & \varrho_{12} & . . & \varrho_{1m} \\ \varrho_{12} & 1 & . . & \varrho_{2m} \\ . & . & . . & . \\ . & . & . . & . \\ \varrho_{1m} & \varrho_{2m} & . . & 1 \end{pmatrix} \begin{pmatrix} \sigma_1 & 0 & . . & 0 \\ 0 & \sigma_2 & 0 . & 0 \\ 0 & 0 & . . & \\ . & . & . . & 0 \\ 0 & , . & . 0 & \sigma_m \end{pmatrix}.$$

EXAMPLE I.2.11: COVARIANCE AND CORRELATION MATRICES

Find the annual covariance matrix when three assets have the volatilities and correlations shown in Table I.2.1.

Table I.2.1   Volatilities and correlations

Asset 1 volatility	20%	Asset 1 – asset 2 correlation	0.8
Asset 2 volatility	10%	Asset 1 – asset 3 correlation	0.5
Asset 3 volatility	15%	Asset 3 – asset 2 correlation	0.3

SOLUTION   We have

$$\mathbf{D} = \begin{pmatrix} 0.2 & 0 & 0 \\ 0 & 0.1 & 0 \\ 0 & 0 & 0.15 \end{pmatrix}, \quad \mathbf{C} = \begin{pmatrix} 1 & 0.8 & 0.5 \\ 0.8 & 1 & 0.3 \\ 0.5 & 0.3 & 1 \end{pmatrix}.$$

So the annual covariance matrix $\mathbf{DCD}$ is

$$\begin{pmatrix} 0.2 & 0 & 0 \\ 0 & 0.1 & 0 \\ 0 & 0 & 0.15 \end{pmatrix} \begin{pmatrix} 1 & 0.8 & 0.5 \\ 0.8 & 1 & 0.3 \\ 0.5 & 0.3 & 1 \end{pmatrix} \begin{pmatrix} 0.2 & 0 & 0 \\ 0 & 0.1 & 0 \\ 0 & 0 & 0.15 \end{pmatrix} = \begin{pmatrix} 0.04 & 0.016 & 0.015 \\ 0.016 & 0.01 & 0.0045 \\ 0.015 & 0.0045 & 0.0225 \end{pmatrix}.$$

I.2.4.2   Portfolio Risk and Return in Matrix Notation

In Section I.1.4 we proved that the percentage return R on a linear portfolio is a weighted sum of the percentage returns on its constituent assets, i.e.

$$R = \sum_{i=1}^{k} w_i R_i. \tag{I.2.21}$$

It is convenient to write this relationship in matrix form. Let $\mathbf{r}$ denote the $k \times 1$ vector of asset returns and let $\mathbf{w}$ denote the $k \times 1$ vector of portfolio weights. That is

$$\mathbf{w} = (w_1, \ldots w_k)' \quad \text{and} \quad \mathbf{r} = (R_1, \ldots, R_k)'.$$

Then the matrix equivalent of (I.2.21) is

$$R = \mathbf{w}'\mathbf{r}. \tag{I.2.22}$$

The risk of an asset or a portfolio can be measured by its standard deviation, i.e. the square root of its variance. Taking the variance of (I.2.21) and using the properties of the variance operator (see Section I.3.2.6), we obtain the following expression for the variance of the portfolio returns:

$$V(R) = \sum_{i=1}^{k} w_i^2 V(R_i) + \sum_{i=1}^{k}\sum_{j=1}^{k} w_i w_j \, \text{Cov}\left(R_i, R_j\right). \tag{I.2.23}$$

Hence the variance of a portfolio is a quadratic function of the variances and covariances on the constituent assets. However, (I.2.23) is a very cumbersome expression. It is much more convenient to write the portfolio variance in matrix form and when we do this we see that the portfolio variance is a quadratic form, with the vector being the vector of portfolio weights and the matrix being the covariance matrix of the asset returns. That is,

$$V(R) = \mathbf{w'Vw}. \tag{I.2.24}$$

Note that (I.2.20) gives another way to write the portfolio variance, as

$$V(R) = \mathbf{x'Cx}, \quad \mathbf{x = Dw}. \tag{I.2.25}$$

Thus the variance of the portfolio returns can be expressed as either

- a quadratic form of the covariance matrix and the portfolio weights vector $\mathbf{w}$, or
- a quadratic form of the correlation matrix and the vector $\mathbf{x}$ where each weight is multiplied by the standard deviation of that asset return.

The result will be the same, as shown in Example I.2.12 below. In this example we use the term *volatility*. Volatility is the same as standard deviation, except it is quoted in annualized terms. Under a constant weights assumption the volatility of the portfolio P&L is the returns volatility times the current value of the portfolio.

EXAMPLE I.2.12: VOLATILITY OF RETURNS AND VOLATILITY OF P&L

Let the return on asset 1 have volatility 10% and the return on asset 2 have volatility 20% and suppose the asset returns have a correlation of 0.5. Write down their correlation matrix and their annual covariance matrix and hence calculate the volatility of the return and the volatility of the P&L for a portfolio in which €2 million is invested in asset 1 and €3 million is invested in asset 2.

SOLUTION   With these volatilities the annual variances of the assets are 0.01 and 0.04 and their annual covariance is $0.5 \times 0.1 \times 0.2 = 0.01$. Hence the annual covariance matrix is

$$\mathbf{V} = \begin{pmatrix} 0.01 & 0.01 \\ 0.01 & 0.04 \end{pmatrix} = \begin{pmatrix} 1 & 1 \\ 1 & 4 \end{pmatrix} \times 10^{-2}.$$

The portfolio weights vector is $\mathbf{w} = \begin{pmatrix} 0.4 \\ 0.6 \end{pmatrix}$ and so the annual variance of the portfolio return is

$$\mathbf{w'Vw} = \begin{pmatrix} 0.4 & 0.6 \end{pmatrix} \begin{pmatrix} 1 & 1 \\ 1 & 4 \end{pmatrix} \begin{pmatrix} 0.4 \\ 0.6 \end{pmatrix} \times 10^{-2} = \begin{pmatrix} 0.4+0.6 & 0.4+0.6 \times 4 \end{pmatrix} \begin{pmatrix} 0.4 \\ 0.6 \end{pmatrix} \times 10^{-2}$$

$$= \begin{pmatrix} 1 & 2.8 \end{pmatrix} \begin{pmatrix} 0.4 \\ 0.6 \end{pmatrix} \times 10^{-2} = (0.4 + 2.8 \times 0.6) \times 10^{-2} = 2.08 \times 10^{-2}.$$

Equivalently we could use (I.2.25) with

$$\mathbf{x} = \begin{pmatrix} 0.4 \times 0.1 \\ 0.6 \times 0.2 \end{pmatrix} = \begin{pmatrix} 0.04 \\ 0.12 \end{pmatrix} \text{ and } \mathbf{C} = \begin{pmatrix} 1 & 0.5 \\ 0.5 & 1 \end{pmatrix}.$$

Then

$$\mathbf{x}'\mathbf{C}\mathbf{x} = \begin{pmatrix} 0.04 & 0.12 \end{pmatrix} \begin{pmatrix} 1 & 0.5 \\ 0.5 & 1 \end{pmatrix} \begin{pmatrix} 0.04 \\ 0.12 \end{pmatrix} = \begin{pmatrix} 0.1 & 0.14 \end{pmatrix} \begin{pmatrix} 0.04 \\ 0.12 \end{pmatrix}$$

$$= 0.004 + 0.0168 = 0.0208.$$

Either way the portfolio return's volatility is the square root of 0.0208, i.e. 14.42%, and the portfolio's P&L has volatility $0.1442 \times €5$ million $= €721,000$.

I.2.4.3 Positive Definiteness of Covariance and Correlation Matrices

A quadratic form $\mathbf{x}'\mathbf{V}\mathbf{x}$ represents the variance of a portfolio when $\mathbf{V}$ is a covariance matrix and the nature of $\mathbf{x}$ is linked to that of $\mathbf{V}$. For instance, if $\mathbf{V}$ is the covariance matrix of *percentage* returns on the asset then $\mathbf{x}$ is a vector of portfolio weights, or if $\mathbf{V}$ is the covariance matrix of *absolute* returns (i.e P&L) on risk factors then $\mathbf{x}$ is a vector of portfolio sensitivities measured with respect to changes in risk factors. The relationship between $\mathbf{x}$ and $\mathbf{V}$ depends on the asset type and whether we are measuring all the risk or just the 'systematic' risk, i.e. the risk attributed to variations in risk factors. This complex relationship will be the focus of many chapters in Volume IV.

The elements of $\mathbf{x}$ do not need to be positive, but the variance of every portfolio must be positive. Hence the condition that all quadratic forms are positive merely states that every portfolio, whatever the weights, must have positive variance. Obviously we should require this. In other words, every covariance matrix should be positive definite.[11]

A covariance matrix is positive definite if and only if its associated correlation matrix is positive definite. To see this, recall that we can write a covariance matrix of a set of returns (or P&Ls) as

$$\mathbf{V} = \mathbf{DCD} \tag{I.2.26}$$

where $\mathbf{D}$ is a diagonal matrix of standard deviations and $\mathbf{C}$ is the associated correlation matrix. Then

$$\mathbf{w}'\mathbf{V}\mathbf{w} = \mathbf{w}'\mathbf{DCD}\mathbf{w} = \mathbf{x}'\mathbf{C}\mathbf{x} \text{ with } \mathbf{x} = \mathbf{D}\mathbf{w}.$$

That is, $\mathbf{x}$ is the vector whose ith element is w_i multiplied by the standard deviation of the ith asset return.

Since the standard deviations along the diagonal are all positive, $\mathbf{w} \neq 0 \Rightarrow \mathbf{x} \neq 0$. Hence,

$$\mathbf{w}'\mathbf{V}\mathbf{w} > 0 \text{ for any } \mathbf{w} \neq 0 \Rightarrow \mathbf{x}'\mathbf{C}\mathbf{x} > 0 \text{ for any } \mathbf{x} \neq 0.$$

The converse implication can also be proved, on noting that

$$\mathbf{C} = \mathbf{D}^{-1}\mathbf{V}\mathbf{D}^{-1}. \tag{I.2.27}$$

In summary, the relationship $\mathbf{V} = \mathbf{DCD}$, where $\mathbf{D}$ is the diagonal matrix of standard deviations, implies that $\mathbf{V}$ is positive definite if and only if $\mathbf{C}$ is positive definite.[12]

---

[11] Or at least we should require that all portfolios have non-negative variance. Hence the condition of positive definiteness that we apply to covariance matrices is sometimes relaxed to that of positive semi-definiteness.
[12] Note that $\mathbf{D}$ will always be positive definite since it is a diagonal matrix with positive elements on its diagonal.

Every 2×2 correlation matrix is positive semi-definite, and is strictly positive definite when the correlation is not equal to $+1$ or -1. But when the dimension increases not all matrices that *look like* a correlation matrix can in fact be one, since every correlation matrix must be positive semi-definite. This is illustrated by the following example.

EXAMPLE I.2.13: A NON-POSITIVE DEFINITE 3×3 MATRIX

Show that the matrix

$$\begin{pmatrix} 1 & -0.9 & -0.8 \\ -0.9 & 1 & -0.5 \\ -0.8 & -0.5 & 1 \end{pmatrix}$$

is not positive semi-definite. Hence it cannot represent a correlation matrix.

SOLUTION   We use the Excel add in, as in Example I.2.10, to find the eigenvalues, which are

$$1.9840, 1.4948 \text{ and } -0.4788.$$

Since one of the eigenvalues is negative the matrix is not positive semi-definite. Indeed, the eigenvalues have different signs, so it is not definite at all.

Most methods for estimating covariance or correlation matrices will ensure that the matrix is positive definite or at least positive semi-definite. But during the stress testing of portfolios, volatilities and correlations are changed in a subjective fashion and there is a chance that the perturbed matrix will not be positive semi-definite. In that case it cannot represent a correlation matrix.

I.2.4.4   Eigenvalues and Eigenvectors of Covariance and Correlation Matrices

The eigenvectors and eigenvalues of covariance and correlation matrices play a crucial role in principal component analysis, which is a standard technique for market risk assessment in highly correlated systems such as a term structure of interest rates. This will be explained in Section I.2.6. But first we shall provide some illustrative examples of positive definiteness of covariance and correlation matrices and find their eigenvalues and eigenvectors.

We can test whether a covariance matrix $\mathbf{V}$ is positive definite by finding its eigenvalues and seeing whether they are all positive. Also, since a covariance matrix is positive definite if, and only if, its corresponding correlation matrix $\mathbf{C}$ is also positive definite, it does not really matter whether we find the eigenvalues of $\mathbf{V}$ or those of $\mathbf{C}$.

It is easy to find the eigenvalues and eigenvectors of a 2×2 correlation matrix. We have seen above that

$$\begin{pmatrix} 1 & \varrho \\ \varrho & 1 \end{pmatrix}\begin{pmatrix} 1 \\ 1 \end{pmatrix} = (1+\varrho)\begin{pmatrix} 1 \\ 1 \end{pmatrix} \text{ and } \begin{pmatrix} 1 & \varrho \\ \varrho & 1 \end{pmatrix}\begin{pmatrix} 1 \\ -1 \end{pmatrix} = (1-\varrho)\begin{pmatrix} 1 \\ -1 \end{pmatrix}.$$

Hence the eigenvalues are $1+\varrho$ and $1-\varrho$. This shows that the matrix must be positive definite, unless the correlation is ± 1, in which case it will be positive semi-definite. The eigenvectors belonging to these eigenvalues are

$$\begin{pmatrix} 1 \\ 1 \end{pmatrix} \text{ for the eigenvalue } 1+\varrho$$

and

$$\begin{pmatrix} 1 \\ -1 \end{pmatrix}$$ for the eigenvalue $1 - \varrho$.

But these eigenvectors have length $\sqrt{2}$, not length 1. In fact the orthonormal matrix of eigenvectors is

$$\mathbf{W} = \begin{pmatrix} \dfrac{1}{\sqrt{2}} & \dfrac{1}{\sqrt{2}} \\ \dfrac{1}{\sqrt{2}} & -\dfrac{1}{\sqrt{2}} \end{pmatrix} = \frac{1}{\sqrt{2}} \begin{pmatrix} 1 & 1 \\ 1 & -1 \end{pmatrix}.$$

Note that since $\mathbf{W}$ is symmetric and orthogonal $\mathbf{W} = \mathbf{W}' = \mathbf{W}^{-1}$ and we may write:

$$\frac{1}{2} \begin{pmatrix} 1 & 1 \\ 1 & -1 \end{pmatrix} \begin{pmatrix} 1 & \varrho \\ \varrho & 1 \end{pmatrix} \begin{pmatrix} 1 & 1 \\ 1 & -1 \end{pmatrix} = \begin{pmatrix} 1 + \varrho & 0 \\ 0 & 1 - \varrho \end{pmatrix}.$$

This is a specific example of the *spectral decomposition* (I.2.30) for the case of a 2×2 correlation matrix. See the next section for more details.

Now consider a 2×2 covariance matrix

$$\mathbf{V} = \begin{pmatrix} \sigma_1^2 & \varrho\sigma_1\sigma_2 \\ \varrho\sigma_1\sigma_2 & \sigma_2^2 \end{pmatrix}.$$

Note that if $\sigma_1 = \sigma_2 = \sigma$, say, then $\mathbf{V} = \sigma^2\mathbf{C}$ and then $\mathbf{V}$ and $\mathbf{C}$ have the same eigenvectors, with the eigenvalues of $\mathbf{V}$ being just a multiple σ^2 of the eigenvalues of $\mathbf{C}$. However, in general there is no simple relationship between the eigenvectors and eigenvalues of covariance and correlation matrices, as the following example shows.

EXAMPLE I.2.14: EIGENVECTORS AND EIGENVALUES OF A 2×2 COVARIANCE MATRIX

Find the eigenvalues and eigenvectors of the annual covariance matrix of returns on two assets that have correlation 0.5 and volatilities 20% and 25%, respectively.

SOLUTION   We have

$$\mathbf{V} = \begin{pmatrix} 0.04 & 0.025 \\ 0.025 & 0.0625 \end{pmatrix} = 10^{-2} \begin{pmatrix} 4 & 2.5 \\ 2.5 & 6.25 \end{pmatrix},$$

so we can find the eigenvalues of the matrix

$$\begin{pmatrix} 4 & 2.5 \\ 2.5 & 6.25 \end{pmatrix}$$

and then multiply them by 10^{-2}. The characteristic equation for this matrix is

$$(4 - \lambda)(6.25 - \lambda) - 2.5^2 = \lambda^2 - 10.25\lambda + 18.75 = 0,$$

which has roots 7.87664 and 2.38354.

Hence the eigenvalues are $\lambda_1 = 0.0787$ and $\lambda_2 = 0.0238$. The corresponding eigenvectors are found using (I.2.14) for each value of λ. For λ_1 we have to solve

$$4x + 2.5y = 7.87664x$$

$$2.5x + 6.25y = 7.87664y.$$

Thus $y = 1.5466x$, so $(1, \ 1.5466)'$ is an eigenvector and the normalized eigenvector for λ_1 is $(0.543, \ 0.840)'$. The calculation of the normalized eigenvector for λ_2 is left to the reader.

So although one might imagine otherwise, there is no simple relationship between the eigenvectors and eigenvalues of C and those of the associated covariance matrix $V = DCD$. We only know that all eigenvalues of C are positive if and only if all eigenvalues of V are positive. And both matrices should have positive eigenvalues. They must at least be positive semi-definite. D is always positive definite so V is positive semi-definite if and only if C is positive semi-definite. Hence the positive semi-definiteness of V only depends on the way we construct the correlation matrix.

It is quite a challenge to generate meaningful, positive semi-definite correlation matrices that are large enough for managers to be able to net the risks across all positions in a firm. Simplifying assumptions are necessary. For example, the RiskMetrics™ data described in Section II.3.8.6 cover hundreds of risk factors for global financial markets, but they are estimated in a very simple way, using moving averages.

I.2.5   MATRIX DECOMPOSITION

In this section we introduce various ways to decompose a matrix into a product of two (or more) other matrices. These decompositions will prove very useful in later chapters. For instance, the *spectral decomposition* forms the basis of principal component analysis, as we shall see in Section I.2.6. And the *Cholesky decomposition*, and the LU decomposition, can be used for generating correlated simulations, as we shall see in Section I.5.7.

I.2.5.1   Spectral Decomposition of a Symmetric Matrix

A square matrix A has a simple representation in terms of its eigenvectors and eigenvalues. Denote by Λ the diagonal matrix of eigenvalues of A. That is, Λ has the eigenvalues along its main diagonal and zeros elsewhere. If we ensure that the eigenvalues in Λ have the same order as the eigenvectors in W, then we can express the eigenvector–eigenvalue condition (I.2.14) in matrix form as

$$AW = W\Lambda. \tag{I.2.28}$$

If all the eigenvalues of A are non-zero and distinct (i.e. no two eigenvalues are the same) then the eigenvectors belonging to different eigenvalues are linearly independent. Hence W is invertible, and (I.2.28) can be written

$$A = W\Lambda W^{-1}. \tag{I.2.29}$$

Since W is orthogonal, i.e. $W^{-1} = W'$, when the eigenvectors have unit length (I.2.29) becomes

$$A = W\Lambda W'. \tag{I.2.30}$$

The relationship (I.2.30) is called the *spectral decomposition* of a square, symmetric matrix A.[13]

EXAMPLE I.2.15: SPECTRAL DECOMPOSITION OF A CORRELATION MATRIX

Verify (I.2.30) for the correlation matrix in Example I.2.11.

SOLUTION   The spreadsheet for Example I.2.15 verifies the spectral decomposition for an arbitrary 3×3 correlation matrix.

---

[13] If an eigenvalue is repeated r times then there are r linearly independent eigenvectors belong to this eigenvalue. It can be shown that these eigenvectors can be normalized in such a way that each is of length unity and they are mutually orthogonal. Thus even in the presence of multiple eigenvectors there exists an orthogonal matrix W such that $W'AW$ is a diagonal matrix displaying all eigenvalues, each with its multiplicity.

I.2.5.2 Similarity Transforms

The *trace* of a square matrix $\mathbf{A}$, denoted tr $(\mathbf{A})$, is the sum of the diagonal elements of $\mathbf{A}$. It has the property that

$$\text{tr}\,(\mathbf{A}) = \text{tr}\left(\mathbf{P}^{-1}\mathbf{A}\mathbf{P}\right) \tag{I.2.31}$$

for any invertible matrix $\mathbf{P}$ of the same dimension as $\mathbf{A}$.

A transformation of the type $\mathbf{P}^{-1}\mathbf{A}\mathbf{P}$ is called a similarity transform, and the matrices $\mathbf{A}$ and $\mathbf{P}^{-1}\mathbf{A}\mathbf{P}$ are called *similar matrices*. When two matrices are similar they have the same trace and they also have the same eigenvalues, the same determinant and the same rank. Because of this property these qualities – trace, determinant, rank and eigenvalues – are sometimes called *matrix invariants*.

From the relationship (I.2.29) we know that a square matrix $\mathbf{A}$ is similar to its diagonal matrix of eigenvalues. Thus by (I.2.31) the sum of the eigenvalues of any square matrix $\mathbf{A}$ is equal to the sum of the diagonal elements of $\mathbf{A}$. For instance, the sum of the eigenvalues of $\mathbf{C}$ is equal to the dimension of the matrix, whereas the sum of the eigenvalues of $\mathbf{V}$ is equal to the total variance.

I.2.5.3 Cholesky Decomposition

A square matrix is called *upper triangular* if it has only zeros below the main diagonal and *lower triangular* if it has only zeros above the main diagonal. If a symmetric matrix $\mathbf{A}$ is positive definite then there exists a lower triangular square matrix $\mathbf{Q}$ of the same dimension as $\mathbf{A}$ such that

$$\mathbf{A} = \mathbf{Q}\mathbf{Q}'. \tag{I.2.32}$$

This matrix is called the *Cholesky matrix* of $\mathbf{A}$. It acts like the *square root* of a matrix and, just as the square root of a real number only exists (in the real numbers) if the number is non-negative, the Cholesky matrix only exists if the matrix is positive semi-definite.

EXAMPLE I.2.16: THE CHOLESKY MATRIX OF A 2×2 MATRIX

Find a Cholesky matrix for the matrix

$$\mathbf{A} = \begin{pmatrix} 1 & -1 \\ -1 & 2 \end{pmatrix}.$$

SOLUTION   Let $\mathbf{Q} = \begin{pmatrix} a & 0 \\ b & c \end{pmatrix}$ and solve (I.2.32). Thus:

$$\begin{pmatrix} 1 & -1 \\ -1 & 2 \end{pmatrix} = \begin{pmatrix} a & 0 \\ b & c \end{pmatrix} \begin{pmatrix} a & b \\ 0 & c \end{pmatrix} = \begin{pmatrix} a^2 & ab \\ ab & b^2 + c^2 \end{pmatrix}.$$

Hence $a^2 = 1$, $ab = -1$, $b^2 + c^2 = 2$ and solving these equations gives four possible Cholesky matrices:

$$\begin{pmatrix} 1 & 0 \\ -1 & 1 \end{pmatrix}; \begin{pmatrix} -1 & 0 \\ 1 & 1 \end{pmatrix}; \begin{pmatrix} 1 & 0 \\ -1 & -1 \end{pmatrix}; \text{ and } \begin{pmatrix} -1 & 0 \\ 1 & -1 \end{pmatrix}.$$

EXAMPLE I.2.17: THE CHOLESKY MATRIX OF A 3×3 MATRIX

Find a Cholesky matrix for the matrix

$$\mathbf{A} = \begin{pmatrix} 1 & -1 & -2 \\ -1 & 5 & 4 \\ -2 & 4 & 6 \end{pmatrix}.$$

SOLUTION   Using the same method as in the preceding example, we write

$$\begin{pmatrix} a & 0 & 0 \\ b & c & 0 \\ d & e & f \end{pmatrix} \begin{pmatrix} a & b & d \\ 0 & c & e \\ 0 & 0 & f \end{pmatrix} = \begin{pmatrix} a^2 & ab & ad \\ ab & b^2+c^2 & bd+ec \\ ad & bd+ec & d^2+e^2+f^2 \end{pmatrix} = \begin{pmatrix} 1 & -1 & -2 \\ -1 & 5 & 4 \\ -2 & 4 & 6 \end{pmatrix}.$$

Since $a^2 = 1$ we must have $a = 1$ or $a = -1$. Suppose $a = 1$. Then since $ab = -1$ and $ad = -2$ we have $b = -1$ and $d = -2$. Since $b^2 + c^2 = 5$ we have $c = 2$ or $c = -2$. Suppose $c = 2$. Then the relations imply that $e = 1$ and $f = 1$ or -1. This gives a Cholesky matrix

$$\mathbf{Q} = \begin{pmatrix} 1 & 0 & 0 \\ -1 & 2 & 0 \\ -2 & 1 & 1 \end{pmatrix}.$$

However, this is only unique up to the signs on its columns. That is, we can multiply any column of $\mathbf{Q}$ by -1 and it will still be a Cholesky matrix.

EXAMPLE I.2.18: FINDING THE CHOLESKY MATRIX IN EXCEL

Find a Cholesky matrix of

$$\mathbf{A} = \begin{pmatrix} 1 & 2 & 0 & 3 \\ 2 & 13 & 9 & 12 \\ 0 & 9 & 13 & 8 \\ 3 & 12 & 8 & 30 \end{pmatrix}.$$

SOLUTION   We first check that $\mathbf{A}$ is positive definite by finding its eigenvalues (using the Excel add-in as above). These are: 41.11, 11.75, 3.83 and 0.31 and since they are all positive the matrix is indeed positive definite and we can find the Cholesky matrix. The add-in command MCholesky (array) gives the Cholesky matrix as:

$$\mathbf{Q} = \begin{pmatrix} 1 & 0 & 0 & 0 \\ 2 & 3 & 0 & 0 \\ 0 & 3 & 2 & 0 \\ 3 & 2 & 1 & 4 \end{pmatrix}.$$

This has eigenvalues 4, 3, 2 and 1. The spreadsheet also verifies the relationship (I.2.32).

The above example demonstrates that the eigenvalues of the Cholesky matrix are *not* equal to the square root of the eigenvalues of $\mathbf{A}$.

I.2.5.4   LU Decomposition

Cholesky decomposition is a special case of LU decomposition. LU decomposition can be applied to several types of square matrices, but the Cholesky decomposition is restricted to positive definite matrices. An LU decomposition of a square matrix $\mathbf{A}$ takes the form

$$\mathbf{A} = \mathbf{LU} \qquad\qquad (I.2.33)$$

where **L** is a lower triangular matrix and **U** is an upper triangular matrix, of the same dimension as **A**.

The matrix does not need to be non-singular to have an LU decomposition, and non-singular matrices do not always have an LU decomposition. In fact a matrix of rank k has an LU decomposition if and only if the first k principal minors are non-zero.

EXAMPLE I.2.19: FINDING THE LU DECOMPOSITION IN EXCEL

Find the LU decomposition of

$$A = \begin{pmatrix} 1 & 2 & 0 & 1 \\ 2 & 2 & 2 & -3 \\ 0 & 1 & 3 & 8 \\ 1 & -1 & 8 & -2 \end{pmatrix}.$$

SOLUTION   This matrix is not positive definite because one of its diagonal elements is negative. In the spreadsheet for this example we use the add-in command MLU to obtain the matrices

$$L = \begin{pmatrix} 1 & 0 & 0 & 0 \\ 0.5 & 1 & 0 & 0 \\ 0 & -0.5 & 1 & 0 \\ 0.5 & -0.5 & 0.38 & 1 \end{pmatrix} \quad U = \begin{pmatrix} 2 & 2 & 2 & -3 \\ 0 & -2 & 7 & -0.5 \\ 0 & 0 & 6.5 & 7.75 \\ 0 & 0 & 0 & -0.73 \end{pmatrix},$$

and then we verify the relationship (I.2.33).[14]

We cannot always guarantee the existence of an LU decomposition for a square matrix, but there are various alternatives that may be used. For instance, any square matrix will have an LU decomposition if we permute of the rows or columns of **L** and **U**. Further details can be found on: http://en.wikipedia.org/wiki/LU_decomposition.

I.2.6   PRINCIPAL COMPONENT ANALYSIS

Principal component analysis is based on the spectral decomposition of a covariance matrix or a correlation matrix. That is, we use the relationship

$$A = W \Lambda W',$$

where **A** is either a covariance matrix or the corresponding correlation matrix. If PCA is performed on a correlation matrix then the results will only be influenced by the correlations of returns, but if the input to PCA is a covariance matrix then the results will be influenced by the volatility of the returns as well as the correlations of returns. In the previous section we saw that there is no general relationship between the spectral decomposition of a covariance matrix and the spectral decomposition of the corresponding correlation matrix. Hence, there is no general relationship between the principal components of a covariance matrix and those of its correlation matrix.

PCA is the simplest of many orthogonalization techniques that transform a set of correlated variables into a set of uncorrelated variables, and it is currently the most popular of these techniques for financial risk management applications. PCA can be applied to any set of

---

[14] It is not always the case that $A = LU$, but it is always true that $PA = LU$ for some permutation matrix **P**.

stationary time series, however high or low their correlation, but it works best on highly correlated systems such as a set of zero coupon returns of different maturities, a set of commodity
futures returns of different maturities, or an implied volatility surface. In short, PCA works
best for term structures.

PCA can achieve many things and, as a result, has many purposes. Its statistical applications include the filling of missing data, and orthogonal regression to cope with the problem
of collinear explanatory variables. Financial applications include multi-factor option pricing models, predicting the movements in implied volatility surfaces and quantitative fund
management strategies. In this book we shall focus on its many applications to market risk
management. PCA is commonly used to compute the large-dimensional covariance matrices
that are used for market risk assessment (see Section II.4.6) and to reduce dimensionality
for stress testing and scenario analysis (see Chapter IV.7).

I.2.6.1   Definition of Principal Components

Denote by X the $T \times n$ matrix of time series of the different stationary variables to be
analysed by PCA. Thus T is the number of data points used in the analysis and n is the
number of variables. The variables of interest here are financial variables such as asset,
portfolio or risk factor returns.

The columns of X are denoted x_1, x_2, ..., x_n . These are time series of data on a (more
or less) correlated set of returns. That is, each x_j (for $j = 1, ..., n$) is a $T \times 1$ vector, where
T is the number of observations on each return and the data cover the same period and are
measured at the same frequency for each variable. Now the input data to PCA is a $T \times n$
matrix X, whose jth column is x_j. We assume each column of X has zero mean.

The sample variances and covariances of these data are summarized by a matrix,

$$V = T^{-1}X'X. \qquad (\text{I.2.34})$$

Note that V represents the correlation matrix of the returns if we normalize the data so
that each time series of observations x_j has variance 1 as well as mean 0. We can do this
normalization by dividing by the sample standard deviation after subtracting the sample
mean from each observation.

In some applications it may be that $T < n$. For instance, we may have only a few years of
monthly data from which to extract the common trend in mutual fund returns. In that case V
will have one or more zero eigenvalues because it will be a singular matrix. Then a full set
of n principal components cannot be determined. This does not necessarily matter because,
as we shall see below, we require only the first few 'most important' principal components
to represent the system. When $T \geq n$ all the eigenvalues of V should be positive, because V
should be positive definite. That is, V will have n positive eigenvalues λ_1, λ_2, ..., λ_n.

We define each *principal component* to be a linear combination of the columns of X, where
the weights are chosen in such a way that:

- the principal components are *uncorrelated* with each other; and
- the first principal component explains the *most variation* (i.e. the greatest amount of the
  total variation in X) and the second component explains the greatest amount of the
  remaining variation, etc.

Denote by Λ the diagonal matrix of eigenvalues of V and by W the orthogonal matrix of
eigenvectors of V. In Λ we order the eigenvalues (and their corresponding eigenvectors in W)

from largest to smallest. That is, $\lambda_1 \geq \lambda_2 \geq \ldots \geq \lambda_n$. The matrix of principal components of V is a $T \times n$ matrix P defined as the product of the matrix of input data X with the eigenvector matrix of V:

$$P = XW. \tag{I.2.35}$$

The mth principal component of V is defined as the mth column of P. It may be written as

$$\mathbf{p}_m = w_{1m}\mathbf{x}_1 + w_{2m}\mathbf{x}_2 + \ldots + w_{nm}\mathbf{x}_n, \tag{I.2.36}$$

where $\mathbf{w}_m = (w_{1m}, w_{2m}, \ldots, w_{nm})'$ is the eigenvector corresponding to λ_m, the mth largest eigenvalue of V. That is, $\mathbf{w}_m$ is the mth column of W. Thus $\mathbf{p}_1$ belongs to the first and largest eigenvalue λ_1, $\mathbf{p}_2$ belongs to the second largest eigenvalue λ_2, and so on. Each principal component is a time series, i.e. a $T \times 1$ vector.

The covariance matrix $T^{-1}P'P$ of the principal components is Λ. This can be seen on observing that

$$T^{-1}P'P = T^{-1}W'X'XW = W'VW = W'W\Lambda = W^{-1}W\Lambda = \Lambda, \tag{I.2.37}$$

where we have used (I.2.28) and (I.2.18). This shows that

- the covariance matrix is diagonal, i.e. the principal components are uncorrelated; and
- the variance of the mth principal component is λ_m, the mth largest eigenvalue of V.

The *total variation* in X is the sum of the eigenvalues of V, i.e. $\lambda_1 + \lambda_2 + \ldots + \lambda_n$. Hence the proportion of this total variation that is explained by the mth principal component is

$$\frac{\lambda_m}{\lambda_1 + \ldots + \lambda_n}. \tag{I.2.38}$$

From our observations about the trace of a matrix in Section I.2.5.2 it follows that the sum of the eigenvalues of a correlation matrix is the number of variables in the system, so if V represents the correlation matrix then $\lambda_1 + \lambda_2 + \ldots + \lambda_n = n$.

In a highly correlated system the first (i.e. the largest) eigenvalue will be much larger than the others, so the first principal component alone can explain a very large part of the movements in returns. The first principal component (i.e. the one given by the eigenvector belonging to the largest eigenvalue) explains most of the variation, followed by the second component, and so on.

I.2.6.2   Principal Component Representation

Since $P = XW$ and $W' = W^{-1}$, we have

$$X = PW'. \tag{I.2.39}$$

In other words, we can write each of the original returns that are input to the PCA as a linear combination of the principal components, as

$$\mathbf{x}_i = w_{i1}\mathbf{p}_1 + w_{i2}\mathbf{p}_2 + \ldots + w_{ik}\mathbf{p}_k.$$

In a highly correlated system there are only a few independent sources of variation. Hence, most of the variation in the system can be explained by approximating each of the input returns $\mathbf{x}_i$ using only the first few principal components in the above representation, as these are the most important ones. For instance, a representation using the first three principal components is

$$\mathbf{x}_i \approx w_{i1}\mathbf{p}_1 + w_{i2}\mathbf{p}_2 + w_{i3}\mathbf{p}_3. \tag{I.2.40}$$

In matrix notation the above *principal component representation* is written

$$\mathbf{X} \approx \mathbf{P}^* \mathbf{W}^{*\prime}, \tag{I.2.41}$$

where $\mathbf{X}$ is the $T \times n$ matrix of returns, $\mathbf{P}^*$ is a $T \times k$ matrix with columns being the first k principal components, and $\mathbf{W}^*$ is a $n \times k$ matrix with k columns given by the first k eigenvectors. It is this type of principal component representation of the original variables, in terms of only a few uncorrelated factors, that lies at the core of PCA models. Only the first few principal components are used because, in a highly correlated system, they are sufficient to explain most of the variation.

PCA is a useful technique for reducing dimensions in highly correlated systems where n is very large and $k \ll n$. Even without this dimension reduction the calculation of a large covariance matrix can be greatly facilitated by the orthogonal representation of the returns: the principal components are uncorrelated so their unconditional covariance matrix is diagonal. For instance, this technique will be applied in Section II.4.6 to generate large covariance matrices in highly correlated systems of returns, such as those from term structures of interest rates or commodity futures.

I.2.6.3 Case Study: PCA of European Equity Indices

Readers will find many case studies based on PCA in every volume of this work. In this section we take weekly data on six European equity indices (AEX 25, CAC 40, DAX 30, FTSE 100, IBEX 35, MIB 30) from 2 January 2001 until 17 July 2006, which were downloaded from Yahoo! Finance. Figure I.2.4 illustrates the evolution of these indices over this time period where, for comparison, we have set all indices to have value 100 on 2 January 2001.

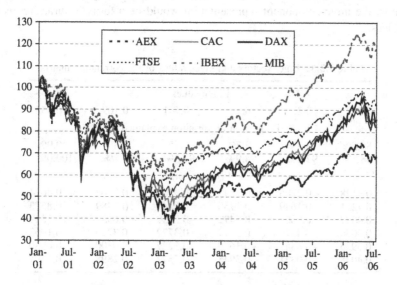

Figure I.2.4   Six European equity indices

We shall perform a PCA on the equally weighted correlation matrix of the weekly returns to these indices. This matrix is shown in Table I.2.2. The spreadsheet for this case study also contains the results when PCA is applied to the equally weighted covariance matrix, but we shall not discuss these results in detail in the text. We have used the Excel add-in, as in Section I.2.3.5. Then the principal components are calculated using (I.2.35) and we shall use the properties of the eigenvalues and eigenvectors of the matrix to discuss what, if anything, the principal components represent. In fact we shall see that only the first component has a meaningful interpretation in this case.[15] The interpretation of the first principal component will be linked to the high correlation of the returns, which is evident from Table I.2.2.

Table I.2.2   The correlation matrix of weekly returns

Correlation	AEX	CAC	DAX	FTSE	IBEX	MIB
AEX	1	0.937	0.884	0.865	0.823	0.855
CAC	0.937	1	0.912	0.893	0.847	0.896
DAX	0.884	0.912	1	0.837	0.830	0.863
FTSE	0.865	0.893	0.837	1	0.790	0.856
IBEX	0.823	0.847	0.830	0.790	1	0.833
MIB	0.855	0.896	0.863	0.856	0.833	1

The eigenvalues and (normalized) eigenvectors of this correlation matrix are shown in Table I.2.3. The proportion of variation explained by each principal component is given by (I.2.38). Thus the first principal component explains 88.5% of the variation, the second explains 3.7% of the variation and so on. The cumulative variation explained is shown below these figures, and we see that a principal component representation (I.2.41) with three components would explain 95% of the variation of the whole system over the period. In other words, the three-component representation would be a fairly accurate representation of the indices.

Table I.2.3   Eigenvectors and eigenvalues of the correlation matrix

		Eigenvalues			
5.309	0.223	0.165	0.141	0.109	0.053
		Proportion of variation explained			
88.5%	3.7%	2.7%	2.4%	1.8%	0.9%
88.5%	92.2%	94.9%	97.3%	99.1%	100.0%
		Eigenvectors			
0.4128	0.2205	0.3892	0.3109	0.5607	0.4674
0.4221	0.1649	0.1750	0.0441	0.1889	−0.8523
0.4097	0.0007	0.5472	−0.2859	−0.6532	0.1559
0.4030	0.4579	−0.5797	0.3772	−0.3720	0.1062
0.3935	−0.8447	−0.1630	0.3227	−0.0300	0.0080
0.4078	−0.0321	−0.3948	−0.7572	0.2898	0.1397

---

[15] But readers will see that in later volumes PCA is applied to *term structures* and then all the components have a meaningful interpretation.

The three-component representation (I.2.40) is therefore:

$$\mathbf{R}_{aex} = 0.4128\mathbf{p}_1 + 0.2205\mathbf{p}_2 + 0.3893\mathbf{p}_3$$
$$\mathbf{R}_{cac} = 0.4221\mathbf{p}_1 + 0.1649\mathbf{p}_2 + 0.1750\mathbf{p}_3$$
$$\mathbf{R}_{dax} = 0.4097\mathbf{p}_1 + 0.0007\mathbf{p}_2 + 0.5472\mathbf{p}_3$$
$$\mathbf{R}_{ftse} = 0.4030\mathbf{p}_1 + 0.4579\mathbf{p}_2 - 0.5797\mathbf{p}_3 \qquad \text{(I.2.42)}$$
$$\mathbf{R}_{ibex} = 0.3935\mathbf{p}_1 - 0.8447\mathbf{p}_2 - 0.1630\mathbf{p}_3$$
$$\mathbf{R}_{mib} = 0.4078\mathbf{p}_1 - 0.0321\mathbf{p}_2 - 0.3948\mathbf{p}_3$$

where $\mathbf{R}_i$ denotes the $T \times 1$ vector (i.e. time series) of returns on the ith equity index. From the representation (I.2.42) we note that all the returns have a similar coefficient on the first component, P_1. Thus when the first principal component changes and the other components remain unchanged then all the returns will change by approximately the same amount. In other words, the first component captures the *common trend* that is shared by these stock indices and which is evident from Figure I.2.4.

Note that this interpretation of the first component is only possible here because the returns happen to be very highly correlated. The higher the correlation between the variables the more similar will be the elements of the first eigenvector and the more variation that is explained by a representation with just one component. In this case, 88.5% of the variation would be explained by a representation such as (I.2.42) but with only P_1 on the right-hand side.

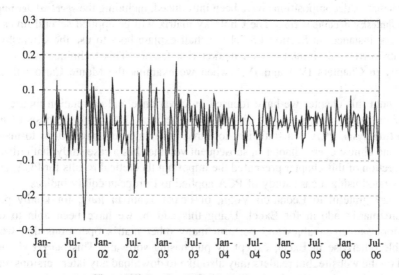

Figure I.2.5 The first principal component

The first principal component is shown in Figure I.2.5. Its features are those that are common to all the returns in the system. Hence, we can see that these stock indices were very volatile during the first few years, until they began to trend upward again in January 2004.

I.2.7   SUMMARY AND CONCLUSIONS

A good understanding of linear algebra is essential for modelling financial instruments. Readers will have learned from this chapter how to represent systems of variables using vectors and matrices and how to operate with these quantities, including taking products, inverses and evaluating the quadratic forms that represent the variance of a system of returns or P&L.

The *eigenvectors* of a square matrix are those special vectors that are simply scaled when the matrix is applied to them, and the *eigenvalues* are the scaling constants. A matrix of order k has k eigenvalues, but the eigenvectors belonging to each eigenvalue are not unique. There are infinitely many eigenvectors belonging to each eigenvalue. We often take a normalized eigenvector, which has unit distance from the origin but even then it is not unique because multiplying this vector by -1 yields another eigenvector with unit distance from the origin.

The concept of *positive definiteness* has been defined and we have explained how the positive definiteness of a covariance matrix depends on that of the correlation matrix, and that these matrices must always be positive definite, or at least positive semi-definite. A positive definite matrix must have positive diagonal elements and a negative definite matrix must have negative diagonal elements. However, examining the diagonal elements is not a test for positive or negative definiteness. There is a determinant test for definiteness but this is rather lengthy for large matrices and it is much easier to test whether any given square matrix is positive or negative definite by examining its eigenvalues. A square matrix is positive definite if and only if all its eigenvalues are positive, and negative definite if and only if all its eigenvalues are negative. If some eigenvalues are zero but the others all positive (negative) then the matrix is positive (negative) semi-definite.

Various matrix decompositions have been introduced, including the *spectral decomposition* and the *Cholesky decomposition*. The Cholesky matrix will be applied several times later in the text. For instance, in Section I.5.7.4 we shall explain how to use the Cholesky matrix to generate correlated simulations on market risk factors. This technique will be applied extensively in Chapters IV.4 and IV.5 when we examine the Monte Carlo value at risk model.

Throughout this chapter we have focused on covariance and correlation matrices and in particular on their eigenvalues and eigenvectors, because this forms the basis of *principal component analysis*. PCA is a statistical tool that has numerous applications to market risk analysis, and almost every chapter in subsequent volumes has a case study that utilizes PCA. The last section of this chapter presented the important theoretical results for PCA, and these were illustrated using a case study of PCA applied to European equity indices.

I am very grateful to Leonardo Volpi, of Foxes Team in Italy, for kindly providing a freeware matrix add-in for Excel. Using this add-in, we have been able to compute eigenvectors and eigenvalues and perform many other matrix operations that would not be possible otherwise in Excel, except by purchasing software. This *matrix.xla* add-in is included on the website, but readers may also like to download any later versions, currently available free from: http://digilander.libero.it/foxes (e-mail: leovlp@libero.it).

I.3
Probability and Statistics

I.3.1 INTRODUCTION

This chapter describes the probabilistic and statistical models that we use to analyse the evolution of financial asset prices or interest rates. Prices or returns on financial assets, interest rates or their changes, and the value or P&L of a portfolio are some examples of the *random variables* used in finance. A random variable is a variable whose value could be observed today and in the past, but whose future values are unknown. We may have some idea about the future values, but we do not know exactly which value will be realized in the future. This is what we mean by *uncertainty*. For instance, we cannot say that the return on an investment over the next year *will* be 25%, we can only say that there is some probability that the return will be 25%. When we write '$P(R = 25\%) = 1/2$' we mean that there is a 50:50 chance that the investment will make a return of 25%.

Most of the random variables we consider are assumed to be *real continuous random variables*. Loosely speaking, this means that we assume their value can be anything within a defined range of real numbers. By contrast, *discrete random variables* can only take certain discrete values such as 0, 1, 2, ... Any real numbers are allowed, not just non-negative integers, provided that the possibilities are discrete.

Since P&L, returns, prices and interest rates are usually regarded as continuous random variables the statement $P(R = 25\%) = 1/2$ is nonsense, because for any continuous random variable the probability that it actually equals a given value is always 0. For continuous random variables we can only make a probabilistic statement about a *range* of values, i.e. an interval within which it may fall. For instance $P(R < 0) = 0.1$ means that there is a 10% chance that the investment will make a negative return and $P(25\% < R < 75\%) = 0.4$ means that there is a 40% chance that the investment will return between 25% and 75%.

Beginning with the basic concepts, this chapter states the basic laws of probability and then introduces the concept of a *probability distribution* for a random variable. Distributions may be characterized by their expectation, variance, skewness, kurtosis and higher *moments*. The moments of a sample and of a distribution and the meaning of the terms *percentile* and *quantile* are all defined in Section I.3.2.

In Section I.3.3 we provide a catalogue of the most important probability distributions for financial applications. Common univariate distributions include the families of *normal distributions, lognormal distributions, normal mixture distributions, Student t distributions* and *extreme value distributions*. We describe the theoretical properties of each distribution and give examples of practical applications to finance. We also define what is meant by a *stable distribution* and why this property can help to aggregate risks over time. Finally, we explain how an empirical distribution can be represented in non-parametric form using a *kernel* estimator.

Section I.3.4 introduces *joint distributions* and their associated *marginal distributions* and *conditional distributions*. Starting with the case of two random variables, we explain what is meant by saying that the variables are *independent* and how this relates to their correlation. The limitations of correlation as a dependency measure are emphasized. The only joint distributions described here are the multivariate normal and the multivariate Student t distributions. This lays the foundation for Chapter II.6 on *copulas*, which are special joint distributions that allow one to build a multitude of other joint distributions.

Section I.3.5 provides an introduction to statistical inference, i.e. *confidence intervals* and *hypothesis testing*. Inferences on variance or volatility are particularly important for market risk analysis and we shall make considerable use of the theory learned in this section in Chapter II.3, when we build confidence intervals for volatility forecasts based on time series models. This section is also required reading for Chapter I.4 on *regression models*. Then in Section I.3.6 we describe the *likelihood function* that is associated with a sample and a functional form for the distribution, and how to estimate the parameters of a distribution using *maximum likelihood estimation*. Readers interested in estimating the parameters of a GARCH model when they come to Chapter II.4 will need to understand maximum likelihood estimation.

Section I.3.7 shows how to model the evolution of financial asset prices and returns using a *stochastic process* in both discrete and continuous time. The translation between discrete and continuous time, and the relationship between the continuous time representation and the discrete time representation of a stochastic process, is very important indeed. The theory of finance requires an understanding of both discrete time and continuous time stochastic processes. Section I.3.8 summarizes and concludes.

Some prior knowledge of basic calculus and elementary linear algebra is required to understand this chapter. Specifically, an understanding of Sections I.1.3 and I.2.4 is assumed. As usual, we have made great use of Excel in the examples and applications, all of which are in the workbooks for this chapter.

I.3.2   BASIC CONCEPTS

This section introduces the foundations of probability and statistics, the fundamental laws of probability, the concept of a probability distribution and the density function associated with this distribution, if it exists. We define the joint, conditional and unconditional distributions, the notion of independence, and the moments and percentiles of probability distributions. Then we turn to basic sample statistics, describing how the sample moments are calculated and how they are related to the moments of a random variable's distribution.

I.3.2.1   Classical versus Bayesian Approaches

The classical approach to probability, pioneered by Irving Fisher (1867–1947), identifies a probability with a *relative frequency*. For instance, if we threw a fair die 600 times we would expect to get a five 100 times. Thus, because we observe that there is 1 chance in 6 of getting a five when a fair die is thrown, we say that the *probability* of this event is 1/6.

But long before the relative frequentist theory came to dominate our approach to probability and statistics, a more general *Bayesian approach* to probability and statistics had been pioneered by Thomas Bayes (1702–1761). The classical approach is based on objective information culled from experimental observations, but Bayes allowed subjective assessments of probabilities to be made, calling these assessments the *prior beliefs*.

In fact, the classical approach is just a simple case of Bayesian probability and statistics, where there is no subjective information and so the prior distribution is uniform.

It is unfortunate that classical probability and statistics have come to dominate so much of the analysis we do today, especially in finance. Classical statistics is rooted in the belief that observations on experiments in the real world are all that matter. This may be all very well for a scientist who is able to replicate precise conditions of experiments. But in market risk analysis the use of classical statistics is limited to those who believe that history is an accurate representation of the future. Of course historical data have a role to play, but they are not the only useful information. Indeed, regulators are continually giving warnings that historical events are not to be relied upon, so they agree that we should arrive at probability distributions using historical information *and* our beliefs. Of course, our beliefs may be based on historical data, but they need not be. Unfortunately it will be some years before market risk analysis has developed to such an extent that Bayesian analysis is commonplace. And since this is a general text I suppress my Bayesian tendencies and present the classical approach in this chapter.

I.3.2.2 Laws of Probability

In this section we define the basic laws of probability with respect to abstract events. In the case of finance, an *event* A may be something like '25% < R < 75%', i.e. my investment returns between 25 and 75% as in the example given in the introduction. Other examples of events include: a price is less than £10; volatility exceeds 20%; and interest rates increase.

Law 1. The probability of an event A is a number between 0 and 1:

$$P(A) \in [0, 1].\tag{I.3.1}$$

If an event has probability 1 it is certain to occur.

Law 2. Suppose A and B are two *mutually exclusive events*, which means that they cannot both occur at the same time. Then the probability of *either* A occurring *or* B occurring is the sum of their probabilities. That is,

$$P(A \text{ or } B) = P(A) + P(B),\tag{I.3.2}$$

for mutually exclusive events A and B. The probability that either event occurs or that it does not occur is 1. The event that A does not occur is called the *complement* of A and is denoted $\bar{A}$.[1] Hence a consequence of this law is that

$$P(A) + P(\bar{A}) = 1.\tag{I.3.3}$$

For instance the probability of getting a six from a throw of a fair die is 1/6, and the probability of getting a number other than six is 5/6.

Law 3: The *joint probability* of two events A and B occurring is

$$P(A \text{ and } B) = P(A \mid B) P(B).\tag{I.3.4}$$

Here $P(A \mid B)$ is the *conditional probability* of the event A occurring, given that the event B occurs. It is 0 if the events are mutually exclusive. The conditional probability should be distinguished from $P(A)$, the 'stand-alone' probability of A without having any information about B – we call this the *marginal probability* of A.

---

[1] The complement of the event A is the event 'not A'. Some authors denote the complement by A^c or by $\neg A$ where $\neg$ is the logical symbol for 'not'.

To illustrate Law 3, consider the probability of getting a six when a die is thrown *given* that the number shown is an even number. If we let A be 'a six is thrown' and B be 'the number shown is even', then $P(A) = 1/6$ and $P(B) = 1/2$. Given the number is even there are only three possibilities, so the probability that we get a six *given* that the number is even is $P(A|B) = 1/3$. Thus,

$$P(A \text{ and } B) = P(A|B)\,P(B) = \frac{1}{3} \times \frac{1}{2} = \frac{1}{6}.$$

Or, put another way, $P(B|A) = 1$ and so

$$P(A \text{ and } B) = P(B|A)\,P(A) = 1 \times \frac{1}{6} = \frac{1}{6}.$$

This makes sense: we know that the number will be even if we get a six, so the probability that we get a six *and* the number is even is $1/6$.

Note that Law 3 implies that

$$P(A|B) = \frac{P(A \text{ and } B)}{P(B)} \tag{I.3.5}$$

and also that

$$P(A \text{ and } B) = P(B|A)\,P(A).$$

Law 3 is sometimes turned around quoted in a form that is commonly known as *Bayes' rule*:

$$P(A|B) = \frac{P(B|A)\,P(A)}{P(B)}. \tag{I.3.6}$$

The left-hand side of (I.3.6) is referred to as the *posterior probability* of A, i.e. the probability of A given that we have some information B. In the numerator on the right-hand side $P(B|A)$ is called the *likelihood* of our information and $P(A)$ is the *marginal probability* of A, also called the *prior probability* because we have no information on B when we form this probability. The marginal probability of B, $P(B)$ appears in the denominator.

Two events are *independent* if and only if $P(A|B) = P(A)$, or equivalently if and only if $P(B|A) = P(B)$. For instance, the probability of getting a six is independent of the event 'the die is blue with red spots' but it is not independent of the event 'the number shown on the die is greater than 3'. Hence, by Law 3, if two events are independent then the probability that they both occur is just the product of their marginal probabilities,

$$P(A \text{ and } B) = P(A)\,P(B). \tag{I.3.7}$$

Law 4: Let A and B be *any* two events. Then the probability of *either* A occurring *or* B occurring is the sum of their probabilities *less* the probability that they both occur. That is,

$$P(A \text{ or } B) = P(A) + P(B) - P(A \text{ and } B). \tag{I.3.8}$$

Thus Law 4 generalizes Law 2 to include the possibility that $P(A \text{ and } B)$ is not 0, as it is for mutually exclusive events. The reason why we subtract $P(A \text{ and } B)$ from the right-hand side in (I.3.8) is that we count this event *twice* when A and B are not mutually exclusive, and this is depicted in the *Venn diagram* shown in Figure I.3.1.

To illustrate Law 4, consider again the events $A = $ 'a six is thrown' and $B = $ 'the number shown is even'. Then the probability of getting a six *or* an even number is

$$P(A \text{ or } B) = \frac{1}{6} + \frac{1}{2} - \frac{1}{6} = \frac{1}{2}.$$

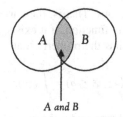

A and B

Figure I.3.1   Venn diagram

I.3.2.3   Density and Distribution Functions

A random variable is a variable whose values are *stochastic*. This means that there is uncertainty about the values that the variable can take. A random variable should be distinguished from a *deterministic variable* whose values are completely determined by the information we currently hold. A *realization* (also called an *observation*) on a random variable X may be thought of as a number that is associated with a chance outcome. Since every outcome is determined by a chance event, every outcome has a measure of probability associated with it. The set of all outcomes and their associated probabilities is called a *probability measure*.

One way of representing a probability measure on a random variable is via a probability *distribution function*. This function gives the probability that X takes a value *less than or equal to* x. Sometimes we call the distribution function the *cumulative* distribution function. Another way to represent a probability measure is via a probability *density function* of the random variable. Later we shall see that there is a relationship between the distribution function and the density function and that we do not need both to describe the behaviour of the variable.

If the random variable is discrete and can only take a finite number of values then the density function can be represented by a table, as shown for example in Table I.3.1. But in standard discrete distributions, such as the binomial distribution or the Poisson distribution, the values of $P(X = x)$ are given by a formula. Note that the probabilities must add up to 1, because X has to take one of these values. Cumulating the values of the density function in Table I.3.1 gives the distribution function shown in Table I.3.2.

Table I.3.1   Example of the density of a discrete random variable

x	-3	-2	-1	0	1	2	3
$P(X = x)$	0.05	0.1	0.2	0.3	0.2	0.1	0.05

Table I.3.2   Distribution function for Table I.3.1

x	-3	-2	-1	0	1	2	3
$P(X \leq x)$	0.05	0.15	0.35	0.65	0.85	0.95	1

For our purposes a random variable will be real-valued and, unless it represents a frequency (such as the number of defaults or the number of upward price movements), most random variables used in finance are continuous. That is, the variable can take any value x that lies in a range of real numbers. Its density function, if it exists, is given by an integrable function f of x which is never negative and has the property that

$$P(a \leq X \leq b) = \int_a^b f(x)dx. \tag{I.3.9}$$

Since $P(-\infty < X < \infty) = 1$ the total area under the curve of a continuous density must be 1. Also, since there is no area under the density function defined by the inequality $a \leq X \leq a$, every continuous random variable has the property that $P(X = a) = 0$ for any real number a. This, of course, also means that $P(X \leq a) = P(X < a)$ and $P(X \geq a) = P(X > a)$ for any real number a, and that $P(a < X < b) = P(a \leq X \leq b)$.

Given a probability density function $f(x)$, the corresponding distribution function is

$$F(x) = P(X \leq x) = \int_{-\infty}^x f(y)dy. \tag{I.3.10}$$

In other words, the distribution function is the area under the density curve to the left of x. Also, combining (I.3.9) and (I.3.10) yields

$$P(a \leq X \leq b) = F(b) - F(a). \tag{I.3.11}$$

It is not really necessary to specify both the density and distribution functions. For discrete random variables the distribution is the sum of the density, and the density is the difference of the distribution. For continuous variables the distribution function is the integral of the density function, and the density is the first derivative of the distribution with respect to x, $f(x) = F'(x)$, if this exists. Often it is easier to specify the density function (e.g. for normal or lognormal distributions) but sometimes it is easier to specify the distribution function (e.g. for extreme value distributions).

Figure I.3.2 illustrates the typical shapes for density and distribution functions of (a) a discrete and (b) a continuous random variable X. In the discrete case the value of the distribution function at $X = x$ is the cumulative sum of the densities up to and including x. In the continuous case the value of the distribution function at $X = x$ is the area under the density curve to the left of x. In each case we indicate the probability that the random variable takes a value less than or equal to 0.1, i.e.

$$P(X \leq 0.1) = \begin{cases} \sum_{x=-\infty}^{0.1} P(X = x), & \text{for discrete } X, \\ \int_{-\infty}^{0.1} f(x)dx, & \text{for continuous } X. \end{cases}$$

I.3.2.4   Samples and Histograms

A *histogram* is a discrete density function that is obtained from observations on the value of a random variable. We call any set of observations on one or more random variables a *sample*. A sample of size n has n observations, often denoted $\{x_1, \ldots, x_n\}$. For instance, a sample could be a set of returns on a financial asset, observed at a particular frequency (e.g. daily or weekly) over a given time period. We call such a sample a set of *historical* returns.

To build a histogram from a sample we first bucket the observations into 'cells' or 'bins' of equal width. For instance, the cells could be $\{-1$ or less; -1 to -0.9; -0.9 to -0.8; \ldots;

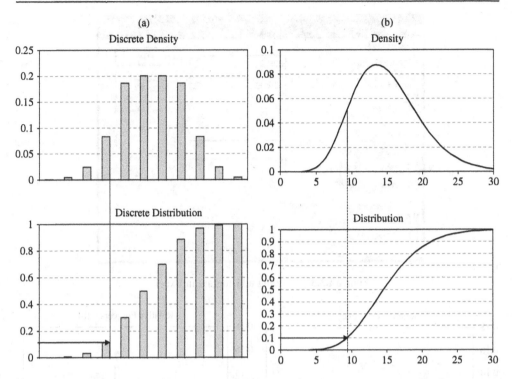

Figure I.3.2 Density and distribution functions: (a) discrete random variable; (b) continuous variable

0.8 to 0.9, 0.9 to 1, greater than 1}.[2] We then count the number of observations in each cell, and divide by the total number of observations (i.e. the sample size) to obtain the proportion or *relative frequency* of observations in each cell. A plot of these relative frequencies is called the histogram. Thus the histogram relates to an *empirical distribution* rather than to a theoretical distribution.

EXAMPLE I.3.1: BUILDING A HISTOGRAM

Using daily data on the S&P 500 index from 31 December 2004 to 30 December 2005, construct two histograms of the daily log returns, one with cell width 0.001 and the other with cell width 0.002.

SOLUTION   We use the Excel data analysis tool 'histogram' to automatically bucket the log returns into a predefined 'bin range', as illustrated in Figure I.3.3. The result is the frequency density, so we must divide by the sample size (252 in this case) to obtain the *relative frequency densities* shown in Figure I.3.4. A sample histogram gives an idea of the shape of the probability density function for the whole population. The larger the sample, the better the approximation is. However, this example shows that the choice of cell width influences the shape of the histogram. How does one choose the best cell width, i.e. the cell width that gives us the closest representation of the population density? See Section I.3.3.12 for the answer.

---

[2] If an observation falls on a boundary we normally use the convention that it is placed in the lower bin. Thus 0.9 is in the bin 0.8 to 0.9, not in the bin 0.9 to 1 in this example.

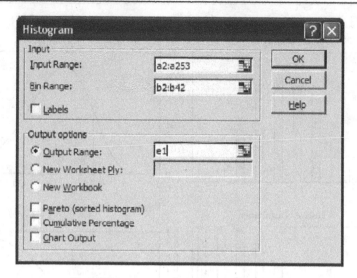

Figure I.3.3   Building a histogram in Excel

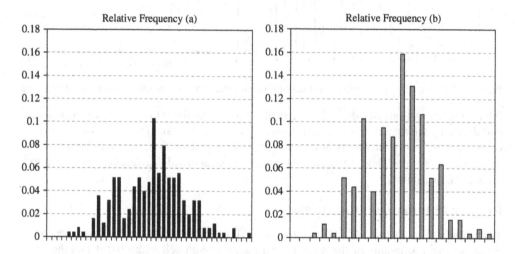

Figure I.3.4   The effect of cell width on the histogram shape

I.3.2.5   Expected Value and Sample Mean

The *first moment* of the probability distribution of a random variable X is called the *expected value* or the *expectation* of X. This is denoted $E(X)$ if we use the *operator notation* or μ if we use the *parameter notation*. The expected value represents the *centre of location* of the distribution. Formally,[3]

$$\mu = E(X) = \sum_{-\infty}^{\infty} x P(X = x) \tag{I.3.12}$$

---

[3] Naturally X need not have a range that goes from $-\infty$ to $+\infty$. The range depends on the random variable. But we can use $-\infty$ to $+\infty$ as the range and thereby use the same formula for all random variables, since the density is zero for values of x outside its range.

when X is discrete, or

$$\mu = E(X) = \int_{-\infty}^{\infty} x f(x) \, dx \qquad (I.3.13)$$

when X is continuous with density function $f(x)$.

The expectation operator is a *linear operator*, i.e. for random variables X and Y and constants a and b,

$$E(aX + bY) = aE(X) + bE(Y). \qquad (I.3.14)$$

For example,

$$E(2X - 3Y) = 2E(X) - 3E(Y).$$

Since $E(X)$ is a real number and not a random variable,

$$E(E(X)) = E(X). \qquad (I.3.15)$$

This property is sometimes referred to as the *tower law for expectations*.

The *sample mean* is the arithmetic average of the observations in sample. For instance, the expectation of the sample $\{1, 2, 3, 4, 5\}$ is 3. Denoting a sample with n observations on a random variable X by $\{x_1, \ldots, x_n\}$, the sample mean is given by the formula

$$\bar{x} = n^{-1} \sum_{i=1}^{n} x_i. \qquad (I.3.16)$$

It can be shown that this is an *unbiased estimate* of the expected value of the distribution. That is,

$$E(\bar{X}) = E(X) = \mu.$$

Here $\bar{X}$ is the random variable formed by repeatedly taking samples of size n from the population and calculating the sample means. The sample mean $\bar{X}$ is a special sort of random variable because its uncertainty arises from differences between samples. In other words, $\bar{X}$ is a *sampling random variable*. Its distribution depends on the size of the sample. Whilst $\bar{X}$ always has the same expected value (the population mean, μ) the variability depends on the size of the sample. The larger is n, the less the variability of $\bar{X}$. We shall return to this point in Section I.3.5.2.

I.3.2.6 Variance

The variance of the probability distribution of a random variable X is denoted $V(X)$ in operator notation or σ^2 in parameter notation. It represents the dispersion about the centre of the density. Formally,

$$\sigma^2 = V(X) = \sum_{-\infty}^{\infty} (x - \mu)^2 P(X = x) \qquad (I.3.17)$$

when X is discrete, or

$$\sigma^2 = V(X) = \int_{-\infty}^{\infty} (x - \mu)^2 f(x) dx \qquad (I.3.18)$$

when X is continuous with density function $f(x)$. It follows from this definition that

$$V(X) = E([X - E(X)]^2).$$ (I.3.19)

For this reason we call the variance the *second moment about the expectation*, or the second *central moment* of the distribution. Note that (I.3.15) and (I.3.19) together give a simple relationship between variance and expectation, i.e.

$$V(X) = E(X^2) - E(X)^2.$$ (I.3.20)

This property often simplifies the calculation of a variance.

Another property of the variance operator, which we have already used in Section I.2.4, is that for any constants a and b and any random variables X and Y,

$$V(aX + bY) = a^2 V(X) + b^2 V(Y) + 2ab \, \text{Cov}(X, Y)$$ (I.3.21)

where $\text{Cov}(X, Y)$ denotes the *covariance* between X and Y. We formally introduce the covariance operator, and its relationship with the correlation operator, in Section I.3.4.

The square root of the variance is called the *standard deviation* or, in the case where the random variable is a sampling random variable, the *standard error*. We often quote the standard deviation as the measure of dispersion rather than the variance. This is because it is in the same units of measurement as the expectation.

The two density functions shown in Figure I.3.5 have the same expectation, but the density function shown by the black line has greater standard deviation than the density shown by the grey line.

Corresponding to the population parameters we have the sample statistics s^2 (sample variance) and s (sample standard deviation). Given a sample $\{x_1, \ldots, x_n\}$ with n observations on a random variable X, we calculate the sample variance using the formula

$$s^2 = (n-1)^{-1} \sum_{i=1}^{n} (x_i - \bar{x})^2.$$ (I.3.22)

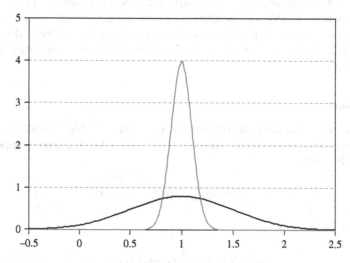

Figure I.3.5 Two densities with the same expectation but different standard deviations

Note that we divide by $n-1$ and not by n because only then will (I.3.22) be an *unbiased estimator* of the population variance, i.e.

$$E(s^2) = \sigma^2. \tag{I.3.23}$$

An example in the next section computes the variance of a sample and its square root s, the sample standard deviation.

I.3.2.7 Skewness and Kurtosis

The variance is the second central moment of the random variable. The variance could also be denoted μ_2, a notation that makes clear the extension to higher moments. The kth *central moment* is defined by

$$\mu_k = E\left([X - \mu]^k\right). \tag{I.3.24}$$

The *skewness* and *kurtosis* are the third and fourth standardized central moments, where a standardized central moment is the kth central moment divided by σ^k. We may as well use parameter notation rather than operator notation for these because, unlike the expectation and variance, the skewness and kurtosis operators do not obey simple rules. Thus the skewness τ and kurtosis κ are respectively given by

$$\tau = \frac{\mu_3}{\sigma^3}, \quad \kappa = \frac{\mu_4}{\sigma^4}. \tag{I.3.25}$$

EXAMPLE I.3.2: CALCULATING MOMENTS OF A DISTRIBUTION

Calculate the first four moments of the distribution with density function given in Table I.3.1.

SOLUTION   The expectation of the random variable X with this distribution is zero:

$$E(X) = -3 \times 0.05 - 2 \times 0.1 - 1 \times 0.2 + 0 \times 0.3 + 1 \times 0.2 + 2 \times 0.1 + 3 \times 0.05 = 0.$$

That this is so could have been seen immediately, on observing that the density is symmetric and its centre is located at zero. The variance is

$$V(X) = 9 \times 0.05 + 4 \times 0.1 + 1 \times 0.2 + 0 \times 0.3 + 1 \times 0.2 + 4 \times 0.1 + 9 \times 0.05 = 2.1,$$

and so the standard deviation is 1.45. We can tell immediately that the skewness is 0, because the density is symmetric. But the fourth central moment (remembering that in this case the centre happens to be at zero) is

$$\mu_4 = (-3)^4 \times 0.05 + (-2)^4 \times 0.1 + (-1)^4 \times 0.2 + 0 \times 0.3$$
$$+ 1^4 \times 0.2 + 2^4 \times 0.1 + 3^4 \times 0.05 = 11.7$$

so the kurtosis is $11.7/2.1^2 = 2.65$.

In a standard normal distribution the skewness is 0 and the kurtosis is 3 (see Section I.3.3.4). For this reason we often subtract 3 from the kurtosis, and call this the *excess kurtosis*. Then a normal distribution has zero skewness and zero excess kurtosis. If the excess kurtosis is positive the distribution has heavier tails than the normal distribution and if it is negative the distribution has lighter tails.

Biased sample estimates of skewness and kurtosis are given by[4]

$$\hat{\tau} = (n-1)^{-1} \sum_{i=1}^{n} \left(\frac{x_i - \bar{x}}{s} \right)^3,$$

$$\hat{\kappa} = (n-1)^{-1} \sum_{i=1}^{n} \left(\frac{x_i - \bar{x}}{s} \right)^4.$$

(I.3.26)

Thus in general, sample moments are calculated using equal weighting of the observations, but we compute the moments of a distribution by weighting observations by their probability as we did in Example I.3.2 above.

EXAMPLE I.3.3: CALCULATING MOMENTS OF A SAMPLE

Calculate the expectation, standard deviation, skewness and excess kurtosis of the sample

$$\{ -3, 1, 4, -2, 0, 5, 6, 2, -3, -1, 0, -3, -2, 4, 7 \}.$$

How do the results compare with those obtained using the Excel functions?

SOLUTION   The spreadsheet for this example applies the formulae (I.3.16), (I.3.22) and (I.3.26) and also applies the Excel functions AVERAGE, STDEV, SKEW and KURT to obtain the results shown in Table I.3.3. The sample mean is 1 and the variance is 12, and this agrees with the Excel computations. However, the sample skewness and excess kurtosis differ because Excel applies a bias correction to the formulae (I.3.26). The bias correction is also shown in the spreadsheet, where we adjust the skewness and excess kurtosis obtained from (I.3.26) to equate with the unbiased results given by Excel.

Table I.3.3 Biased and unbiased sample moments

Method	Expectation	Standard Deviation	Skewness	Excess Kurtosis
Formula	1	3.464	0.3505	−1.369
Excel	1	3.464	0.4045	−1.260

A *leptokurtic density* is one that has a higher peak than a normal density. Since the total area under the curve must be 1, a higher peak implies that the tails of a unimodal density are also heavier. Hence a unimodal leptokurtic density has heavy tails, i.e. positive excess kurtosis. An example of a leptokurtic density is depicted in Figure I.3.6(a).[5]

A density has *positive skewness* if the upper (right-hand) tail is heavier – i.e. has more probability weight – than the lower (left-hand) tail. Similarly, it has *negative skewness* if

---

[4] Many different definitions of sample skewness and kurtosis such as those used in Excel are based on small-sample adjustments so that the estimates are unbiased. For instance, see Joanes and Gill (1998).

[5] Karl Pearson, the famous classical statistician, introduced the term *leptokurtic* in 1905 to describe densities with high kurtosis. Leptokurtic is Greek for 'thin arch'. He also used the terms *mesokurtic* and *platykurtic* to describe densities with medium and low kurtosis (i.e. excess kurtosis around zero and negative, respectively).

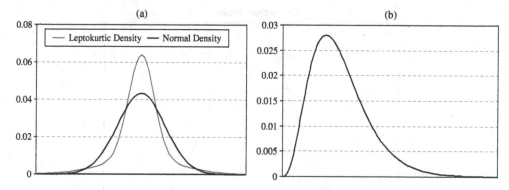

Figure I.3.6 (a) A normal density and a leptokurtic density; (b) a positively skewed density

the lower tail is heavier than the upper tail. Figure I.3.6(b) illustrates a density with positive skewness.

The returns on most financial assets are skewed and leptokurtic random variables, although the extent of leptokurtosis depends on the sampling frequency and the market in question. A negative skewness is often evident in daily equity index and stock returns because large price falls are often succeeded by further price falls as investors try to close out positions to limit losses. The opposite is the case in commodity markets: here price rises are 'bad news' for consumers, who may increase demand for futures forcing prices to rise even further. Nevertheless, the standard analysis of financial asset returns most often begins with an assumption that returns are normally distributed. In fact it is only relatively recently that significant advances have been made in returns analysis based on non-normal assumptions.

I.3.2.8 Quantiles, Quartiles and Percentiles

Any value x of X cuts the distribution of X into two parts: the part that lies to the left of x and that which lies to the right of x. When the area under the density to the left of x is α then the area under the density to the right is $1 - \alpha$. We call x the α *quantile* of the distribution.

Formally, the realization x_α is an α quantile of X if $P(X \leq x_\alpha) = \alpha$. The α quantile of a continuous random variable is the value x_α of X that exactly cuts off a certain area α under and to the left of the density curve. But for a discrete random variable the quantile value is that value x_α of X for which the sum of the probabilities less than or equal to x_α equals α. Quantiles can be illustrated as in Figure I.3.7. In this figure the 0.1 quantile is at -5%, meaning that $P(X \leq -5\%) = 0.1$.

Certain quantiles have special names, for instance the 0.25, 0.50 and 0.75 quantiles are called the first, second and third *quartiles*. The $0.01, 0.02, \ldots, 0.98, 0.99$ quantiles are called the first, second, third, $\ldots$, ninety-eighth, and ninety-ninth *percentiles*. A shorthand for the percentile with, say, $\alpha = 0.01$ is the '1st percentile'. The small percentiles refer to the *lower tail* of the distribution and the high percentiles refer to the *upper tail*.

Percentiles may be computed in Excel using the function PERCENTILE (array,α) where α is a number between 0 and 1. For instance, if the array is $\{1, 2, 3, \ldots, 10\}$ then the Excel percentile refers to a random variable X that is equally likely to take any of these 10 values. For instance, the 10th percentile is the number x in this array such that $P(X \leq x) = 0.1$. That is, PERCENTILE ($\{1, 2, 3, \ldots, 10\}, 0.1) = 1$, yes?

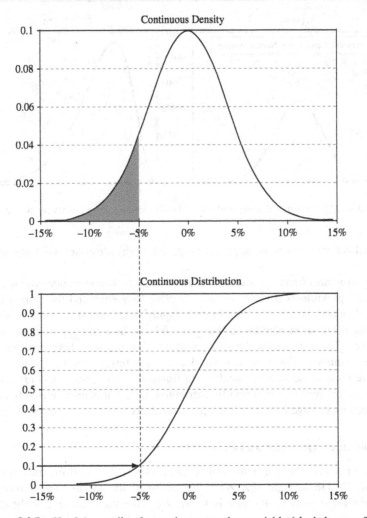

Figure I.3.7 The 0.1 quantile of a continuous random variable (shaded area $= 0.1$)

Er. . . actually, no. Excel does something rather strange with its percentile function because PERCENTILE $(\{1, 2, 3, \ldots, 10\}, 0.1) = 1.9$ and how it gets to this answer is difficult to follow. Obviously Excel uses some sort of interpolation between values, so it automatically assumes that discrete data are realizations of a continuous random variable, which is not necessarily the case. So the 10th percentile is the number x, not necessarily from amongst those in the array, such that $P(X < x) = 0.1$. Secondly, it seems to ignore the largest value in the range. For instance, as you can verify for yourself, PERCENTILE $(\{1, 2, 3, \ldots, 10, 11\}, 0.1) = 2$, which is indeed rather odd.

Percentiles have a particularly nice property: they are invariant under (strictly) monotonic transformations. For instance, suppose that $g(x)$ is a strictly monotonic increasing function, which means that g never decreases as x increases. Then

$$P(X < x) = P(g(X) < g(x)).\qquad\qquad (I.3.27)$$

For example, if $P(X < 1) = 0.4$ then we know that $P(\ln(X) < 0) = 0.4$, because the natural log is a strictly monotonic increasing function and $\ln(1) = 0$. Similarly, percentiles are invariant under any monotonic decreasing transformation. For example, if $P(X < 1) = 0.4$ then we know that $P(\exp(-X) > 0.367879) = 0.4$, because $\exp(-X)$ is a strictly monotonic decreasing function and $\exp(-1) = 0.367879$.[6]

I.3.3 UNIVARIATE DISTRIBUTIONS

Financial practitioners need to understand calculus to price financial instruments and to map portfolios to their risk factors and they need some linear algebra to handle the multivariate systems that represent the risk and return on portfolios. But more than anything they need an understanding of statistics, because the study of the evolution of financial variables is essentially a statistical analysis. This section introduces the standard distributions such as the binomial, uniform, normal, lognormal and Student t distributions, as well as some popular alternative distributions in the normal mixture and extreme value families. Sampling distributions are also included, as we shall require these for hypothesis testing. We discuss the *stable* property that is a feature of the normal, Cauchy and Lévy distributions, since this property has important implications for aggregating returns over time. We also explain how kernel functions are applied to fit empirical distributions. Kernel fitting is an essential tool for constructing an historical simulation.

I.3.3.1 Binomial Distribution

A *Bernoulli trial* is an experiment, such as tossing a coin, that has only *two* outcomes. The outcomes are traditionally labelled 'success' and 'failure'. The binomial distribution is the distribution of the number of successes in N independent Bernoulli trails, where the probability of a success is a constant, p. Its main application in finance is to lattice-based methods for pricing options, and we shall discuss this in detail in Section I.5.6.

For example, when a fair die is rolled during a board game there is a probability of 1/6 of a 'success', for instance getting a six. Moreover, the probability of getting a six on one throw is independent of the probability of getting a six on any other throw. So the random variable $X =$ 'the number of sixes in three rolls of a fair die' has a binomial distribution with parameter $N = 3$ and $p = 1/6$. Three sixes occur only when a six is thrown each time:

$$P(X = 3) = (1/6)^3.$$

But what about one six? There are three ways this can happen (on either the first, second, or third throw) and for each sequence of throws the probability is $(1/6) \times (5/6)^2$. Hence

$$P(X = 1) = 3 \times (1/6) \times (5/6)^2.$$

Finally, two sixes can also happen in three ways (*not* a six on either the first, second or third throw), so

$$P(X = 2) = 3 \times (1/6)^2 \times (5/6).$$

Similarly, no sixes occur with probability

$$P(X = 0) = (5/6)^3.$$

We summarize this in Table I.3.4.

---

[6] If g is monotonic decreasing then $x < y \Leftrightarrow g(x) > g(y)$.

Table I.3.4 The $B(3, 1/6)$ distribution

X	0	1	2	3
Number of ways	1	3	3	1
Probability of each way	$(1/6)^3$	$(1/6)(5/6)^2$	$(1/6)^2(5/6)$	$(1/6)^3$

The number of ways that X can take a given value m is called the *binomial coefficient*. For arbitrary values of N, and any integer m between 0 and N, these coefficients are given by

$$\binom{N}{m} = \frac{N!}{m!\,(N-m)!}. \tag{I.3.28}$$

Here the '!' notation stands for the *factorial*, i.e. for any non-negative integer x,

$$x! = x \times (x-1) \times (x-2) \times \ldots \times 3 \times 2 \times 1,$$

and where we define $0! = 1$.

The probability of obtaining m successes in N Bernoulli trails is therefore

$$P(X = m) = \binom{N}{m} p^m (1-p)^{N-m} \quad m = 0, 1, \ldots, N, \tag{I.3.29}$$

and this is the *binomial density function*. Note that it is straightforward to verify that, if a random variable X has a binomial distribution with parameters N and p, written $X \sim B(N, p)$ for short, then

$$E(X) = Np \quad \text{and} \quad V(X) = Np(1-p). \tag{I.3.30}$$

Three binomial densities are depicted in Figure I.3.8 for the case $N = 20$ and for $p = 0.1$, 0.25 and 0.5. The figure was drawn using the Excel function BINOMDIST(x, 20, p, false) for $x = 0, 1, \ldots, 20$ and for the three different values of p.

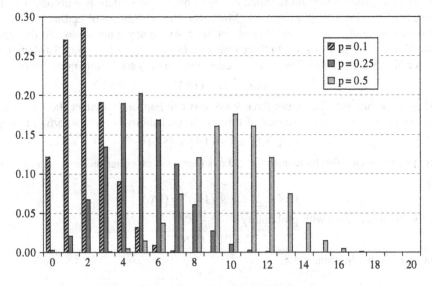

Figure I.3.8 Some binomial density functions

EXAMPLE I.3.4: EVOLUTION OF AN ASSET PRICE

A stock has price 50 pence today but tomorrow and on each subsequent day the price moves, either up by a multiplicative factor of 1.25 or down by a factor of 0.8 every day.[7] If the probability that the price moves up on any day is 0.7, what are the possible prices and the probabilities associated with these prices 4 days from now? What is the expected stock price in 4 days time?

SOLUTION   Figure I.3.9 depicts the evolution of the stock price over the next four days, the number of *paths* that lead to each price after 4 days, and uses the Excel binomial function to compute the probability of each price on the fourth day. For instance, the probability that the price will still be 50 after 4 days corresponds to two successes (i.e. up moves) and two failures (i.e. down moves). Let X denote the binomial random variable denoting the number of up moves over a four-day period. The probability of success is 0.7 and there are six possible ways of having two up moves and two down moves (i.e. there are six paths that lead to 50 in the tree) so we have

$$P(X=2) = 6 \times 0.7^2 \times 0.3^2 = 0.2646.$$

Given the possible terminal prices and the probabilities associated with these outcomes, we can compute the expectation of the terminal prices. Thus if S denotes the stock price at the terminal nodes then

$$E(S) = 122.07 \times 0.2401 + 78.125 \times 0.4116 + 50 \times 0.2646$$

$$+ 32 \times 0.0756 + 20.48 \times 0.0081 = 77.28.$$

				Prices	No. of Paths	Probability
				122.07	1	0.2401
			97.6563			
		78.125		78.125	4	0.4116
	62.5		62.5			
50		50		50	6	0.2646
	40		40			
		32		32	4	0.0756
			25.6			
				20.48	1	0.0081

Figure I.3.9   A binomial tree for a stock price evolution

I.3.3.2   Poisson and Exponential Distributions

The distribution introduced by the French mathematician and philosopher Poisson (1781–1840) is a common distribution for modelling the frequency of events during a fixed time interval. If a discrete random variable X has a Poisson distribution we write $X \sim \wp(\mu)$. The distribution has a single parameter, μ, which is the expected number of events during the time interval. We shall see below that it is related to another parameter, λ, the expected

---

[7] In this example we take $d = u^{-1}$ as is standard in a binomial tree.

number of events per *unit* time and which is called the *intensity* or *arrival rate* of a Poisson process and which is defined below.

The Poisson distribution is commonly used in operational risk to model the number of operational loss events, and in credit risk to model the number of credit defaults, during a time interval such as 1 year. In market risk we use a Poisson process to model waiting times between trades in high frequency data,[8] and to model jumps in asset prices when pricing options on these assets.[9]

The Poisson distribution has density function

$$P(X=x) = \frac{\exp(-\mu)\mu^x}{x!} \quad x=0, 1, 2, \ldots. \tag{I.3.31}$$

This has the property that

$$E(X) = V(X) = \mu. \tag{I.3.32}$$

The values of the Poisson density are calculated in Excel via the POISSON(x, μ, false) function. For instance, Table I.3.5 shows the Poisson probabilities for $\mu = 2.5$. Note that μ does not need to be an integer.

Table I.3.5   A Poisson density function

x	0	1	2	3	4	5	6	7	8	9	10
$P(X=x)$	0.0821	0.2052	0.2565	0.2138	0.1336	0.0668	0.0278	0.0099	0.0031	0.0009	0.0002

A *Poisson process* is a time series associated with Bernoulli trials, i.e. trials with two possible outcomes: the event occurs and we label this a 'success' or it does not occur and we label this a 'failure'. The Poisson process is defined by three basic assumptions:

1. The probability of one success during a very small time interval of length Δt is $\lambda \Delta t$.
2. The probability of more than one success during an interval of length Δt is negligible.
3. The probability of a success during any such time interval does not depend on what has happened before.

The constant parameter $\lambda > 0$ is called the *arrival rate* or the *intensity* of the Poisson process. Specifically, when the Poisson distribution relates to a time interval of length t then the expected number of events during this time interval is $\mu = \lambda t$.

The *waiting time* is the time between successes. To measure the waiting time in a Poisson process the independence property (property 3 above) implies that we take an arbitrary point in time, which we label time 0, and then ask how long we have to wait until the next success occurs. We now show that the *waiting time distribution* associated with a Poisson process is the *exponential distribution*.

To derive this, we first use the definition of the Poisson density function (I.3.31) with expected number of events $\mu = \lambda t$ to write:

$$P(\text{No events occur between time 0 and time } t) = P(X=0) = \frac{\exp(-\lambda t)\lambda t^0}{0!} = \exp(-\lambda t).$$

---

[8] See Section II.7.7.2.
[9] See Section I.3.7.4 and Section III.4.5.8.

The complement of this is:

$$P(\text{the first occurrence is before time } t) = 1 - \exp(-\lambda t).$$

In other words, if Y denotes the *continuous* random variable corresponding to the waiting time between events, then

$$P(Y < t) = 1 - \exp(-\lambda t). \tag{I.3.33}$$

This is the distribution function for the exponential distribution. Its associated density function is obtained by differentiating (I.3.33):

$$f(t) = \lambda \exp(-\lambda t), \quad \lambda > 0, t > 0. \tag{I.3.34}$$

I.3.3.3   Uniform Distribution

As its name suggests, the uniform distribution arises when there is the same probability of the random variable taking any value, within a given range. Continuous uniform variables and the standard uniform variable in particular have important applications to simulation, which is an essential tool in market risk analysis.[10]

The *standard uniform distribution* is the distribution of a random variable X that can take any value between 0 and 1 with the same probability. The density function of the standard uniform random variable $X \sim U[0, 1]$ is depicted in Figure I.3.10.

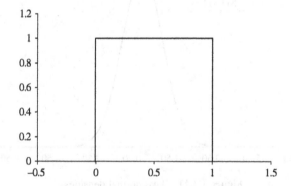

Figure I.3.10   The standard uniform distribution

It is straightforward to show that if $X \sim U[0, 1]$ then $E(X) = 1/2$ and $V(X) = 1/12$.

A set of independent observations from the standard uniform distribution is called a set of *random numbers*. The Excel function RAND() generates a random number, although the random number generator used in Excel is not the best. More generally, we can define a continuous uniform variable $X \sim U[a, b]$ for *any* real numbers a and b, with $a < b$. The density function is

$$f(x) = \begin{cases} (b-a)^{-1} & \text{if } x \in [a, b], \\ 0 & \text{otherwise,} \end{cases} \tag{I.3.35}$$

and $E(X) = \frac{1}{2}(b+a)$, $V(X) = (b-a)^2/12$.

---

[10] The connection between the uniform distribution and simulation is described in Section I.5.7.

I.3.3.4   Normal Distribution

The random variable X has a normal distribution if it has the density function

$$\varphi(x) = \frac{1}{\sqrt{2\pi\sigma^2}} \exp\left(-\frac{(x-\mu)^2}{2\sigma^2}\right) \qquad (I.3.36)$$

for $-\infty < x < \infty$. This gives the familiar symmetric bell-shaped curve that is centred on the expectation μ and has a dispersion that is determined by the standard deviation σ. When X is normally distributed with expectation μ and standard deviation σ we write $X \sim N(\mu, \sigma^2)$.

Figure I.3.11 depicts the $N(1, 4)$ density function and the standard normal density function. The *standard normal distribution* has expectation 0 and standard deviation 1. We often use the letter Z to denote a standard normal random variable. Any normal random variable can be transformed into a standard normal variable using the *standard normal transformation*,

$$Z = \frac{X-\mu}{\sigma}. \qquad (I.3.37)$$

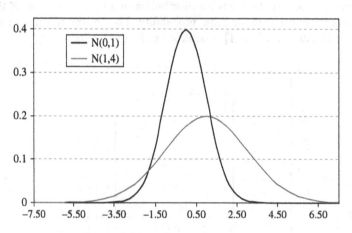

Figure I.3.11   Two normal densities

EXAMPLE I.3.5: NORMAL PROBABILITIES

The annual return on an investment is assumed to have a normal distribution. The expected return is 10% and the volatility is 20%. What is the probability that the annual return will be negative?

SOLUTION   Let X denote the annual return. We calculate $P(X < 0)$ when $X \sim N(0.1, 0.04)$ using the standard normal transformation (I.3.37) as follows:

$$P(X < 0) = P\left(\frac{X-0.1}{0.2} < \frac{-0.1}{0.2}\right) = P(Z < -0.5)$$

where $Z \sim N(0, 1)$. The Excel function gives $P(Z < -0.5)$ as

$$\text{NORMSDIST}(-0.5) = 0.30854.$$

Hence the probability that the investment return is negative is 0.30854.

In fact Excel offers an array of normal distribution functions that are easy to use:

- NORMSDIST(x) is the value of $P(Z < z)$ when Z has a standard normal distribution,
- NORMDIST(x, μ, σ, true) is the value of $P(X < x)$ when $X \sim N(\mu, \sigma^2)$,
- NORMDIST(x, μ, σ, false) is the value of the density function $\varphi(x)$ when $X \sim N(\mu, \sigma^2)$,
- NORMSINV(u) is $\Phi^{-1}(u)$ for the standard normal distribution Φ and some $u \in [0, 1]$.

For example, for $X \sim N(0, 1)$,
NORMSINV$(0.95) = 1.6449$ and NORMSDIST$(1.6449) = P(X < 1.6449) = 0.95$;
NORMSINV$(0.01) = -2.3263$ and NORMSDIST$(-2.3263) = P(X < -2.3263) = 0.01$;
NORMDIST$(3, 1, 2, \text{true}) = P(X < 3) = 0.8413$ for $X \sim N(1, 4)$;
NORMDIST$(-2, 1, 3, \text{false}) = \varphi(-2) = 0.08066$ for $X \sim N(1, 9)$.

A normal density has zero skewness because it is symmetric. In fact all the odd order higher moments are zero. However, the even order moments are not zero – they are related to σ. For instance, we can show that

$$E([X - \mu]^4) = 3\sigma^4 \qquad (\text{I.3.38})$$

when $X \sim N(\mu, \sigma^2)$. Hence the kurtosis of any normal variable is 3. We often subtract 3 from the kurtosis and call this result the *excess kurtosis* so that a normal variable has zero excess kurtosis as well as zero skewness.

Normal distributions have nice properties, which is the main reason why we use them so extensively. First, they have only two parameters: the expectation μ and the variance σ^2. So if we know the values of these parameters we know the entire distribution. Secondly, the normal distribution is a *stable distribution*. The stable property is formally defined in Section I.3.3.11 below. Informally, it means that the sum of normal random variables is another normal variable, so the expectation and variance of the new normal variance can be found using the rules for the expectation and variance operators.

EXAMPLE I.3.6: NORMAL PROBABILITIES FOR PORTFOLIO RETURNS

An investor holds a portfolio of two assets, with \$1 million invested in X and \$3 million invested in Y. Each asset's annual return is assumed to be normally distributed and the two returns have a correlation of 0.5.[11] The return on X has expectation 24% and volatility 20% and the return on Y has expectation 16% and volatility 10%.

(i) What is the distribution of the annual returns on the investor's portfolio?
(ii) What is the probability that he will make a loss over the year?
(iii) If the target return is 20%, what is the probability that the portfolio will meet or exceed the target?

SOLUTION

(i) By the stable property the portfolio return R is also normally distributed, and it will have expectation 18% and volatility 10.9%. To see why, note that:

$$E(0.25X + 0.75Y) = 0.25 \times 0.24 + 0.75 \times 0.16 = 0.18,$$

---

[11] Correlation is formally defined only later in this chapter, but readers will be familiar with the use of correlation from Section I.2.4.

and

$$V(0.25X + 0.75Y) = 0.25^2 \times 0.2^2 + 0.75^2 \times 0.1^2 + 2 \times 0.25 \times 0.75 \times 0.5 \times 0.2 \times 0.1$$
$$= 0.011875$$

so the volatility is the square root of this, i.e. 10.9%.

(ii) The probability of a negative return is[12]

$$P(R < 0) = P\left(\frac{R - 0.18}{0.109} < \frac{-0.18}{0.109}\right) = P(Z < -1.65179) = 0.049288,$$

where Z is a standard normal variable. Hence there is approximately a 5% chance that the return on the portfolio will be negative.

(iii) Similarly,

$$P(R > 0.2) = P\left(\frac{R - 0.18}{0.109} > \frac{0.2 - 0.18}{0.109}\right) = P\left(Z > \frac{0.02}{0.109}\right)$$

$$= P\left(Z > \frac{0.02}{0.109}\right) = P(Z > 0.1835) = 0.4272,$$

where Z is a standard normal variable. So there is a 42.72% chance that the portfolio will meet or exceed the target.

In the above example we assumed the target return was fixed. But in most cases the performance of a fund is measured against a benchmark that is itself a random variable. In this case the normality assumption greatly facilities calculations, as illustrated in the next example.

EXAMPLE I.3.7: NORMAL PROBABILITIES FOR ACTIVE RETURNS

The annual returns on a fund and its benchmark are assumed to be normally distributed with a correlation of 0.75. The fund and the benchmark have expected annual returns of 10% and 8% respectively, but the fund return X has a greater volatility. The volatility of the fund's return is 25% whereas that of the benchmark return Y is only 15%. On the basis of this information what is the probability that the fund will underperform the benchmark this year?

SOLUTION   The active return on the fund is (under continuous compounding) the difference between the fund return and the benchmark return. Hence the expected active return is 2%, and the variance of the active return is

$$V(X - Y) = V(X) + V(Y) - 2\text{Cov}(X, Y)$$

$$= 0.25^2 + 0.15^2 - 2 \times 0.75 \times 0.25 \times 0.15 = 0.02875.$$

The volatility of the active return is $\sqrt{0.02875} = 16.96\%$. Hence the probability that the fund will underperform the benchmark is,

$$P(X - Y < 0) = P\left(Z < \frac{0 - 0.02}{0.1696}\right) = P(Z < -0.11795) = 0.453,$$

where Z is a standard normal variable. So there is a 45.3% chance that the fund will underperform the benchmark.

---

[12] NORMDIST(0,0.18,SQRT(0.011875),true) gives the same result.

I.3.3.5   Lognormal Distribution

A random variable is lognormally distributed when its logarithm is normally distributed. That is, Y has a lognormal distribution if and only if $X = \ln Y$ has a normal distribution. Put another way, if X has a normal distribution then $\exp(X)$ has a lognormal distribution.

The lognormal density function is

$$f(y) = \frac{1}{y\sqrt{2\pi\sigma^2}} \exp\left(-\frac{(\ln(y) - \mu)^2}{2\sigma^2}\right) \tag{I.3.39}$$

for $0 < y < \infty$ where μ and σ^2 are the expectation and variance of $\ln Y$. In (I.3.39) it must be stressed that μ and σ are the expectation and variance of the associated *normal* density function. However, the expectation and variance of Y are simple to derive from μ and σ. It can be shown that

$$E(Y) = \exp(\mu + \tfrac{1}{2}\sigma^2) \tag{I.3.40}$$

and

$$V(Y) = \exp(2\mu + \sigma^2)\left(\exp(\sigma^2) - 1\right). \tag{I.3.41}$$

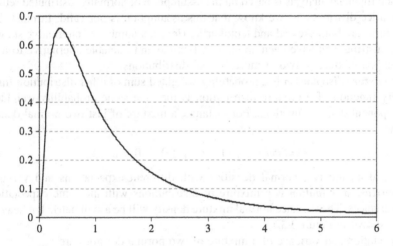

Figure I.3.12   Lognormal density associated with the standard normal distribution

The density function (I.3.39) is not symmetrical. For instance, Figure I.3.12 illustrates the lognormal density associated with the standard normal distribution. Its expectation and variance are $\sqrt{e}$ and $e(e - 1)$, respectively.

Financial asset prices are observed in the present, and will have been observed in the past, but it is not possible to determine exactly which value they will take in the future. Hence financial asset prices, and their returns, are random variables. Since a lognormal variable can only take positive values it is commonly assumed that financial asset prices are better represented by a lognormal than by a normal random variable. However, investors compare financial assets on the basis of their returns because returns are comparable whatever the price of the underlying asset. The simplest assumption we can make is that log returns are normally distributed; and if the log return over a time interval of length t is normally distributed then the future price at time t will have a lognormal distribution.

To see why asset prices have a lognormal distribution when log returns are assumed to be normally distributed, we need only note that

$$\ln\left(\frac{S(t)}{S(0)}\right) \sim N(\mu, \sigma^2) \Leftrightarrow \ln S(t) \sim N(\mu + \ln S(0), \sigma^2). \tag{I.3.42}$$

This is because we can observe the current price, so it is no longer a random variable and can be treated like a constant. The relationship (I.3.42) shows that if the t-period log return is normally distributed then the future asset price at time t has a lognormal distribution, and conversely.

The normal log returns assumption is very common for both discrete and continuous time models. It may not be very representative of their observed behaviour but it is consistent with the Black–Scholes–Merton option pricing formula, where prices are assumed to have a lognormal distribution. Another reason for the lognormal assumption is that models based on log returns are very tractable for the simple reason that the sum of h consecutive one-period log returns is equal to the h-period log return.

I.3.3.6 Normal Mixture Distributions

Whilst much financial analysis is based on the assumption of normally distributed returns and lognormal price distributions, we know that this assumption is not valid. In most financial markets returns are both skewed and leptokurtic. Hence, a number of alternative skewed and leptokurtic distributions have been applied. A flexible and tractable alternative to a normal distribution is a mixture of two or more normal distributions.

A finite *mixture distribution* is a probability-weighted sum of other distribution functions. The density function of a mixture distribution is then the same probability-weighted sum of the component density functions. For instance, a mixture of just two normal densities is defined by:

$$g(x) = \pi \varphi_1(x) + (1 - \pi) \varphi_2(x), \quad 0 < \pi < 1, \tag{I.3.43}$$

where φ_1 and φ_2 are two normal densities with different expectations and variances. A *variance mixture distribution* is a mixture of distributions with the same expectations but different variances. The variance normal mixture density will be a symmetric but heavy-tailed density, as shown in Figure I.3.13.

The expectation and variance of a mixture of two normal densities are

$$\mu = \pi \mu_1 + (1 - \pi) \mu_2,$$
$$\sigma^2 = \pi \sigma_1^2 + (1 - \pi) \sigma_2^2 + \pi \mu_1^2 + (1 - \pi) \mu_2^2 - (\pi \mu_1 + (1 - \pi) \mu_2)^2. \tag{I.3.44}$$

Suppose the expectation of X is zero under φ_1 and φ_2. Then the variance of X under g is just the probability-weighted sum of the variances under φ_1 and φ_2, i.e.

$$\sigma^2 = \pi \sigma_1^2 + (1 - \pi) \sigma_2^2. \tag{I.3.45}$$

Also, the kurtosis of X under g is given by

$$\kappa = 3\left(\frac{\pi \sigma_1^4 + (1 - \pi) \sigma_2^4}{[\pi \sigma_1^2 + (1 - \pi) \sigma_2^2]^2}\right). \tag{I.3.46}$$

The following example illustrates the fact that a normal variance mixture has a greater kurtosis than the normal density of the same variance.

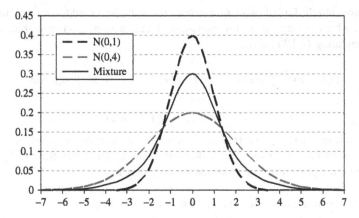

Figure I.3.13   A variance mixture of two normal densities

EXAMPLE I.3.8: VARIANCE AND KURTOSIS OF A ZERO-EXPECTATION NORMAL MIXTURE

A random variable X has a density that is a mixture of two zero-mean normal densities, one with standard deviation 3% and another with standard deviation 4% and the mixing probability in (I.3.43) is 0.5. Calculate the standard deviation of X and the kurtosis of X.

SOLUTION   By (I.3.45),

$$\sigma^2 = 0.5 \times 3^2 + 0.5 \times 4^2 = 12.5.$$

Hence X has standard deviation $\sqrt{12.5} = 3.536\%$ under the normal mixture density. For the kurtosis we use (I.3.46) to obtain a kurtosis of

$$\kappa = 3\left(\frac{0.5 \times 0.03^4 + 0.5 \times 0.04^4}{[0.5 \times 0.03^2 + 0.5 \times 0.04^2]^2} \right) = 3.235.$$

This is greater than the kurtosis of a normal density, which has a kurtosis of 3.

The definitions above have the obvious extensions to more than one normal component in the mixture. A general finite normal mixture of n normal density functions is

$$g(x) = \pi_1 \varphi_1(x) + \pi_2 \varphi_2(x) + \ldots + \pi_n \varphi_n(x), \quad \sum_{i=1}^{n} \pi_i = 1, \pi_i \geq 0. \qquad \text{(I.3.47)}$$

When X has such a density we write $X \sim \mathrm{NM}(\pi_1, \ldots, \pi_n; \mu_1, \ldots, \mu_n, \sigma_1^2, \ldots, \sigma_n^2)$ and we call the probability vector

$$\pi = (\pi_1, \ldots, \pi_n)' \qquad \text{(I.3.48)}$$

the *mixing law*. When the expectations are 0 and there are only two components, we write $X \sim \mathrm{NM}(\pi; \sigma_1^2, \sigma_2^2)$ for short.

If all the normal densities $\varphi_1, \ldots, \varphi_n$ in (I.3.47) have expectation 0 then the variance and kurtosis under the normal mixture g are given by

$$\sigma^2 = \pi_1 \sigma_1^2 + \pi_2 \sigma_2^2 + \ldots + \pi_n \sigma_n^2 \qquad \text{(I.3.49)}$$

and

$$\kappa = 3\left(\frac{\pi_1 \sigma_1^4 + \pi_2 \sigma_2^4 + \ldots + \pi_n \sigma_n^4}{\left[\pi_1 \sigma_1^2 + \pi_2 \sigma_2^2 + \ldots + \pi_n \sigma_n^2 \right]^2} \right). \qquad \text{(I.3.50)}$$

Normal mixtures inherit lots of other nice properties from their component normal densities. One property, which is very useful for value-at-risk calculations, concerns their distribution functions. Integrating (I.3.47) gives

$$P(X < x) = \int_{-\infty}^{x} g(x)dx = \pi_1 \int_{-\infty}^{x} \varphi_1(x)dx + \ldots + \pi_n \int_{-\infty}^{x} \varphi_n(x)dx$$

$$= \pi_1 P_1(X < x) + \ldots + \pi_n P_n(X < x).$$

(I.3.51)

That is, the normal mixture distribution function is a probability-weighted sum of the component distribution functions. The following example illustrates how (I.3.51) may be used to compute the percentiles of a normal mixture density.

EXAMPLE I.3.9: PROBABILITIES OF NORMAL MIXTURE VARIABLES

Consider a random variable X whose density function is a normal mixture with two components: the first normal component has expectation 1 and standard deviation 4, the second normal component has expectation -2 and standard deviation 5 and the probability weight on the first of these components is 0.25. Find the probability that X is less than -1.

SOLUTION   Applying the standard normal transformation:

$$P_1(X < -1) = P(\frac{X-1}{4} < \frac{-1-1}{4}) = P(Z < -0.5)$$

$$P_2(X < -1) = P\left(\frac{X+2}{5} < \frac{-1+2}{5}\right) = P(Z < 0.2)$$

where Z is a standard normal variable. Hence, by (I.3.51),

$$P(X < -1) = 0.25 \times P(Z < -0.5) + 0.75 \times P(Z < 0.2)$$

$$= 0.25 \times 0.30854 + 0.75 \times 0.57926 = 0.51158.$$

The kurtosis is always greater than 3 in any mixture of two zero-mean normal components, so the mixture of two zero-mean normal densities always has a higher peak and heavier tails than the normal density of the same variance. The same comment applies when we take any number of component normal densities in the mixture, provided they all have the same expectation. More generally, taking several components of different expectations and variances in the mixture can lead to almost any shape for the density,[13] whilst retaining the tractability of the analysis under normality assumptions. Even a mixture of just two normal densities can have positive or negative skewness, and light or heavy tails. Figure I.3.14 illustrates one such normal mixture, which has a negative skew and positive excess kurtosis.

Normal mixture distributions also have an intuitive interpretation when markets display regime-specific behaviour. A typical example is the return on an equity index. We might assume the return is normally distributed, but that the expectation and variance of the returns distribution depends on the market regime. When markets are stable the expected return is relatively small and positive and the volatility is relatively low, but around the time of a market crash the expected return is relatively large and negative and the returns volatility

---

[13] Maclachlan and Peel (2000) provide pictures of many interesting examples.

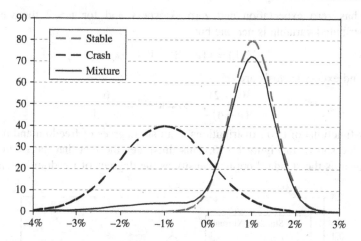

Figure I.3.14   A skewed, leptokurtic normal mixture density

is much larger than it is when markets are stable. For instance, suppose the returns during a stable market regime, which occurs 90% of the time, have expectation 1% and standard deviation 0.5%. However, 10% of the time the market is in turmoil with an expected return of −1% and a standard deviation of 1%. Then the normal mixture distribution of daily returns has the density function depicted by the black line in Figure I.3.13 and the distributions under the stable and crash regimes have density functions depicted by the dotted lines.

In Section I.5.4.4 we apply the *EM algorithm* to estimate the parameters of normal mixture distributions for equity index and exchange rate returns. We find that the FTSE 100 and S&P 500 equity indices exhibit marked regime-specific behaviour that is captured very well by a normal mixture distribution. However, the evidence for regime-specific behaviour in the £/$ exchange rate is much less pronounced than it is for equity indices and a Student t distribution may provide a better model for these returns.

I.3.7   Student t Distributions

The Student t distribution is so called because the employer of the statistician who introduced it would not allow him to publish under his own name. His real name was William Gosset, and he introduced the distribution in 1908 using the pen name 'Student'. The t distribution is closely related to the normal distribution: it is a symmetric curve that converges to the standard normal density as the *degrees of freedom* increase. The 'degrees of freedom' is the only parameter in the t distribution and the lower the degrees of freedom the lower the peak of the distribution and the longer the tails.

The density function for the Student t distribution with ν degrees of freedom is

$$f_\nu(t) = (\nu\pi)^{-1/2} \Gamma\left(\frac{\nu}{2}\right)^{-1} \Gamma\left(\frac{\nu+1}{2}\right) \left(1 + \frac{t^2}{\nu}\right)^{-\left(\frac{\nu+1}{2}\right)}, \tag{I.3.52}$$

where the *gamma function* Γ is an extension of the factorial function $n!$ to non-integer values.[14] When a random variable T has the Student t distribution we write $T \sim t_\nu$. The

---

[14] When x is an integer then $\Gamma(x) = (x-1)!$. See Section I.3.4.8 for further details about the gamma function.

distribution has zero expectation and zero skewness and for $\nu > 2$ the variance of a Student t distributed variable is *not* one but

$$V(T) = \nu(\nu - 2)^{-1} \text{ if } T \sim t_\nu. \tag{I.3.53}$$

Its kurtosis and excess kurtosis are

$$\kappa = \frac{3(\nu - 2)}{(\nu - 4)}, \quad \varkappa = \kappa - 3 = \frac{6}{\nu - 4}. \tag{I.3.54}$$

The density functions of two t distributions, with six degrees of freedom and three degrees of freedom, are shown in Figure I.3.15. This illustrates the fact that the t density (I.3.52) converges towards the standard normal density as the degrees of freedom increase.

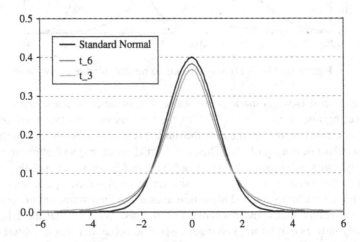

Figure I.3.15   Comparison of Student t densities and standard normal

We emphasize that the Student t distribution (I.3.52) does *not* have unit variance, it has variance given by (I.3.53). So Figure I.3.15 is misleading: it gives the impression that the t distribution has a peak that is too low compared with the normal density. However, in Figure I.3.16 we compare a Student t density function with six degrees of freedom with the normal density having the *same* variance, i.e. the normal with mean 0 and variance 1.5, and then the leptokurtic character of the Student t density is evident.

Generalized t distributions are obtained from linear transformations of the distribution (I.3.52). If we set

$$X = \mu + \sigma T,$$

then X has a *generalized t distribution* with density function

$$f_\nu(x \,|\, \mu, \beta) = (\beta \nu \pi)^{-1/2} \Gamma\left(\frac{\nu}{2}\right)^{-1} \Gamma\left(\frac{\nu + 1}{2}\right) \left(1 + \frac{(x - \mu)^2}{\beta \nu}\right)^{-\left(\frac{\nu+1}{2}\right)}. \tag{I.3.55}$$

Also X has expectation μ, the skewness and kurtosis are unchanged from above and the variance of X is

$$\sigma^2 = \beta \nu(\nu - 2)^{-1}. \tag{I.3.56}$$

This is equal to 1 when $\beta \nu = \nu - 2$.

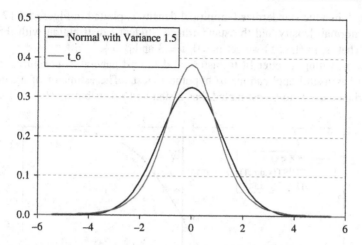

Figure I.3.16 Comparison of Student t density and normal with same variance

Setting $\mu = 0$ and $\beta v = v - 2$ in (I.3.55) gives the density for the *standardized Student t distribution*, i.e. the Student t distribution with zero expectation and unit variance. This has density function

$$f_v(x) = ((v - 2)\pi)^{-1/2} \Gamma\left(\frac{v}{2}\right)^{-1} \Gamma\left(\frac{v+1}{2}\right)\left(1 + \frac{x^2}{v-2}\right)^{-\left(\frac{v+1}{2}\right)}. \qquad (I.3.57)$$

When a random variable X has the standardized Student t distribution with density function (I.3.57) we write $X \sim t_v(0, 1)$. Be careful not to confuse this with the *standard* Student t distribution which has density (I.3.52).

In Figure I.3.17 we compare three distributions of some high frequency data on the €/\$ exchange rate. The empirical returns are standardized to have zero expectation and unit

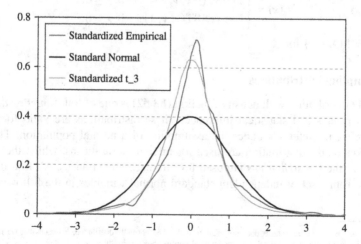

Figure I.3.17 Comparison of standardized empirical density with standardized Student t density and standard normal density

variance,[15] and then the standardized empirical density is plotted in Figure I.3.17 along with the standard normal density and the standardized Student t distribution with three degrees of freedom. That is, in (I.3.55) we set $\mu = 0$, $\nu = 3$ and $\beta = \frac{1}{3}$.

As well as providing a better fit to historical data on financial asset returns, the Student t distribution has useful applications to hypothesis tests. The estimator of a sample mean, when the variance needs to be estimated, has a standard t distribution.[16]

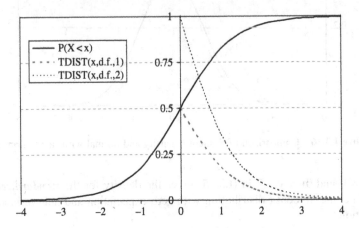

Figure I.3.18   The Excel t distribution function

Using the t distribution in Excel is unfortunately rather complex. Excel has a function for the cumulative distribution of the standard t distribution but not for its density. However, the log of the gamma function is given by Excel, so the density function (I.3.55) can be written as an Excel formula as in the spreadsheets for Figures I.3.17 and I.3.18. Moreover, Excel does not provide a very nice format for the standard t distribution function. Figure I.3.18 shows the Excel function TDIST which is implicitly defined as

$$t_\nu(x) = \begin{cases} \text{TDIST}(-x, \nu, 1), & \text{if } x \leq 0, \\ 1 - \text{TDIST}(x, \nu, 1), & \text{if } x > 0, \end{cases} \qquad (I.3.58)$$

where $t_\nu(x) = P(X < x)$ for $X \sim t_\nu$.

I.3.3.8   Sampling Distributions

The standard t distribution with density function (I.3.52) is one of four *sampling distributions* that are used in classical statistical inference. These distributions are valid for hypothesis tests and confidence intervals under the assumption of a normal population. The standard normal and standard t distribution are used for inferences on means, whilst the *chi-squared distributions* or the *F distributions* are used for inference on variances. All four distributions may be built from a set of independent standard normal variables in the following way:[17]

---

[15] We emphasize that to *standardize* returns does not mean to make then normally distributed. It means that we make their mean zero and their variance one. We may also call the standardized returns *normalized* returns.
[16] Similar types of *t ratios* are standard output from regression models. See Section I.3.5 and Chapter I.4 for further details.
[17] We use the notation NID(0, 1) to denote a set of independent standard normal variables.

- The sum of squares of k independent standard normal variables is a *chi-squared* variable with k degrees of freedom:

$$X = Z_1^2 + \ldots + Z_k^2, \quad Z_i \sim \text{NID}(0, 1), \ i = 1, \ldots, k \Rightarrow X \sim \chi_k^2. \tag{I.3.59}$$

- A standard t distributed variable with k degrees of freedom is the ratio of a standard normal variable Z to the square root of a chi-squared variable X with k degrees of freedom divided by k:

$$Y = \frac{Z}{(X/k)^{1/2}}, \quad Z \sim N(0, 1) \text{ and } X \sim \chi_k^2 \Rightarrow Y \sim t_k \tag{I.3.60}$$

where X is independent of Z.

- A variable having the *F-distribution* with k_1 degrees of freedom in the numerator and k_2 degrees of freedom in the denominator is the ratio of a chi-squared variable X_1 with k_1 degrees of freedom divided by k_1 to another independent chi-squared variable X_2 with k_2 degrees of freedom divided by k_2:

$$F = \frac{X_1/k_1}{X_2/k_2}, \quad X_i \sim \chi_{k_i}^2, \ i = 1, 2 \Rightarrow F \sim F_{k_1, k_2}. \tag{I.3.61}$$

I.3.3.9   Generalized Extreme Value Distributions

Extreme value theory relates to a class of distributions that are derived from considering the extreme values in a sample. However, some of these distributions can be used to model the entire distribution of a random variable and not just the tails of the distribution. Extreme value distributions are commonly used to quantify probabilities of exceptional losses and to improve the accuracy of estimates of very low quantiles, such as the 0.001 quantile or even smaller. There are two types of extreme value distribution:

- the *generalized extreme value* (GEV) *distributions* that can be used to fit any set of data and whose name arises from their derivation as the distribution of a sample maximum (or minimum);
- the *generalized Pareto distribution* (GPD) that applies only to a specific tail, i.e. to excesses over a pre-defined threshold.

We begin by deriving the GEV distributions as the distributions of the *maximal loss* over a certain interval of time.[18] The extreme value is defined as the maximum (or minimum) of a sample $\{x_1, x_2, \ldots, x_n\}$. For example, one might model the maximum daily loss experienced during a trading week, as in Figure I.3.19, in which case $n = 5$. Figure I.3.19 depicts how to obtain the maximal loss data: the underlying time series is a series of daily P&Ls, and we assume the P&L value for each day of the week is generated by a sequence of five *independent and identically distributed* (i.i.d.) random variables $X_1, \ldots, X_5$.[19] During each non-overlapping week in the sample period we record the maximal loss (i.e. the largest negative P&L).

---

[18] We can derive results for the maximum in a sample without loss of generality: the results can easily be converted to results for the minimum because $\min\{x_1, \ldots, x_n\} = -\max\{-x_1, \ldots, -x_n\}$.
[19] See Section I.3.7.1 for the formal definition of an i.i.d. process.

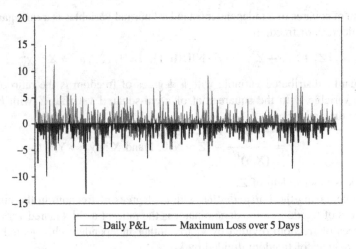

Figure I.3.19 Filtering data to derive the GEV distribution

We assume that each observation in the sample is an observation on a random variable X_i and that $X_1, \ldots, X_n$ are i.i.d. Let $M_n = \max\{X_1, \ldots, X_n\}$. What is the distribution of M_n? Suppose each X_i has distribution $F(x)$. Since

$$P(M_n < x) = P(X_1 < x \text{ and } X_2 < x \text{ and } \ldots \text{ and } X_n < x)$$
$$= P(X_1 < x)\, P(X_2 < x) \ldots P(X_n < x)$$

the distribution function of M_n is $F^n(x)$. Hence the limiting distribution of M_n as $n \to \infty$ is degenerate. For this reason M_n is transformed, by subtracting its location parameter and dividing the result by its scale parameter. After this transformation the extreme values have a non-degenerate distribution. In fact there are only three possible limiting distributions and all three may be expressed in the single formula below; hence the term 'generalized' extreme value distributions for this type of distribution.

The GEV distribution depends on the *location* and *scale* parameters δ and β and a parameter ξ which is called the *tail index* because it defines the shape of the tail of the GEV distribution.[20] The GEV distribution function is

$$F(x) = \begin{cases} \exp\left(-\exp\left(-\dfrac{x-\delta}{\beta}\right)\right), & \xi = 0, \\[2mm] \exp\left(-\left(1 + \xi\left(\dfrac{x-\delta}{\beta}\right)\right)^{-\xi^{-1}}\right), & \xi \neq 0, \xi\left(\dfrac{x-\delta}{\beta}\right) > -1. \end{cases} \tag{I.3.62}$$

And the corresponding density function is

$$f(x) = \begin{cases} \beta^{-1} \exp\left(-\dfrac{x-\delta}{\beta}\right) \exp\left(-\exp\left(-\dfrac{x-\delta}{\beta}\right)\right), & \xi = 0, \\[2mm] \beta^{-1}\left(1 + \xi\left(\dfrac{x-\delta}{\beta}\right)\right)^{-1-\xi^{-1}} \exp\left(-\left(1 + \xi\left(\dfrac{x-\delta}{\beta}\right)\right)^{-\xi^{-1}}\right), & \xi \neq 0, \xi\left(\dfrac{x-\delta}{\beta}\right) > -1. \end{cases} \tag{I.3.63}$$

---

[20] Sometimes we refer to ξ^{-1} as the *shape parameter* in the GEV.

Note that the condition $\xi((x - \delta)/\beta) > -1$ is a condition on the possible range for x, specifically,

$$x > \delta - \beta\xi^{-1}, \quad \text{if } \beta\xi > 0,$$
$$x < \delta - \beta\xi^{-1}, \quad \text{if } \beta\xi < 0.$$

There are three types of GEV, corresponding to different values of the tail index ξ:

- If $\xi = 0$ we have the *Gumbel distribution*. The corresponding density function has a mode at 0, positive skew and declines exponentially in the tails.
- If $\xi < 0$ we have the *Weibull distribution*. This has a density that converges to a mass at δ as $\xi \rightarrow -\infty$. The lower tail remains finite in the Weibull density.
- If $\xi > 0$ we have the *Fréchet distribution*. This also has a density that converges to a mass at δ, this time as $\xi \rightarrow \infty$. But it converges more slowly than the Weibull density since the tail in the Fréchet declines by a power law.

Figure I.3.20 depicts the GEV density for $\beta = 5$, $\delta = 10$ and $\xi = 1$. Readers may use the spreadsheet to explore the density function for other GEV distributions with $\xi \neq 0$.

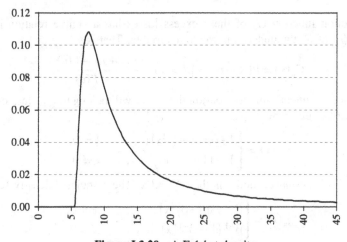

Figure I.3.20   A Fréchet density

Although we have derived the GEV distributions as distributions of sample maxima it is important to note that their application is not limited to this type of random variable. In fact GEV distributions are often used to fit the entire empirical density of financial asset returns because, with three parameters, their fit is flexible and they can accommodate different types of tail behaviour.

I.3.3.10   Generalized Pareto Distribution

Now let us turn to the case where extreme values are based on the *peaks-over-threshold* model. Here all excess losses (or negative returns) over a high and pre-defined threshold u are recorded, as depicted in Figure I.3.21. In this figure the threshold u is -2%.[21] We regard the excesses over this threshold as observations on another random variable $X - u$.

---

[21] We state results only in terms of the excesses over a positive threshold, i.e. with $u > 0$, but results for a negative threshold follow by symmetry.

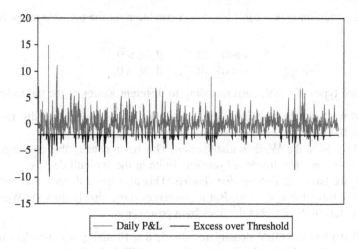

Figure I.3.21   Filtering data in the peaks-over-threshold model

The distribution function G_u of these excess losses has a simple relationship with the distribution $F(x)$ of X, the underlying random variable. That is,

$$G_u(x) = P(X - u < x \mid X > u) = \frac{F(x+u) - F(u)}{1 - F(u)}. \qquad (I.3.64)$$

For many choices of underlying distribution the above will belong to the class of *generalized Pareto distributions* given by

$$G_u(x) = \begin{cases} 1 - \exp(-\beta^{-1}x), & \xi = 0, \\ 1 - \left(1 + \beta^{-1}\xi x\right)^{-\xi^{-1}}, & \xi \neq 0. \end{cases} \qquad (I.3.65)$$

where β is the *scale parameter* and ξ is the *tail index*. The associated density function is

$$g_u(x) = \begin{cases} \beta^{-1} \exp(-\beta^{-1}x), & \xi = 0, \\ \beta^{-1} \left(1 + \beta^{-1}\xi x\right)^{-\xi^{-1}-1}, & \xi \neq 0. \end{cases} \qquad (I.3.66)$$

As the scale parameter β increases so does the effective range for the density function. As for the GEV distributions, the effect of an increasing tail index ξ is to increase the weight in the tails.

Many statistical packages such as Matlab have in-built functions for fitting extreme value distributions.

The *mean excess loss* over a threshold u is defined by

$$e(u) = E(X - u \mid X > u). \qquad (I.3.67)$$

If the excess over threshold has a generalized Pareto distribution (I.3.65) then the mean excess loss has a simple functional form,

$$e(u) = \frac{\beta + \xi u}{1 - \xi}. \qquad (I.3.68)$$

Generalized Pareto distributions have useful applications to value at risk (VaR) measurement. In particular, if the portfolio returns have a GPD distribution there are analytic expressions for the VaR and the *expected tail loss* (ETL), which is the average of all losses that exceed VaR.

Expected tail loss (also called *conditional VaR*) is often used for internal VaR measurement because it is a 'coherent' risk measure.[22] By definition of the mean excess loss,

$$ETL = VaR + e(VaR). \qquad (I.3.69)$$

So to calculate the ETL from historical loss data we take the losses in excess of the VaR level, estimate the parameters β and ξ of a generalized Pareto distribution and compute the quantity (I.3.68) with $u = VaR$. Adding this quantity to the VaR gives the ETL. Some examples of computing VaR and ETL under the generalized Pareto distribution are given in Sections IV.3.4 and IV.3.6.

I.3.3.11 Stable Distributions

In Section IV.3.2 we consider how to scale a VaR estimate. For instance, how is the 10-day VaR estimate related to the 1-day VaR estimate? We can answer this question using the concept of a *stable* distribution. A random variable X has a stable distribution if the sum of N independent copies of X is a random variable that has the same type of distribution. For instance, the normal distribution is stable because the sum of N independent normal variables is another normal variable.[23] Apart from the normal there are two other parametric forms for stable distributions: the *Cauchy distribution*, with density function

$$f(x) = \pi^{-1} \left(\frac{\beta}{(x-\delta)^2 + \beta^2} \right), \quad -\infty < x < \infty; \qquad (I.3.70)$$

and the *Lévy distribution*, with density function

$$f(x) = \sqrt{\frac{\beta}{2\pi}} (x-\delta)^{-3/2} \exp\left(-\frac{\beta}{2(x-\delta)} \right), \quad \delta < x < \infty. \qquad (I.3.71)$$

The parameters δ and β are the location and scale parameters. The Cauchy density is symmetric with a maximum value at $x = \delta$ and the Lévy density is highly skewed. Both these distributions have infinite variance and very heavy tails.

The precise definition of a stable distribution depends on a parameter which is related to the tail index of heavy tailed distributions. A random variable X with zero expectation has a *ξ-stable distribution* if[24]

$$\sum_{i=1}^{h} X_i \overset{d}{=} h^{1/\xi} X, \quad \text{for } \xi \in (0, 2], \qquad (I.3.72)$$

where the notation $\overset{d}{=}$ stands for 'has the same distribution as' and $\{X_1, \ldots, X_h\}$ are independent copies of X.

It may be shown that the Cauchy distribution (I.3.70) is stable with $\xi = 1$ and the Lévy distribution (I.3.71) is stable with $\xi = 1/2$. The normal distribution is stable with $\xi = 2$. To see why, note that (I.3.87) implies that the sum of h independent normal variables with zero expectation and variance σ^2 has variance $h\sigma^2$. Hence, the right-hand side of (I.3.72) must be $\sqrt{h}X$, since this has variance $h\sigma^2$.

---

[22] See Section IV.1.5 for further details about 'coherent' risk metrics.

[23] In fact normal variables do not even have to be independent for their sum to remain normal.

[24] Assuming zero expectation is no restriction to the definition, since we can always subtract μ from X. If (I.3.72) holds for a random variable with non-zero expectation, the distribution is called *strictly stable*. The usual terminology is actually 'α-stable distribution' and not 'ξ-stable distribution'. However, we use the notation α for the significance of a VaR estimate. Also the terminology 'ξ-stable distribution' makes clear the association with the tail index.

The definition (I.3.72) should be distinguished from the *square-root-of-time* scaling rule for standard deviation that applies to any set of i.i.d. returns provided their variance is finite.[25] When VaR is estimated by simulation (either historical or Monte Carlo) it is measured as a percentile, not by a standard deviation. Hence, the square-root-of-time rule cannot always be applied to scale the VaR. Instead we may try to estimate the *scale exponent* ξ^{-1} in (I.3.72) as described in Section IV.3.2 to determine the scaling law for a VaR estimate, assuming the empirical evidence is that returns do have a stable distribution.

A simple example of a scaling law is when the daily log returns are normally distributed. Then the h-day log returns are also normally distributed and one simply has to scale the daily log returns distribution by the factor $h^{1/2}$ to obtain the distribution of h-day log returns. So if daily log returns are normally distributed then the h-day VaR estimate of a linear portfolio is just $h^{1/2}$ times the 1-day VaR estimate. The square-root-of-time scaling rule applies only to scaling a standard deviation under the assumption that there is an i.i.d. process for returns. The stable property refers to the scaling of percentiles and the entire distribution, but it applies only to random variables with stable distributions.

I.3.3.12 Kernels

A market risk manager's prime concern is to quantify the potential for a portfolio – and the firm as a whole – to incur extreme losses. For this he needs to have useful tools for forecasting the likelihood and magnitude of extreme negative returns. This is exactly what VaR models aim to achieve by forecasting the lower tail of a portfolio's return distribution. Any VaR methodology uses some sort of historical data, indeed the Basel recommendations are for at least 1 year of historical data to be taken into account when forecasting portfolio returns over the next ten days. These data can be applied in the form of a covariance matrix of returns on the portfolio's risk factors, as in the linear and Monte Carlo VaR methodologies. But in the historical VaR model, simulations of portfolio returns are based on a set of historical asset or risk factor returns. Historical VaR can be a very powerful tool for forecasting extreme losses, but a significant challenge to implementing an historical VaR model is the derivation of an empirical portfolio returns distribution that captures the tails of the distribution adequately.

The aim of kernel fitting is to derive a smooth curve from a random sample that provides the best possible representation of the probability density of the random variable. In other words, kernel fitting is a way to infer the *population* density from an *empirical* density function.[26] Given a random sample $\{x_1, x_2, \ldots, x_n\}$ on a random variable X, the kernel approximation to the density of X is defined as

$$\hat{f}_h(x) = (nh)^{-1} \sum_{i=1}^{n} K(u), \quad \text{with } u = \frac{x - x_i}{h}, \tag{I.3.73}$$

where K is the *kernel function* and h is the *bandwidth*. The bandwidth is equivalent to the cell width of a histogram and the object of a kernel estimation algorithm is to find the optimal

---

[25] The square-root-of-time rule is derived in Section II.3.2.1. The Cauchy and Lévy distributions both have infinite variance.

[26] We know from Section I.3.2.4 that a histogram can take on an altogether different shape when we change the cell width, and secondly its shape can change if we shift the start and end points of the cells. Thus it is not possible to infer much about the population density from a histogram unless the cell width becomes very small and the sample becomes very large.

choice of bandwidth. This is chosen to minimize the *asymptotic mean integrated square error*, an objective function that can be thought of as the sum of the squared errors between the empirical density and the fitted density.

When the kernel function is a normal density function we have the *Gaussian kernel*. This is commonly used in finance because it is straightforward and intuitive, though it is not necessarily the best kernel for forecasting the tails of a distribution. In the Gaussian kernel the density is approximated by a mixture of normal density functions with different expectations and variances.[27] Another very popular kernel is the *Epanechnikov kernel*, where

$$K(u) = \begin{cases} \dfrac{3}{4}\left(1 - u^2\right), & \text{if } -1 \leq u \leq 1, \\ 0, & \text{otherwise.} \end{cases} \qquad (I.3.74)$$

A wide variety of other kernel functions are commonly used. For instance, the free kernel estimation software provided by Wessa (2006) applies the Gaussian, Epanechnikov and five other kernels. The graphs in Figure I.3.22 used this software to compare the Gaussian kernel with the Epanechnikov kernel. Both kernels are applied to the daily data on the S&P 500 index from 31 December 2004 to 30 December 2005 that was used in Example I.3.1. The optimal bandwidth for these kernels was computed to be 0.0019288. Note that which kernel is chosen seems to matter very little, provided a sensible choice is made. For instance, trying to use a lognormal kernel when data are relatively normal may produce misleading results.

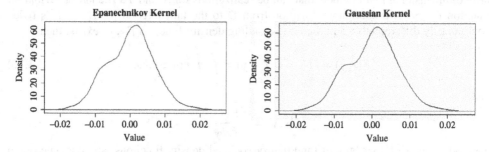

Figure I.3.22   Kernel estimates of S&P 500 returns

I.3.4   MULTIVARIATE DISTRIBUTIONS

This section begins with a discussion of the general properties of bivariate distributions, i.e. the *joint, marginal and conditional distributions* of a pair of continuous random variables. Then these concepts are extended to multivariate distributions for an arbitrary finite number of continuous random variables.[28] We explain what it means to say that two random variables are *independent* and introduce *covariance* and *correlation* as a measure of dependency between

---

[27] See Section I.3.3.6 for further details on normal mixture distributions.
[28] We assume the distributions are continuous here because most market risk management applications of bivariate and multivariate distributions are for continuous random variables. The general concepts of joint, marginal and conditional distributions carry over to discrete random variables. However, in Chapter II.6 when we introduce a particular type of distribution called a *copula* the continuous assumption will become necessary.

two random variables. Then three specific types of multivariate distributions will be analysed in detail: the bivariate and multivariate normal and Student t distributions and the bivariate normal mixture distributions. We describe these here because they have many applications to finance, including the computation of VaR and pricing multi-asset options, and they also provide the statistical foundation for regression analysis.

I.3.4.1   Bivariate Distributions

A positive real-valued function f of two continuous variables is a *bivariate density function* if it is integrable, never negative and the total area underneath the surface that it describes is 1. The joint probability that X takes values in one range and Y takes values in another range simultaneously is the area under the surface defined by these two ranges:[29]

$$P(x_a < X < x_b, y_a < Y < y_b) = \int_{y_a}^{y_b} \int_{x_a}^{x_b} f(x, y) \, dxdy. \tag{I.3.75}$$

A bivariate density may be visualized as a 'mountain' and (I.3.75) as the volume of a rectangular vertical shaft in the mountain. The shape of the mountain depends on two things, the *marginal* density functions $h(x)$ and $g(y)$ and the type of *dependence* between the two variables.[30]

Suppose that X and Y are defined on a domain D. For our purposes the domain is the set of two-dimensional real numbers that can be realizations for X and Y. The *joint distribution* function $F(x, y)$ is a continuous function from D to the unit interval $[0, 1]$. If F is twice continuously differentiable and the corresponding density function $f(x, y)$ exists, then

$$F(x, y) = P(X < x, Y < y) = \int_{-\infty}^{y} \int_{-\infty}^{x} f(u, v) \, dudv \tag{I.3.76}$$

and

$$f(x, y) = \frac{\partial^2 F(x, y)}{\partial x \partial y}. \tag{I.3.77}$$

Two other types of distributions (and their associated density functions) are associated with a bivariate distribution. These are the *marginal distributions* and the *conditional distributions*. There are two marginal distributions, one for each variable, and we denote these by $H(x)$ and $G(y)$. These are the distributions of X and Y alone, ignoring any information about the other variable.[31] We can derive the marginal distributions from the joint distribution as

$$H(x) = F(x, \infty) \text{ and } G(y) = F(\infty, y). \tag{I.3.78}$$

The *marginal densities* if they exist are given by

$$h(x) = \int_{-\infty}^{\infty} f(x, y) \, dy \text{ and } g(y) = \int_{-\infty}^{\infty} f(x, y) \, dx, \tag{I.3.79}$$

---

[29] To shorten the general notation, when there are n variables the probability that X_1 *and* X_2 both lie in some range, i.e. $P(X_1 < x_1$ and $X_2 < x_2)$ is written as $P(X_1 < x_1, X_2 < x_2)$.

[30] Dependence is represented by their *copula*. The special case of the Gaussian copula gives *correlation* as the dependence measure. But otherwise dependence is a much more general concept than correlation.

[31] They are called *marginals* because if the joint distribution is laid out in a table with X_1 along the rows and X_2 along the columns, then the marginal distribution of X_1 is given by the row sums and the marginal distribution of X_2 is given by the column sums, and these sums are easily put in the margins of the table.

and we have the usual relationships between marginal distributions and densities:

$$H(x) = \int_{-\infty}^{x} h(s)ds \text{ and } h(x) = H'(x),$$

(I.3.80)

$$G(y) = \int_{-\infty}^{y} g(s)ds \text{ and } g(y) = G'(y).$$

For any two random variables with joint distribution $F(x, y)$ the *conditional distribution* of Y given that X takes a fixed value is the distribution that is obtained by taking a 'slice' through the joint distribution parallel to the y axis at the point x where X is fixed. In other words, the conditional distribution of Y given X is the *first partial derivative* of the joint distribution with respect to y. Similarly, the first derivative with respect to x gives the conditional distribution of X given Y. We denote the conditional distributions of X given Y as $F(x|y)$, and similarly $F(y|x)$ are the conditional distributions of Y given X. Thus

$$F(x|y) = \frac{F(x, y)}{H(x)} \text{ and } F(y|x) = \frac{F(x, y)}{G(x)}.$$

(I.3.81)

The *conditional densities* are given by the following relationship between the density functions:

$$f(y|x) = \frac{f(x, y)}{h(x)} \text{ and } f(x|y) = \frac{f(x, y)}{g(y)}.$$

(I.3.82)

I.3.4.2   Independent Random Variables

Following the definition of independent events in Section I.3.2.2, we say that two random variables X and Y are *independent* if and only if their joint distribution function is the product of the marginal distribution of X and the marginal distribution of Y. That is, X and Y are independent if and only if

$$F(x, y) = H(x)G(y),$$

(I.3.83)

where $F(x, y)$ denotes the joint distribution and $H(x)$ and $G(y)$ denote the two marginal distributions. When the random variables are independent the conditional distributions for X are all the same, and are equal to the marginal distribution $H(x)$. Similarly, the conditional distributions for Y are all equal to $G(y)$.

It follows that the density functions, if they exist, also obey a similar rule, i.e. two random variables are independent if and only if

$$f(x, y) = h(x)g(y),$$

(I.3.84)

where $f(x, y)$ denotes the joint density and $h(x)$ and $g(y)$ are the two marginal densities. When the random variables are independent the conditional densities for X are all the same, and are equal to the marginal density $h(x)$. Similarly, the conditional densities for Y are all equal to $g(y)$.

When variables are not independent their densities are still related to the joint density, and their distributions are still related to the joint distribution, but we require a *copula* to account for the dependency between X and Y. The most commonly used copula is the Gaussian copula, which has *correlation* as the dependency metric. However, this is not a very good metric to use for dependencies between financial assets, for reasons that will be explained in Chapter II.3. To define correlation we first introduce *covariance*, which is the first moment of the bivariate distribution function. Then correlation is introduced as a standardized form of covariance.

I.3.4.3 Covariance

The covariance is the first central moment of the joint density function of X and Y, i.e.

$$\mathrm{Cov}(X, Y) = E[(X - \mu_X)(Y - \mu_Y)], \tag{I.3.85}$$

where $\mu_X = E(X)$ and $\mu_Y = E(Y)$ are the expectations of X and Y. Using the properties of the expectation operator, we also have

$$\mathrm{Cov}(X, Y) = E(XY) - E(X)E(Y) \tag{I.3.86}$$

or, in parameter notation,

$$\sigma_{XY} = \mu_{XY} - \mu_X \mu_Y.$$

EXAMPLE I.3.10: CALCULATING A COVARIANCE

Calculate the covariance between X and Y given they have the joint density shown in Table I.3.6.

Table I.3.6 A simple bivariate density

x	−20	−10	5	10	20
y	0	−20	40	30	−10
$P(X = x$ and $Y = y)$	0.2	0.1	0.3	0.25	0.15

SOLUTION   First calculate the expectations of the marginal densities using the method shown in the previous section. This gives $\mu_X = 2$ and $\mu_Y = 16$. Then we can either use (I.3.86) or work straight from the definition (I.3.85). Using the form (I.3.86) requires calculating the expectation of the product XY, as shown in Table I.3.7. So

$$\mu_{XY} = 0.2 \times 0 + 0.1 \times 200 + 0.3 \times 200 + 0.25 \times 300 - 0.15 \times 200 = 125,$$

and the covariance is

$$\sigma_{XY} = 125 - 2 \times 16 = 93.$$

Table I.3.7 Distribution of the product

$z = xy$	0	200	200	300	−200
$P(XY = z)$	0.2	0.1	0.3	0.25	0.15

Alternatively, use the definition (I.3.85). This requires calculating the product of the mean deviations, as shown in Table I.3.8. Thus the covariance is

$$\sigma_{XY} = 352 \times 0.2 + 432 \times 0.1 + 72 \times 0.3 + 112 \times 0.25 - 468 \times 0.15 = 93$$

as before.

Table I.3.8   Calculating a covariance

$x - \mu_X$	-22	-12	3	8	18
$y - \mu_Y$	-16	-36	24	14	-26
Product	352	432	72	112	-468
Probabilities	0.2	0.1	0.3	0.25	0.15

Properties of the Covariance Operator

In Section I.3.2.6 we stated a property of the variance operator that is used very extensively in market risk analysis. This property, which also involves the covariance operator, is that for any random variables X and Y and constants a and b,

$$V(aX + bY) = a^2 V(X) + b^2 V(Y) + 2ab\,\mathrm{Cov}(X, Y). \tag{I.3.87}$$

For instance,

$$V(3X - Y) = 9V(X) + V(Y) - 6\mathrm{Cov}(X, Y).$$

Other properties follow directly from the definition of covariance. For instance,

$$\mathrm{Cov}(aX, bY) = ab\,\mathrm{Cov}(X, Y) \tag{I.3.88}$$

and, for random variables X, Y and Z,

$$\mathrm{Cov}(X, Y + Z) = \mathrm{Cov}(X, Y) + \mathrm{Cov}(X, Z). \tag{I.3.89}$$

If X and Y are independent then their covariance and their correlation will be 0. But the converse is not true. Full independence places conditions on *all* the moments of the joint density but the covariance is only the first moment.

I.3.4.4   Correlation

Covariance is determined not only by the degree of dependency between X and Y but also by the size of X and Y. For example, monthly returns are of a much greater order of magnitude than daily returns, so the covariance of any monthly returns will normally be greater than the covariance of any daily returns on the same asset. For this reason we often prefer to work with an associated statistic, which is called the correlation.

Correlation is the most common measure of dependency between two random variables X and Y. Loosely speaking, if X tends to increase when Y increases and tends to decrease when Y decreases, then X and Y have positive correlation. If X tends to decrease when Y increases and tends to increase when Y decreases, they have negative correlation. If movements in X have no association with movements in Y, they have zero correlation.

Many financial market models analyse the correlation between time series of returns over a period of time. From this one could, if desired, infer a correlation of *changes* in prices or P&L. But it is nonsense to measure correlation on time series of prices themselves. There are many assumptions that must be made in order to use correlation and covariance as a measure of dependency. The very least of our assumptions is that the underlying data are generated by a set of *stationary* stochastic processes.[32] So we do *not* take the covariance

---

[32] See Section I.3.7 for further information about stationary processes.

or correlation between prices, or any other variable that follows a random walk. This is a surprisingly common mistake.[33] Prices are, typically, non-stationary variables and as such will be dominated by a trend.

When estimating covariance and correlation the returns can be measured in absolute (e.g. P&L) or percentage (e.g. log returns) terms. It is not easy to define a percentage return on a long-short portfolio, so absolute returns may be used. We often take absolute returns for interest rate and volatility risk factors. Price risk factor returns can be measured in either percentage or absolute terms.

Figure I.3.23 shows some *scatter plots* where synchronous observations on each of the returns are plotted along the two axes. A scatter plot is a sample from the joint density of the two returns series. If the returns have positive correlation the joint density will have a ridge sloping upwards, as in Figure I.3.23(a) where the correlation is 0.75. With zero correlation their scatter plot will be symmetrically dispersed like the one in Figure I.3.23(b). If they have negative correlation the joint density will have a downwards sloping ridge as in Figure I.3.23(c), which shows returns with correlation −0.75. In this case when one variable has a high value the other will tend to have a low value, and vice versa.

Since covariance is not independent of the units of measurement, it is a difficult measure to use for comparisons. It is better to use the correlation, which is a standardized form of covariance that is independent of the units of measurement. In fact, the formal definition of correlation is

$$\text{Corr}(X, Y) = \frac{\text{Cov}(X, Y)}{\sqrt{V(X)V(Y)}}. \tag{I.3.90}$$

That is, the correlation is just the covariance divided by the product of the standard deviations. Equivalently, using parameter notation rather than operator notation,

$$\varrho_{XY} = \frac{\sigma_{XY}}{\sigma_X \sigma_Y}. \tag{I.3.91}$$

EXAMPLE I.3.11: CALCULATING A CORRELATION

Calculate the correlation in the joint density given in Table I.3.6.

SOLUTION   We know from Example I.3.10 that $E(X) = 2$, $E(Y) = 16$ and $\text{Cov}(X, Y) = 93$. Moreover,

$$E(X^2) = (-20)^2 \times 0.2 + \ldots + 20^2 \times 0.15 = 182.5,$$

$$V(X) = E(X^2) - E(X)^2 = 182.5 - 4 = 178.5$$

and, similarly, $V(Y) = 504$. Hence,

$$\text{Corr}(X, Y) = \frac{93}{\sqrt{178.5 \times 504}} = 0.31.$$

From the definition of correlation, and from (I.3.87), we see that

$$\text{Corr}(aX, bY) = \begin{cases} \text{Corr}(X, Y), & \text{if } ab > 0, \\ -\text{Corr}(X, Y), & \text{if } ab < 0. \end{cases} \tag{I.3.92}$$

---

[33] One can always ask a spreadsheet to produce a number according to some formula, but if the data put into the formula are not the right type of data the result will be nonsense. For instance, it can happen that attempting to measure a correlation on two price series gives a result of 0.9 when the changes in these prices have no association whatsoever.

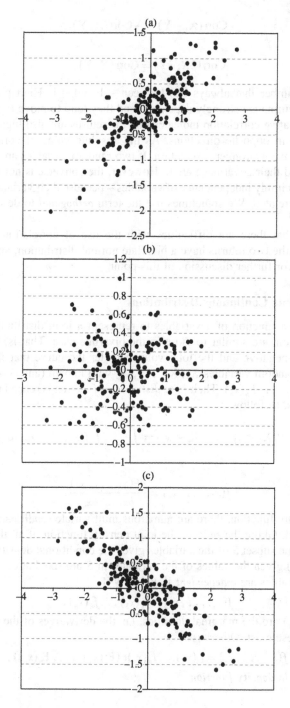

Figure I.3.23   Scatter plots from a paired sample of returns: (a) correlation +0.75; (b) correlation 0; (c) correlation −0.75

Thus, for instance,

$$\text{Corr}(X, -Y) = -\text{Corr}(X, Y)$$

and

$$\text{Corr}(2X, 3Y) = \text{Corr}(X, Y).$$

Correlation is a number that always lies between -1 and $+1$. High positive correlation indicates that the returns are strongly dependent and they tend to move together in the same direction. High negative correlation indicates that the returns are also highly dependent, but they tend to move in opposite directions. As the absolute value of correlation increases, random variables have a stronger association. If two random variables are independent then their correlation and their covariance are 0. However, the converse is not true. That is, zero correlation does not imply independence of variables – because their variances or their higher moments could be related. We sometimes use the term *orthogonal* to describe uncorrelated random variables.[34]

We emphasize that there are difficulties with the use of correlation as a measure of dependence unless the two returns have a bivariate normal distribution, and refer the reader to Section II.3.3.2 for further discussion of this point.

I.3.4.5   Multivariate Continuous Distributions

The conditions for a function of n variables to represent a joint distribution function, or a joint density function, are similar to those in the bivariate case. That is, the function must be integrable, non-negative and the total volume under the curve that it defines must be unity. Consider n random variables $X_1, X_2, \ldots, X_n$ with known (and continuous) marginal distributions $F_1(x_1), \ldots, F_n(x_n)$. Their *joint distribution function* is related to the *joint density function*, if it exists, as follows:

$$F(x_1, \ldots, x_n) = P(X_1 < x_1, \ldots, X_n < x_n) = \int_{-\infty}^{x_n} \cdots \int_{-\infty}^{x_1} f(x_1, \ldots, x_n)\, dx_1 \ldots dx_n \quad \text{(I.3.93)}$$

and

$$f(x_1, \ldots, x_n) = \frac{\partial F(x_1, \ldots, x_n)}{\partial x_1 \ldots \partial x_n}. \quad \text{(I.3.94)}$$

Given a joint density function, there are numerous multivariate *conditional* densities associated with it. Indeed, taking the ratio of the joint density function of all the variables to the joint density of some subset S of the variables gives the conditional density of the remaining variables (not in S) given the values of the variables in S are fixed at certain levels.

The random variables are *independent* if and only if

$$f(x_1, \ldots, x_n) = f_1(x_1) \ldots f_n(x_n), \quad \text{(I.3.95)}$$

where $f_i(x_i) = F_i'(x_i)$ are the marginal densities, i.e. the derivatives of the marginal distributions, assuming these exist. Otherwise

$$f(x_1, \ldots, x_n) = f_1(x_1) \ldots f_n(x_n) c\,(F_1(x_1), \ldots, F_n(x_n)),$$

where c is the *copula density function*.[35]

---

[34] Do not be confused with the term *orthogonal* as applied in linear algebra, where it means that the dot product of two vectors is zero (i.e. they are perpendicular).
[35] See Section II.6.3 for further details.

I.3.4.6   Multivariate Normal Distributions

A common assumption in market risk analysis is that a set of returns has a multivariate normal distribution. This implies that each return has a normal distribution and that the set of returns may have non-zero pairwise correlations. Suppose there are k returns, $\mathbf{x} = (x_1, \ldots, x_k)'$, with expectations $\boldsymbol{\mu} = (\mu_1, \ldots, \mu_k)'$ and (symmetric) covariance matrix

$$
\mathbf{V} = \begin{pmatrix}
\sigma_1^2 & \sigma_{12} & \cdots & \cdots & \sigma_{1k} \\
\sigma_{21} & \sigma_2^2 & \cdots & \cdots & \sigma_{2k} \\
\sigma_{31} & \sigma_{32} & \sigma_3^2 & \cdots & \sigma_{3k} \\
\cdots & \cdots & \cdots & \cdots & \cdots \\
\sigma_{k1} & \cdots & \cdots & \cdots & \sigma_k^2
\end{pmatrix}.
$$

The *multivariate normal density* function is

$$
\varphi(\mathbf{x}) = (2\pi)^{-k/2} |\mathbf{V}|^{-1/2} \exp\left(-\tfrac{1}{2}(\mathbf{x} - \boldsymbol{\mu})' \mathbf{V}^{-1}(\mathbf{x} - \boldsymbol{\mu})\right), \tag{I.3.96}
$$

and we write $\mathbf{X} \sim N_k(\boldsymbol{\mu}, \mathbf{V})$ for the vector random variable that has a k-dimensional multivariate normal distribution.

The multivariate *standard* normal density function is

$$
\varphi(\mathbf{x}) = (2\pi)^{-k/2} |\boldsymbol{\Sigma}|^{-1/2} \exp\left(-\frac{1}{2}\mathbf{x}'\boldsymbol{\Sigma}^{-1}\mathbf{x}\right), \tag{I.3.97}
$$

where $\boldsymbol{\Sigma}$ is the (symmetric) matrix of correlations between the variables

$$
\boldsymbol{\Sigma} = \begin{pmatrix}
1 & \varrho_{12} & \cdots & \cdots & \varrho_{1k} \\
\varrho_{21} & 1 & \cdots & \cdots & \varrho_{2k} \\
\varrho_{31} & \varrho_{32} & 1 & \cdots & \varrho_{3k} \\
\cdots & \cdots & \cdots & \cdots & \cdots \\
\varrho_{k1} & \cdots & \cdots & \cdots & 1
\end{pmatrix}.
$$

An important property of multivariate normal distributed returns is that every portfolio containing these assets will have a normal distribution. If the portfolio weights vector is $\mathbf{w} = (w_1, \ldots, w_k)'$ then the portfolio return is

$$
R = w_1 x_1 + \ldots + w_k x_k = \mathbf{w}'\mathbf{x},
$$

and so

$$
R \sim N(\mu, \sigma^2) \quad \text{with} \quad \mu = \mathbf{w}'\boldsymbol{\mu} \quad \text{and} \quad \sigma^2 = \mathbf{w}'\mathbf{V}\mathbf{w}, \tag{I.3.98}
$$

where $\boldsymbol{\mu}$ is the vector of expected returns on the assets and $\mathbf{V}$ is the asset returns covariance matrix. We have already used this property in Example I.3.6.

The bivariate form of (I.3.96) forms the basis of the normal linear regression models that are introduced in the next chapter. The bivariate normal distribution has a single parameter ϱ, the correlation between two normal variables X and Y. The bivariate normal density function is a symmetrical bell-shaped surface in three dimensions, and similar symmetry properties also hold for higher dimensions. The *level sets*, or contours, of the bivariate normal density form ellipses, as do the contours of a bivariate Student t density. For this reason we call these distributions *elliptical distributions*.

When two random variables have a bivariate normal distribution they are independent *if and only if* their correlation is 0.[36] Suppose X and Y are standard normal variables with correlation $\varrho_{XY} > 0$ and that their joint density is the bivariate standard normal density.[37] Then the conditional distributions are normal distributions, but they are *not* standard normal distributions. In fact when X and Y are bivariate standard normal variables with correlation ϱ then the conditional expectation and conditional variance of Y given X are

$$E(Y\,|X) = \varrho X \quad \text{and} \quad V(Y\,|X) = 1 - \varrho^2. \tag{I.3.99}$$

More generally, suppose X and Y have a bivariate normal distribution with expectations μ_x and μ_y, standard deviations σ_x and σ_y and correlation ϱ_{XY}. Then the conditional distribution $F(Y\,|X)$ is normal with[38]

$$E(Y\,|X) = \mu_Y + \varrho_{XY}\frac{\sigma_Y}{\sigma_X}(X - \mu_X) \quad \text{and} \quad V(Y\,|X) = \sigma_Y^2\left(1 - \varrho_{XY}^2\right). \tag{I.3.100}$$

This result lays the foundations for simple linear regression. The expectation and variance of the other conditional normal distribution $F(X\,|Y)$ are clear from the above, by symmetry.

I.3.4.7 Bivariate Normal Mixture Distributions

Consider two normal mixture variables where we assume for simplicity that there are only two normal components in each distribution. We may write their marginal density functions as

$$h(x) = \pi_1\varphi\left(x; \mu_{11}, \sigma_{11}^2\right) + (1 - \pi_1)\,\varphi\left(x; \mu_{12}, \sigma_{12}^2\right),$$

$$g(y) = \pi_2\varphi\left(y; \mu_{21}, \sigma_{21}^2\right) + (1 - \pi_2)\,\varphi\left(y; \mu_{22}, \sigma_{22}^2\right),$$

where φ is the normal density function. When correlation is used as the dependency metric their joint density will be a *bivariate normal mixture density* of the form

$$f(x, y) = \pi_1\pi_2\varphi(x, y; \boldsymbol{\mu}_1, \mathbf{V}_1) + (1 - \pi_1)\,\pi_2\varphi(x, y; \boldsymbol{\mu}_2, \mathbf{V}_2)$$
$$+ \pi_1(1 - \pi_2)\,\varphi(x, y; \boldsymbol{\mu}_3, \mathbf{V}_3) + (1 - \pi_1)(1 - \pi_2)\,\varphi(x, y; \boldsymbol{\mu}_4, \mathbf{V}_4), \tag{I.3.101}$$

where φ is the bivariate normal density function.

The bivariate normal *mixture* density has four component bivariate normal densities with expectation vectors

$$\boldsymbol{\mu}_1 = \begin{pmatrix} \mu_{11} \\ \mu_{21} \end{pmatrix}, \quad \boldsymbol{\mu}_2 = \begin{pmatrix} \mu_{12} \\ \mu_{21} \end{pmatrix}, \quad \boldsymbol{\mu}_3 = \begin{pmatrix} \mu_{11} \\ \mu_{22} \end{pmatrix}, \quad \boldsymbol{\mu}_4 = \begin{pmatrix} \mu_{12} \\ \mu_{22} \end{pmatrix}$$

---

[36] This only happens when they have a bivariate normal distribution. With other types of bivariate distributions the random variables have zero correlation when they are independent, but *not* the other way around. For instance, we shall see in Section II.3.3.2 that with some bivariate distributions the variables can be highly dependent and still have a zero correlation.

[37] That X and Y are correlated standard normal variables does *not* necessarily imply that their joint distribution is a bivariate normal distribution. For further details see our discussion on copulas in Chapter II.6.

[38] See Miller and Miller (1999) for a proof.

and covariance matrices given by

$$\mathbf{V}_1 = \begin{pmatrix} \sigma_{11}^2 & \varrho_1 \sigma_{11} \sigma_{21} \\ \varrho_1 \sigma_{11} \sigma_{21} & \sigma_{21}^2 \end{pmatrix}, \quad \mathbf{V}_2 = \begin{pmatrix} \sigma_{12}^2 & \varrho_2 \sigma_{12} \sigma_{21} \\ \varrho_2 \sigma_{12} \sigma_{21} & \sigma_{21}^2 \end{pmatrix},$$

$$\mathbf{V}_3 = \begin{pmatrix} \sigma_{11}^2 & \varrho_3 \sigma_{11} \sigma_{22} \\ \varrho_3 \sigma_{11} \sigma_{22} & \sigma_{22}^2 \end{pmatrix}, \quad \mathbf{V}_4 = \begin{pmatrix} \sigma_{12}^2 & \varrho_4 \sigma_{12} \sigma_{22} \\ \varrho_4 \sigma_{12} \sigma_{22} & \sigma_{22}^2 \end{pmatrix}.$$

This distribution has useful applications to portfolio analysis of assets that display regime-specific behaviour. For instance, consider a portfolio with weights $\mathbf{w} = (w, 1 - w)'$ on two assets with returns X_1 and X_2 that have a bivariate normal mixture distribution. The portfolio return is

$$R = wX_1 + (1 - w) X_2.$$

Now the portfolio returns distribution is a mixture of *four* normal distributions with mixing law

$$\pi = (\pi_1 \pi_2, (1 - \pi_1) \pi_2, \pi_1 (1 - \pi_2), (1 - \pi_1)(1 - \pi_2))'. \qquad (I.3.102)$$

The component expectations are

$$\{\mathbf{w}'\boldsymbol{\mu}_1, \mathbf{w}'\boldsymbol{\mu}_2, \mathbf{w}'\boldsymbol{\mu}_3, \mathbf{w}'\boldsymbol{\mu}_4\}, \qquad (I.3.103)$$

and the component variances are

$$\{\mathbf{w}'\mathbf{V}_1\mathbf{w}, \mathbf{w}'\mathbf{V}_2\mathbf{w}, \mathbf{w}'\mathbf{V}_3\mathbf{w}, \mathbf{w}'\mathbf{V}_4\mathbf{w}\}. \qquad (I.3.104)$$

We shall apply this result in Section IV.2.8 when we derive a simple formula for calculating the VaR of a linear portfolio (i.e. one that contains no options) under the assumption that the risk factor returns have a normal mixture distribution.

I.3.4.8 Multivariate Student t Distributions

The standard univariate Student t distribution with expectation 0 and variance $v(v-2)^{-1}$ was introduced in Section I.3.3.7. We can generalize this to the *multivariate Student t distribution*, which has density function

$$f(\mathbf{x}) = k |\boldsymbol{\Sigma}|^{-1/2} \left(1 + v^{-1} \mathbf{x}' \boldsymbol{\Sigma}^{-1} \mathbf{x}\right)^{-(v+n)/2}, \qquad (I.3.105)$$

where $|\boldsymbol{\Sigma}|$ denotes the determinant of the correlation matrix and

$$k = \Gamma\left(\frac{v}{2}\right)^{-1} \Gamma\left(\frac{v+n}{2}\right) (v\pi)^{-n/2},$$

in which Γ is the gamma function.

If x is a positive integer, $\Gamma(x) = (x-1)!$. When ν and n are positive even integers then

$$\Gamma\left(\frac{\nu}{2}\right) = \left(\frac{\nu}{2}-1\right)! \quad \text{and} \quad \Gamma\left(\frac{\nu}{2}\right)^{-1}\Gamma\left(\frac{\nu+n}{2}\right) = \left(\frac{\nu+n}{2}-1\right)\cdots\left(\frac{\nu}{2}+1\right)\cdot\frac{\nu}{2},$$

so when $n=2$,

$$\Gamma\left(\frac{\nu}{2}\right)^{-1}\Gamma\left(\frac{\nu+n}{2}\right) = \frac{\nu}{2}$$

and if ν is an even positive integer, $k = (2\pi)^{-1}$.

The multivariate t distribution has very useful applications which will be described in Volumes II and IV. Its most important market risk modelling applications are to:

- multivariate GARCH modelling,
- generating copulas, and
- simulating asset prices.

I.3.5 INTRODUCTION TO STATISTICAL INFERENCE

A statistical model will predict well only if it is properly specified and its parameter estimates are robust, unbiased and efficient. *Unbiased* means that the expected value of the estimator is equal to the true model parameter and *efficient* means that the variance of the estimator is low, i.e. different samples give similar estimates. When we set up a statistical model the implicit assumption is that this is the 'true' model for the population. We estimate the model's parameters from a sample and then use these estimates to infer the values of the 'true' population parameters. With what degree of confidence can we say that the 'true' parameter takes some value such as 0?[39] Do two random variables have the same distribution? The true population parameter, denoted by a Greek letter, has a value that we will never know for sure, but what is a *range* of values that we are reasonably confident contains the true parameter? These questions are examples of *statistical inference* and their answers – and answers to similar questions – will be addressed in this section.[40]

I.3.5.1 Quantiles, Critical Values and Confidence Intervals

When a random variable X has a known distribution function $F(x)$ we can find the *quantiles* of X by inverting this distribution function. For instance, the lower 5% quantile of X is $F^{-1}(0.05)$ and this point cuts off an area of 5% in the lower tail of the distribution. Put another way, $P(X < F^{-1}(0.05)) = 5\%$ and, more generally,

$$P(X < F^{-1}(\alpha)) = \alpha \tag{I.3.106}$$

where $F^{-1}(\alpha)$ denotes the α quantile of X, i.e. the inverse of the distribution function at α.

When X is a sampling random variable, the upper and lower percentiles of X are called its *critical values*. We can find these values in statistical tables or in statistical packages such

---

[39] The hypothesis $\beta = 0$ is a particularly interesting inference in a regression model, because it implies that the associated explanatory variable has no effect on the dependent variable.
[40] Non-linear hypotheses require statistical methods that are beyond the scope of this book, but they are well covered in econometrics texts such as Campbell et al. (1997).

as Excel. For instance, in Excel the function NORMSINV(α) returns the α of a standard normal random variable. Because the standard normal distribution is symmetric about zero.

$$-\text{NORMSINV}(\alpha) = \text{NORMSINV}(1 - \alpha)$$

So $\text{NORMSINV}(0.025) = -1.96$ or, using mathematical notation,

$$\Phi^{-1}(0.025) = -1.96 \text{ and } \Phi^{-1}(0.975) = 1.96$$

where $\Phi^{-1}(u)$ is the inverse value of the standard normal distribution function at u for $0 < u < 1$.

The following critical values are very useful for all types of statistical inference and will also be used extensively in Chapter IV.2 to calculate the value at risk of a linear portfolio:

$$\Phi^{-1}(0.999) = 3.09 \quad \Rightarrow P(Z < -3.09) = 0.001 \quad \text{and } P(Z > 3.09) = 0.001,$$
$$\Phi^{-1}(0.995) = 2.5758 \Rightarrow P(Z < -2.5758) = 0.005 \text{ and } P(Z > 2.5758) = 0.005,$$
$$\Phi^{-1}(0.99) = 2.3263 \quad \Rightarrow P(Z < -2.3263) = 0.01 \quad \text{and } P(Z > 2.3263) = 0.01,$$
$$\Phi^{-1}(0.975) = 1.96 \quad \Rightarrow P(Z < -1.96) = 0.025 \quad \text{and } P(Z > 1.96) = 0.025,$$
$$\Phi^{-1}(0.95) = 1.645 \quad \Rightarrow P(Z < -1.645) = 0.05 \quad \text{and } P(Z > 1.645) = 0.05.$$

$$(\text{I.3.107})$$

As its name suggests, a *confidence interval* is a range within which one is fairly confident the true parameter lies. So (A, B) is a 95% confidence interval for θ if $P(A < \theta < B) = 0.95$. The range of the confidence interval depends on the degree of confidence and the distribution of the parameter estimator.

EXAMPLE I.3.12: NORMAL CONFIDENCE INTERVALS

(*i*) An area of 0.6827 lies under the curve described by a normal density function between $\mu - \sigma$ and $\mu + \sigma$. That is, approximately two-thirds of the time a realization of the normal random variable will lie in the range $[\mu - \sigma, \mu + \sigma]$. Put another way,

$$P(\mu - \sigma < X < \mu + \sigma) = 0.6827.$$

Hence $[\mu - \sigma, \mu + \sigma]$ is a 68.27% confidence interval for X.

(*ii*) An area of 0.9545 lies under the normal density function between $\mu - 2\sigma$ and $\mu + 2\sigma$, so approximately 95% of the time a realization of a normal random variable will lie in the range $[\mu - 2\sigma, \mu + 2\sigma]$. That is,

$$P(\mu - 2\sigma < X < \mu + 2\sigma) = 0.9545$$

and $[\mu - 2\sigma, \mu + 2\sigma]$ is a 95.45% confidence interval for X.

The confidence intervals above are called *two-sided confidence intervals* and in this case the range for the variable given by the confidence interval is symmetric. We may also consider *one-sided confidence intervals*, where the range runs from $-\infty$ to a finite value, or from a finite value to $+\infty$. Naturally, if the random variable can only take positive values, such as a lognormal random variable, the lower one-sided confidence interval would cover a range starting from 0.

To find a two-sided 90% confidence interval for a normal variable we must find the value of c such that $P(\mu - c\sigma < X < \mu + c\sigma) = 0.90$. Applying the standard normal transformation (I.3.37) gives

$$P(\mu - c\sigma < X < \mu + c\sigma) = P(-c < Z < c) = 0.90.$$

This gives $c = 1.645$, since this is the upper 5% critical value of the standard normal distribution. Clearly, a two-sided 90% confidence interval for X is

$$P(\mu - 1.645\sigma < X < \mu + 1.645\sigma) = 0.90$$

Similarly a one-sided upper 95% confidence interval for X is

$$P(\mu - 1.645\sigma < X < \infty) = 0.95.$$

EXAMPLE I.3.13: ONE- AND TWO-SIDED CONFIDENCE INTERVALS

If $X \sim N(1, 4)$, find

(i)   a two-sided 99% confidence interval for X,
(ii) a one-sided lower 99% confidence interval for X,
(iii) a one-sided lower 99% confidence interval for $y = \exp(X)$.

SOLUTION

(i)   From standard normal tables we find:

$$P(-2.56 < Z < 2.56) = 0.99$$

$$\Rightarrow P(-2.56\sigma + \mu < X < 2.56\sigma + \mu) = 0.99$$

$$\mu = 1, \sigma = 2 \Rightarrow P(-4.12 < X < 6.12) = 0.99.$$

(ii) Again from standard normal tables we find:

$$P(-\infty < Z < 2.3263) = 0.99$$

$$\Rightarrow P(-\infty < X < 2.3263\sigma + \mu) = 0.99$$

$$\mu = 1, \sigma = 2 \Rightarrow P(-\infty < X < 5.6527) = 0.99.$$

(iii) We take the exponential of the limits in (ii) above. Since the exponential is a monotonic increasing transformation, this will not change the probability, which remains 0.99. So we obtain

$$P(0 < Y < \exp(5.6527)) = P(0 < Y < 285) = 0.99.$$

This is how we obtain confidence intervals for lognormally distributed variables.

I.3.5.2   Central Limit Theorem

Suppose we have a sequence $\{X_1, \ldots, X_n\}$ of i.i.d. random variables with finite expectation μ and finite variance σ^2. Consider their mean,

$$\overline{X}_n = \frac{X_1 + \ldots + X_n}{n}. \tag{I.3.108}$$

Applying the expectation and variance operators to (I.3.108) gives:

$$E(\overline{X}_n) = \mu \tag{I.3.109}$$

and

$$V(\overline{X}_n) = n^{-1}\sigma^2. \qquad (\text{I.3.110})$$

To derive (I.3.110) we have used (I.3.87) and the assumption that the variables are independent, so that their covariance is 0.

Taking the square root of (I.3.110) gives the *standard error* of the sample mean as $\sigma/\sqrt{n}$. Note that here we have used the term 'standard error', rather than standard deviation, because the sample mean has a sampling distribution. Also note that (I.3.109) and (I.3.110) hold irrespective of the distribution of $X_1, \ldots, X_n$ provided only that their expectation and variance are finite. In particular, the random variables do not need to be normally distributed for (I.3.109) and (I.3.110) to hold.

A random sample $\{x_1, \ldots, x_n\}$ can be regarded as a set of observations on n i.i.d. random variables $X_1, \ldots, X_n$, one observation from each variable. If the population has expectation μ and variance σ^2 then the sample mean has expectation and variance given by (I.3.109) and (I.3.110), respectively. But what is the shape of the distribution of the sample mean? Since normal distributions are stable, the sum of n independent normal random variables with expectation μ and variance σ^2 is another normal variable. But what if the underlying population is not normally distributed?

The central limit theorem states that the distribution of (I.3.108) will *converge* to a normal distribution as $n \to \infty$. In other words, if the sample is truly random and its size is sufficiently large, then the sample mean $\overline{X}_n$ is approximately normally distributed, whatever the distribution of x.

Formally,

$$\overline{X} \xrightarrow{d} N\left(\mu, \frac{\sigma^2}{n}\right) \qquad (\text{I.3.111})$$

where the notation $\xrightarrow{d}$ stands for *converges in distribution* as the sample size $n \to \infty$.[41] Put another way,

$$\lim_{n \to \infty} P\left(\frac{\overline{X}_n - \mu}{\sigma/\sqrt{n}} < z\right) = \Phi(z) \qquad (\text{I.3.112})$$

where $\Phi(z)$ is the value of the standard normal distribution function at z.

The result (I.3.112) implies the following approximate two-sided confidence interval for an unknown population mean:[42]

$$P\left(\overline{X}_n - \Phi^{-1}\left(\frac{1+\alpha}{2}\right) \times \frac{\sigma}{\sqrt{n}} < \mu < \overline{X}_n + \Phi^{-1}\left(\frac{1+\alpha}{2}\right) \times \frac{\sigma}{\sqrt{n}}\right) = \alpha. \qquad (\text{I.3.113})$$

For instance, if $n = 25$, $\alpha = 0.95$ and the sample mean is 5 then

$$P\left(5 - 1.96 \times \frac{\sigma}{5} < \mu < 5 + 1.96 \times \frac{\sigma}{5}\right) = 0.95.$$

Given a sample of size n, we can compute a value for the sample mean $\overline{X}_n$ in (I.3.113). But we do not know σ and hence we cannot apply (I.3.113) to obtain a confidence interval for the true population mean μ. We need to estimate σ, and because of this (I.3.113) no longer holds. Instead we need to use the Student t critical values, as explained in the next subsection.

---

[41] This is a rather weak form of convergence. It means that a variable does not converge to a specific value but that its distribution converges to a certain distribution, in this case a normal distribution, with known mean and variance.
[42] One-sided confidence intervals can be deduced similarly.

I.3.5.3 Confidence Intervals Based on Student t Distribution

It follows from the construction of sampling distributions in Section I.3.3.8 that when we replace the true variance by an estimated variance the normal statistic $\overline{X}_n$ becomes t distributed. Thus in place of (I.3.112) we have

$$P\left(\frac{\overline{X}_n - \mu}{s/\sqrt{n}} < x\right) \approx t_{n-1}(x),\tag{I.3.114}$$

where $t_{n-1}(x)$ is the value of the standard Student t distribution function with $n-1$ degrees of freedom at the point x.[43] And in place of (I.3.113) we have an approximate confidence interval for the population mean:

$$P\left(\overline{X}_n - t_{n-1}^{-1}\left(\frac{1+\alpha}{2}\right) \times \frac{s}{\sqrt{n}} < \mu < \overline{X}_n + t_{n-1}^{-1}\left(\frac{1+\alpha}{2}\right) \times \frac{s}{\sqrt{n}}\right) = \alpha,\tag{I.3.115}$$

where $t_{n-1}^{-1}(u)$ denotes the u *quantile* of the standard t distribution with $n-1$ degrees of freedom.

For instance, if $n=25$, $\alpha=0.95$, the sample mean is 5 and the sample standard deviation is 2 then, since $t_{24}^{-1}(0.975) = 2.0639$

$$P\left(5 - 2.0639 \times \frac{2}{5} < \mu < 5 + 2.0639 \times \frac{2}{5}\right) = 0.95.$$

Hence

$$P(5 - 0.82556 < \mu < 5 + 0.82556) = 0.95,$$

that is, a 95% confidence interval for the population mean is $(4.17444, 5.82556)$.

Critical Values of the Student t Distribution

Unfortunately the inverse t distribution function in Excel returns the two-tailed probability. This makes it rather difficult to use when calculating critical values for Student t distributed variables. For instance, we know that

$$t_\nu^{-1}(u) \to \Phi^{-1}(u) \text{ as } \nu \to \infty,$$

but putting some large value of ν such as 200 in Excel gives

$$\text{TINV}(0.1, 200) \approx 1.64485 = -\text{NORMSINV}(0.05).$$

Hence,

$$\text{TINV}(0.1, 200) \neq \text{NORMSINV}(0.05).$$

In fact whenever we want to find critical values for the t distribution we must use the following rather horrible formula:

$$t_\nu^{-1}(u) = \begin{cases} -\text{TINV}(2u, \nu), & \text{if } u \leq 0.5, \\ \text{TINV}(2(1-u), \nu), & \text{if } u > 0.5. \end{cases}\tag{I.3.116}$$

The critical values of the standard Student t distribution can be found in statistical tables, or using the Excel function TINV(α) as explained above. Like the standard normal critical

---

[43] We lose one degree of freedom because we have to estimate the sample mean. Note that (I.3.114) follows from the relationships between sampling distributions stated in Section I.3.3.8.

values they are symmetric about zero, but at high significance levels they are greater than the standard normal critical values. For instance, if X has a standard Student t distribution with ten degrees of freedom then:

$$t_{10}^{-1}(0.999) = 4.1437 \quad \Rightarrow P(X < -4.1437) = 0.001 \quad \text{and} \quad P(X > 4.1437) = 0.001,$$

$$t_{10}^{-1}(0.995) = 3.1693 \quad \Rightarrow P(X < -3.1693) = 0.005 \quad \text{and} \quad P(X > 3.1693) = 0.005,$$

$$t_{10}^{-1}(0.99) = 2.7638 \quad \Rightarrow P(X < -2.7638) = 0.01 \quad \text{and} \quad P(X > 2.7638) = 0.01,$$

$$t_{10}^{-1}(0.975) = 2.2281 \quad \Rightarrow P(X < -2.2281) = 0.025 \quad \text{and} \quad P(X > 2.2281) = 0.025,$$

$$t_{10}^{-1}(0.95) = 1.8125 \quad \Rightarrow P(X < -1.8125) = 0.05 \quad \text{and} \quad P(X > 1.8125) = 0.05.$$

$$(\text{I.3.117})$$

By symmetry of the t distribution,

$$t_\nu^{-1}(1 - u) = -t_\nu^{-1}(u) \tag{I.3.118}$$

for any u between 0 and 1. Thus, for instance,

$$t_{10}^{-1}(0.025) = -t_{10}^{-1}(0.975) = -2.2281.$$

EXAMPLE I.3.14: CONFIDENCE INTERVAL FOR A POPULATION MEAN

A sample with 11 observations has a sample mean of 8 and a sample standard deviation of 2. Find an approximate 99% two-sided confidence interval for the population mean.

SOLUTION   From (I.3.115) and using (I.3.117) with $\nu = 10$ and $\alpha = 0.99$ we have

$$P\left(8 - 3.1693 \times \frac{2}{\sqrt{11}} < \mu < 8 + 3.1693 \times \frac{2}{\sqrt{11}}\right) = 0.99.$$

Hence an approximate 99% two-sided confidence interval for the population mean is

$$[6.09, \ 9.91].$$

I.3.5.4   Confidence Intervals for Variance

Confidence intervals for a variance σ^2 are constructed in a similar way to those above, but they are based on the statistic

$$\frac{(n-1)s^2}{\sigma^2} \sim \chi_{n-1}^2. \tag{I.3.119}$$

The critical values of the chi-squared distribution can be found in statistical tables or using the Excel function CHIINV(α, ν), where ν denotes the degrees of freedom.

Unfortunately, Excel switches around the usual notation again. For instance, CHIINV(0.05, 10) = 18.307 and CHIINV(0.95, 10) = 3.940, so

$$P(X < 3.940) = 0.05 \text{ and } P(X < 18.307) = 0.95.$$

But, following standard notation for quantiles,

$$P\left(X < (\chi_\nu^2)^{-1}(u)\right) = u$$

where $(\chi_\nu^2)^{-1}$ denotes the inverse distribution function for the chi-squared distribution.

Hence, to find $(\chi_\nu^2)^{-1}(u)$ for some u between 0 and 1 we use the Excel command CHIINV($1 - u$, ν) and not, as one might suppose, CHIINV(u, ν).

It follows from (I.3.119) that a one-sided $100\alpha\%$ confidence interval for a variance is

$$P\left(\sigma^2 < \frac{(n-1)s^2}{\left(\chi^2_{n-1}\right)^{-1}(1-\alpha)}\right) = \alpha, \tag{I.3.120}$$

and a two-sided $\alpha\%$ confidence interval for a population variance is:

$$P\left(\frac{(n-1)s^2}{\left(\chi^2_{n-1}\right)^{-1}(\alpha/2)} < \sigma^2 < \frac{(n-1)s^2}{\left(\chi^2_{n-1}\right)^{-1}(1-\alpha/2)}\right) = \alpha. \tag{I.3.121}$$

For instance, if we obtain $s^2 = 1$ based on a sample of size 11 then a 90% confidence interval for the population variance is [0.546, 2.538] because

$$P\left(\frac{10}{18.307} < \sigma^2 < \frac{10}{3.94}\right) = P(0.546 < \sigma^2 < 2.538) = 0.90. \tag{I.3.122}$$

I.3.5.5 Hypothesis Tests

The framework for hypothesis tests is conceptually very simple:

1. *Set up the null and alternative hypotheses, H_0 and H_1.* The null hypothesis H_0 consists of one or more restrictions on the true model parameters. The alternative hypothesis H_1 may be either one-sided ($<$ or $>$) or two sided ($\neq$).
2. *State the test statistic, X.* Often a variety of test statistics is available. The most common parametric test statistics fall into one of three categories: *Wald* tests, *Lagrange multiplier* (LM) tests or *likelihood ratio* (LR) tests. These tests have different power properties and different distributions in small samples, although they are asymptotically equivalent.[44]
3. *Choose a significance level α.* The level of significance with which one can state results determines the 'size' of the test, which is the probability of a type I error. A *type I error* is the rejection of a true null hypothesis. Increasing the significance level reduces the size of the test but also increases the probability of a type II error and so reduces the power of the test. A *type II error* is the acceptance of a false null hypothesis.
4. *Determine the critical region.* The critical values of the test statistic X depend on the chosen significance level α. For a fixed α and for a two-sided alternative, upper and lower critical values $CV_U(X, \alpha)$ and $CV_L(X, \alpha)$ give the critical region

$$CR(X, \alpha) = \{(-\infty, CV_L(X, \alpha)] \quad \text{and} \quad [CV_U(X, \alpha), \infty)\}.$$

A one-sided alternative ($<$) has the critical region $(-\infty, CV_L(X, \alpha)]$ and a one-sided alternative ($>$) has the critical region $[CV_U(X, \alpha), \infty)$. In each case the size of the test is the area above the critical region under the density function of the test statistic as shown in Figure I.3.24. In the majority of cases the critical values of a test statistic are tabulated.[45]

---

[44] The *power* of a test is the probability that it will reject a false null hypothesis. When more than one test is available it is preferable to choose the most powerful test of any given size.

[45] In fact many test statistics have one of four standard sampling distributions under the null hypothesis: the normal distribution, the t distribution, the chi-squared distribution or the F distribution.

Critical Region of a One-Sided Statistical Test

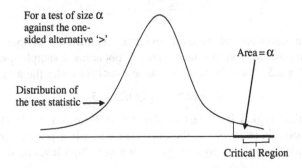

For a test of size α against the one-sided alternative '>'

Area = α

Distribution of the test statistic →

Critical Region

Critical Region of a Two-Sided Statistical Test

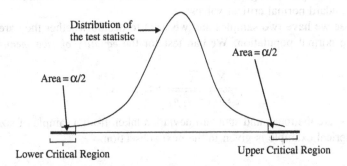

Distribution of the test statistic →

Area = $\alpha/2$

Area = $\alpha/2$

Lower Critical Region

Upper Critical Region

Figure I.3.24   Critical regions for hypothesis tests

5. *Evaluate the test statistic.* The value that we get for the test statistic, X^*, will be based on sample data and it is also (often but not always) based on the values of model parameters that are given by the null hypothesis. For instance, LR tests use both unrestricted values and values that are restricted by the null hypothesis.[46]
6. *Apply the decision rule.* The test is 'reject H_0 in favour of H_1 at $100\alpha\%$ if $X^* \in CR(X, \alpha)$'.

I.3.5.6   Tests on Means

Assume that the population from which a sample is drawn has a normal distribution but that we know neither the expectation nor the variance of this distribution. How can we infer the values of these parameters from a sample? From Section I.3.5.3 we know that the sample mean has a t distribution when the population variance is unknown. Hence a t test may be used to test the null hypothesis $H_0 : \mu = \mu_0$ where μ_0 is a specific value, e.g. 0, 1, or any other number. Suppose we wish to test

$$H_0 : \mu = 0 \quad \text{vs} \quad H_1 : \mu < 0.$$

---

[46] See Section I.4.4.6.

The test statistic is

$$t = \frac{\overline{X}_n - \mu}{s/\sqrt{n}} \sim t_{n-1},$$

(I.3.123)

where $\overline{X}_n$ and s are the mean and standard deviation taken from a sample of size n.

For instance, suppose we take a sample size 10, obtaining a sample mean $\overline{x} = 2.5$ and a sample variance $s^2 = 2.5$. Then the value of the test statistic under the null hypothesis is

$$t^* = (2.5 - 0)/\sqrt{0.25} = 5.$$

The one-sided critical region for a test of size 5% is $(-\infty, -1.83)$.[47] Hence, we cannot reject the null hypothesis in favour of the one-sided alternative $\mu < 0$. However, we could reject the null in favour of the alternative $\mu > 0$ at a very high level of significance – even at 0.1%!

Since the t distribution converges to a standard normal distribution, if the sample size is 'large' we use the normal distribution for the test and call it a Z test. How large is 'large' in this case? For sample sizes greater than 120 the Student t critical values are virtually the same as the standard normal critical values.

Now suppose we have two samples and we want to decide whether they are both drawn from the same normal population. We can test for the *equality of two means* using the t statistic

$$\frac{\overline{X}_1 - \overline{X}_2}{\sqrt{s_1^2/n_1 + s_2^2/n_2}} \sim t_{n_1+n_2-2},$$

(I.3.124)

where $\overline{X}_i$ and s_i are the mean and standard deviation taken from a sample of size n_i for $i = 1$ and 2. A numerical example is given in the next subsection.

I.3.5.7 Tests on Variances

Tests on *variances* from normal populations use the chi-squared test statistic (I.3.119). For instance, suppose we want to test the hypothesis that the variance of the sample above is 0.5, against a one-sided alternative:

$$H_0 : \sigma^2 = 0.5 \quad \text{vs} \quad H_1 : \sigma^2 < 0.5.$$

Under the assumption that the population is normal and under the null hypothesis, the test statistic X has a chi-squared distribution with $n - 1$ degrees of freedom.

In our case the sample size $n = 10$, and the sample variance $s^2 = 0.25$, so our value of the test statistic is

$$X^* = \frac{9 \times 0.25}{0.5} = 4.5.$$

The 5% critical value for the χ_9^2 variable is 3.33 and so the critical region is $(0, 3.33)$ because the chi-squared density always takes positive values. The 10% critical value is 4.17 and the critical region is $(0, 4.17)$.[48] Since our value of the test statistic lies in neither of these regions, we cannot reject the null hypothesis even at 10%.

---

[47] We can find the value of 1.83 using the Excel command TINV(0.1,9).
[48] Using Excel, CHIINV(0.95, 9) = 3.33 and CHIINV(0.9,9) = 4.17. Note that Excel uses a probability value for the upper tail, not the lower tail.

F tests are used to test the joint significance of several explanatory variables in a linear regression model, and, to test whether restrictions on parameters hold. [49] They are also used to test the *equality of two variances*, based on the statistic

$$\frac{s_1^2}{s_2^2} \sim F_{n_1-1, n_2-1}, \qquad (I.3.125)$$

where n_1 and s_1^2 are the sample size and sample variance in the first sample and n_2 and s_2^2 are the sample size and sample variance in the second sample. Again (I.3.125) only holds under the null hypothesis that the two populations are normal with equal variances.

EXAMPLE I.3.15: TESTING FOR EQUALITY OF MEANS AND VARIANCES

Two samples are drawn from (assumed) normal populations with statistics shown in Table I.3.9. Test whether the samples could be drawn from the same populations.

Table I.3.9   Sample statistics

Sample	Number of observations	Sample mean	Sample variance
1	25	1.0	3.0
2	35	2.0	8.0

SOLUTION   The value of the F-statistic (I.3.125) for equality of variances is the ratio of the variances, i.e.

$$F^* = 3/8 = 0.375.$$

This value has a cumulative probability of 0.007 under the F distribution with (24, 34) degrees of freedom (using the FDIST function in Excel). In other words, this value falls into the lower 1% tail of the F distribution. Hence we can reject the hypothesis that the variances are equal in favour of the one-sided alternative that the second sample is drawn from a population with a larger variance.

To test for equality of means we calculate (I.3.124) as follows:

$$t^* = \frac{1-2}{\sqrt{\frac{3}{25} + \frac{8}{35}}} = -1.697.$$

The 10% two-tailed critical value of the t distribution with 58 degrees of freedom is 1.67 and the 5% critical value is approximately 2 (using the TINV function in Excel). Hence we can reject the hypothesis that the means are the same only at 10%, not at 5%. We conclude that the two samples are drawn from different populations, mainly because the second sample has a significantly larger variance than the first sample.

I.3.5.8   Non-Parametric Tests on Distributions

We often need to test whether two distributions are significantly different from each other, for instance when evaluating different hedging models or different models for predicting

---

[49] See Section I.4.4.6 for further details.

portfolio risk and returns, or simply when testing which type of distribution fits the sample data best. So far we have described how to conduct hypothesis tests on population parameters, and how to construct confidence intervals for population parameters, always under the assumption that the populations have normal distributions. In this case we need only test the equality of means and variances to decide whether two populations are identical. However, normal distributions are rare in empirical analysis.

In the following we describe the basic *Kolmogorov–Smirnoff* tests for the equality of distributions, and one of its generalizations, and we explain how to simulate the critical values of these statistics. Note that these tests make no assumption about the shape of the distributions, i.e. they are *non-parametric* tests. This means that we can apply them to any type of distributions at all. The test statistic itself is very flexible, because in most cases we find the critical values by simulation.

Kolmogorov–Smirnoff Test

As with the mean and variance tests above, the Kolmogorov–Smirnoff test has both one-sample and two-sample versions. The one-sample version is most often used to test the *goodness of fit* of a parametric distribution to the empirical distribution, i.e. the distribution calculated directly from the sample data. The two-sample test is used to decide whether there are any significant differences between two empirical distributions. Both tests are based on two cumulative distribution functions, $F_1(x)$ and $F_2(x)$. The null hypothesis is that the two distributions are the same and in the goodness-of-fit tests one of the distributions is the empirical distribution, which is commonly fitted using a kernel.

The *Kolmogorov–Smirnoff* test statistic is

$$KS = \max_x |F_1(x) - F_2(x)|.$$ (I.3.126)

That is, KS is the maximum of the vertical differences between two cumulative distribution functions. For large samples an approximate critical value for KS at the $\alpha\%$ level is

$$C_\alpha = c_\alpha \sqrt{\frac{n_1 + n_2}{n_1 n_2}},$$ (I.3.127)

where c_α is a constant that depends on the significance level as follows:

α	0.1%	1%	5%	10%
c_α	1.95	1.63	1.36	1.22

In small samples the critical values of KS are obtained by simulation, for instance using a similar method to that described for the Anderson–Darling test critical values below. KS critical values are calculated automatically by statistical software that implements Kolmogorov–Smirnoff test procedures. See also Peter Lee's homepage, where many non-standard distributions are tabulated.[50]

---

[50] Currently (February 2008) at http://www.york.ac.uk/depts/maths/tables/welcome.htm.

Anderson–Darling Test

In the Kolmogorov–Smirnoff test the KS statistic focuses on the fit between the two distributions around their means. If we want to shift the focus of the test to the fit between two distributions in their *tails* then we can apply a modified version of the KS test called the Anderson–Darling test.

Let $F_E(x)$ denote the empirical distribution and $F_H(x)$ denote an hypothesized distribution, such as a Student t distribution that has been fitted to the sample. The null hypothesis is that the two distributions are the same and the Anderson–Darling statistic is[51]

$$AD = \max_x \left(\frac{|F_E(x) - F_H(x)|}{\sqrt{F_H(x)\,(1 - F_H(x))}} \right). \tag{I.3.128}$$

The critical values for the Anderson–Darling test depend on the specific distribution that is being tested, and critical values are computed by simulation. Tabulated values of the AD critical values have been published only for a few specific distributions (see Stephens, 1976).

A general procedure for simulating critical values of non-standard test statistics is outlined in Section II.8.2.3. Here we explain how the procedure is implemented in order to generate critical values for the Anderson–Darling test. Suppose the empirical and fitted distributions are based on a sample of size n. To find critical values for the AD statistic we take the fitted distribution $F_H(x)$ with parameters estimated from the sample and apply Monte Carlo simulations as follows:

1. Simulate a random number u between 0 and 1.[52]
2. Apply the inverse cumulative distribution function to u and set $x = F_H^{-1}(u)$;
3. Do n repetitions of steps 1 and 2, thus simulating a sample of size n.
4. Find the empirical distribution $F_E(x)$ and the re-fitted hypothesized distribution $F_H(x)$ *both* based on the simulated sample.
5. Compute the AD test statistic (I.3.128).[53]
6. Return to step 1 and repeat a large number of times (e.g. 10,000 times) to obtain a simulated distribution of the test statistic under the null hypothesis.[54]
7. The $100\alpha\%$ critical value is the α quantile of the distribution simulated at step 6.

The KS and AD statistics focus on the fit in the centre and in the tails, respectively. Since the tests have critical values that are computed by simulation we can modify the statistics in many ways. For instance, to better reflect the overall fit between two distributions we could take the *average* difference between the distribution functions in (I.3.126) and (I.3.128) rather than the maximum over the sample. To simulate new critical values for the test statistic after this modification, use the procedure outlined above but with the modified test statistic in place of (I.3.126) or (I.3.128).

---

[51] This formulation is non-standard but is increasingly used for financial applications. See Malevergne and Sornette (2003).
[52] In Excel, use the RAND() command.
[53] Or the KS statistic (I.3.126).
[54] Or more or less than 10,000 times depending on the accuracy you require.

I.3.6 MAXIMUM LIKELIHOOD ESTIMATION

Maximum likelihood estimation (MLE) is a general method for estimating the parameters of a distribution. It is used extensively because maximum likelihood estimators are *consistent*. That is, the distribution of the estimator converges to the true value of the parameter as the sample size increases. MLE may also be applied to estimate parameters of regression models, and we shall be using MLE to estimate the parameters of GARCH models in Chapter II.4. But there is no need for likelihood methods when estimating linear regression models under the classical assumptions, because ordinary least squares estimation and maximum likelihood estimation are equivalent.

The MLE process is based on the construction of a *likelihood function*, which depends on the parametric form that is assumed for the distribution and on the sample data. Then the parameters of the distribution are chosen to maximize this function. These values are the maximum likelihood estimators.

I.3.6.1 The Likelihood Function

The *likelihood* of an observation x on a random variable is the value of its density function at x. The likelihood of a sample $\mathbf{x} = (x_1, \ldots, x_n)'$ is the *product* of the values of the density function at each observation x_i. In Figure I.3.25 we assume we have a fixed sample, indicated by the points on the horizontal axis, and depicts how the value of a likelihood function depends on the value of the distribution's parameters. For two different values of a parameter vector θ, say θ_0 and θ_1, the likelihood of the sample is greater when the parameters take the values θ_0.

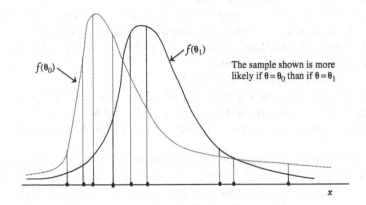

$f(\theta_0)$

$f(\theta_1)$

The sample shown is more likely if $\theta = \theta_0$ than if $\theta = \theta_1$

x

Figure I.3.25   The dependence of the likelihood on parameters

Different sample data will give different values of the likelihood. Thus, if the density function has parameters θ then the likelihood of $\mathbf{x}$ is written

$$L(\theta \,|\, \mathbf{x}) = \prod_{i=1}^{n} f(x_i, \theta). \tag{I.3.129}$$

The greater the value of the likelihood, the more probable are the parameters' values, based on the given sample data. But the values of the parameters that generate the highest likelihood

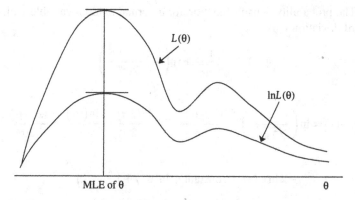

Figure I.3.26   The likelihood and the log likelihood functions

will depend on the choice of the sample data. As θ ranges over all possible values of the parameters the likelihood function describes a surface that is highly dependent on the sample.

The *maximum likelihood estimator* of θ is the value of θ that maximizes the likelihood function. For example, when there is a single parameter θ the likelihood function describes a curve $L(\theta)$, such as that shown in Figure I.3.26. And the MLE is the value of θ where this function achieves a maximum, as depicted in the figure.

I.3.6.2   Finding the Maximum Likelihood Estimates

The likelihood function is, by definition, a *product* of density functions and differentiating products is not easy. It is much easier to differentiate the log of the likelihood function, because this is a *sum* (of log densities):

$$\ln L(\theta\,|\mathbf{x}) = \sum_{i=1}^{n} \ln f(x_i, \theta). \qquad (I.3.130)$$

Since the log is a monotonic increasing function, the *same* value of θ that maximizes the likelihood also maximizes the log likelihood, as depicted in Figure I.3.26. Hence, we usually find the maximum likelihood estimate by maximizing the log likelihood function rather than the likelihood function itself.

EXAMPLE I.3.16: LOG LIKELIHOOD OF THE NORMAL DENSITY

Show that minimizing the function

$$n \ln(\sigma^2) + \sum_{i=1}^{n} \left(\frac{x_i - \mu}{\sigma}\right)^2 \qquad (I.3.131)$$

with respect to μ and σ^2 yields the maximum likelihood estimators for a normal density, and consequently show that the maximum likelihood estimators for a normal density are given by

$$\hat{\mu} = \bar{x} = \frac{1}{n}\sum_{i=1}^{n} x_i \quad \text{and} \quad \hat{\sigma}^2 = \frac{1}{n}\sum_{i=1}^{n}(x_i - \bar{x})^2. \qquad (I.3.132)$$

SOLUTION   The probability density function for a normal random variable with expectation μ and standard deviation σ is

$$\varphi(x) = \frac{1}{\sqrt{2\pi\sigma^2}} \exp\left(-\frac{(x-\mu)^2}{2\sigma^2}\right). \qquad (I.3.133)$$

Hence

$$\ln \varphi(x) = \ln\left(\frac{1}{\sqrt{2\pi\sigma^2}}\right) - \frac{(x-\mu)^2}{2\sigma^2} = -\frac{\ln(2\pi)}{2} - \frac{\ln(\sigma^2)}{2} - \frac{(x-\mu)^2}{2\sigma^2}$$

i.e.

$$-2\ln \varphi(x) = \text{constant} + \ln(\sigma^2) + \left(\frac{x-\mu}{\sigma}\right)^2.$$

Given a sample $x = (x_1, \ldots, x_n)'$, maximizing the likelihood is equivalent to minimizing -2 times the log likelihood, i.e. minimizing

$$-2\ln L = -2\sum_{i=1}^{n} \ln \varphi(x_i) = \text{constant} + n\ln(\sigma^2) + \sum_{i=1}^{n}\left(\frac{x_i - \mu}{\sigma}\right)^2.$$

We can ignore the constant, as it will not affect the optima. This proves the first part of the question.

Differentiating (I.3.131) with respect to μ and with respect to σ^2 yields the two first order conditions

$$\sum_{i=1}^{n}(x_i - \mu) = 0,$$

$$\sum_{i=1}^{n}(x_i - \mu)^2 = n\sigma^2,$$

and solving the above gives (I.3.132). For the second order condition it can be shown that the Hessian matrix of second partial derivatives of (I.3.131) is

$$\begin{pmatrix} n\sigma^{-2} & 0 \\ 0 & 2^{-1}n\sigma^{-4} \end{pmatrix}$$

which is positive definite, so the stationary point found is a local minimum.

EXAMPLE I.3.17: FITTING A STUDENT t DISTRIBUTION BY MAXIMUM LIKELIHOOD

Figure I.3.27 shows the FTSE 100 index from 2 January 2004 to 20 August 2007. Fit a Student t distribution to the daily log returns on the index using MLE.

SOLUTION   The spreadsheet for this example computes the sample of daily log returns, and then standardizes the observations to have a sample mean of 0 and a sample variance of 1. Then we assume a value for the degrees of freedom and calculate the log likelihood for the standardized t distribution, based on the density function (I.3.57) for each observation. Summing the log likelihood of each observation gives us a value for the log likelihood function based on our assumed value for the degrees of freedom. Finally, we apply the Excel Solver to find the degrees-of-freedom parameter which maximizes our log likelihood function.

The sample mean log return is 0.033% (which is equivalent to an annualized mean log return of 8.13%) and the sample standard deviation of log returns is 0.746% (which is

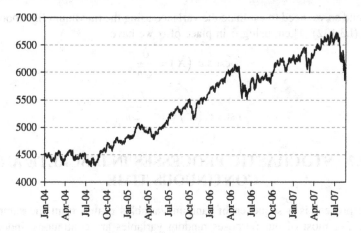

Figure I.3.27 FTSE 100 index

equivalent to a volatility of 11.19%). Using these values to normalize the sample, we then construct the log likelihood function as explained above and maximize it using the Solver. The result is a degrees-of-freedom estimate of 4.73.

I.3.6.3 Standard Errors on Mean and Variance Estimates

Hypothesis tests and confidence intervals based on MLE require the use of standard errors of the maximum likelihood estimates, and if the test involves more than one parameter we may also need the covariances of the maximum likelihood estimates. The variances and covariances of the maximum likelihood estimators are given by the inverse of the information matrix of the estimators, and the standard errors of the maximum likelihood estimators are found by taking the square root of the variances, which lie along the diagonal of the inverse information matrix.

The *information matrix* $I(\theta)$ is the matrix of expected values of the negative of the second derivatives of the log likelihood. For a normal density the matrix of second derivatives of the log likelihood is

$$-\begin{pmatrix} n\sigma^{-2} & \sum(x_i - \mu)\sigma^{-4} \\ \sum(x_i - \mu)\sigma^{-4} & \sum(x_i - \mu)^2\sigma^{-6} - 2^{-1}n\sigma^{-4} \end{pmatrix}$$

and the information matrix, being the expected value of the negative of this matrix, is thus

$$I(\theta) = \begin{pmatrix} n\sigma^{-2} & 0 \\ 0 & 2^{-1}n\sigma^{-4} \end{pmatrix}.$$

The *inverse* of the information matrix is the covariance matrix of the maximum likelihood estimates. This matrix may be used to make inference on models estimated by MLE. For instance, under a normal distribution the inverse information matrix is

$$I(\theta)^{-1} = \begin{pmatrix} n^{-1}\sigma^2 & 0 \\ 0 & 2n^{-1}\sigma^4 \end{pmatrix}. \tag{I.3.134}$$

From this it follows that the standard errors of the maximum likelihood estimators of the sample mean and variance given in (I.3.132) are $\sigma/\sqrt{n}$ and $\sigma^2\sqrt{2/n}$, respectively. But we do not know σ and so we need to estimate the variance using the maximum likelihood estimator $\hat{\sigma}^2$ given by (I.3.132). Then, using $\hat{\sigma}$ in place of σ we have

$$\text{est.s.e.}\left(\overline{X}\right) = \frac{\hat{\sigma}}{\sqrt{n}} \tag{I.3.135}$$

and

$$\text{est.s.e.}\left(\hat{\sigma}^2\right) = \hat{\sigma}^2\sqrt{2/n} \tag{I.3.136}$$

I.3.7 STOCHASTIC PROCESSES IN DISCRETE AND CONTINUOUS TIME

A stochastic process is a sequence of random variables drawn from the same family of distributions. For most of our purposes random variables are continuous, indeed they are often assumed to be normal, but the sequence may be over continuous or discrete time. That is, we consider *continuous state processes* in both continuous and discrete time.

- The study of discrete time stochastic processes is called *time series analysis*. In the time domain the simplest time series models are based on regression analysis, which is introduced in the next chapter. A simple example of a time series model is the *first order autoregression*, and this is defined below along with a basic test for stationarity. We shall introduce the general *autoregressive moving average* time series models for stationary processes and analyse their properties in Section II.5.2.
- Continuous time stochastic processes are represented as *stochastic differential equations* (SDEs). The most famous example of an SDE in finance is *geometric Brownian motion*. This is introduced below, but its application to option pricing is not discussed until Chapter III.3.

The first two subsections define what is meant by a stationary or 'mean-reverting' stochastic process in discrete and continuous time. We contrast this with a particular type of non-stationary process which is called a 'random walk'. Then Section I.3.7.3 focuses on some standard discrete and continuous time models for the evolution of financial asset prices and returns. The most basic assumption in both types of models is that the prices of traded assets follow a random walk, and from this it follows that their returns follow a stationary process.

I.3.7.1 Stationary and Integrated Processes in Discrete Time

This section introduces the time series models that are used to model stationary and integrated processes in discrete time. Then we explain why prices of financial assets are usually integrated of order 1 and the associated returns are therefore stationary. A more formal and detailed treatment of these concepts is given in Section II.5.2.

A discrete time stochastic process is a sequence of random variables from the same distribution family and we denote the process, indexed by time t, as $\{X_1, X_2, \ldots, X_T\}$ or $\{X_t\}_{t=1}^{T}$ for short. It is *stationary* if:

$E(X_t)$ is a finite constant;

$V(X_t)$ is a finite constant; $\tag{I.3.137}$

the joint distribution of (X_t, X_s) depends only on $|t - s|$.

The first two conditions in (I.3.137) are straightforward. The constant expectation condition implies that the expected value of a stationary process does not trend; in fact it does not change at all over time. The finite constant variance condition means that most realizations will be 'close' to expected value; how close depends on the size of this variance. The third condition implies that the joint distribution between adjacent variables in the process is the same at any point in time; similarly, the joint distribution between the variables in the process that are two steps apart is the same at any point in time; similarly for the variables that are three steps apart, and so on. Often this condition is weakened to require only that the *covariance* is independent of the time at which it is measured, rather than the whole joint distribution. In that case we call the process *weakly stationary*.

A common assumption for a stationary process is that the random variables are *independent and identically distributed (i.i.d.)*. The independence assumption implies that there is no autocorrelation in the process and the identical distribution assumption implies that the random variables all have the same distribution parameters. In particular the variance is the same at all points in time, and we call such a process *homoscedastic*. The i.i.d. assumption is commonly applied to the error process in a regression model.[55] The additional assumption that i.i.d. random variables are also standard normal is written

$$X_t \sim \text{NID}(0, 1),$$

so if $\varepsilon_t = \sigma X_t$ and $X_t \sim NID(0, 1)$ then $\varepsilon_t \sim NID(0, \sigma^2)$.

An *autoregression* is a regression of a stationary process on its own lags. A *first order autoregression*, or AR(1) for short, is a regression on the first lag only. Similarly, a second order autoregression or AR(2) is a regression on the first two lags, and so forth. The first order autoregressive model is:

$$X_t = \alpha + \varrho X_{t-1} + \varepsilon_t, \quad \varepsilon_t \sim \text{i.i.d.} \left(0, \sigma^2\right). \tag{I.3.138}$$

The coefficient ϱ on the lagged X is called the *first order autocorrelation coefficient*.

In Section II.5.2 it is shown that:

$$E(X_t) = \frac{\alpha}{1 - \varrho}, \ V(X_t) = \frac{\sigma^2}{1 - \varrho^2} \quad \text{and} \quad \varrho = \frac{\text{Cov}(X_t, X_{t-1})}{V(X_t)}. \tag{I.3.139}$$

Thus the expectation and variance are both finite constants if $|\varrho| < 1$. But if $\varrho = 1$ then the expectation and variance in (I.3.139) are infinite and the process is *non-stationary*. When $\varrho = 1$ the AR(1) model (I.3.138) becomes

$$X_t = \alpha + X_{t-1} + \varepsilon_t, \quad \varepsilon_t \sim \text{i.i.d.} \left(0, \sigma^2\right). \tag{I.3.140}$$

This is the *discrete time random walk model* with drift α and volatility σ.

When the drift is positive the process has an upward trend and when it is negative there is a downward trend over time. Without the stochastic part (the error term) the process would run along a straight line sloping upward if $\alpha > 0$ and sloping downward if $\alpha < 0$. But since the process *does* have a stochastic part, when the volatility σ is not negligible the trend may not be noticeable to the eye.

Loosely speaking, a time series process is *integrated of order* 1 (or just *integrated*, for short) if it is not stationary but its first difference is stationary.[56] Hence the random walk (I.3.140)

---

[55] See Section I.4.3 for a discussion about this assumption.

[56] More specifically, the first difference has a stationary ARMA representation – see Section II.5.2 for more details.

is a particular type of integrated process. Two (or more) integrated time series are said to be *cointegrated* if some linear combination of them is stationary.

Statistical tests for integration and cointegration are based on *unit root tests*, i.e. tests for stationarity. For instance, the basic *Dicky–Fuller test* is performed as follows:

- Regress ΔX_t on a constant and X_{t-1} using OLS.[57]
- The test statistic is the ratio of the estimated coefficient on X_{t-1} to its estimated standard error.
- The critical values are given in Dickey–Fuller tables. They are larger than standard t critical values and are negative, because the test is one-sided.
- If the test statistic falls in the critical region (i.e. it is more negative than the critical value) then reject the null hypothesis that X is integrated in favour of the alternative that X is stationary.

The rationale for this test can be seen on rewriting (I.3.138) as

$$\Delta X_t = \alpha + \beta X_{t-1} + \varepsilon_t \quad \text{with} \quad \beta = \varrho - 1.$$

So a test for $\beta = 0$ is equivalent to the test that $\varrho = 1$, i.e. the null hypothesis is that the process is integrated and the one-sided alternative hypothesis $\beta < 0$ is equivalent to $\varrho < 1$, i.e. the process is stationary. Further detail on unit root tests is given in Section II.5.3.

I.3.7.2 Mean Reverting Processes and Random Walks in Continuous Time

A continuous time stochastic process has dynamics that are represented by a stochastic differential equation. There are two parts to this representation: the first term defines the deterministic part and the second term defines the stochastic part. A *Wiener process*, also called a *Brownian motion*, describes the stochastic part when the process does not jump. Thus a Wiener process is a continuous process with stationary, independent normally distributed increments. The increments are normally distributed so we often use any of the notations $W(t)$, $B(t)$ or $Z(t)$ for such a process. The *increments* of the process are the total change in the process over an infinitesimally small time period; these are denoted $dW(t), dB(t)$ or $dZ(t)$, with

$$E(dW) = 0 \quad \text{and} \quad V(dW) = dt$$

Now we are ready to write the equation for the dynamics of a continuous time stochastic process $X(t)$ as the following SDE:

$$dX(t) = \alpha dt + \sigma dZ(t) \tag{I.3.141}$$

where α is called the *drift* of the process and σ is called the *process volatility*. The model (I.3.141) is called *arithmetic Brownian motion*.

Arithmetic Brownian motion is the continuous time version of a random walk. To see this, we first note that the discrete time equivalent of the Brownian increment $dZ(t)$ is a standard normal independent process: i.e. as we move from continuous to discrete time,

$$dZ(t) \to Z_t \sim \text{NID}(0, 1).$$

---

[57] OLS, or ordinary least squares, is introduced in Section I.4.2.2.

Also the increment $dX(t)$ in continuous time becomes a first difference $\Delta X_t = X_t - X_{t-1}$ in discrete time.[58] Using these discrete time equivalents gives the following discretization of (I.3.141):

$$\Delta X_t = \alpha + \varepsilon_t \quad \text{where } \varepsilon_t = \sigma Z_t \text{, so } \varepsilon_t \sim \text{NID}(0, \sigma^2).$$

But this is the same as $X_t = \alpha + X_{t-1} + \varepsilon_t$, which is the discrete time random walk model (I.3.140).

So (I.3.141) is non-stationary. However a *stationary* continuous time process can be defined by introducing a *mean reversion* mechanism to the drift term. Now in place of (I.3.141) we write

$$dX(t) = \varphi(\theta - X(t))dt + \sigma dB(t). \tag{I.3.142}$$

The parameter φ is called the *rate of mean reversion* and the parameter θ is called the *long term* value of X. In Section II.5.3.7 we prove that the discrete time version of (I.3.142) is a *stationary* AR(1) model.

I.3.7.3   Stochastic Models for Asset Prices and Returns

Time series of asset prices behave quite differently from time series of returns. In efficient markets a time series of prices or log prices will follow a random walk. More generally, even in the presence of market frictions and inefficiencies, prices and log prices of tradable assets are *integrated* stochastic processes. These are fundamentally different from the associated returns, which are generated by *stationary* stochastic processes.

Figures I.3.28 and I.3.29 illustrate the fact that prices and returns are generated by very different types of stochastic process. Figure I.3.28 shows time series of daily prices (left-hand scale) and log prices (right-hand scale) of the Dow Jones Industrial Average (DJIA)

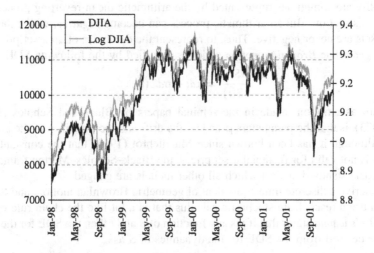

Figure I.3.28   Daily prices and log prices of DJIA index

---

[58] This is not the only possible discretization of a continuous increment. For instance, we could use a forward difference instead of a backward difference.

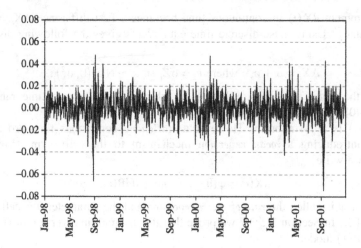

Figure I.3.29 Daily log returns on DJIA index

stock index. Clearly they have similar characteristics. Indeed, the log price is like a 'scaled down' version of the price series. Both are usually integrated of order 1.

Figure I.3.29 depicts the daily log returns, i.e. the first differences in the log price series shown in Figure I.3.28. This has very different characteristics to the price and log price series. The mean return appears to be constant and the variance appears to be finite. Indeed, it seems reasonable to assume that these returns are stationary. Again, see Section II.5.3 for a formal test of this hypothesis.

We now introduce the standard models for the prices of tradable assets and their returns in discrete and continuous time. Non-tradable assets such as interest rates, credit spreads and even volatility are sometimes represented by the arithmetic mean reverting process defined in the previous section. But an arithmetic process can become *negative*, whilst the prices of tradable assets are never negative. Thus, to represent the dynamics of an asset price we very often use a *geometric Brownian motion* which is specified by the following SDE:

$$\frac{dS(t)}{S(t)} = \mu dt + \sigma dZ(t). \tag{I.3.143}$$

The standard assumption, made in the seminal papers by Black and Scholes (1973) and Merton (1973), is that the parameters μ and σ (the drift and the volatility of the process) are constant. Although it has been known since Mandlebrot (1963) that the constant volatility assumption is not valid for financial asset prices, the Black–Scholes–Merton framework still remains a basic standard against which all other models are gauged.

Now we derive a discrete time equivalent of geometric Brownian motion, and to do this it will help to use a result from stochastic calculus that is a bit like the chain rule of ordinary calculus.[59] *Itô's lemma* states that if f is any function of S and t then the SDE for the dynamics of f may be derived from the SDE for the dynamics of S as

$$df(S,t) = \left\{ f_t(S,t) + \mu S(t) f_s(S,t) + \tfrac{1}{2}\sigma^2 S(t)^2 f_{SS}(S,t) \right\} dt + f_s(S,t)\,\sigma S(t)\,dZ(t), \tag{I.3.144}$$

where the subscripts denote the partial derivatives with respect to S and t.

---

[59] The chain rule is given in Section I.1.3.2. In Section III.3.2.1 we derive the general form of Itô's lemma.

Application of Itô's lemma with $f = \ln S$ shows that a continuous time representation of geometric Brownian motion that is equivalent to the geometric Brownian motion (I.3.143) but is translated into a process for *log* prices is the *arithmetic* Brownian motion,

$$d \ln S(t) = \left(\mu - \tfrac{1}{2}\sigma^2\right) dt + \sigma dW(t). \tag{I.3.145}$$

We already know what a discretization of (I.3.145) looks like. The change in the log price is the log return, so using the standard discrete time notation P_t for a price at time t we have

$$d \ln S(t) \rightarrow \Delta \ln P_t.$$

Hence the discrete time equivalent of (I.3.145) is

$$\Delta \ln P_t = \alpha + \varepsilon_t, \quad \varepsilon_t \sim \mathrm{NID}\left(0, \sigma^2\right), \tag{I.3.146}$$

where $\alpha = \mu - \tfrac{1}{2}\sigma^2$. This is equivalent to a discrete time random walk model for the *log* prices, i.e.

$$\ln P_t = \alpha + \ln P_{t-1} + \varepsilon_t, \quad \varepsilon_t \sim \mathrm{NID}\left(0, \sigma^2\right). \tag{I.3.147}$$

To summarize, the assumption of geometric Brownian motion for *prices* in continuous time is equivalent to the assumption of a random walk for *log prices* in discrete time.

I.3.7.4   Jumps and the Poisson Process

A Poisson process, introduced in Section I.3.3.2, is a stochastic process governing the occurrences of events through time. For our purposes the event will be a jump in a price, or a jump in another financial variable such as an interest rate, a credit spread or a volatility. Suppose the jumps follow a Poisson process and let $n(t)$ be the number of jumps from time 0 to time t. Then the defining property of the Poisson process is that $n(t_2) - n(t_1)$ has a Poisson distribution for any times t_1 and t_2 with $t_2 > t_1$. Put another way, the number of jumps in any time interval has a Poisson distribution.

The Poisson process has a single parameter λ, the expected number of events per unit time and which is called the *intensity* or *arrival rate* of the process. Then

$$P(n(t+dt) - n(t) = x) = \frac{\exp(-\lambda dt)(\lambda dt)^x}{x!} \quad x = 0, 1, 2, \ldots. \tag{I.3.148}$$

The process $n(t)$ is an example of a *counting process*: it counts the number of jumps from time 0 to time t. An alternative formulation of a Poisson process uses an *indicator process* $q(t)$ instead of $n(t)$. Thus $q(t)$ is a continuous time process which is unity if a jump occurs at time t and zero otherwise. Then if the jumps follow a Poisson process with intensity λ the probability of a jump during an interval of length dt is λdt. Hence the probability of no jump during an interval of length dt is $(1 - \lambda)dt$.

We can apply the Poisson process to model asset prices using a *jump diffusion* process of the form

$$\frac{dS(t)}{S(t)} = \mu dt + \sigma dW(t) + J(t) dq(t), \tag{I.3.149}$$

where the size of the jump $J(t)$ is a random variable. See Section III.4.5.8 for further details and examples.

I.3.8   SUMMARY AND CONCLUSIONS

This chapter began with an introduction to the fundamental *laws of probability* and introduced the concept of a probability distribution of a random variable. We described the first four *moments* of a probability distribution and showed how to estimate these moments from a sample of observations on the random variable. The first two moments are: the *expectation*, which measures the location of the distribution, i.e. the general 'size' of the values of a random variable; and the *variance*, which measures the dispersion of the distribution, i.e. how spread out these values are. The third moment is called the *skewness*, which is non-zero when the density function is asymmetric, and the fourth is the *kurtosis*, which measures the probability weight in the tails of the distribution. Further basic concepts included the definition and properties of the *quantiles* of a distribution $F(x)$: the α quantile of F is $F^{-1}(\alpha)$, in other words $P(X < F^{-1}(\alpha)) = \alpha$.

The next section provided a long catalogue of the univariate distributions commonly used in finance. Most of the distributions analysed here represent a continuous random variable and a common assumption, because it leads to a tractable analysis, is that returns on financial assets have a *normal distribution*. A normal density function is a symmetric bell-shaped curve with zero skewness and zero excess kurtosis, so the distribution can be fully characterized by knowing only its expectation and variance. The *excess kurtosis* is the kurtosis minus 3, and this is zero for a normal distribution. A leptokurtic distribution is one that has positive excess kurtosis and hence has more weight in the tails than a normal distribution with the same variance. The empirical distributions of returns on a financial asset are usually both skewed and leptokurtic, hence they are not well captured by normal distributions even though this assumption is often made for simplicity.

We have described some useful distributions that can be skewed and leptokurtic, including the *Student t distribution* and the family of *normal mixture* distributions. The Student *t* distribution is one of four classical *sampling distributions*, which are distributions of variables whose uncertainty arises from variations between different samples. The other sampling distributions are the standard normal, *chi-squared* and *F* distributions. These four distributions are used in classical hypothesis testing under the assumption that the underlying population is normal. Normal mixture distributions can be leptokurtic, mesokurtic, symmetric, or positively or negatively skewed, depending on the choice of normal components. They also retain the analytic tractability associated with normal densities. Normal mixture distributions are intuitive, since they capture *regime-dependent behaviour* which is often exhibited by financial asset returns. They have very useful applications to option pricing and hedging as well as to market risk analysis. Other types of distributions that will be applied in subsequent volumes, and in Volume IV in particular, are *stable distributions* and *extreme value distributions*.

The section on multivariate distributions defined the *joint, conditional* and *marginal distributions* that characterize the behaviour of two or more random variables. We also introduced the notion of *independence* between two random variables. Random variables that are not independent have a dependency that can be characterized, albeit rather crudely, by their *covariance* and *correlation*. These associated operators were defined and their properties were characterized. We then introduced the multivariate normal, multivariate Student *t* and bivariate normal mixture distributions. The bivariate normal distribution underlies the theory of regression analysis which is covered in Chapter I.4. And the multivariate normal mixture distribution will be used to generalize the linear VaR model to non-normal risk factor returns in Chapter IV.2. Multivariate normal and Student *t* distributions can be used to define *copu-*

las, which are a special type of multivariate distribution that can be used to construct a wide variety of other joint distributions. A long chapter on copulas is provided in Volume II.

The elementary principles of statistical inference have been covered, including the *central limit theorem*, confidence intervals and hypothesis tests on means and variances. We also introduced two non-parametric tests on the proximity between two distribution functions, the *Kolmogorov–Smirnoff* test and a modification of this called the *Andersen–Darling* test. The statistics, which are based on a distance metric between two distribution functions, have critical values that must usually be obtained by simulation.

We have described how to estimate the parameters of a distribution using *maximum likelihood estimation*. This is a very general method that always provides consistent estimators of the distribution parameters. We gave an example of the estimation of a Student t distribution here, and in Volume II we shall provide many more empirical examples where maximum likelihood estimation is used to estimate the parameters of regression models.

Finally, we provided an informal introduction to *stochastic processes* in discrete and continuous time. Discrete time processes, which are also called *time series*, are often represented by regression models. Here we introduced the simplest first order autoregression model for a stationary time series, but much more detail on time series models is given in Chapter II.5. The first order autoregression allowed us to illustrate the concept of a stationary time series, following its formal definition. It also allowed us to describe a simple test for stationarity.

By applying *Itô's lemma* we demonstrated the equivalence between the continuous time *geometric Brownian motion* model for asset prices and the discrete time *random walk* model for log prices. We also introduced *arithmetic Brownian motion* and *mean reverting* models for financial asset prices, and jumps that are governed by the *Poisson process*. The aim of this section was to make the first important connection between discrete and continuous time models. This lays the foundation for continuous time option pricing models, which are covered in Chapters III.3 and III.5, and discrete time series analysis, which is the subject of Chapter II.5.

I.4
Introduction to Linear Regression

I.4.1 INTRODUCTION

A regression model is a statistical model of the influence of one (or more) random variables on another random variable. Usually we assume a simple linear relationship between the variables of the form

$$Y = \beta_1 X_1 + \beta_2 X_2 + \ldots + \beta_k X_k.$$

On the left of the above equality is the *dependent variable*, often denoted Y. On the right of the equality we have:

- k *independent variables*, $X_1, X_2, \ldots, X_k$. These are often called *explanatory variables* because they are put into the model to explain the behaviour of the dependent variable. Almost all models contain a *constant term*, which means that $X_1 = 1$.
- k *coefficients* $\beta_1, \beta_2, \ldots, \beta_k$. These are not random variables and usually they are assumed to be constant. The coefficients are some of the model parameters that will be estimated using data on the dependent and independent variables.[1] Each coefficient measures the effect that a change in its independent variable will have upon Y. So if an estimated coefficient is insignificantly different from 0 then its explanatory variable can be excluded from the regression model.

The estimated model can be used to:

- predict or forecast values of the dependent variable using scenarios on the independent variables;
- test an economic or financial theory;
- estimate the quantities of financial assets to buy or sell when forming a diversified portfolio, a hedged portfolio or when implementing a trading strategy.

The outline of this chapter is as follows. Section I.4.2 introduces the simplest possible linear regression model, i.e. one with just one explanatory variable. We describe the best method to estimate the model parameters when certain assumptions hold. This is called *ordinary least squares* (OLS) estimation. Then we explain how to test some simple hypotheses in the simple linear model. Section I.4.3 analyses the assumptions that we make when using OLS and the properties of OLS estimators under these assumptions.

A more general framework is introduced in Section I.4.4. Here we analyse the multivariate linear regression model, i.e. the linear model with more than one explanatory variable. The formulae for the analysis of variance (ANOVA) and the OLS estimators are straightforward

---

[1] The data, which must consist of an equal number of observations on each variable, may be time series (indexed by the subscript t), cross sectional (indexed by the subscript i), or panel data (which is a mixture of cross section and time series, indexed by the subscript i, t).

generalizations of the simple linear model formulae, but now they are represented in matrix notation. A simple case study shows how to apply the formulae and how to estimate a regression using Excel. We also discuss hypothesis tests (at considerable length), the construction of confidence intervals, and the problem of *multicollinearity* and how to deal with it.

Section I.4.5 explains what happens when the OLS assumptions are violated, either because the error process has *autocorrelation* or because it has *heteroscedasticity* – or both. We explain the meaning of these terms, the causes of these problems and some standard statistical tests for their presence. In finance we often estimate regression models using very large samples and robust standard errors, in which case autocorrelation and heteroscedasticity do not cause significant problems for the use of OLS. However, if the sample is small it is better to use *generalized least squares* (GLS) in the presence of autocorrelation or heteroscedasticity.

We end the chapter with a survey of the most common applications of standard linear regression models in finance. There are so many applications of regression to finance that we can provide only a brief overview here, but we shall be exploring these applications in further detail in later chapters and other volumes of *Market Risk Analysis*. Throughout this chapter we shall assume readers have a basic understanding of statistics and linear algebra and we refer to the relevant sections in Chapters I.2 and I.3 where necessary. As usual, all but the most trivial of examples are illustrated in Excel.[2]

I.4.2 SIMPLE LINEAR REGRESSION

In this section we make the very simple assumption that the dependent variable has a linear relationship with just one explanatory variable, such as would be the case in the capital asset pricing model or the single index model, both of which are introduced in Chapter I.6.

I.4.2.1 Simple Linear Model

The simplest case of linear relationship is $Y = \alpha + \beta X$. This is the equation of a straight line: the parameter α is called the *regression constant* and represents the intercept of the line with the vertical (Y) axis, and the *regression coefficient* β represents the slope of the line.[3]

Take an arbitrary sample of T observations on X and Y and denote this

$$\{(X_t, Y_t); t = 1, \ldots, T\}.$$

In the following we implicitly assume the sample is a historical sample taken over some period of time, i.e. a *time series*. For instance, the data on Y may be the weekly returns on a stock and the data on X may be the weekly returns on the index, taken over identical historical periods. However, the concepts below apply equally well to *cross sectional data* taken at one particular point in time. For instance, Y may be the annual returns on all 100 stocks in the FTSE100 index during 2008 – so we have $T = 100$ data points – and X may be the price–earnings ratios on these 100 stocks in January 2008.

A *scatter plot* of the data records each pair (X_t, Y_t) as a point in the $X - Y$ plane, as depicted in Figure I.4.1. Here we show the scatter plot of daily log returns on the Amex

---

[2] Note that readers need to add in the data analysis tools, if not already added in, to access the regression function in Excel.
[3] For this notation to be consistent with the multiple regression model (I.4.34) we set $\beta_1 = \alpha$ and $\beta_2 = \beta$ to conform with standard notation. The number of coefficients to be estimated, including the constant, is $k = 2$.

stock and the corresponding daily log returns on the S&P 500 index. The data period covered is from 3 January 2005 to 31 December 2007, a total of 754 data points.[4]

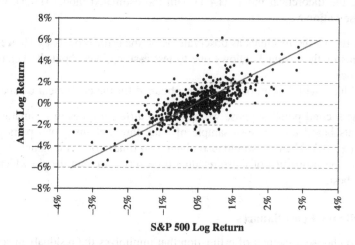

Figure I.4.1   Scatter plot of Amex and S&P 500 daily log returns

The points will not lie exactly along a line (unless X and Y are perfectly correlated) so in the *simple linear model* we include an error term so that the points do not need to lie exactly along a line. Thus we write

$$Y_t = \alpha + \beta X_t + \varepsilon_t, \quad t = 1, \ldots, T, \qquad (I.4.1)$$

where ε_t is called the *error process*. A low correlation between X and Y implies that the error process has a relatively high variance; a high correlation between X and Y implies that the error process has a relatively low variance.

The properties of the error process define the best method for estimating the equation of the best fitting line through the scatter plot. We discuss these properties in Section I.4.2.3. First, we define the basic concepts and introduce our terminology.

We need some notation for the best fitting line through the scatter plot. We adopt the standard caret (^) notation to denote an estimator. Then the fitted line, such as the line indicated in grey on Figure I.4.1, is denoted

$$\hat{Y} = \hat{\alpha} + \hat{\beta}X, \qquad (I.4.2)$$

where $\hat{\alpha}$ and $\hat{\beta}$ denote the estimates of the line *intercept* α and *slope* β.

The difference between the actual value of Y and the fitted value of Y for the observation at time t is denoted e_t and this is called the *residual* at time t. That is:

$$e_t = Y_t - \hat{Y}_t. \qquad (I.4.3)$$

With this definition the data point for Y at time t is the fitted model value plus the residual, i.e.

$$Y_t = \hat{\alpha} + \hat{\beta}X_t + e_t, \quad t = 1, \ldots, T. \qquad (I.4.4)$$

---

[4] Data were downloaded from Yahoo! Finance with the look-up symbols AXP and ^GSPC. Note that an index requires a caret (^) before the symbol, but a stock does not.

Assuming the sample $\{(X_t, Y_t)\}$ are time series data, the residuals will also be a time series $\{e_t\}$ over the same historical period.

Comparing the theoretical model (I.4.1) with the estimated model (I.4.4), we make the following observations:

- We can regard the residuals as observations on the error process ε_t. Hence, testing the properties of the residuals allows one to test assumptions about the behaviour of the error process.
- The residuals will depend on the values obtained for the coefficient estimates $\hat{\alpha}$ and $\hat{\beta}$.

Regarding the second point, suppose we apply two *different* types of estimator to estimate the coefficients based on the *same* sample of data, thus obtaining two pairs of estimates $(\hat{\alpha}_1, \hat{\beta}_1)$ and $(\hat{\alpha}_2, \hat{\beta}_2)$. Then we would also obtain two time series of residuals $\{e_{1t}\}$ and $\{e_{2t}\}$. By comparing the properties of these residual time series we can decide which method of estimation is best.

I.4.2.2   Ordinary Least Squares

It is logical to choose a method of estimation that minimizes the residuals in some manner, because then the predicted values of the dependent variable will be as close as possible to the observed values. But choosing the estimates to minimize the sum of the residuals will not work because large positive residuals would cancel large negative residuals. The sum of the absolute residuals could be minimized, as they are in quantile regression (see Section II.7.2). However, the easiest way to obtain estimators that have simple mathematical properties is to minimize the variance of the residuals, or equivalently to *minimize the sum of the squared residuals*.[5] This is the *ordinary least squares* optimization criterion.

The sum of the squared residuals, also called the *residual sum of squares* and denoted RSS, may be expressed as

$$RSS = \sum_{t=1}^{T} e_t^2 = \sum_{t=1}^{T} (Y_t - (\alpha + \beta X_t))^2. \tag{I.4.5}$$

Hence the OLS estimators $\hat{\alpha}$ and $\hat{\beta}$ are found by solving the optimization problem

$$\min_{\alpha, \beta} \sum_{t=1}^{T} (Y_t - (\alpha + \beta X_t))^2. \tag{I.4.6}$$

This is the OLS criterion.

By differentiating (I.4.6) with respect to α and with respect to β and setting these derivatives to 0, it can be shown that the OLS estimators of the coefficients in the simple linear model (I.4.1) are given by

$$\hat{\beta} = \frac{\sum_{t=1}^{T} (X_t - \overline{X})(Y_t - \overline{Y})}{\sum_{t=1}^{T} (X_t - \overline{X})^2} \quad \text{and} \quad \hat{\alpha} = \overline{Y} - \hat{\beta}\overline{X}, \tag{I.4.7}$$

where $\overline{X}$ and $\overline{Y}$ denote the means (arithmetic averages) of the observations on X and Y. Note that the expression for $\hat{\alpha}$ implies that the mean residual $\overline{e} = 0$.

---

[5] Minimizing the residual sum of squares implies that the mean residual will be zero, hence it is equivalent to minimizing the variance because when the sample mean is zero the sample variance is the average of the sum of the squared observations.

EXAMPLE I.4.1: USING THE OLS FORMULA

Use formula (I.4.7) to calculate the OLS estimates for the simple linear model, given the following data:

$$Y: \quad 10 \quad 13 \quad 19 \quad 18 \quad 20$$
$$X: \quad 1 \quad 2 \quad 3 \quad 4 \quad 5$$

SOLUTION   We have $\overline{X} = 3$ and $\overline{Y} = 16$. We lay out the calculations in Table I.4.1.

Table I.4.1   Calculation of OLS estimates

Y_t	10	13	19	18	20	Sum
$Y_t - \overline{Y}$	−6	−3	3	2	4	
X_t	1	2	3	4	5	
$X_t - \overline{X}$	−2	−1	0	1	2	
$(X_t - \overline{X})^2$	4	1	0	1	4	10
$(X_t - \overline{X})(Y_t - \overline{Y})$	12	3	0	2	8	25

Thus, by (I.4.7) we have

$$\hat{\beta} = 25/10 = 2.5 \quad \text{and} \quad \hat{\alpha} = 16 - 3 \times 2.5 = 8.5,$$

so the fitted model is $\hat{Y} = 8.5 + 2.5X$.

The OLS estimator of the slope has a simple relationship with the sample correlation and with the relative volatility of the variables. To understand this, note that (I.4.7) implies that the OLS estimate $\hat{\beta}$ is the ratio of the sample covariance to the sample variance:

$$\hat{\beta} = \frac{s_{XY}}{s_X^2} = \frac{\text{est.Cov}(X, Y)}{\text{est. } V(X)}. \tag{I.4.8}$$

But the covariance is the product of the correlation, the standard deviation of X and the standard deviation of Y, as we know from Section I.3.4.4. That is, $s_{XY} = r_{XY} s_X s_Y$. So we have

$$\hat{\beta} = r_{XY}\left(\frac{s_Y}{s_X}\right) = \text{correlation} \times \text{relative volatility}. \tag{I.4.9}$$

EXAMPLE I.4.2: RELATIONSHIP BETWEEN BETA AND CORRELATION

A stock has a market beta of 1.2 and a volatility of 30%. If the market volatility is 20%, what is the correlation between the stock return and the market return?

SOLUTION   Assuming the market beta is calculated using OLS, we can use (I.4.9) to obtain

$$\text{market correlation} = 1.2 \times \frac{0.2}{0.3} = 0.8.$$

Note that the stock beta can be *any* positive or negative number (or 0) but the market correlation of every stock must be between −1 and +1.

Now recall the properties of the bivariate normal distribution and the property (I.3.99) in particular. This tells us that the conditional expectation of Y given X is

$$E(Y|X) = \mu_Y + \varrho_{XY}\frac{\sigma_Y}{\sigma_X}(X - \mu_X), \qquad (I.4.10)$$

which may be rewritten in the form $\hat{Y} = \hat{\alpha} + \hat{\beta}X$ with

$$\hat{Y} = E(Y|X), \quad \hat{\beta} = \varrho_{XY}\frac{\sigma_Y}{\sigma_X} \quad \text{and} \quad \hat{\alpha} = \mu_Y - \hat{\beta}\mu_X. \qquad (I.4.11)$$

In other words, if the data used to estimate the coefficients are generated by bivariate normal variables then the OLS regression line defines the *conditional expectation* of Y, given a specific value for X. For this reason we sometimes call an OLS linear regression the *conditional mean equation*.

I.4.2.3   Properties of the Error Process

We now discuss the error process in the simple linear model (I.4.1). Later we shall prove that the OLS estimation method – i.e. to minimize the residual sum of squares – is optimal when the error is generated by an independent and identically distributed (i.i.d.) process.[6] So for the moment we shall assume that

$$\varepsilon_t \sim \text{i.i.d.}\left(0, \sigma^2\right). \qquad (I.4.12)$$

It makes sense of course to assume that the expectation of the error is zero. If it were not zero we would not have a random error, we would have a systematic bias in the error and the regression line would not pass through the middle of the scatter plot. So the definition (I.4.12) is introducing the variance of the error process, σ^2, into our notation. This is the third and final parameter of the simple linear model.

The OLS estimate of σ^2 is

$$s^2 = \frac{RSS}{T-2}, \qquad (I.4.13)$$

where the numerator in (I.4.13) is understood to be the residual sum of squares that has been minimized by the choice of the OLS estimates.[7] The square root of (I.4.13) is called the *standard error of the regression*. It plays a crucial role in statistical inference, as we shall see later in this section.

EXAMPLE I.4.3: ESTIMATING THE OLS STANDARD ERROR OF THE REGRESSION

Estimate the standard error of the regression using the data given in Example I.4.1.

SOLUTION   We use the OLS estimates calculated in Example I.4.1 to obtain the fitted values of Y as $\hat{Y}_t = 8.5 + 2.5X_t$ for $t = 1, \ldots, 5$. Then we subtract the actual values from the fitted values to obtain the residuals. Then summing the squared residuals and dividing the result

---

[6] See Section I.3.7.1 for the definition of i.i.d.
[7] The reason we use $T - 2$ in the denominator here is clarified in the next subsection.

Table I.4.2 Estimating the residual sum of sqaures and the standard error of the regression

Y_t	10	13	19	18	20	Sum
X_t	1	2	3	4	5	
$\hat{Y}_t$	11	13.5	16	18.5	21	
$e_t = \hat{Y}_t - Y_t$	1	0.5	−3	0.5	1	0
e_t^2	1	0.25	9	0.25	1	11.5

by $T - 2 = 3$ gives the square of the standard error of the regression. The calculations are laid out in Table I.4.2. Hence,

$$s^2 = \frac{RSS}{T-2} = \frac{11.5}{3} = 3.8333 \Rightarrow s = 1.958.$$

Notice two things about this example:

- The sum of the residuals is 0, and therefore so also is the mean residual, i.e. $\bar{e} = 0$.
- The regression line, i.e. the line of the points $\left(\hat{X}_t, \hat{Y}_t \right)$, passes through the sample mean (3, 16).

This is always the case with OLS regression.

I.4.2.4   ANOVA and Goodness of Fit

The standard error of the regression, which is derived from the residual sum of squares, measures the goodness of fit of the regression model. A small standard error indicates a good fit, but how small is 'small'? This depends on the *total sum of squares* (denoted TSS) which is given by

$$TSS = \sum_{t=1}^{T}(Y_t - \bar{Y})^2. \tag{I.4.14}$$

TSS measures the amount of variation in the dependent variable Y that we seek to explain by the regression model. It is directly related to the sample variance of Y – indeed,

$$TSS = (T-1)s_Y^2. \tag{I.4.15}$$

There are $T - 1$ degrees of freedom associated with the total sum of squares.

The *explained sum of squares* (ESS) is the amount of variation in Y that is explained by the regression. It is obtained by subtracting RSS from TSS:

$$ESS = TSS - RSS. \tag{I.4.16}$$

There are $T - 2$ degrees of freedom associated with the residual sum of squares, and the number of degrees of freedom associated with the explained sum of squares is the number of explanatory variables in the regression model, which is 1 in this case.[8]

---

[8] One degree of freedom is lost for every constraint on the data that is necessary to calculate the estimates. Since we must estimate α and β before we can calculate RSS, it has T-2 degrees of freedom.

The decomposition of the total variance of the dependent variable into the variance explained by the model and the residual variance is called the *analysis of variance* or ANOVA for short. The results of ANOVA can be summarized succinctly in a single statistic which is called the *regression* R^2. This is given by

$$R^2 = \frac{ESS}{TSS}. \tag{I.4.17}$$

So the regression R^2 takes a value between 0 and 1 and a large value indicates a good fit for the model. The regression R^2 is the square of the correlation between the fitted value $\hat{Y}$ and Y and in the simple linear model this is just the square of the correlation between X and Y.[9]

We can perform a statistical test of the significance of the R^2 from a simple linear regression model, using the F statistic:

$$F = \frac{ESS}{RSS/(T-2)} \sim F_{1,T-2}. \tag{I.4.18}$$

The next example illustrates the method.

EXAMPLE I.4.4: ANOVA

Find TSS, RSS and ESS for the regression model considered in the previous examples. Hence, compute the regression R^2 and test whether this is significantly different from 0.

SOLUTION   The calculation of TSS is set out in Table I.4.3 and the result is 74.

Table I.4.3   Estimating the total sum of squares

Y_t	10	13	19	18	20	Sum
$Y_t - \overline{Y}$	−6	−3	3	2	4	
$(Y_t - \overline{Y})^2$	36	9	9	4	16	74

We already know from Example I.4.3 that RSS is 11.5. Since RSS is relatively small compared with TSS, the regression line seems to be quite a good fit to the data. Indeed, the ESS is 62.5 and so the regression R^2 is

$$R^2 = \frac{62.5}{74} = 0.845.$$

The goodness of fit test statistic (I.4.18) is

$$F = \frac{62.5}{3.8333} = 16.30.$$

The upper 5% critical value of the $F_{1,3}$ distribution is found from statistical tables, or using the Excel function FINV(0.05, 1, 3), giving 10.128. But the upper 1% critical value is 34.116, so our value of F lies between the 5% and the 1% critical values of the test statistic. Hence, we can only conclude a moderately good fit for the model, a fit that is significant at 5% but not at 1%.

---

[9] When there are several explanatory variables the regression R^2 is the square of the correlation between the fitted values of Y and the actual values of Y.

I.4.2.5   Hypothesis Tests on Coefficients

Having estimated the simple linear regression, we can perform hypothesis tests on the true value of a coefficient. Such tests are useful for determining whether the explanatory variable is significant enough to be included in the regression, where the null and alternative hypotheses are

$$H_0 : \beta = 0 \quad \text{vs} \quad H_1 : \beta \neq 0. \tag{I.4.19}$$

Additionally, we can test whether the true coefficient takes a particular value, such as would be the case when we are testing a theory. For instance we might test

$$H_0 : \alpha = 0 \quad \text{vs} \quad H_1 : \alpha > 0.$$

The alternative hypothesis can be one-sided as above or two-sided as in (I.4.19). The computation of the value of the test statistic is the same in either case, and the only thing that changes is the critical region of the test statistic. See Section I.3.5.5 for further details.

The test statistics for the coefficients in a linear regression have a Student t distribution (see Section I.3.3.7). They are given by the difference between the coefficient estimate and its hypothesized value, divided by the estimated standard error of the estimator. The standard errors of the coefficient estimators depend on the sample size. The more observations used to estimate the regression coefficients the more accurate they are and the lower their standard errors.

In the simple linear regression model the t tests for the coefficient parameters are

$$t = \frac{\hat{\alpha} - \alpha_0}{\text{est.s.e.}(\hat{\alpha})} \sim t_{T-2} \quad \text{and} \quad t = \frac{\hat{\beta} - \beta_0}{\text{est.s.e.}(\hat{\beta})} \sim t_{T-2}, \tag{I.4.20}$$

where α_0 and β_0 are the values of α and β under the null hypothesis,

$$\text{est s.e.}(\hat{\beta}) = \frac{s}{s_X \sqrt{T-1}},$$

and

$$\text{est s.e.}(\hat{\alpha}) = \text{est s.e.}(\hat{\beta})\left(T^{-1}\sum_{t=1}^{T}X_t^2\right)^{1/2}. \tag{I.4.21}$$

We illustrate the application of these formulae by testing some hypotheses in the next example.

EXAMPLE I.4.5: HYPOTHESIS TESTS IN A SIMPLE LINEAR MODEL

Using the model that has been estimated in the previous example test the hypotheses:

(a) $H_0 : \beta = 1 \quad \text{vs} \quad H_1 : \beta \neq 1$;

(b) $H_0 : \alpha = 0 \quad \text{vs} \quad H_1 : \alpha > 0$.

SOLUTION   We estimate the standard errors of the coefficient estimates using (I.4.21). We know that $s = 1.958$ but we have not yet calculated the sample standard deviation of the explanatory variable s_X. Since

$$s_X^2 = \frac{\sum_{t=1}^{5}(X_t - \overline{X})^2}{4} = \frac{10}{4} = 2.5,$$

we have $s_X = \sqrt{2.5} = 1.581$, and so

$$\text{est s.e.} \left(\hat{\beta} \right) = \frac{s}{s_X \sqrt{T-1}} = \frac{1.958}{1.581 \times 2} = 0.619$$

and

$$\text{est s.e.} \left(\hat{\alpha} \right) = \text{est s.e.} \left(\hat{\beta} \right) \left(5^{-1} \sum_{t=1}^{5} X_t^2 \right)^{1/2} = 0.619 \times \sqrt{55/5} = 2.053.$$

Now we can compute the t ratios for each test as follows:

$$\text{(a) } t = \frac{2.5 - 1}{0.619} = 2.423,$$

$$\text{(b) } t = \frac{8.5}{2.053} = 4.139.$$

To make our decision we need the critical values of the test statistics. For a t distribution with 3 degrees of freedom the one-sided and two-sided critical values are computed using the TINV function in Excel and these are shown in Table I.4.4.

Table I.4.4   Critical values of t_3

Significance Level	10%	5%	1%
Two-sided	2.353	3.182	5.841
One-sided	1.638	2.353	4.540

Test (a) is a two-sided test and since our value for t does not exceed the 5% critical value we can accept the null hypothesis that the true slope coefficient is 1. Test (b) is a one-sided test and our value for t exceeds the 5% critical value but not the 1% critical value. Therefore we have some evidence to reject the null hypothesis that the intercept is zero against the alternative that it is positive.

I.4.2.6   Reporting the Estimated Regression Model

Once we have the coefficient estimates we can derive the t ratios for any simple hypothesis from the estimated standard errors of the coefficients. Alternatively, if we know the t ratio for the hypothesis that the coefficient is 0 we can calculate the estimated standard error of the coefficient estimate on dividing the estimate by the t ratio. It is standard to report an estimated model by putting below the estimated coefficient either the t ratio for the hypothesis that the coefficient is 0 or the estimated standard error of the coefficient estimate.

For instance we could report the fitted model that has been estimated in the preceding examples as either

$$\hat{Y} = \underset{(4.139)}{8.5} + \underset{(4.038)}{2.5} \, X$$

with t ratios in parentheses or, with estimated standard errors in parentheses.

$$\hat{Y} = \underset{(2.053)}{8.5} + \underset{(0.619)}{2.5} \, X$$

Putting the t ratios under the coefficient estimates is useful because it gives one an immediate idea about the significance of the constant term and the explanatory variable; putting the estimated standard errors below the coefficient estimates instead of the t ratios is useful because we do not then need to derive these from the t ratio and the coefficient estimate if we want to perform hypotheses tests other than the standard hypothesis that the coefficient is 0.

I.4.2.7   Excel Estimation of the Simple Linear Model

Excel provides OLS estimates of linear regressions via its *data analysis tools*. We shall illustrate how to perform a simple linear regression in Excel using the Amex and S&P 500 data shown in Figure I.4.1. Here the dependent variable is the Amex daily log return and the explanatory variable is the S&P 500 index return. The completed dialog box is shown in Figure I.4.2.

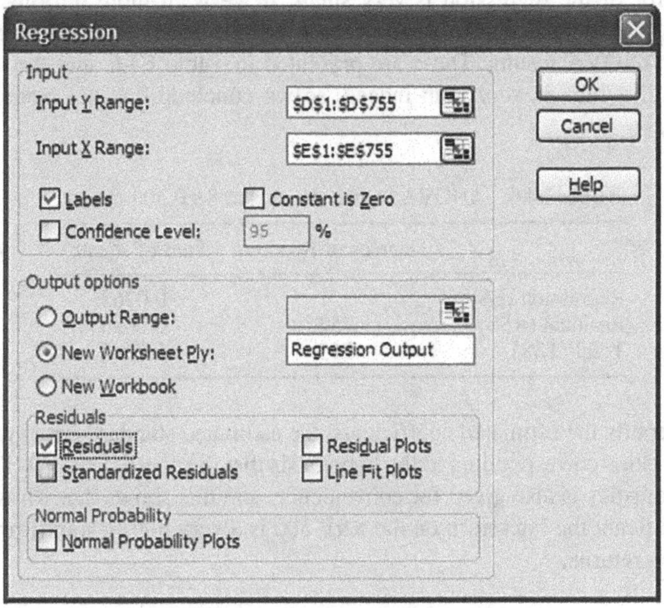

Figure I.4.2   Dialog box for Excel regression

Here we have checked the box for saving the residuals because in the next section we shall perform a number of diagnostic tests on the residuals to determine whether OLS is really the best method for estimation on these data.

The regression results will be shown in the spreadsheet labelled Regression Output and the replication of these results is left as an exercise to the reader. We abstract only some of the Excel regression output, in Table I.4.5, and discuss the meaning of its content.

The regression R^2 given by formula (I.4.17) is 0.5476. The *multiple R* is just the square root of R^2: $\sqrt{0.5476} = 0.7400$. The *adjusted R^2* is the R^2 after an adjustment to take account of the fact that the more variables in the model, the better the fit. It is always less than the regression R^2 but is higher for *parsimonious* models which use as few variables as possible to capture the variation in Y. Table I.4.5 also shows the estimated standard error of the

Table I.4.5 Some of the Excel output for the Amex and S&P 500 model

Multiple R	0.7400
R Square	0.5476
Adjusted R Square	0.5470
Standard Error	0.0092
Observations	754

regression, i.e. the square root of the s^2 given by (I.4.13), so here we have $s = 0.0092$. Finally, we have the number of observations, $T = 754$.

These results already give a good indication that the model fits the data very well. The correlation between the log returns on Amex and the log returns on S&P 500 is 0.74 and the standard error of the regression is very small. If we want more information about the goodness of fit, and in particular to perform the F test for goodness of fit given by (I.4.18), we look at the ANOVA results. These are presented in Table I.4.6, and the value of the F statistic is 910.22 which is very high indeed, so we conclude that the model fits the data extremely well.

Table I.4.6 ANOVA for the Amex and S&P 500 model

	Degrees of freedom	Sum of squares
Regression (ESS)	1	0.0762
Residual (RSS)	752	0.0630
Total (TSS)	753	0.1392

Table I.4.7 reports the estimated coefficients, the estimated standard errors of these coefficients and the t ratios corresponding to the hypothesis that the coefficient is 0. The probability value of the t statistics is also given for convenience, and this shows that whilst the constant term is not significant the log return on the S&P 500 is a very highly significant determinant of the Amex log returns.

Table I.4.7 Coefficient estimates for the Amex and S&P 500 model

	Coefficients	Standard error	t stat	p value
Intercept	−0.0002	0.0003	−0.6665	0.5053
S&P 500 rtn	1.2885	0.0427	30.1698	0.0000

Following the results in Table I.4.7, we may write the estimated model, with t ratios in parentheses, as

$$\hat{Y} = \underset{(-0.6665)}{-0.0002} + \underset{(30.1698)}{1.2885}\,X,$$

where X and Y are the daily log returns on the S&P 500 and on Amex, respectively. The Excel output automatically tests whether the explanatory variable should be included in the model, and with a t ratio of 30.1698 this is certainly the case. But we may also test other hypotheses, such as the hypothesis

$$H_0 : \beta = 1 \quad \text{vs} \quad H_1 : \beta > 1.$$

The test statistic is

$$t = \frac{1.2885 - 1}{0.0427} = 6.76.$$

So we can reject the hypothesis and there is evidence to suggest Amex is a *high risk stock*, i.e. a stock with a market beta greater than 1.

I.4.3   PROPERTIES OF OLS ESTIMATORS

In this section we discuss the properties of the OLS estimators under the assumption that the error process is i.i.d. and when this assumption is violated. We also clarify the assumptions under which the hypothesis tests introduced in the previous section are valid.

I.4.3.1   Estimates and Estimators

When applying OLS, or any other estimation method, it should be understood that there is only one theoretical model but there may be any number of estimated models corresponding to different data and/or different estimation methods. There is only one OLS estimator for each coefficient in the model, and in the simple linear model the OLS estimators are given by the formulae (I.4.7) for the coefficients and (I.4.13) for the error variance. However, there will be many different OLS estimates of any coefficient, because different data give different estimates, and when the estimated coefficients change, so do the residuals.

For instance, in Section I.4.2.7 we would have obtained different coefficient estimates if we had used data from 3 January 2006 to 31 March 2007, instead of from 3 January 2005 to 31 March 2006. And the OLS residuals would be different. Indeed, they would be covering a different data period in this case. However, the OLS estimators, i.e. the formulae used to obtain the estimates, remain the same.

The model coefficients are not random variables (although their values will always be unknown) but the estimators *are* random variables. Thus β is not a random variable but $\hat{\beta}$ is, because different data give different estimates. Hence, the distributions of the OLS estimators arise from differences in samples. In other words, the OLS estimators have *sampling* distributions.

We emphasize that two different types of random variables are present in the context of regression:

- the error processes, which are assumed to have theoretical (often normal and i.i.d.) distributions; and
- the coefficient estimators, which are random variables because different data sources, frequencies of observations, or time periods yield different values.

The properties of the estimator distributions follow from the properties of the error distributions. For instance, if the error process is normal and i.i.d. then the OLS estimators will have normal distributions. This is a very convenient assumption, because it allows one to use classical statistical inference, such as t tests and F tests, on the true value of the model parameters.

I.4.3.2   Unbiasedness and Efficiency

The sampling distributions of the estimators may or may not have desirable properties. This depends on both the method of estimation employed, OLS or otherwise, and the assumptions made about the distribution of the error process. Two desirable properties for estimator distributions are *unbiasedness* and *efficiency*. Unbiasedness means that the expected value of the estimator equals the true value of the parameter, and efficiency means that the variance of the estimator is as small as possible.

Figure I.4.3 illustrates the distributions of four different estimators of the coefficient β. The estimator with the distribution shown by the solid black curve is the best of the four because it is unbiased and more efficient than the other unbiased estimator, whose distribution is depicted by the solid grey curve. The other two estimators with distributions shown in the figure are biased downward. More often than not we would underestimate the true value of β using one of these estimators.

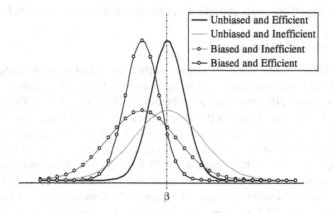

Figure I.4.3   Unbiasedness and efficiency

If many different estimates were obtained from an unbiased and efficient estimator, using different samples each time, they would all be near the true parameter value. On the other hand, these estimates could be very far from the true parameter value if the distribution of the estimator is biased, or inefficient, or both. For an inefficient estimator, the estimates arising from small differences in samples are likely to vary considerably. Thus estimates will not be robust even to small changes in the data. Parameter estimates may change considerably, for no obvious reason, when a slightly different sample is used. Perhaps the worst case is severely biased and efficient estimators, where most estimates will lie far away from the true value. In this case estimates will be quite robust, changing little even when the sample data change a lot. But they will almost always be far from the true model parameter.

In many financial markets it is possible to obtain hundreds if not thousands of data points. The *asymptotic properties of estimators* are therefore particularly relevant to models of financial markets. A *consistent* estimator has a distribution that converges to the true value of the parameter as the sample size tends to infinity. The estimator may be biased and/or inefficient for small sample sizes, but as the number of observations used to make the estimate increases the distribution converges in probability to the true parameter value. Figure I.4.4 depicts what happens to the distribution of a consistent estimator as the same size increases.

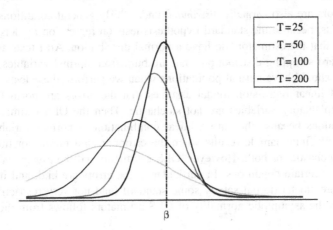

Figure I.4.4 Distribution of a consistent estimator

I.4.3.3 Gauss–Markov Theorem

OLS will only give the 'best' linear estimates, in the sense that they are unbiased and the most efficient linear estimators available, under certain conditions. The *Gauss–Markov theorem* states that if the residuals are i.i.d. then the OLS estimators are the *best linear unbiased estimators* (BLUE):

- 'Best' means that the OLS estimators are more efficient than any other linear unbiased estimators.
- 'Linear' means that the OLS formula is a linear function of the data, in other words it can be expressed in terms of matrix operations on the variables. We shall do this in the next section.
- 'Unbiased' means that the expectation of the estimator is the true value of the coefficient.
- 'Estimator' is a method for estimating parameters – recall the difference between *estimate* and *estimator* discussed above.

This is the reason why we save the residuals when we perform a linear regression. We must analyse the model residuals to see whether the i.i.d. assumption could be violated. If it is, then OLS may not be the best estimation method to use. The estimates we obtain using formula (I.4.7) may be biased and/or inefficient if the residuals are not i.i.d.

The Gauss–Markov theorem also assumes that the explanatory variables are not stochastic. That is, X is assumed to be a time trend or some other type of deterministic variable. But of course explanatory variables *are* stochastic, so the theorem is of limited use in practice.

I.4.3.4 Consistency and Normality of OLS Estimators

Although the Gauss–Markov theorem has its limitations, OLS estimators will always be *consistent* provided that the error process is stationary. This is good news for us, because we often have plenty of data available in market risk analysis. The reason why OLS is so widely used is that it does provide consistent estimators in fairly general circumstances.

OLS estimators are also *normally distributed* under fairly general conditions. This is also good news for us, because the standard hypothesis tests on regression models are based on the assumption that the estimators do have a normal distribution. All t tests and F tests are based on standard sampling distributions that are built from normal variables.[10] This is the reason why we should have normal populations when we perform these tests.

The classical linear regression model assumes that the errors are normally distributed and that the explanatory variables are not stochastic. Then the OLS estimators will have normal distributions because they are a linear combination of normal variables. It is difficult to state any finite sample results when the errors are not normal or the explanatory variables are stochastic, or both. However, OLS estimators will be *asymptotically* normally distributed under certain conditions. In particular, if the errors are i.i.d. and if the explanatory variables are stochastic but satisfy some standard (and not very restrictive) regularity conditions, then the asymptotic normality of OLS estimators follows from the central limit theorem.

I.4.3.5   Testing for Normality

The *Jarque–Bera normality test* is a simple test that can be applied to the OLS residuals. Unfortunately, it only applies to large samples and we already know that OLS estimators are asymptotically normal under fairly general conditions. However, the Jarque–Bera test also applies to *any* random variable whenever we need to justify an assumption of normality.

The test is based on the estimates $\hat{\tau}$ and $\hat{\varkappa}$ of the skewness and excess kurtosis in a sample.[11] The Jarque–Bera test statistic is given by

$$JB = \left(\frac{\hat{\tau}}{\text{est.s.e.}(\hat{\tau})}\right)^2 + \left(\frac{\hat{\varkappa}}{\text{est.s.e.}(\hat{\varkappa})}\right)^2 \overset{asy}{\sim} \chi_2^2, \qquad (I.4.22)$$

where, under the null hypothesis of normality, and for large T

$$\text{est.s.e.}(\hat{\tau}) \approx \sqrt{\frac{6}{T}} \quad \text{and} \quad \text{est.s.e.}(\hat{\varkappa}) \approx \sqrt{\frac{24}{T}}. \qquad (I.4.23)$$

Note that the distribution of JB is only specified asymptotically. That is, under the null hypothesis that the distribution is normal, as $T \to \infty$ the distribution of JB converges to a chi-squared distribution with two degrees of freedom.

I.4.4   MULTIVARIATE LINEAR REGRESSION

We begin this section by writing the simple linear regression model in matrix form. Then we illustrate the application of the matrix version of the OLS formulae by repeating the simple example discussed in Section I.4.2. Then we introduce the general linear model, write it in matrix form, state the general formulae for ANOVA and OLS estimators and illustrate their application in a case study of a multiple regression model for Billiton, a general mining corporation stock. The case study shows how to estimate a multivariate regression using matrix operations and using the linear regression tool in Excel. We also use this case study

---

[10] See Section I.3.3.8.
[11] See Section I.3.2.7.

to discuss statistical inference and the potential for multicollinearity in a general linear model.

I.4.4.1 Simple Linear Model and OLS in Matrix Notation

The simple linear model (I.4.1) written out in full is

$$Y_1 = \alpha + \beta X_1 + \varepsilon_1$$
$$\vdots \tag{I.4.24}$$
$$Y_T = \alpha + \beta X_T + \varepsilon_T.$$

But these are just T simultaneous linear equations, and we know from Section I.2.2.6 how to write them in matrix form. Indeed, (I.4.24) is equivalent to

$$y = X\beta + \varepsilon, \tag{I.4.25}$$

where $\varepsilon_t \sim \text{i.i.d.} \left(0, \sigma^2\right)$ and

$$y = \begin{pmatrix} Y_1 \\ \vdots \\ Y_T \end{pmatrix}, \quad X = \begin{pmatrix} 1 & X_1 \\ \vdots & \vdots \\ 1 & X_T \end{pmatrix}, \quad \beta = \begin{pmatrix} \alpha \\ \beta \end{pmatrix} \quad \text{and} \quad \varepsilon = \begin{pmatrix} \varepsilon_1 \\ \vdots \\ \varepsilon_T \end{pmatrix}.$$

That is, the vector y is the $T \times 1$ column of data on the independent variable; the $T \times 2$ matrix X is the matrix with 1s in the first column and the data on the explanatory variable in the second column; β is the 2×1 coefficient vector; and the error term ε is a $T \times 1$ vector.

The matrix version of the OLS formula (I.4.7) is

$$\hat{\beta} = (X'X)^{-1} X'y. \tag{I.4.26}$$

We may also express the ANOVA formulae in matrix notation as follows:

- The *total sum of squares* is the sum of the squared mean deviations of the dependent variable, that is,

$$TSS = y'y - T\bar{Y}^2. \tag{I.4.27}$$

- The *residual sum of squares* is the sum of the squared residuals,

$$RSS = e'e = y'y - \hat{\beta}'X'y. \tag{I.4.28}$$

- The *explained sum of squares* measures the amount of variation in Y that is captured by the model. Since $RSS = TSS - ESS$:

$$ESS = \hat{\beta}'X'y - T\bar{Y}^2. \tag{I.4.29}$$

As before, the *regression* R^2 is the proportion of variance that the model can explain, i.e.

$$R^2 = \frac{ESS}{TSS}. \tag{I.4.30}$$

The OLS estimator of the error variance σ^2 is

$$s^2 = \frac{RSS}{T-2}. \tag{I.4.31}$$

Finally, the estimated covariance matrix of the OLS estimators is

$$\text{est.} V\left(\hat{\beta}\right) = s^2 (X'X)^{-1}. \tag{I.4.32}$$

EXAMPLE I.4.6: SIMPLE REGRESSION IN MATRIX FORM

Use the data from Example I.4.1 to estimate the simple linear model by OLS and to perform the ANOVA, this time using matrix notation. Also estimate the covariance matrix of the OLS estimators.

SOLUTION   The data are repeated here for convenience:

$$Y: \quad 10 \quad 13 \quad 19 \quad 18 \quad 20$$
$$X: \quad 1 \quad 2 \quad 3 \quad 4 \quad 5$$

Hence

$$\mathbf{X'y} = \begin{pmatrix} 80 \\ 265 \end{pmatrix}, \quad \mathbf{X'X} = \begin{pmatrix} 5 & 15 \\ 15 & 55 \end{pmatrix}, \quad (\mathbf{X'X})^{-1} = \frac{1}{50} \begin{pmatrix} 55 & -15 \\ -15 & 5 \end{pmatrix},$$

and

$$\hat{\beta} = \frac{1}{50} \begin{pmatrix} 55 & -15 \\ -15 & 5 \end{pmatrix} \begin{pmatrix} 80 \\ 265 \end{pmatrix} = \begin{pmatrix} 8.5 \\ 2.5 \end{pmatrix}.$$

For the ANOVA,

$$TSS = \mathbf{y'y} - T\bar{Y}^2 = 1354 - 5 \times 16^2 = 1354 - 1280 = 74.$$

And since

$$\hat{\beta}'\mathbf{X'y} = (8.5, 2.5) \begin{pmatrix} 80 \\ 265 \end{pmatrix} = 1342.5,$$

we have

$$RSS = 1354 - 1342.5 = 11.5$$

and

$$ESS = 74 - 11.5 = 62.5.$$

Now $s^2 = 11.5/(5-2) = 11.5/3$, so

$$\text{est} V\left(\hat{\beta}\right) = \left(\frac{11.5}{3 \times 50}\right) \begin{pmatrix} 55 & -15 \\ -15 & 5 \end{pmatrix} = \begin{pmatrix} 4.216 & -1.149 \\ -1.149 & 0.3833 \end{pmatrix}. \tag{I.4.33}$$

Note that the estimated covariance matrix of the OLS estimators gives the estimated standard errors of the estimates as the square root of its diagonal elements. We have already calculated these in Example I.4.5 and now we can calculate them from the matrix (I.4.33). We have

$$\text{est.s.e.} (\hat{\alpha}) = \sqrt{4.216} = 2.053,$$

$$\text{est.s.e.} \left(\hat{\beta}\right) = \sqrt{0.3833} = 0.619,$$

which of course is exactly the same result as in Example I.4.5. But the main point to note about the matrix (I.4.33) it that is also gives the estimated covariance of the OLS estimators on the off-diagonal. Indeed, we have

$$\text{est.Cov}\left(\hat{\alpha}, \hat{\beta}\right) = -1.149.$$

In the simple linear model this covariance will always be negative. That is because higher estimates of the intercept are always associated with lower estimates of the slope.

The fact that $\hat{\alpha}$ has greater estimated variance than $\hat{\beta}$ does not imply that $\hat{\alpha}$ is a less accurate estimate than $\hat{\beta}$. The elements of the covariance matrix and the coefficient estimates themselves are always in units of measurement determined by those of the corresponding variables. Changing units of measurement will not affect the properties of the model but parameter estimates and their variances and covariances *do* depend on the units of measurement. For instance, if we divided each observation on X by 10 and then re-estimated the model, the result would be a slope coefficient estimate that is 10 times larger than before. This is why we investigate the accuracy of the coefficient estimates in a regression model using t ratios. Both the coefficient estimate and its standard error are in the same units of measurement, so the t ratio is a *unitless* measure of association between the explanatory variable and the dependent variable.

I.4.4.2   General Linear Model

The general linear statistical model includes more than one explanatory variable:

$$Y_t = \beta_1 X_{t1} + \beta_2 X_{t2} + \ldots + \beta_k X_{tk} + \varepsilon_t, \qquad \varepsilon_t \sim \text{i.i.d}(0, \sigma^2), \qquad (\text{I.4.34})$$

for $t = 1, \ldots, T$. In most models $X_1 = 1$ so the first coefficient β_1 is the *constant term*, like α in the simple linear regression. There are T equations in the k unknown parameters $\{\beta_1, \ldots, \beta_k\}$, one equation for each data vector. Model estimation or 'fitting' the model involves choosing a method for solving these equations and then using data to obtain estimates $\left\{\hat{\beta}_1, \ldots, \hat{\beta}_k\right\}$ of the model parameters. The fitted value of Y is

$$\hat{Y}_t = \hat{\beta}_1 X_{t1} + \hat{\beta}_2 X_{t2} + \ldots + \hat{\beta}_k X_{tk},$$

for $t = 1, \ldots, T$. Again the difference between the actual and predicted value of Y_t is the residual e_t, therefore

$$Y_t = \hat{\beta}_1 X_{t1} + \hat{\beta}_2 X_{t2} + \ldots + \hat{\beta}_k X_{tk} + e_t, \qquad (\text{I.4.35})$$

for $t = 1, \ldots, T$. Care should be taken to distinguish (I.4.35), where the values estimated for the coefficients and residuals depend on the data employed, from the theoretical model (I.4.34).

The general linear model may also be written using matrix notation. Let the $T \times 1$ column vector of dependent variable data be $\mathbf{y}$ and arrange the data on the independent variables into a matrix $\mathbf{X}$, so that the ith column of $\mathbf{X}$ is the data on X_i. The first column of $\mathbf{X}$ will be a column of 1s, assuming there is a constant term in the model. Denote by $\boldsymbol{\beta} = (\beta_1, \ldots, \beta_k)'$ the vector of true parameters and by $\boldsymbol{\varepsilon}$ the vector of error terms. Then we can write the matrix form of the general linear model as

$$\mathbf{y} = \mathbf{X}\boldsymbol{\beta} + \boldsymbol{\varepsilon}, \qquad \varepsilon_t \sim \text{i.i.d}(0, \sigma^2), \qquad (\text{I.4.36})$$

where the $T \times k$ matrix $\mathbf{X}$ has first column all 1s and subsequent columns containing the data on the explanatory variables. This notation allows one to express the formulae for the OLS estimators in a succinct manner, as before. That is,

$$\hat{\boldsymbol{\beta}} = (\mathbf{X}'\mathbf{X})^{-1}\mathbf{X}'\mathbf{y}. \qquad (\text{I.4.37})$$

The covariance matrix of the OLS estimators is given by

$$V\left(\hat{\boldsymbol{\beta}}\right) = \sigma^2 (\mathbf{X}'\mathbf{X})^{-1}. \qquad (\text{I.4.38})$$

However, formula (I.4.38) cannot be used in practice because the variance of the error process is unknown. Thus, we use the following unbiased estimate of σ^2:

$$s^2 = \nu^{-1} RSS,\tag{I.4.39}$$

where the number $\nu = T - k$ is called the *degrees of freedom* for the regression and RSS is given by (I.4.28). Indeed, all the ANOVA formulae in matrix form are exactly as quoted in Section I.4.4.1. The estimated covariance matrix of the OLS estimators is

$$\text{est.}V\!\left(\hat{\beta}\right) = s^2 (\mathbf{X}'\mathbf{X})^{-1}.\tag{I.4.40}$$

This is a $k \times k$ matrix with the estimated variance of the estimators along the diagonal and the estimated covariances of the estimators in the off-diagonal elements. This matrix, along with the estimated coefficient matrix (I.4.37), will be used for inference on the true model parameters later on in this section.

I.4.4.3 Case Study: A Multiple Regression

BHP Billiton Limited is an Australian corporation engaging in mining, drilling, and processing mineral resources. It operates through seven segments: Petroleum, Aluminium, Base Metals, Carbon Steel Materials, Diamonds and Specialty Products, Energy Coal, and Stainless Steel Materials. In this case study we apply a multiple regression to explain the changes in the Billiton stock price using the Amex Oil and Gold indices. All data are weekly and cover the period from 6 January 1997 to 31 December 2007, a total of 572 returns on each series.[12]

Figure I.4.5 depicts the price data used in the study. All series are normalized to be 100 on 6 January 1997. The Gold index and Oil index are shown on the left-hand scale and the Billiton stock price is on the right-hand scale.

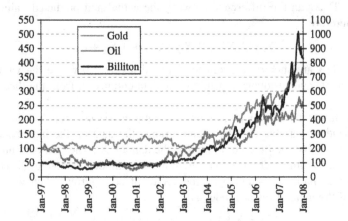

Figure I.4.5 Billiton share price, Amex Oil index and CBOE Gold index

These data are converted into weekly returns and then we estimate the multivariate linear regression model:

$$R_{Bt} = \alpha + \beta R_{Gt} + \gamma R_{Ot} + \varepsilon_t,\tag{I.4.41}$$

---

[12] Data were downloaded from Yahoo! Finance: symbols BHP (Billiton), ^XOI (Oil index) and ^HUI (Gold index).

where R_B denotes the weekly returns on Billiton stocks, R_G denotes the weekly returns on the Amex Gold index and R_O denotes the weekly returns on the Amex Oil index. We can write the model in matrix form as $\mathbf{y} = \mathbf{X}\beta + \varepsilon$, where $\mathbf{y}$ is a column of data on Billiton returns, the $\mathbf{X}$ matrix has first column all 1s, second column the Gold index returns and third column the Oil index returns, and $\beta = (\alpha, \beta, \gamma)'$.

In the workbook for this case study the 'Returns and OLS' spreadsheet applies ANOVA using formulae (I.4.27)–(I.4.30) and applies the OLS formulae (I.4.37) and (I.4.40) using Excel's matrix functions. The fitted model is, with t statistics in parentheses below the coefficient estimates:

$$\hat{R}_B = \underset{(1.5538)}{0.0025} + \underset{(5.7542)}{0.1709} R_G + \underset{(10.6341)}{0.5969} R_O,$$

$$R^2 = 0.2594, \tag{I.4.42}$$

$$s = 0.0378.$$

With 572 data points, any t statistic in excess of about 2 indicates a significant explanatory variable. Hence, both the Gold index and the Oil index are significant determinants of the changes in the Billiton share price. The Oil index has a much larger and more significant effect than the Gold index. This case study will be continued in empirical examples throughout this and the next section.

I.4.4.4   Multiple Regression in Excel

The Excel dialog box shown in Figure I.4.2 can also be used to perform multiple regressions. It is important to note that the data on the explanatory variables must be in adjacent columns. Thus if there are three explanatory variables each with 100 data points (and a label in row 1) and these data are in columns C, D and E then we enter C1:E101 in the 'Input X Range' box, ticking the 'Labels' box below.

The completed dialog box for the Billiton case study is shown in Figure I.4.6 and the regression output is contained in the spreadsheet labelled Excel output. Readers can verify that it is identical to the calculations reported in the previous subsection. However, an advantage of performing a multiple regression 'by hand' as in the previous subsection, is that we can estimate the entire covariance matrix of the OLS estimators, which is useful for hypothesis testing, and this matrix is *not* provided in the Excel output.

I.4.4.5   Hypothesis Testing in Multiple Regression

The standard goodness-of-fit test for a multiple regression is simply an extension of the goodness-of-fit test (I.4.18) for a simple regression. The R^2 of the regression is calculated in exactly the same way, as the ratio of *ESS* to *TSS*, but in the general model the degrees of freedom for *ESS* are not 1 as in the simple linear model but $k - 1$, i.e. the number of explanatory variables *not* including the constant. Hence, the general F test for goodness of fit has the test statistic

$$F = \frac{(k-1)^{-1} ESS}{v^{-1} RSS} \sim F_{k-1, v}, \tag{I.4.43}$$

where $v = T - k$ as above. Clearly this is related to the regression R^2, and indeed after some algebra we find that an alternative form of (I.4.43) is

$$F = \frac{(k-1)^{-1} R^2}{v^{-1} (1 - R^2)} \sim F_{k-1, v}. \tag{I.4.44}$$

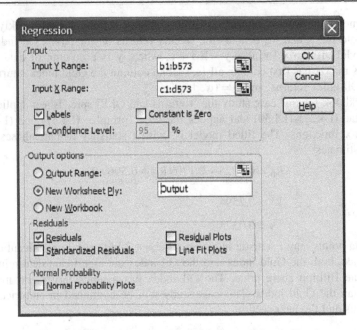

Figure I.4.6 Dialog box for multiple regression in Excel

EXAMPLE I.4.7: GOODNESS-OF-FIT TEST IN MULTIPLE REGRESSION

Test the overall fit of the Billiton regression performed in Section I.4.4.4.

SOLUTION   The ANOVA for the regression is reported in Table I.4.8. Since there are two explanatory variables not including the constant the F statistic (I.4.43) is

$$F = \frac{0.28492/2}{0.81336/569} = 99.659.$$

This has the $F_{2,569}$ distribution, which has an upper 0.1% critical value of approximately 6.992. Hence the overall fit of the regression is very highly significant.

Table I.4.8 ANOVA for Billiton regression

TSS	1.09828
RSS	0.81336
ESS	0.28492
R^2	0.25942
s.e. regression	0.03781

Hypothesis tests on the value of individual parameters are performed exactly as described in Section I.4.2.5 except for two important modifications. Firstly, the test statistics have a Student t distribution with $T-k$ degrees of freedom, instead of $T-2$ degrees of freedom. That is, for the null hypothesis $H_0 : \beta = \beta_0$, the t test statistic is

$$t = \frac{\hat{\beta} - \beta_0}{\text{est.s.e.}\left(\hat{\beta}\right)} \sim t_{T-k}. \tag{I.4.45}$$

Secondly, the estimated standard errors of the estimators are no longer given by formula (I.4.21). Instead we find them by taking the square root of the appropriate diagonal element of the estimated covariance matrix of the estimators. The following example illustrates.

EXAMPLE I.4.8: TESTING A SIMPLE HYPOTHESIS IN MULTIPLE REGRESSION

Test the hypothesis that a 1% change of the Oil index is associated with a 0.5% change (in the same direction) of the Billiton share price.

SOLUTION   Using a two-sided alternative we can write the hypothesis as

$$H_0 : \gamma = 0.5 \quad \text{vs} \quad H_1 : \gamma \neq 0.5.$$

The estimated standard error of $\hat{\gamma}$ is the square root of the bottom right element of the estimated covariance matrix, which is calculated in the spreadsheet as

$$s^2 (\mathbf{X}'\mathbf{X})^{-1} = \begin{pmatrix} 0.0252 & -0.0144 & -0.0716 \\ -0.0144 & 8.82388 & -4.89593 \\ -0.0716 & -4.89593 & 31.5022 \end{pmatrix} \times 10^{-4}.$$

Hence,

$$\text{est.s.e.} (\hat{\gamma}) = \sqrt{31.5022} \times 10^{-2} = 0.0561$$

and so the test statistic (I.4.45) takes the value

$$t = \frac{0.5969 - 0.5}{0.0561} = 1.7257.$$

Thus we cannot reject the null hypothesis. But we would, for instance, reject the null hypothesis that a 1% change in the Oil index is associated with a 1% change in the share price, against the one-sided alternative that the share price response is *less* than 1%.

The testing of *linear restrictions* is also possible using the t distribution, provided we know the entire estimated covariance matrix of the regression estimates (I.4.40) and not just the estimated standard errors of the coefficients. We may test

$$H_0 : f(\beta) = 0 \quad \text{vs} \quad H_1 : f(\beta) \neq 0,$$

where f is any linear function, using the test statistic

$$\frac{f(\hat{\beta})}{\text{est.s.e.} f(\hat{\beta})} \sim t_{T-k} \tag{I.4.46}$$

and (I.4.40) is needed to find the denominator of this expression.

EXAMPLE I.4.9: TESTING A LINEAR RESTRICTION

A linear regression model has the following output based on 64 observations:

$$\hat{\beta} = \begin{pmatrix} 0.05 \\ 0.97 \\ -0.55 \\ 1.23 \end{pmatrix} \quad \text{est.} \mathbf{V}(\hat{\beta}) = \begin{pmatrix} 0.005 & -0.001 & 0.002 & 0.003 \\ -0.001 & 0.04 & 0.005 & 0.003 \\ 0.002 & 0.005 & 0.03 & -0.003 \\ 0.003 & 0.003 & -0.003 & 0.05 \end{pmatrix}.$$

Test the hypothesis

$$H_0 : \beta_1 + \beta_2 = \beta_3 + \beta_4 \quad \text{vs} \quad H_1 : \beta_1 + \beta_2 \neq \beta_3 + \beta_4.$$

SOLUTION   The test statistic is

$$\frac{\left(\hat{\beta}_1 + \hat{\beta}_2 - \hat{\beta}_3 - \hat{\beta}_4\right)}{\text{est.s.e.}\left(\hat{\beta}_1 + \hat{\beta}_2 - \hat{\beta}_3 - \hat{\beta}_4\right)} \sim t_{60}.$$

Now using the matrix formula for the variance of a sum (see Section I.2.4.2) we have

$$V\left(\hat{\beta}_1 + \hat{\beta}_2 - \hat{\beta}_3 - \hat{\beta}_4\right) = (1,\ 1,\ -1,\ -1) \begin{pmatrix} 0.005 & -0.001 & 0.002 & 0.003 \\ -0.001 & 0.04 & 0.005 & 0.003 \\ 0.002 & 0.005 & 0.03 & -0.003 \\ 0.003 & 0.003 & -0.003 & 0.05 \end{pmatrix} \begin{pmatrix} 1 \\ 1 \\ -1 \\ -1 \end{pmatrix}$$

$$= 0.091.$$

Hence, the above t statistic becomes

$$\frac{0.05 + 0.97 + 0.55 - 1.23}{\sqrt{0.091}} = \frac{0.34}{0.3017} = 1.13,$$

and this is clearly not large enough to reject the hypothesis even at the 10% level, because the critical value of t_{60} at 10% is 1.67.

I.4.4.6   Testing Multiple Restrictions

Complex hypotheses involving more than two parameters may be formulated as a set of linear restrictions. It is convenient to write these in matrix form as

$$\mathbf{R\beta} = \mathbf{q} \tag{I.4.47}$$

and if p denotes the number of restrictions on the parameters then $\mathbf{R}$ will be a $p \times k$ matrix and $\mathbf{q}$ is a $p \times 1$ vector of constants. For example, the null hypothesis

$$H_0 : \beta_1 = \beta_2, \quad \beta_1 + \beta_3 = 0, \quad \beta_2 + 2\beta_3 = \beta_1 + 2$$

may be written as

$$\begin{pmatrix} 1 & -1 & 0 \\ 1 & 0 & 1 \\ -1 & 1 & 2 \end{pmatrix} \begin{pmatrix} \beta_1 \\ \beta_2 \\ \beta_3 \end{pmatrix} = \begin{pmatrix} 0 \\ 0 \\ 2 \end{pmatrix}.$$

Hypotheses of this type may be tested using the statistic

$$\frac{p^{-1}(RSS_R - RSS_U)}{v^{-1}RSS_U} \sim F_{p,v}, \tag{I.4.48}$$

where p is the number of restrictions and $v = T - k$ is the sample size less the number of variables in the regression including the constant. The regression model is estimated twice, first with no restrictions giving the *unrestricted* residual sum of squares RSS_U and then after imposing the restrictions in the null hypothesis to obtain the *restricted* residual sum of squares RSS_R.

A special case of (I.4.47) is the hypothesis[13]

$$H_0 : \beta_2 = \ldots = \beta_k = 0$$

This hypothesis test is the goodness-of-fit test for the whole regression. The restricted model is just

$$Y_t = \beta_1 + \varepsilon_t,$$

so $RSS_R = TSS$. Hence, (I.4.48) reduces to the test statistic (I.4.43) in this case.

For the statistic (I.4.48) to have an F distribution it is necessary to assume that the error process is normally distributed. When errors are not normal but the sample is large we may use a *Wald test*, a *Lagrange multiplier* (LM) *test* or a *likelihood ratio* (LR) *test*. These test statistics are all chi-squared distributed with p degrees of freedom (assuming the null hypothesis is true) and are summarized in Table I.4.9.

Table I.4.9   Wald, LM and LR statistics

Test	Statistic
Wald	$\dfrac{RSS_R - RSS_U}{\nu^{-1} RSS_U}$
LM	$\dfrac{RSS_R - RSS_U}{(\nu + p)^{-1} RSS_U}$
LR	$T \times (\ln(RSS_R) - \ln(RSS_U))$

Wald, LM and LR tests are very general. They may also be applied to *non-linear hypotheses* and to parameter tests with general statistical distributions (e.g. for testing restrictions on general covariance matrices).[14] Note that these tests do *not* require errors to be normally distributed in general. The form of LR test given above does assume normal errors, but the general LR test statistic can be defined in terms of any likelihood function. For further details see Greene (2007).

I.4.4.7   Confidence Intervals

We use the t distribution to find approximate confidence intervals for the true value of a regression model coefficient. The Student t distribution applies because although the OLS estimators are normally distributed we only know the *estimated* standard errors of model parameter estimates. These are given in the estimated covariance matrix. In fact we know from Section I.4.2.5 that

$$\frac{\hat{\beta} - \beta}{\text{est.s.e. } \hat{\beta}} \sim t_\nu, \tag{I.4.49}$$

where the degrees-of-freedom parameter $\nu = T - k$.

---

[13] Again assuming the model has a constant term.
[14] See Chapter II.8 for further details on the applications of these tests, for instance to Markov switching regression models.

This t statistic also forms the basis of confidence intervals for the true value of a regression coefficient β. Denote by $t_\nu^{-1}(0.975)$ the 97.5% critical value of the standard t distribution on ν degrees of freedom. Since

$$P\left(\frac{\hat{\beta}-\beta}{\text{est.s.e. }\hat{\beta}} < -t_\nu^{-1}(0.975)\right) = 0.025 \quad \text{and} \quad P\left(\frac{\hat{\beta}-\beta}{\text{est.s.e. }\hat{\beta}} > t_\nu^{-1}(0.975)\right) = 0.025,$$

we have

$$P\left(\hat{\beta} - t_\nu^{-1}(0.975) \times \text{est.s.e. }\hat{\beta} < \beta < \hat{\beta} + t_\nu^{-1}(0.975) \times \text{est.s.e. }\hat{\beta}\right) = 0.95.$$

Hence the two-sided 95% confidence interval is

$$\left(\hat{\beta} - t_\nu^{-1}(0.975) \times \text{est.s.e. }\hat{\beta}, \hat{\beta} + t_\nu^{-1}(0.975) \times \text{est.s.e. }\hat{\beta}\right).$$

In general, a two-sided $100\alpha\%$ confidence interval for β is[15]

$$\left(\hat{\beta} - t_\nu^{-1}\left(\frac{1+\alpha}{2}\right) \times \text{est.s.e. }\hat{\beta}, \hat{\beta} + t_\nu^{-1}\left(\frac{1+\alpha}{2}\right) \times \text{est.s.e. }\hat{\beta}\right). \tag{I.4.50}$$

EXAMPLE I.4.10: CONFIDENCE INTERVAL FOR REGRESSION COEFFICIENT

Find a 95% confidence interval for the coefficient on the Gold index return in the Billiton regression.

SOLUTION   Recall from Section I.4.4.4 that the estimated model is

$$\hat{R}_B = \underset{(1.5538)}{0.0025} + \underset{(5.7542)}{0.1709\,R_G} + \underset{(10.6341)}{0.5969\,R_O}.$$

Following Example I.4.8, we have the estimated covariance matrix

$$s^2(\mathbf{X}'\mathbf{X})^{-1} = \begin{pmatrix} 0.0252 & -0.0144 & -0.0716 \\ -0.0144 & 8.82388 & -4.89593 \\ -0.0716 & -4.89593 & 31.5022 \end{pmatrix} \times 10^{-4}.$$

So the estimated standard error for the estimated coefficient on the Gold index return is

$$\text{est.s.e. }\hat{\beta} = \sqrt{8.82388} \times 10^{-2} = 0.0297.$$

Thus a 95% confidence interval for the true coefficient β is

$$P\left(0.1709 - t_{569}^{-1}(0.975) \times 0.0297 < \beta < 0.1709 + t_{569}^{-1}(0.975) \times 0.0297\right) = 0.95.$$

With 569 degrees of freedom in this regression, the critical values are the same as the normal critical values and the 2.5% critical value is 1.96. So the required 95% confidence interval is

$$[0.1709 - 1.96 \times 0.0297, 0.1709 + 1.96 \times 0.0297] = [0.1126, 0.2293].$$

---

[15] A one-sided upper $100\alpha\%$ confidence interval for β is $\left(\hat{\beta} - t_\nu^{-1}(\alpha) \times \text{est.s.e. }\hat{\beta}, \infty\right)$. Put another way,

$$P\left(\beta > \hat{\beta} - t_\nu^{-1}(\alpha) \times \text{est.s.e. }\hat{\beta}\right) = \alpha.$$

Similarly, a lower $100\alpha\%$ confidence interval is $\left(-\infty, \hat{\beta} + t_\nu^{-1}(\alpha) \times \text{est.s.e. }\hat{\beta}\right)$, which is another way of saying that

$$P\left(\beta < \hat{\beta} + t_\nu^{-1}(\alpha) \times \text{est.s.e. }\hat{\beta}\right) = \alpha.$$

These confidence intervals are automatically output in the Excel regression analysis tool.

Another type of confidence interval in regression is a *conditional confidence interval*, i.e. a confidence interval for the value of the dependent variable given that the independent variables take certain values. Thus the fitted model may be used in scenario analysis, where we assume certain values for the explanatory variables and deduce the possible range for the dependent variable.

Suppose the explanatory variables take some specified values, denoted by the vector

$$\mathbf{x}_0 = (x_{10}, \ldots, x_{k0}).$$
(I.4.51)

Then, under the assumption that the error process is i.i.d. $(0, \sigma^2)$, the Gauss–Markov theorem tells us that the best linear unbiased predictor of Y given these values is

$$\hat{y}_0 = \mathbf{x}_0 \hat{\boldsymbol{\beta}}.$$
(I.4.52)

That is, $\hat{y}_0 = E(Y | X_1 = x_{10}, \ldots, X_k = x_{k0})$. The variance of the prediction error about this mean prediction is

$$V(y_0 - \hat{y}_0 | X_1 = x_{10}, \ldots, X_k = x_{k0}) = \sigma^2 + \mathbf{x}_0 V\left(\hat{\boldsymbol{\beta}}\right) \mathbf{x}_0',$$

and we can estimate this using s^2 to estimate the variance σ^2 of the error. This gives the estimated variance of the prediction error as

$$\text{est.} V(y_0 - \hat{y}_0 | X_1 = x_{10}, \ldots, X_k = x_{k0}) = s^2 + \mathbf{x}_0\left(s^2 (\mathbf{X}'\mathbf{X})^{-1}\right) \mathbf{x}_0'.$$
(I.4.53)

This contains two terms: the first term s^2 is the variance of the residuals, i.e. the estimated variance of the regression error process, and the second term is the estimated variance of the prediction *mean* $\hat{y}_0$. Adding them and taking the square root gives the estimated *standard error of the prediction*, which we denote by est.s.e. $(y_0 - \hat{y}_0)$. This may be used to construct confidence intervals for predictions in the usual way. Thus,

$$P\left(\hat{y}_0 - t_\nu^{-1}\left(\frac{1+\alpha}{2}\right) \times \text{est.s.e.} (y_0 - \hat{y}_0) < y_0 < \hat{y}_0 + t_\nu^{-1}\left(\frac{1+\alpha}{2}\right) \times \text{est.s.e.} (y_0 - \hat{y}_0)\right) = \alpha.$$
(I.4.54)

EXAMPLE I.4.11: PREDICTION IN MULTIVARIATE REGRESSION

Use the regression model estimated in the case study of Section I.4.4.4 to predict the return on Billiton if the Oil index fell by 20% at the same time as the Gold index fell by 10%. Then find a 90% confidence interval for your prediction.

SOLUTION   We have $\mathbf{x}_0 = (1, -0.1, -0.2)$ and

$$\hat{\boldsymbol{\beta}} = \begin{pmatrix} 0.0025 \\ 0.1709 \\ 0.5969 \end{pmatrix}.$$

Thus the best linear unbiased predictor is

$$\hat{y}_0 = (1, -0.1, -0.2) \begin{pmatrix} 0.0025 \\ 0.1709 \\ 0.5969 \end{pmatrix} = -0.1340.$$

So our best prediction of the effect on the Billiton share price is that it falls by 13.4%.

Now we construct a 90% confidence interval around this prediction by first estimating the prediction error variance using (I.4.53) with $s^2 = 0.00143$ and estimated covariance matrix

$$s^2 (\mathbf{X'X})^{-1} = \begin{pmatrix} 0.0252 & -0.0144 & -0.0716 \\ -0.0144 & 8.82388 & -4.89593 \\ -0.0716 & -4.89593 & 31.5022 \end{pmatrix} \times 10^{-4}.$$

That is,

$$\text{est.} V(y_0 - \hat{y}_0 | X_1 = -0.1, X_2 = -0.2)$$
$$= 0.00143 + (1, -0.1, -0.2) \begin{pmatrix} 0.0252 & -0.0144 & -0.0716 \\ -0.0144 & 8.82388 & -4.89593 \\ -0.0716 & -4.89593 & 31.5022 \end{pmatrix} \begin{pmatrix} 1 \\ -0.1 \\ -0.2 \end{pmatrix} \times 10^{-4}$$
$$= 0.00155.$$

Hence est.s.e. $(y_0 - \hat{y}_0) = \sqrt{0.00155} = 0.0394$. Thus there is almost a 4% standard error on our prediction. A 90% confidence interval for the effect of the Oil and Gold price scenario on the Billiton share price is therefore

$$P(-0.1340 - 1.645 \times 0.0394 < y_0 < -0.1340 + 1.645 \times 0.0394) = 0.9. \qquad (\text{I.4.55})$$

That is, the 90% confidence interval is $[-19.88\%, -6.92\%]$. Put another way, given our regression model, we are 90% confident that the Billiton share price would fall by between 6.92% and 19.88% if the Amex Oil index were to fall by 10% at the same time as the CBOE Gold index fell by 20%.

I.4.4.8 Multicollinearity

A potential problem with multiple linear regressions is that explanatory variables may have a high degree of correlation between themselves. In this case it may not be possible to determine their individual effects. The problem is referred to as *multicollinearity*. Perfect multicollinearity occurs when two (or more) explanatory variables are perfectly correlated. In this case the OLS estimators do not even exist. To see why, consider the extreme case where two variables X_1 and X_2 are perfectly correlated. Then X_1 is linearly related to X_2, say $X_1 = 2X_2$ for example. In that case the linear regression model relating Y to X_1 and X_2 can be written in an infinite number of ways. For example, if $Y = 1.2X_1 + 0.6X_2$ then also $Y = 0.2X_1 + 2.6X_2$ or $Y = 2X_1 - X_2$ and so on. So it is impossible to know which values for the regression coefficients are correct.

But perfect multicollinearity only occurs when the analyst has made a mistake in the model specification: some linear transform of one or more of the explanatory variables has been included as another explanatory variable. The real problem arises when there is a high *degree* of multicollinearity: not perfect correlation but a high correlation between some explanatory variables. The OLS estimators do exist and they are still the most efficient of all linear unbiased estimators. But that does not mean that their variances and covariances are small. They may be 'most efficient' but when there is a high degree of multicollinearity the problem is that 'most efficient' is still not very efficient.

The problem with multicollinearity is that if some of the explanatory variables are highly correlated then the estimated covariance matrix of the OLS estimators (I.4.40) will have some very large elements on the diagonals corresponding to these variables and some very small elements on the diagonals of the elements corresponding to the variables that are not highly correlated with these variables. In other words, the estimated standard errors for the coefficients will be biased. Often the t ratios will indicate that positively correlated variables are less significant than they really are, but they can also indicate that collinear variables are more significant than they really are. An example of this is provided by the case study in the next subsection.

If you have ever estimated a regression model and you find that a variable does not appear to be significant unless you add another variable, which itself is not necessarily significant, then you have encountered multicollinearity. If the significance of X_1 depends on including another variable X_2 which itself may or may not be significant, then the apparent significance of X_1 may be an artefact of the high (positive or negative) correlation between X_1 and X_2.

But the false significance of variables that really do not explain the dependent variable is not the only sign of multicollinearity. If X_1 and X_2 are highly correlated then it is possible that they are both doing a good job of explaining Y, but it is impossible to estimate their separate coefficients precisely. Then the estimated coefficients on these variables could change a lot when we change the input data only a little, a problem that is referred to as a lack of *robustness* in the coefficient estimates.

Multicollinearity is not an 'all or nothing' issue, it is a question of degree, so there is no formal test for multicollinearity. If the correlations between certain explanatory variables are too high then multicollinearity can be severe enough to distort the model estimation procedure.[16] In that case there are a number of possible solutions:

- Use different data – either over a different period or with a different frequency. It is possible that the problem variables will be less correlated in a different sample.
- Drop the least significant (or least important) of the collinear variables, and if there are more collinear variables left continue to throw them out of the model until multi-collinearity is no longer a problem.
- Use a *ridge estimator*, which is obtained by using the OLS formula but artificially increasing the diagonal elements of the $X'X$ matrix corresponding to the collinear variables. The problem here is that the OLS estimators are no longer unbiased.
- Apply *principal component analysis* (PCA) to the set of explanatory variables and use the first few principal components as independent variables in the regression instead of the original variables. This technique is called *orthogonal regression* because principle components have zero correlation by construction.[17]

I.4.4.9   Case Study: Determinants of Credit Spreads

In this case study we use multiple regression to test the structural models of credit risk that are based on Merton's (1974) theory of asset pricing. The problem of multicollinearity arises because two of the explanatory variables are extremely highly correlated.

In structural models of credit risk the default of a firm is triggered when the firm's value falls below a certain threshold. The theory suggests the following determinants of credit spreads:

- *Interest rates*. An increase in the risk free interest rate should decrease the default proba-bility (and therefore also the credit spread) because this increases the risk neutral drift in

---

[16] A 'rule of thumb' for the presence of multicollinearity is that the square of the correlation between any two explanatory variables is greater than the R^2 of the regression.
[17] See Section I.4.4.10 below for further details.

the firm value process. Also low interest rates are associated with recession and frequent corporate defaults.

- *Equity prices.* When the market value of the firm decreases, the probability of default will increase because hitting the default threshold becomes more likely. We cannot measure the firm value directly so we use the firm's equity value as a proxy variable.
- *Equity volatility.* By the same token, an increase in equity volatility will increase the likelihood of the firm's value hitting the default threshold and thus increase the credit spread.

Hence we are led to a regression of the form[18]

$$\Delta s_t = \alpha + \beta_1 \Delta r_t + \beta_2 R_t + \beta_3 \Delta \theta_t + \varepsilon_t, \qquad (I.4.56)$$

where Δs denotes the change in the credit spread, α is constant, β_1 is the coefficient on the change in the risk free interest rate r and should be negative, β_2 is the coefficient of the equity return R and should also be negative, and β_3 is the coefficient of the equity implied volatility θ and should be positive.

We now test this theory using daily data from 21 June 2004 to 19 September 2007 on the iTraxx Europe credit spread index, the 1-year euro swap rate, an equity index constructed from the share prices of the 125 firms that are included in the iTraxx index and the implied volatility index for the Eurostoxx index, which is called the Vstoxx.[19] The data are shown in Figure I.4.7, with each series set to 100 on 21 June 2004. After three years of a general downward trend in credit spreads, they returned to their 2004 levels during the sub-prime mortgage crisis in the latter part of 2007. Equity volatility also shot up during this time as

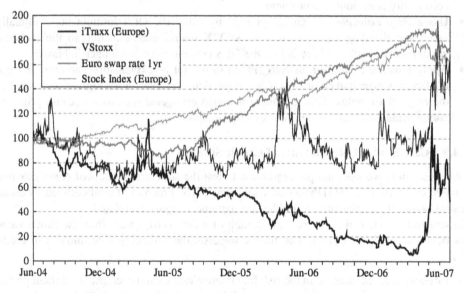

Figure I.4.7   The iTraxx Europe index and its determinants

---

[18] However credit spreads, like many financial variables, appear to switch between tranquil and volatile regimes and a simple linear regression model is unable to capture this. See Alexander and Kaeck (2008) and references therein for further details.

[19] These data were used in Alexander and Kaeck (2008) in a Markov switching regression model of regimes in credit spreads.

the equity index fell, and interest rates were subsequently reduced to alleviate the effects of the credit crunch.

Estimation of the model (I.4.56) is performed using the Excel regression analysis tool and the results are shown in the 'iTraxx Models' spreadsheet of the case study. The fitted model is

$$\Delta \hat{s} = \underset{(0.2832)}{0.1222} - \underset{(-0.9118)}{1.9184}\,\Delta r - \underset{(-5.8720)}{0.3984}\,R + \underset{(2.3669)}{0.1904}\,\Delta\theta. \tag{I.4.57}$$

The coefficients on the equity return and equity volatility are significant and of the correct sign, which supports the structural models of default. But the regression R^2 is only 0.1995 and there is a high degree of multicollinearity between the equity index return and the change in implied volatility. In fact in our sample their correlation is -0.829, and the square of this is 0.687, which far exceeds the regression R^2.

To remedy the multicollinearity problem we can simply drop one of the collinear variables from the regression, using either the equity return or the change in implied volatility in the model, but not both. If we drop the implied volatility from the regression the estimated model becomes

$$\Delta \hat{s} = \underset{(0.6102)}{0.02618} - \underset{(-1.0047)}{2.1181}\,\Delta r - \underset{(-13.9069)}{0.5312}\,R.$$

The equity return alone is actually a more significant determinant of changes in credit spread than the model (I.4.57) would indicate. And if we drop the equity return from the regression, the estimated model becomes

$$\Delta \hat{s} = \underset{(-0.6077)}{-0.0265} - \underset{(-1.0086)}{2.1643}\,\Delta r + \underset{(12.6154)}{0.5814}\,\Delta\theta.$$

Hence, the equity implied volatility alone is a very significant determinant of the credit spread. Its effect was being masked by its collinearity with the equity return in the original model. In fact, the effect of equity implied volatility on the credit spread is almost equal and opposite to the effect of the equity index. However, we do not require both variables in the model since there is only one equity effect, and this may be captured equally well using either variable, but not both of them in the same model.

I.4.4.10   Orthogonal Regression[20]

The idea behind orthogonal regression is very straightforward:

- First put the explanatory variables $\{X_1, \ldots, X_k\}$ through a PCA, saving all of the principal components $\{P_1, \ldots, P_k\}$ and the full matrix of eigenvectors $\mathbf{W}$.
- Then perform an OLS regression of Y on a constant and $\{P_1, \ldots, P_k\}$ and find the OLS estimates:

$$\hat{\beta}_{PCA} = (\mathbf{P}'\mathbf{P})^{-1}(\mathbf{P}'\mathbf{y}), \tag{I.4.58}$$

where the matrix $\mathbf{P}$ has a first column of 1s (for the constant term) and subsequent columns are the principal components.

- Also find their estimated covariance matrix,

$$\mathrm{est.}\,\mathrm{V}\left(\hat{\beta}_{PCA}\right) = s^2 (\mathbf{P}'\mathbf{P})^{-1}, \tag{I.4.59}$$

---

[20] To understand this section readers will need to be familiar with Section I.2.6.

where s is the estimated standard error of the regression. Note that the use of principal components in the regression does not affect the ANOVA, so TSS, ESS, RSS and the estimated standard error of the principal components regression are the same as in the original regression.

We can recover the estimated coefficients for the original regression as

$$\hat{\beta} = \tilde{\mathbf{W}}\hat{\beta}_{PCA} = \tilde{\mathbf{W}}(\mathbf{P'P})^{-1}(\mathbf{P'y}), \tag{I.4.60}$$

and their estimated covariance matrix as:

$$\text{est.}V\left(\hat{\beta}\right) = s^2 \tilde{\mathbf{W}}(\mathbf{P'P})^{-1}\tilde{\mathbf{W}}', \tag{I.4.61}$$

where

$$\tilde{\mathbf{W}} = \begin{pmatrix} 1 & \mathbf{0'} \\ \mathbf{0} & \mathbf{W} \end{pmatrix}.$$

and $\mathbf{0}$ is a $(k+1) \times 1$ vector of zeros. Of course this gives results that are no different from performing OLS on the original regression.

The advantage of orthogonal regression is the ability to perform a regression on the uncorrelated principal components. These are not affected by multicollinearity and they identify the most important sources of risk. Indeed, when there are many explanatory variables and these variables are highly collinear we should use only a *few* of the principal components, enough to explain a large fraction but not all of the variation in the explanatory variables. See Sections I.2.6 and II.1.4 for further details.

Here we illustrate the orthogonal regression method for the case study on the Billiton regression.[21] The results are reported in the spreadsheet labelled 'PCA and OLS'. The orthogonal regression model is:

$$\hat{R}_B = \underset{(1.5538)}{0.0025} + \underset{(10.3108)}{0.2822\,P_1} + \underset{(-9.6440)}{-0.5385\,P_2},$$

$$R^2 = 0.2594, \tag{I.4.62}$$

$$s = 0.0378.$$

Note that the constant term, the R^2 and the standard error of the regression are all unchanged from the ordinary model (I.4.42). The only things that change are the coefficient estimates and the t ratios on the principal components P_1 and P_2.

The first component P_1 captures a common trend in Oil and Gold index prices and we know from the PCA results in the spreadsheet that this component captures 80% of the variation in the explanatory variables. A 10% change in P_1 is associated with a 2.822% change in the Billiton share price in the same direction. The second component, which captures only 20% of the variation in Oil and Gold, is an opposite trend in the prices. A 10% change in P_2 is associated with a 5.385% change in Billiton share price in the opposite direction.

This example is rather simple. With only two explanatory variables – which are, incidentally, not very highly correlated – there is really no point to orthogonal regression. However,

---

[21] Readers require the Excel add-in for principal component analysis – see Section I.2.6.

when there are more explanatory variables and these variables are highly correlated then orthogonal regression is an invaluable tool. A more realistic example of orthogonal regression is provided in Section II.1.4, and in Chapter II.2 we explain how orthogonal regression is used in the APT technology for portfolio optimization. A detailed Excel case study of orthogonal regression in practice is provided in Section II.2.5.

I.4.5   AUTOCORRELATION AND HETEROSCEDASTICITY

The simple goodness-of-fit test (I.4.43) goes some way towards indicating how well a linear model has been specified. But a full *diagnostic analysis* of residuals gives much more information about the possible omission of relevant explanatory variables and the properties of the coefficient estimators. Recall that the Gauss–Markov theorem states that the OLS estimators are BLUE provided that the error process is i.i.d. OLS can be used to estimate the parameters, even in small samples, because the OLS estimators will be unbiased and efficient.

This section examines the tests that we carry out on residuals to decide whether the i.i.d. property is violated, and the causes of any violation of this assumption. We split the i.i.d. property into two parts, asking:

1. Is the error covariance matrix diagonal? If not the errors will be *autocorrelated*.
2. Are the diagonal elements of the error covariance matrix identical, i.e. are the errors *homoscedastic*? In other words, does the error process have a constant variance? If the error process does not have a constant variance we say that it is *heteroscedastic*.

I.4.5.1   Causes of Autocorrelation and Heteroscedasticity

Common causes of autocorrelation and/or heteroscedasticity in residuals include the following:

- *Omitted variables.* This is the prime cause of autocorrelation and/or heteroscedasticity. If the dependent variable has characteristics that are not explained by any of the included explanatory variables those characteristics will show up in the residuals.
- *Structural breaks.* Structural breaks are very common in financial markets, since a market crash or move to a different regime may signify a structural change in the data generation process. If one attempts to fit a linear model to data with structural breaks, residuals may be autocorrelated. The solution is to use a *dummy variable* in the regression, whose precise form depends on the type of structural break.[22] The single model becomes equivalent to two models with different constant terms and/or different slope parameters, depending on how this dummy is incorporated into the model.
- *Fitting an inappropriate functional form.* For instance, Y may be strongly related to the log of X rather than X itself, in which case fitting a linear model will give rise to autocorrelated errors.
- *Over- or under-differencing the data.* The usual method for transforming prices or interest rates into stationary series is first differencing of the log or level variables, respectively.

---

[22] A simple dummy variable takes the values 0 and 1 only; for instance a variable such as $\{0, \ldots, 0, 1, \ldots, 1, 0, \ldots 0\}$ could capture a shift in regime during the centre of the data period.

If this is not done the dependent variable may have a very high degree of positive autocorrelation and if there is no similar explanatory variable to 'balance' the model this autocorrelation will show up in residuals. On the other hand, if first differencing is performed when it is not necessary the dependent variable will have high negative autocorrelation. In either case it is by no means certain that the model could explain such structural autocorrelation. It is a problem with the basic data that should already have been identified when visual plots of the data are examined prior to building the model – plotting the data should be done as a matter of course – never build a model before looking at all the data!

I.4.5.2   Consequences of Autocorrelation and Heteroscedasticity

In large samples the presence of autocorrelation or heteroscedasticity is not particularly damaging to the results of OLS regression. This is because OLS estimators are consistent under quite general conditions. Even in small samples the OLS estimators are still unbiased but their standard errors may be affected so that the OLS estimators are no longer the most efficient of all linear unbiased estimators. In that case we can change the method used to estimate the covariance matrix of the OLS estimators to obtain a covariance matrix that is more robust to the presence of autocorrelation or heteroscedasticity.

If the error process is heteroscedastic we can use *White's robust standard errors* in place of the usual standard errors of the OLS estimators.[23] That is, in place of (I.4.40), we use the estimated covariance matrix

$$\text{est.}V\left(\hat{\beta}\right) = T(\mathbf{X}'\mathbf{X})^{-1}\mathbf{\Sigma}(\mathbf{X}'\mathbf{X})^{-1}, \quad \mathbf{\Sigma} = T^{-1}\sum_{t=1}^{T}e_t^2\mathbf{x}_t\mathbf{x}_t', \tag{I.4.63}$$

where $\mathbf{x}_t$ is the row vector of the observations on the explanatory variables including the constant and e_t is the OLS residual at time t.

If the error process displays autocorrelation then the *Newey–West procedure* may be used to obtain robust standard errors.[24] The procedure is straightforward but the formula for the robust covariance matrix is more complex than the White covariance matrix, so readers are referred to Greene (2007) for further details. Both White's heteroscedasticity robust standard errors and the Newey–West consistent standard errors are automatically output in most econometrics packages.

The next two subsections describe some standard tests for autocorrelation and heteroscedasticity. Excel does not perform these tests automatically but most econometrics packages output these tests in their standard residual diagnostics.

I.4.5.3   Testing for Autocorrelation

The *Durbin–Watson test* is an approximate test for autocorrelation in the residuals in regression. The test statistic is

$$DW = \frac{\sum_{t=2}^{T}(e_t - e_{t-1})^2}{\sum_{t=2}^{T}e_t^2}. \tag{I.4.64}$$

---

[23] See White (1980).
[24] See Newey and West (1987).

Small values of DW indicate positive autocorrelation and large values indicate negative autocorrelation. In large samples DW is approximately equal to $2(1 - r)$ where r is the estimate of the first order autocorrelation in the residuals.

The approximate range for DW is $[0, 4]$ and DW has an expected value of approximately 2 under the null hypothesis of zero autocorrelation. No exact distribution is available, but upper and lower limits D_U and D_L for the significance levels of DW are given in Durbin–Watson tables.

If the null hypothesis for the test is that there is no autocorrelation in the residuals, against the alternative hypothesis of positive autocorrelation the decision rule is

- if $DW < D_L$ then reject the null hypothesis;
- if $DW > D_U$ then do not reject the null; and
- if $D_L < DW < D_U$ the test is inconclusive.

If the alternative hypothesis is that there is negative autocorrelation then substitute $4 - DW$ for DW in the decision rule above.

EXAMPLE I.4.12: DURBIN–WATSON TEST

Test the residuals from the Billiton regression for autocorrelation.

SOLUTION The Durbin–Watson statistic (I.4.64) is computed in cell F26 of the spreadsheet labelled 'Excel output', and the result is 2.265. This is close to the expected value. Indeed, for more than 200 observations $D_U = 1.684$ so we do not reject the null hypothesis of no autocorrelation in favour of either positive or negative autocorrelation.

I.4.5.4 Testing for Heteroscedasticity

A general test for heteroscedasticity, introduced by White (1980) is performed using an *auxiliary regression* of the squared residuals on all the squares and cross products of the explanatory variables. The test statistic is $T\tilde{R}^2$, where T is the number of observations and $\tilde{R}^2$ is the R^2 from the auxiliary OLS regression. It is asymptotically chi-squared distributed with p degrees of freedom, where p is the number of explanatory variables in the auxiliary regression, including the constant.

EXAMPLE I.4.13: WHITE'S HETEROSCEDASTICITY TEST

Test the residuals from the Billiton regression for heteroscedasticity.

SOLUTION The auxiliary regression is a regression of the squared residuals on $p = 6$ variables: a constant, R_G, R_O, $R_G R_O$, R_G^2 and R_O^2. The data on the squared residuals and on these variables are placed in a separate spreadsheet labelled 'White's test' in the case study workbook. The auxiliary regression is performed using the Excel regression analysis tools and the R^2 from this regression is $\tilde{R}^2 = 0.11663$, giving a test statistic $T\tilde{R}^2 = 66.71$. The 0.1% critical value of the chi-squared test with 6 degrees of freedom is 22.46. So we reject the null hypothesis that the residuals have constant variance in favour of the alternative hypothesis that the variance of the residuals changes over time.

Figure I.4.8 plots the residuals from the Billiton regression. From this it is clear that their variance is much larger in the first part of the sample, and this is the reason why we rejected the null hypothesis in White's test for heteroscedasticity.

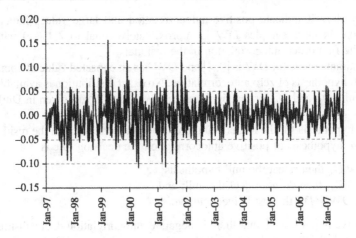

Figure I.4.8   Residuals from the Billiton regression

I.4.5.5   Generalized Least Squares

If residuals are autocorrelated or heteroscedastic and we do not have a large sample, then we need to use an alternative method of estimation to OLS. *Generalized least squares* (GLS) is such a method. The GLS estimator of the coefficients in the multivariate linear model (I.4.34) is

$$\hat{\beta}_{GLS} = \left(\mathbf{X}'\boldsymbol{\Omega}^{-1}\mathbf{X}\right)^{-1}\mathbf{X}'\boldsymbol{\Omega}^{-1}\mathbf{y}, \tag{I.4.65}$$

where

$$V(\varepsilon) = \sigma^2\boldsymbol{\Omega},$$
$$V\left(\hat{\beta}_{GLS}\right) = \sigma^2(\mathbf{X}'\boldsymbol{\Omega}^{-1}\mathbf{X})^{-1}. \tag{I.4.66}$$

Hence, when $\boldsymbol{\Omega} = \mathbf{I}$ then GLS is the same as OLS, otherwise GLS admits a more general structure for the covariance matrix of the error process.

The precise form of $\boldsymbol{\Omega}$ will depend on the nature of the error process. For example, when there is heteroscedasticity but no autocorrelation then $\boldsymbol{\Omega}$ will be a diagonal matrix:

$$\boldsymbol{\Omega} = \begin{pmatrix} \sigma_1^2 & 0 & \cdots & 0 & 0 \\ \vdots & & \ddots & & \vdots \\ 0 & 0 & \cdots & 0 & \sigma_T^2 \end{pmatrix} = \operatorname{diag}\left(\sigma_1^2, \ldots, \sigma_T^2\right). \tag{I.4.67}$$

If there is autocorrelation but no heteroscedasticity then $\boldsymbol{\Omega}$ will take a form that is determined by the type of autocorrelation. For example, if there is *first order autocorrelation* in the error process of the form

$$\varepsilon_t = \varrho\varepsilon_{t-1} + \eta_t \quad \eta_t \sim \text{i.i.d.}\left(0, \sigma_\eta^2\right), \tag{I.4.68}$$

then $\boldsymbol{\Omega}$ will be the *circulant matrix*

$$\boldsymbol{\Omega} = \begin{pmatrix} 1 & \varrho & \varrho^2 & \cdots & \varrho^{T-1} \\ \varrho & 1 & \varrho & \cdots & \varrho^{T-2} \\ \varrho^2 & \varrho & 1 & \cdots & \varrho^{T-3} \\ \cdots & \cdots & \cdots & \cdots & \cdots \\ \varrho^T & \varrho^{T-1} & \cdots & \cdots & 1 \end{pmatrix}.$$

We can obtain GLS estimators by applying OLS to transformed data

$$\mathbf{X}^* = \mathbf{CX} \text{ and } \mathbf{y}^* = \mathbf{Cy},$$

where $\mathbf{C}$ is the Cholesky matrix of $\mathbf{\Omega}^{-1}$. For example, if the model suffers from heteroscedasticity and we assume

$$\sigma_i^2 = \sigma^2 w_i^2$$

for some observable variable W, then by (I.4.67) the transformation matrix is

$$\mathbf{C} = \text{diag}\left(w_1^{-1}, \ldots, w_T^{-1}\right).$$

In other words, the ith row of data in $\mathbf{X}$ and $\mathbf{y}$ must first be divided by w_i and then OLS is applied to these data. This form of GLS is called *weighted least squares*.

I.4.6   APPLICATIONS OF LINEAR REGRESSION IN FINANCE

This section provides a brief survey of the main applications of linear regression in finance. Important applications are to: test a theory; examine the empirical behaviour of financial markets; determine optimal portfolio allocations; hedge an exposure to a security or commodity; and build a trading model. Each application is discussed in general terms but external references and further references to other chapters of this book are provided.

I.4.6.1   Testing a Theory

Economists use regression to test their theories about the behaviour of economic fundamentals. Indeed this was a driving force behind the development of econometrics during the middle of the last century. Empirical researchers in finance also use regression to test theories. For instance, in Section I.4.4.9 we estimated a regression to test the determinants of credit spreads that are implied by the structural models of default. There are many other ways in which regression can be used to test a financial theory and in this section we provide a brief survey of some of the huge literature in this area.

No *arbitrage* implies that the prices of liquid forward contracts are closely tied to the prices of spot assets. Similarly, zero coupon interest rates in the same currency tend to move together over time. And the forward or futures prices of different maturities on the same underlying also move in a highly correlated term structure. Hence, the absence of arbitrage implies many *cointegration* relationships between financial assets and interest rates. Cointegration tests for no arbitrage can be based on regression models, or on an eigenvalue analysis. These are discussed in considerable detail in Chapter II.5.

The *efficient market hypothesis* in its weak form states that no excess returns can be earned by using investment strategies based on historical financial data. The current price of an asset reflects all relevant information, and this implies that the price of a liquid financial asset will follow a random walk. This theory, introduced and developed by Fama (1970), can be tested using a *unit root test* that is based on a simple time series regression called the *Dickey–Fuller regression*, that was introduced in Section I.3.7.1. More advanced unit root tests are surveyed in Phillips and Xiao (1998).

The *capital asset pricing model* (CAPM) introduced by Sharpe (1964) and developed further by Lintner (1965) is described in Section I.6.4. It can be formulated as a regression where the dependent variable is an asset's excess return over the risk free rate of return and the explanatory variable is the excess return of the market portfolio. A test of the theory can be based on a hypothesis test on the constant terms, i.e. that they are zero for all risky assets in the universe. Empirical tests of the CAPM are described in Section I.6.4.4. Readers may also consult Chapter 5 of the book by Campbell et al. (1997) and the many references therein.

More generally, a considerable body of financial econometrics research has focused on discrete time models for the *theory of asset pricing* which depends on the assumptions of no arbitrage, single agent optimality and market equilibrium. Indeed, two out of five of the volumes of classic research papers in financial econometrics collected by Lo (2007) are devoted to this issue.

I.4.6.2 Analysing Empirical Market Behaviour

Market microstructure is the study of price formation and how this is related to trading protocols and trading volume. It is the study of market liquidity, of how prices are formed, of the times between trades and of the determinants of the bid–ask spread. A good survey of research papers in this field is given by Biais et al. (2005).

High quality tic-by-tic data on every trade or quote that is made may be analysed for patterns. Obtaining such data is not easy except from some exchanges. For instance US Exchanges provide a Trade and Quote (TAQ) database, which is a collection of intraday trades and quotes for securities listed on the New York Stock Exchange (NYSE), American Stock Exchange (Amex) and Nasdaq. TAQ provides historical tic-by-tic data of all stocks listed on NYSE back to 1993.[25] Recently some other exchanges – such as the Toronto Stock Exchange – have started to offer similar data. But over-the-counter trades are much more difficult to record. An exception is the MTS Time Series hosted by the ICMA Centre. This covers European sovereign bond markets and includes comprehensive high frequency trade and quote data.

Price discovery refers to the fact that the prices of more liquid instruments respond to news more rapidly than the prices of less liquid instruments traded in the same market. Price discovery most commonly refers to the relationship between futures prices and spot prices. Futures contracts are exchange traded and are usually far more liquid than the spot assets or interest rates on which they are based. For instance, futures on equity indices are very liquid but the spot index is not traded at all.[26] Hence, changes in futures prices tend to lead to changes in the spot price. A test of the price discovery relationship is based on a *Granger causality* time series regression which is described in Section II.5.5.2. For further details on testing the price discovery relationship, see Section III.2.2.6 and references therein.

Financial market integration refers to relationships between broad market indices. There are many reasons why financial markets are becoming more integrated, including the lifting of restrictions on foreign investments in developing countries, the increasing globalization of the financial industry and the growth in large multinational financial conglomerates, economic and monetary union in Europe, advances in technology and electronic trading.

Market integration is often analysed using daily or weekly data. At the daily level it is important to use synchronous data. Not only when the markets are in different time zones, but the futures markets often close slightly later than the spot market and the last 15 or 30 minutes of trading on futures can seriously distort results when daily closing prices are

---

[25] It does not include aggregate indexes, transaction data reported outside the normal hours of operation or pre-opening trades.
[26] Some indices are traded through exchange traded funds, but these still have a tracking error.

used. The possibility of cointegration and/or Granger causal flows between markets has been a topic of interest to financial economists who seek to describe behaviour from a policy perspective rather than any profit-related motive. For a sample of this considerable literature, see Adjaouté and Danthine (2004), Baele et al. (2004), Berben and Jansen (2005), Goetzmann et al. (2005), Kim et al. (2005) and Lumsdaine and Prasad (2003).

I.4.6.3 Optimal Portfolio Allocation

Fund managers allocate investments according to their client's requirements for expected returns and their appetite for risk. The *undiversifiable risk* is the risk that is collinear to a market index and other fundamental factors and which cannot be diversified away by holding a sufficiently large portfolio. It may also be called the *systematic risk* of the factors, i.e. the market index and indices that represent fundamental factors such as growth and value.

The regression model that is used for portfolio allocation takes the form

$$R_t = \alpha + \beta_1 X_{1t} + \ldots + \beta_k X_{kt} + \varepsilon_t, \tag{I.4.69}$$

where R is the return on the asset and the explanatory variables $X_1, \ldots, X_k$ are the returns on the factors.[27] The expected excess return on an asset, over and above the return that the investor would gain by allocating funds to the index and fundamental factors, is identified with the constant term, i.e. the *alpha* of the fitted model (I.4.69). The diversifiable risk is represented by the regression coefficients, i.e. the *betas* of the asset with respect to the factors. The estimated standard deviation of the error process in (I.4.69) is by practitioners, unfortunately termed the *tracking error* although it has little to do with tracking. We discuss this important point in considerable detail in Section II.1.6.

Given a regression of the form (I.4.69) that is fitted to every asset in an investor's universe, the expected return and the diversifiable risk of a portfolio can be immediately derived from the weights. The portfolio alpha is just a weighted sum of the alphas for each asset and the beta with respect to each factor is also a weighted sum of the asset betas, with weights given by the portfolio weights. Thus the portfolio optimization problem is to choose the portfolio weights so that the portfolio alpha and betas satisfy the client's requirements for expected return and risk. We discuss this problem in more detail in Section I.6.3.

A number of fundamental and statistical approaches to the portfolio allocation problem have been developed using specialized *factor model* software that is based on regression analysis. For instance, in Section II.1.5 we describe the foundations of the *Barra model* which links the returns on individual assets to the returns on certain fundamental factors such as growth and value indices. And in Section II.2.5 we describe software that approaches the same problem using orthogonal regression. For further details readers are referred to that section, which contains a case study that implements a statistical factor model for the Dow Jones Industrial Average stocks in Excel.

I.4.6.4 Regression-Based Hedge Ratios

The problem of hedging with futures is introduced in Section III.2.5. Futures hedges were originally intended to remove the risk of price fluctuations for a consumer or producer of

---

[27] Note that our notation here singles out the constant term α because it plays a special role in portfolio allocation. Also, the model may be estimated using cross section or time series data, even though we have used the time subscript in (I.4.69).

a commodity. More generally they may be used by any investor who seeks to immunize himself from changes in the important risk factors.

In Section III.2.5.3 we prove that a *minimum variance hedge ratio* can be estimated by regressing the log return on the spot r^S on the log return on the futures r^F. The regression model is a simple linear model of the form

$$r_t^S = \alpha + \beta r_t^F + \varepsilon_t. \tag{I.4.70}$$

This is estimated using high frequency (usually daily) data and the minimum variance hedge ratio is the beta that is estimated from this regression.

Unfortunately, a disproportionately large academic literature has been devoted to estimating minimum variance hedge ratios. Many hundreds of papers, often published in respectable journals, investigate the 'best' econometric methods for estimating these hedge ratios. For instance, time-varying hedge ratios have been based on GARCH models or even more complex statistical models such as genetic algorithms. Chen et al. (2003) review this literature.

But there are two major problems with this line of academic research. Firstly, the majority of papers have been applied to hedging with financial futures in very liquid markets, for instance to hedging a stock index with the index futures. However, these markets are now so efficient that there is no possibility of improving on the naïve hedge ratios, i.e. where the number of futures contracts exactly matches the spot exposure. See Section III.2.7 and Alexander and Barbosa (2007) for further details of this critique.

A second and far more serious problem is that short-term hedging, where the hedge is placed for only a few days or rebalanced very frequently, is not often used in practice. The only case where traders are interested in a short term hedge is when they have exceeded their exposure limits and therefore wish to place an overnight hedge to reduce their exposure. But in this case they are unlikely to hedge their full exposure and most traders employ a one-for-one hedge ratio rather than a minimum variance hedge ratio.

I.4.6.5 Trading on Regression Models

The fifth and final class of financial applications for regression analysis provides a fruitful avenue for research and development. Linear regression has long been used by mutual fund managers and other investors to track an index using a subset of its constituent assets, and now, with the remarkable growth in hedge funds over the last decade, there are many other opportunities for good econometricians to develop trading models based on regression. New markets, such as the market for variance swaps, also provide excellent opportunities for accurate econometric forecasts to make a profit.

A particularly hot topic of research at the time of writing is to forecast realized variance using high frequency data. We shall see in Section III.4.7 that the pay off to a variance swap depends on the difference between the realized variance over the period of the swap and the fixed swap rate that is agreed at inception. It is easier to forecast variance than to forecast returns, so there is considerable interest in developing high frequency econometric models that provide the most accurate forecasts of realized variance.

In Section II.5.4.6 we describe how to track an index using only a relatively small subset of assets. The *index tracking* regression model has the index return as the dependent variable, and the explanatory variables are the returns on the assets used to track the index. This can be extended to a regression model for *enhanced indexation* by replacing the dependent variable by the index return plus a fixed outperformance. A further extension is to *statistical arbitrage strategies* which take a long position on an enhanced indexation portfolio and a short position on the index futures. A case study on index tracking of the Dow Jones Industrial Average index is presented in Section II.5.4.7 where we use that fact that the tracking portfolio must be cointegrated with the index if the tracking error is to be stationary. In cointegrating regressions the dependent and independent variables are taken in levels rather than in returns.

Pairs trading is a simple example of an arbitrage between two instruments, or between two baskets of instruments. The book by Vidyamurthy (2004) is exclusively devoted to quantitative strategies for pairs trading. Provided the prices of two instruments are cointe-grated the spread will be mean reverting, and it is this mean reversion that traders seek to trade. Whilst it is rare to find a profitable pairs trade between individual securities, the rapid growth in new markets for volatility, weather, real estate, and carbon emissions opens up some new trading opportunities. For instance, in Section II.5.5.3 we describe a pairs trade between the volatility index futures that have recently started trading on the CBOE and Eurex.

Whenever a regression model is used to develop a trading strategy it is very important to backtest the model. *Backtesting* – which is termed *out-of-sample testing* or *post-sample prediction* by academics – is particularly important when considerable sums of money are placed on the output of a regression model. It is absolutely imperative to put the model through the rigorous testing procedure using a long period of historical data.

A simple backtest proceeds as follows:[28]

1. Estimate the regression model on an historical sample of data on the variables, saving subsequent historical data for testing the model.
2. Make an investment that is determined by the estimated model. For instance, in enhanced indexation we would take holdings in the assets that are prescribed by the estimated regression coefficients.
3. Hold the portfolio over the investment horizon. For instance, if trades are made only once a week the trading horizon will be 5 working days.
4. Record the P&L on the portfolio over the investment horizon, including the transactions costs from buying or selling the assets at the beginning of the period.
5. Roll the historical sample forward over the investment horizon. For instance, for a weekly trading strategy the sample will be rolled forward 5 days.
6. Return to step 1 and repeat until all the historical data are exhausted,
7. Then examine the characteristics of the time series of P&L that is generated.

What are the characteristics of P&L that we desire? For trading strategies we may look for strategies that produce a high Sharpe ratio, or that maximize some other risk adjusted performance measure, as outlined in Section I.6.5. But for a pure hedging strategy we should seek a hedge ratio that reduces risk alone, for instance one that minimizes the variance of the P&L.

---

[28] This is an example of the general backtests described in Section II.8.5.

I.4.7 SUMMARY AND CONCLUSIONS

This chapter has laid the foundations of regression analysis in the simple framework of linear models. We focus on the *ordinary least squares* (OLS) estimation criterion since this is optimal under fairly general circumstances when we have large samples of data, as is often the case in market risk analysis. In small samples the distribution of the error process should be investigated by examining the residuals of the fitted model. If these indicate that the error process is not an i.i.d. process then the *Gauss–Markov theorem,* which guarantees unbiasedness and efficiency of the OLS estimators when the errors are i.i.d., is no longer valid. And if the errors are not normally distributed then inference on the model parameters – hypothesis tests and confidence intervals for the true coefficients – is also invalid.

When the errors are not i.i.d. they may have *autocorrelation,* i.e. serial correlation over time, and/or they may have *heteroscedasticity,* i.e. non-constant variance. We have described the basic tests for autocorrelation and heteroscedasticity that are automatically output in econometrics packages. Most econometric packages also allow one to use standard errors on the coefficients that are robust to autocorrelation (*Newey–West standard errors*) and to heteroscedasticity (*White's standard errors*). These robust standard errors increase our reliance on the t ratios that indicate the significance of each explanatory variable.

When there are several coefficients to estimate, the hypotheses on their true values can be quite complex and require an estimate of the entire covariance matrix of the estimators, not just the estimated standard error of each estimator. And when two or more of the explanatory variables are highly correlated this affects the covariance matrix of the estimators, and it may become difficult to distinguish the separate effects of these variables. Then the regression parameter estimates can become unreliable: a problem which is termed *multicollinearity.* One way of dealing with multicollinearity is to use an *orthogonal regression.*

There are numerous applications of regression in finance. They can be used to test a theory, to determine optimal portfolio allocations, to implement a short-term hedge and to build a trading model for a hedge fund. We have provided only a brief survey of these applications here, but all these problems will be discussed in detail later in the book. Linear regression models also form the basis of more advanced econometric models that will be introduced in Volume II. In particular:

- Chapter II.4 deals with *generalized autoregressive conditional heteroscedasticity* (GARCH) models where the conditional mean equation is a simple linear regression and the GARCH process captures the conditional variance, i.e. the time variation of the variance of the error process.
- Chapter II.5 introduces *cointegration* which occurs when the prices of financial assets or interest rates are tied together over the long term, so that the spread is a stationary process. It is only when all the variables in a regression are cointegrated that we can use levels variables to estimate the model, because only in this case will the error process be stationary. Most other regression models are estimated using stationary variables, such as returns on financial assets or instruments or changes in interest rates, credit spreads or volatility.
- Chapter II.7 describes several advanced regression models, including *quantile regressions* where the OLS criterion is replaced by a different objective, which is often more suitable than OLS for risk management; *discrete choice models* that can be easily applied to estimate default probabilities from discrete data; and *Markov switching* models that capture the regime-specific behaviour that we observe in most financial markets.

I.5
Numerical Methods in Finance

I.5.1 INTRODUCTION

An *analytic solution* to a problem is a solution that can be expressed as an explicit formula in terms of well-known functions.[1] Numerical methods are applied when there is no analytic solution. To give just a few common examples:[2]

- The Black–Scholes–Merton (Black and Scholes, 1973; Merton, 1973) model gives an analytic solution for the price of a standard European option under certain (rather unrealistic) assumptions about the behaviour of asset prices. However, it is not possible to invert the Black–Scholes–Merton formula so that we obtain an *analytic* solution for the implied volatility of the option. In other words, the implied volatility is an *implicit function*, not an *explicit function* of the option price (and the other variables that go into the Black–Scholes–Merton formula such as the strike and the maturity of the option). So we use a numerical method to find the implied volatility of an option.
- The allocations to risky assets that give portfolios with the minimum possible risk (as measured by the portfolio volatility) can only be determined analytically when there are no specific constraints on the allocations such as 'no more than 5% of the capital should be allocated to US bonds'.
- The value at risk (VaR) of a portfolio has an analytic solution only under certain assumptions about the portfolio and its returns process. Otherwise we need to use a numerical method – usually simulation – to compute the VaR of a portfolio.
- The yield on a bond is the constant discount rate that, when applied to the future cash flows from the bond, gives its market price. Given the market price of a typical bond, we can only compute its yield using a numerical method.
- When we make realistic assumptions about the evolution of the underlying price, such as that the price process has a stochastic volatility, then the only way that we can find a theoretical price of an American option is using a numerical method such as finite differences or Monte Carlo simulations.

Numerical methods are *resolution techniques*, i.e. techniques for resolving a problem. They need to be applied to virtually all problems in financial analysis once we progress beyond the most basic assumptions about returns processes. The majority of problems in finance

---

[1] An *analytic expression* is a mathematical expression constructed using well-known functions that lend themselves readily to calculation. So also is a *closed-form expression*, but the class of analytic expressions tends to be wider. Closed-form expressions are defined in terms of elementary functions, which exclude infinite series, limits, and continued fractions. But special functions are permitted in analytic expressions. For instance, the Bessel functions and the gamma function are usually allowed, and so are infinite series and continued fractions. However, limits in general and integrals in particular are typically excluded. [Adapted from Wikipedia. See http://en.wikipedia.org/wiki/Analytic_expression.]

[2] There are a huge number of other examples of the applications of numerical methods in finance. This list could have run to several pages.

only have analytic solutions under very simple assumptions, and a very common simple assumption is that returns are generated by independent and identically distributed (i.i.d.) normal variables. However, it is an empirical fact that returns on financial assets and interest rates are not well modelled by independent and identical normal variables. Returns distributions are skewed and leptokurtic, and volatility appears to arrive in 'clusters'. And when we make more realistic assumptions about the data generation processes of returns it is typical that no analytic solution will exist. So we must use a numerical method to resolve the problem.

Here (and many times in later volumes) we shall be applying iterative algorithms to resolve a number of problems, using Excel's *Goal Seek* or, more frequently, the *Solver* optimizer. For instance, in this chapter we use Goal Seek to find the implied volatility of an option and the yield on a bond. But the Excel Solver is a more powerful and more flexible optimizer that is used in numerous other applications in almost every chapter in this and later volumes. For instance, in Chapter III.1 we use Solver to find a cash flow mapping that leaves certain characteristics of a cash flow invariant; in Chapter II.4 we use Solver to estimate the parameters of a GARCH model; and in Chapter IV.3 we use it to estimate the parameters of the Johnson distribution.

This chapter introduces the most common numerical resolution methods used in finance. Section I.5.2 introduces the concept of *iteration* that forms the basis of numerical *optimization* algorithms. We begin at an *initial* or *starting value* for the solution, which is just a guess, and the numerical optimizer should iterate towards the real solution, i.e. it should get closer and closer to the real solution at each step of the algorithm. Section I.5.3 introduces some elementary methods for *interpolation* and *extrapolation*. These are methods that 'fill in the gaps' where data are missing. They are required in many situations: fitting yield curves and implied volatility surfaces being two common examples. Section I.5.4 covers the *optimization* problems that arise in three broad areas of financial analysis: the efficient allocation of resources and applications to portfolio management on capital allocation in particular; the calibration of a model's parameters to market data; and, more generally, the fitting of an assumed statistical distribution to a given data set, which is commonly based on the maximization of a likelihood function.

Section I.5.5 deals with *finite difference* approximations to the values of the first and second derivatives of a function of one or more variables. Finite differences are used to estimate the 'Greeks' of exotic or path-dependent options, to calibrate a local volatility surface, and in any other situation where an analytic formula for the derivative is not available.

A *lattice* or 'tree' is a discretization of time and space that is used to simplify models for the evolution of asset prices and derivative instrument prices. In Section I.5.6 we explain how lattice methods are applied to approximate the price of path-dependent options. For example, we apply a *binomial tree* to price European and American options.

Section I.5.7 describes algorithms for *simulating* prices and returns on financial assets or interest rates. Simulation is a method of 'last resort' because it can always provide a solution, and it is commonly applied to problems where numerical optimization or discretization fails. Simulation is used many times later on in the book, for instance to measure the risk of a barrier option, to estimate the value at risk of an options portfolio and to estimate a portfolio's 'worst case' loss. Finally, Section I.5.8 summarizes and concludes. As usual, illustrations of each method are provided in the associated Excel workbook. Note that it is inadvisable to keep a spreadsheet with simulations open when using the Excel Solver, because the Solver will repeat the simulations at each iteration.

I.5.2   ITERATION

Finding the roots of a non-linear equation $f(x) = 0$ is a common problem in financial analysis. For instance:

- in Chapter III.1 we find the yield y on a bond as a root of the equation $PV(y) - P_{Market} = 0$, where $PV(y)$ and P_{Market} denote the theoretical and market prices of the bond;
- in Chapter III.4 we find the option implied volatility σ as a root of $f_{BSM}(\sigma) - f_{Market} = 0$, where f_{BSM} and f_{Market} denote the Black–Scholes–Merton model price and the observed market price of an option.

We also need to solve an equation of the form $f(x) = 0$ whenever we find the stationary points of a function $g(x)$. This is because the first order conditions for a local maximum or minimum require setting the first derivative to zero (see Section I.1.3.4) and so in this case $f(x) = g'(x) = 0$.

Root-finding problems are solved numerically using an *iterative algorithm*. That is, we find a sequence of values $\{x_1, x_2, \ldots, x_n, x_{n+1}, \ldots\}$ such that $f(x_n)$ gets closer and closer to 0 as n increases. In the following we introduce the iterative algorithms that form the basis of standard optimization routines in Excel and other statistical packages.

I.5.2.1   Method of Bisection

This is a simplistic but slow iterative algorithm. To start we need to find two values of x, labelled x_1 and x_2, such that either $f(x_1) < 0, f(x_2) > 0$ or $f(x_1) > 0, f(x_2) < 0$. In other words, $f(x_1)$ and $f(x_2)$ must have different signs. Set $I = [x_1, x_2]$. 'Bisecting' the interval I means that we take the mid-point $\frac{1}{2}(x_1 + x_2)$. Figure I.5.1 illustrates how the method repeatedly bisects an interval, each time replacing the interval with another that has half the width. This way we 'home in' on a root of the function $f(x)$ provided it is continuous: if the function has a jump the method of bisection is not guaranteed to work.

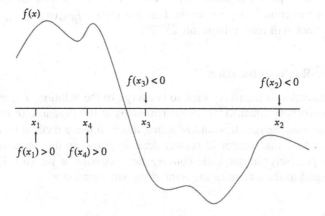

Figure I.5.1   Method of bisection

Without loss of generality we assume $x_1 < x_2$ and $f(x_1) > 0, f(x_2) < 0$. If the opposite inequalities hold then we simply find the root of $-f(x) = 0$, which is obviously the same as the root of $f(x) = 0$. The formal algorithm is as follows:

1. Bisect the interval I and set the midpoint to be x_3.
2. If $f(x_3) = 0$ then stop, we are done.
3. If $f(x_3) > 0$ set $I = [x_3, x_2]$.
4. If $f(x_3) < 0$ set $I = [x_1, x_3]$.
5. Bisect the new interval I and set the midpoint to be x_4.
6. If $f(x_4) = 0$ then stop.
7. If $f(x_4) > 0$ set $I = [x_4, x_n]$, where x_n was the previous interval bound for which $f(x_n) < 0$.
8. If $f(x_4) < 0$ set $I = [x_n, x_4]$, where x_n was the previous interval bound for which $f(x_n) > 0$.
9. Go to step 5 and repeat, i.e. *iterate*, steps 5–8 until we eventually stop at step 6.

Before we proceed to a practical example, it is useful to introduce some general terminology that is applied to iterative methods. The *objective function* is the function for which we wish to find a root, or more generally the function we wish to optimize. The *tolerance level* is related to the *criterion for convergence* of the algorithm. An algorithm to find the roots of an equation $f(x) = 0$ will be deemed to have converged to the solution $x = x^*$ when $|f(x^*)| < T$, where T is the level of tolerance. For instance, if the tolerance level is 0.0001 then the method of bisection will be deemed to have converged to a solution x^* provided that $|f(x^*)| < 0.0001$.

Excel uses the method of bisection in its *Goal Seek* tool. Goal Seek is a very basic algorithm that does not allow you to change convergence criteria or levels of tolerance. The following example uses Goal Seek to find the implied volatility of an option. This is the volatility that is implicit in the observed market price – the higher the market price of the option, the higher the volatility.[3]

EXAMPLE I.5.1: EXCEL'S GOAL SEEK

A call option has a market price of 4 when the underlying price is 100. The strike of the option is 98 and the maturity is 30 days. What is the implied volatility of this option?

SOLUTION   We use the Goal Seek function from the Tools menu with the settings shown in Figure I.5.2. The objective function is just the difference between the two prices. That is, the method of bisection is applied to the function $g(\sigma) = f_{BSM}(\sigma) - f_{Market}$. Readers can verify that Goal Seek will return the result 23.72%.

I.5.2.2   Newton–Raphson Iteration

The method of bisection is relatively slow to converge to the solution. The precision of the solution is approximately equal to the number of steps in the iteration, in other words, the method has *linear convergence*. It would be much faster to use a method that has *quadratic convergence*, i.e. where the number of correct decimal places in the iteration is doubled at each step. More precisely, in quadratic convergence the error at the $(n+1)$th iteration is approximately equal to the square of the error at the nth iteration.

---

[3] See Section III.3.3 for a detailed explanation.

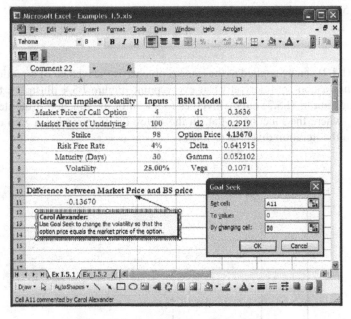

Figure I.5.2   Setting Excel's Goal Seek

We now describe an iterative method called *Newton–Raphson iteration* that has quadratic convergence and which therefore converges to the solution much more quickly than the method of bisection. Let $f(x)$ be a continuous and differentiable function. The slope of the tangent to the function at the point x_n is

$$f'(x_n) = \frac{f(x_n)}{x_n - x_{n+1}}, \tag{I.5.1}$$

where x_{n+1} is the point where the tangent cuts the x-axis.[4] This is illustrated in Figure I.5.3.

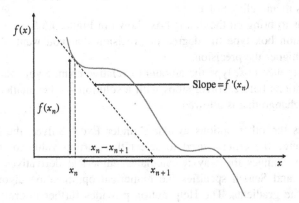

Figure I.5.3   Newton–Raphson iteration

---

[4] For simplicity have used $f'(x_n)$ to denote the derivative of $f(x)$ evaluated at the point x_n.

Turning (I.5.1) around gives the Newton–Raphson iterative scheme:

$$x_{n+1} = x_n - \frac{f(x_n)}{f'(x_n)}. \tag{I.5.2}$$

The iteration (I.5.2) can be applied to the same problems as the method of bisection, provided the function has a non-zero derivative at every point. Figure I.5.4 illustrates the fact that repeated application of (I.5.2) only converges to a root of the function if the iteration leads to no point x_n where the function is flat. In the figure the function has a zero derivative at the point x_4 so the iteration diverges to infinity.

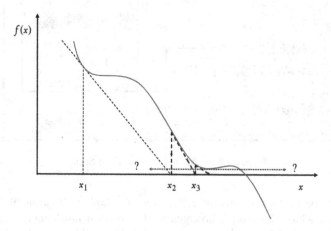

Figure I.5.4   Convergence of Newton–Raphson scheme

Excel *Solver* uses a scheme similar to (I.5.2) which also allows the user to set the precision and convergence criteria, as follows:

- On the Tools menu, click Solver.
- Click Options to bring up the dialog box shown in Figure I.5.5.
- In the Precision box type the degree of precision that you want — the smaller the number, the higher the precision.
- In the Convergence box, type the amount of relative change you want to allow in the last five iterations before Solver stops with a solution — the smaller the number, the less relative change that is allowed.

Figure I.5.5 shows the other options available under Excel Solver: the Estimates option allows one to change the criteria used to select the starting value for the iteration; the Derivatives option changes the way it calculates numerical derivatives using finite difference methods;[5] and Search specifies the numerical optimization algorithm, a Newton method or conjugate gradients. The Help button provides further information on Solver's settings.

---

[5] See Section I.5.5.

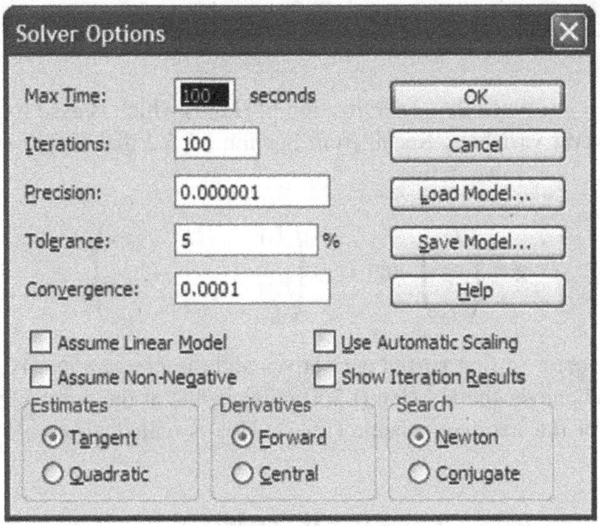

Figure I.5.5   Solver options

EXAMPLE I.5.2: USING SOLVER TO FIND A BOND YIELD[6]

A 4-year bond with annual coupons of 5% has a market price of 92. Find its yield.

SOLUTION   From Section III.1.4.1 we know that the present value of the income received on the bond is given by

$$PV(y) = \sum_{i=1}^{4} \frac{5}{(1+y)^i} + \frac{100}{(1+y)^4},\tag{I.5.3}$$

where y is the yield. In the spreadsheet for this example we set this present value equal to the market price by changing the yield, using the Solver settings shown in the spreadsheet. In the Solver dialog box the target cell contains the objective function, which can be maximized, minimized or set equal to a fixed value such as 0. The cells that will be changed are the variables of the function that we wish to optimize over. We can also apply constraints to the objective function, as explained in Section I.5.4 below. The result is a yield of 7.38%.

I.5.2.3   Gradient Methods

Newton–Raphson iteration may also be used to find the stationary points of a function by applying the iteration to the function $f'(x)$. Rewriting (I.5.2) with $f'(x)$ in place of $f(x)$ gives the iteration

$$x_{n+1} = x_n - \frac{f'(x_n)}{f''(x_n)}.\tag{I.5.4}$$

---

[6] Excel provides a function (called RATE) that is specifically designed to calculate the yield on an annuity. The RATE function may also be used for this problem and we use this function in Chapter III.1, but only when calculating the yield on a standard bond. More general yield calculations can be done using Solver.

Provided the function is twice continuously differentiable and the second derivative $f''(x)$ is nowhere zero, this will converge to a point where $f'(x) = 0$, i.e. a stationary point rather than a root of $f(x)$.

In this section we introduce the generalization of (I.5.4) which is used to find local optima of functions of several variables. Recall from Section I.1.5.2 that if $f(\mathbf{x})$ is a function of m variables $\mathbf{x} = (x_1, \ldots, x_m)'$ we define

$$\mathbf{g} = \begin{pmatrix} f_1 \\ \vdots \\ f_m \end{pmatrix} \text{ and } \mathbf{H} = \begin{pmatrix} f_{11} & \cdots & f_{1m} \\ \vdots & \ddots & \vdots \\ f_{m1} & \cdots & f_{mm} \end{pmatrix} \tag{I.5.5}$$

to be the *gradient* vector of first partial derivatives and the *Hessian* matrix of second partial derivatives of f. Whenever the Hessian (I.5.5) is invertible at the point $\mathbf{x}_n$ we can specify a multivariate form of the iterative scheme (I.5.4). This is called *Newton's method* and it is specified by:

$$\mathbf{x}_{n+1} = \mathbf{x}_n - \mathbf{H}^{-1}(\mathbf{x}_n)\mathbf{g}(\mathbf{x}_n). \tag{I.5.6}$$

Because the iteration is based on the gradient vector, Newton's method is an example of a general class of optimization algorithms that are called *gradient methods*.

The simplest gradient method has the form

$$\mathbf{x}_{n+1} = \mathbf{x}_n - s\, \mathbf{g}(\mathbf{x}_n), \tag{I.5.7}$$

where s is a positive constant called the *step length*. There is a straightforward intuition for a routine of the form (I.5.7). Imagine you are climbing a multi-dimensional hill and are currently at the point with coordinates $\mathbf{x}_n$. To get to the top of the hill as fast as possible you should always take your next step along the path that has the steepest gradient. In (I.5.7) each step is assumed to be of the same length, but naturally you may prefer to take smaller steps when the gradient is steep. Such routines are possible by introducing a *variable* step length s_n and setting

$$\mathbf{x}_{n+1} = \mathbf{x}_n - s_n\, \mathbf{g}(\mathbf{x}_n). \tag{I.5.8}$$

However, the iterations (I.5.7) and (I.5.8) have only linear convergence. To speed up the convergence we could use

$$\mathbf{x}_{n+1} = \mathbf{x}_n - \Theta_n\, \mathbf{g}(\mathbf{x}_n), \tag{I.5.9}$$

where Θ_n is a judiciously chosen $m \times m$ matrix. Newton's method (I.5.6) is a special case of (I.5.9) where Θ_n is the inverse of the Hessian matrix of the function, evaluated at the point $\mathbf{x}_n$ provided this inverse exists. Another special case of (I.5.9) is the *modified Newton method* which adds a variable step length to (I.5.6), i.e. the iteration is

$$\mathbf{x}_{n+1} = \mathbf{x}_n - s_n\, \mathbf{H}^{-1}(\mathbf{x}_n)\mathbf{g}(\mathbf{x}_n). \tag{I.5.10}$$

Although Newton's method and its modification have quadratic convergence, there is a strong condition for convergence, i.e. that the Hessian be invertible everywhere, and this may not be the case. And for high-dimensional systems the calculation of just the Hessian can take considerable computation time, let alone finding its inverse. Some standard optimization routines use a numerical method called *conjugate gradients*, which provide relatively fast and accurate means of computing the Hessian.[7] If the Hessian is not invertible, *quasi-Newton methods* use an approximation to the Hessian that is invertible. Both conjugate gradients and a quasi-Newton method are used by Excel Solver, with the quasi-Newton method as the default option.

I.5.3   INTERPOLATION AND EXTRAPOLATION

Interpolation is a special sort of curve fitting that requires the curve to pass exactly through the given data. The aim is to infer the values of missing data either within the range of existing data (interpolation) or outside the experienced range (extrapolation).

Suppose the 1-year spot rate is 4% and the 2-year spot rate is 6%. Is our best guess of the 18-month interest rate then 5%? It depends on the interpolation method that we use. If we use *linear interpolation* then yes, the 18-month rate should be exactly half way between the 1-year and the 2-year rates. Similarly, the rate at 15 months would be $3/4 \times 4\% + 1/4 \times 6\% = 5.5\%$. But other methods of interpolation are possible and introducing these is one aim of this section.

An associated problem is that of *extrapolation*. What is our best guess of data that are outside our range of observations? For instance, suppose the monthly spot rates from 1 month to 36 months are as shown in Figure I.5.6. How should we 'extrapolate' these data to obtain the spot rates up to 48 months? Since the yield curve is not a straight line, we need to fit a quadratic or higher order polynomial in order to extrapolate to the longer maturities.

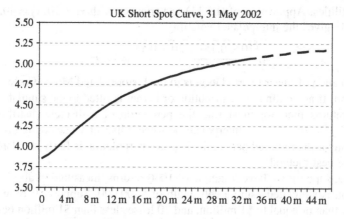

Figure I.5.6   Extrapolation of a yield curve

I.5.3.1   Linear and Bilinear Interpolation

Given two data points, $\{x_1, y_1\}$ and $\{x_2, y_2\}$ with $x_1 < x_2$, linear interpolation gives the value of y at some point $x \in [x_1, x_2]$ as

$$y = \frac{(x_2 - x) y_1 + (x - x_1) y_2}{(x_2 - x_1)}. \qquad (I.5.11)$$

---

[7] See http://en.wikipedia.org/wiki/Conjugate_gradient_method.

For an example of linear interpolation, consider the construction of a constant maturity 30-day futures series from traded futures. On each day in the historical period we take the price P_1 of the *prompt futures*, i.e. the futures contract with expiry date less than or equal to 30 days ahead, and the price P_2 of the first futures with expiry date more than 30 days ahead. If n_1 is the number of days to expiry of the prompt futures contract and n_2 is the number of days to expiry of the next futures contract, then the linearly interpolated 30-day futures price on that day is

$$\frac{(n_2 - 30) P_1 + (30 - n_1) P_2}{n_2 - n_1}.$$

For instance, if the prompt futures price is 10 and it has 5 days until expiry, and the next futures price is 12 and it has 36 days to expiry, then the constant maturity futures price is

$$\frac{6 \times 10 + 25 \times 12}{31} = 11.613.$$

Similarly, linear interpolation can be applied to construct constant maturity implied volatility series from the implied volatilities of options of different maturities. The next example illustrates this application.

EXAMPLE I.5.3: INTERPOLATING IMPLIED VOLATILITY

Suppose we have two options with the same strike but different maturities: option 1 has maturity 10 days and option 2 has maturity 40 days. If the implied volatility of option 1 is 15% and the implied volatility of option 2 is 10%, what is the linearly interpolated implied volatility of an option with the same strike as options 1 and 2 but with maturity 30 days?

SOLUTION   Under the assumption that log returns are i.i.d. it is variances that are additive, not volatilities. Application of (I.5.11) to variances with $x_1 = 10$, $x_2 = 40$, $x = 30$, $y_1 = 0.15^2$, $y_2 = 0.1^2$ gives the interpolated volatility

$$\sqrt{\frac{10 \times 0.15^2 + 20 \times 0.1^2}{30}} = 11.9\%.$$

Another application of linear interpolation is to the historical and Monte Carlo approaches to VaR estimation. If no continuous distribution or kernel is fitted to the simulated distribution of portfolio returns then we must find the percentile of a discrete distribution. In that case we will, typically, need to interpolate between adjacent values of returns to obtain a precise estimate of the required percentile. Linear interpolation is fairly standard, though not necessarily the best method.

For instance, suppose we have a sample of 1000 returns, measured in absolute terms, and the distribution is simulated using a cell width of $100,000. Suppose there are five largest losses, greater than or equal to $1 million, and 20 losses less than $1 million but greater than or equal to $0.9 million. How do we interpolate to find the 1% VaR? With 5 out of 1000 losses at $1 million or more, and 25 out of 1000 losses at $0.9 million or more, we know that the 0.5% VaR is $1 million and the 2.5% VaR is $0.9 million. The 1% VaR therefore lies in between $1 million and $0.9 million, and is closer to $1 million than to $0.9 million. In fact, as shown in Figure I.5.7, the linear interpolation method gives a 1% VaR of $975,000.

EXAMPLE I.5.4: BILINEAR INTERPOLATION

Suppose the closing prices of 1-month and 6-month futures on Monday were 66 and 67 and on Thursday were 60 and 64. What is the linearly interpolated price of 4-month futures on Tuesday?

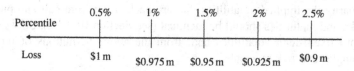

Figure I.5.7 Linear interpolation on percentiles

SOLUTION Here linear interpolation is performed in two stages: first we use linear interpolation to find the prices of the 1-month and 6-month futures on Tuesday, then we use linear interpolation again to find the price of the 4-month futures on Tuesday. Let x, y and z be the prices of the 1-month, 4-month and 6-month futures, and use the subscripts 1 and 2 to denote Monday and Thursday. Then $x_1 = 66$, $x_2 = 60$, $z_1 = 67$, $z_2 = 64$. By linear interpolation over the futures maturities

$$y_1 = \frac{2 \times 66 + 3 \times 67}{5} = 66.6,$$

$$y_2 = \frac{2 \times 60 + 3 \times 64}{5} = 62.4.$$

Using linear interpolation again, now over time, the 4-month futures price on Tuesday is

$$\frac{2 \times 66.6 + 62.4}{3} = 65.2.$$

I.5.3.2 Polynomial Interpolation: Application to Currency Options

Linear and bilinear interpolations are simple but they provide only a crude approximation to the true result because they just consider the two adjacent data points. Looking at more than two points can give a better indication of whether the function we are trying to interpolate is really linear, or whether for instance a quadratic or cubic function would provide a better approximation.

Suppose we are given three data points. Then there is a unique quadratic function that passes through these points and finding this function will allow us to interpolate and extrapolate the data. Similarly, if we have five data points we can find a unique polynomial of degree 4 that passes through all five points. This type of problem is useful for currency options, where prices are quoted in terms of the implied volatilities of certain standard options strategies and usually only three or five implied volatilities are available.

We now provide a very brief definition of these standard options strategies. Readers are referred to Section III.3.5 for more complete details. The most liquid contracts are at-the-money (ATM) forward, '25-delta' and '75-delta' European calls and puts. Much of the trading is on straddles, strangles and risk reversals:

- A *straddle* is a long call and a long put of the same strike, usually ATM. Straddles are quoted as the ATM forward volatility which is the same for the call and the put. This we denote by σ_{ATM} or σ_{50}, since the ATM forward has a delta of 50%.
- A *strangle* is a long out-of-the-money (OTM) put and a long OTM call. Strangles are usually quoted as the spread between the average of the implied volatilities of the put and call components and the ATM forward volatility, and we denote this σ_{ST}.
- A *risk reversal* is a long OTM call and a short OTM put. Risk reversal prices are quoted as the spread between the call and the put volatilities, and are denoted σ_{RR}.

By put–call parity the implied volatilities that are backed out from call and put options of the same strike and maturities should be identical (see Section III.3.3.2). So we can convert everything into fixed delta volatilities and, from the above definitions of the quotes for straddles, strangles and risk reversals,

$$\sigma_{RR,25} = \sigma_{25} - \sigma_{75},$$

$$\sigma_{ST,25} = \tfrac{1}{2}\left(\sigma_{25} + \sigma_{75}\right) - \sigma_{50}.$$

Hence given three quotes on the ATM forward straddle, 25-delta strangle and 25-delta risk reversal, we obtain three implied volatilities, i.e. σ_{50} and

$$\sigma_{25} = \sigma_{50} + \sigma_{ST,25} + \tfrac{1}{2}\sigma_{RR,25},$$

$$\sigma_{75} = \sigma_{50} + \sigma_{ST,25} - \tfrac{1}{2}\sigma_{RR,25}.$$

(I.5.12)

We apply the above in the next example, which illustrates how to interpolate and extrapolate the smile by fitting a quadratic curve to currency option data.

EXAMPLE I.5.5: FITTING A 25-DELTA CURRENCY OPTION SMILE

Fit a smile to the following quotes and hence interpolate the 10-delta and 90-delta volatilities:

ATM forward straddle:	18%
25-delta straddle:	2%
25-delta risk reversal:	1%

SOLUTION   By (I.5.12), $\sigma_{25} = 20.5\%$ and $\sigma_{75} = 19.5\%$. We therefore require a, b and c such that the quadratic $f(x) = ax^2 + bx + c$ passes through the points

$$f(0.25) = 0.205; \quad f(0.50) = 0.18; \quad f(0.75) = 0.195.$$

This leads to the equations

$$a + 4b + 16c = 16 \times 0.205,$$

$$a + 2b + 4c = 4 \times 0.18,$$

$$9a + 12b + 16c = 16 \times 0.195.$$

In the spreadsheet for this example we find the solution

$$a = 0.320, b = -0.340, c = 0.270.$$

Figure I.5.8 plots the fitted implied volatility smile and from this we can read off the interpolated values of the 10-delta and the 90-delta volatilities as 23.9% and 22.3%, respectively.

In general, fitting the quadratic $f(x) = ax^2 + bx + c$ through three points,

$$f(0.25) = \sigma_{25}, \quad f(0.50) = \sigma_{50}, \quad f(0.75) = \sigma_{75},$$

gives the following solution for the coefficients:

$$\begin{pmatrix} a \\ b \\ c \end{pmatrix} = \begin{pmatrix} 1 & 4 & 16 \\ 1 & 2 & 4 \\ 9 & 12 & 16 \end{pmatrix}^{-1} \begin{pmatrix} 16\sigma_{25} \\ 4\sigma_{50} \\ 16\sigma_{75} \end{pmatrix}.$$

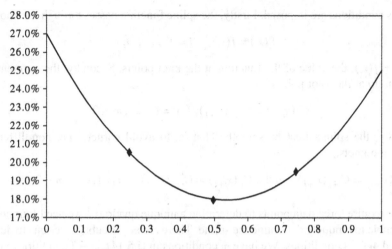

Figure I.5.8   Fitting a currency smile

But when only three implied volatilities are available a quadratic interpolation tends to underestimate the market quotes at more extreme delta values. Hence readers are recommended to use the *vanna–volga* interpolation method described in Castagna and Mercurio (2007).

If further data on 10-delta strangles and risk reversals are available, two more points can be added to the implied volatility smile:

$$\sigma_{10} = \sigma_{50} + \sigma_{ST,10} + \tfrac{1}{2}\sigma_{RR,10},$$
$$\sigma_{90} = \sigma_{50} + \sigma_{ST,10} - \tfrac{1}{2}\sigma_{RR,10}. \tag{I.5.13}$$

A more precise interpolation and extrapolation method is then to fit a *quartic* polynomial to the ATM, 25-delta and 10-delta data: this is left as an exercise to the reader.

I.5.3.3   Cubic Splines: Application to Yield Curves

Spline interpolation is a special type of *piecewise* polynomial interpolation that is usually more accurate than ordinary polynomial interpolation, even when the spline polynomials have quite low degree. In this section we consider cubic splines, since these are the lowest degree splines with attractive properties and are in use by many financial institutions, for instance for yield curve fitting and for volatility smile surface interpolation.

We aim to interpolate a function $f(x)$ using a cubic spline. First a series of *knot points* $\{x_1, \ldots, x_m\}$ are fixed. Then a cubic polynomial is fitted between consecutive knot points. We denote by $C_i(x)$ the cubic polynomial in the segment $[x_i, x_{i+1})$, and joining these together gives the spline function:

$$S(x) = \begin{cases} C_1(x), & x \in [x_1, x_2), \\ \vdots \\ C_{m-1}(x), & x \in [x_{m-1}, x_m]. \end{cases}$$

Various conditions are imposed. Firstly, the spline function passes through the knot points:

$$S(x_i) = f(x_i), \quad i = 1, \ldots, m. \tag{I.5.14}$$

We set $y_i = f(x_i)$, the value of the function at the knot points. Secondly, the segments of the spline join up at the knot points:

$$C_i(x_{i+1}) = C_{i+1}(x_{i+1}), \quad i = 1, \ldots, m-2. \tag{I.5.15}$$

And thirdly, the spline must be smooth. That is, to avoid corners (i.e. non-differentiable points) at the knots:

$$C_i'(x_{i+1}) = C_{i+1}'(x_{i+1}) \quad \text{and} \quad C_i''(x_{i+1}) = C_{i+1}''(x_{i+1}), \quad i = 1, \ldots, m-2. \tag{I.5.16}$$

Just as we require three data points to determine a unique quadratic, we need four conditions for each cubic to uniquely determine the spline. There are $m-1$ cubic functions to determine, so we need $4m-4$ conditions. We have m conditions in (I.5.14), $m-2$ conditions in (I.5.15) and $2(m-2)$ conditions in (I.5.16). That is, we have $4m-6$ conditions. The two further conditions depend on the methodology chosen.

For instance, the *natural* spline imposes the condition that the spline has zero curvature at each of the end points:

$$C_1''(x_1) = C_{m-1}''(x_m) = 0. \tag{I.5.17}$$

The natural spline provides a straightforward interpolation method as follows: First find the distance between the knot points. Denote these distances $h_i = x_{i+1} - x_i$, $i = 1, \ldots, m-1$. Then solve the following iterative equations for $A_1, \ldots, A_m$:

$$h_i A_{i-1} + 2(h_{i-1} + h_i)A_i + h_i A_{i+1} = B_i - B_{i-1},$$

$$\text{where} \quad B_i = \frac{y_{i+1} - y_i}{h_i} \quad \text{and} \quad A_1 = A_m = 0, \tag{I.5.18}$$

and set

$$\alpha_i = \frac{A_{i+1}}{h_i}, \quad \beta_i = \frac{A_i}{h_i}, \quad \gamma_i = \frac{y_{i+1}}{h_i} - A_{i+1}h_i, \quad \delta_i = \frac{y_i}{h_i} - A_i h_i. \tag{I.5.19}$$

Then the cubic polynomials in the spline are given by

$$C_i = \alpha_i(x - x_i)^3 + \beta_i(x_{i+1} - x)^3 + \gamma_i(x - x_i) + \delta_i(x_{i+1} - x). \tag{I.5.20}$$

It is straightforward (but tedious) to verify that the above satisfy conditions (I.5.14) – (I.5.17) for the natural cubic spline.

EXAMPLE I.5.6: INTERPOLATION WITH CUBIC SPLINES

Use a natural cubic spline to interpolate the following forward rate curve from 6-monthly to monthly maturities:

Months x_i	6	12	18	24	30	36	42	48	54	60
% Rate y_i	3.5	3	3.4	3.6	3.8	3.7	3.4	3.3	3	2.8

SOLUTION   We start with forward interest rates that are 6 months apart, so, measuring in months, $x_1 = 6, x_2 = 12, \ldots, x_{10} = 60$, and each $h_i = 6$. Since $h_i = 6$, the equations (I.5.18) to be solved for $\{A_1, \ldots, A_{10}\}$ are easy to write down:

$$A_1 + 4A_2 + A_3 = B_2 - B_1$$

$$\vdots$$

$$A_8 + 4A_9 + A_{10} = B_9 - B_8.$$

The right-hand sides above are obtained in the spreadsheet, using (I.5.18). Since $A_1 = A_m = 0$ the coefficient matrix for the above equations is

$$\begin{pmatrix} 4 & 1 & 0 & 0 & \ldots & \\ 1 & 4 & 1 & 0 & \ldots & \\ 0 & 1 & 4 & 1 & \ldots & \\ \vdots & \vdots & \vdots & & \ddots & \vdots \\ \ldots & \ldots & 0 & 1 & & 4 \end{pmatrix}$$

Inverting this and multiplying by the vectors on the right-hand side gives the solution:

A_2	0.007130
A_3	−0.003521
A_4	0.001398
A_5	−0.002070
A_6	−0.001452
A_7	0.002324
A_8	−0.002286
A_9	0.001266

Now using (I.5.19) we obtain the following cubic spline coefficients:

Spline	Alpha	Beta	Gamma	Delta
C_1	0.0012	0	0.4572	0.5833
C_2	−0.0006	0.0012	0.5878	0.4572
C_3	0.0002	−0.0006	0.5916	0.5878
C_4	−0.0003	0.0002	0.6458	0.5916
C_5	−0.0002	−0.0003	0.6254	0.6458
C_6	0.0004	−0.0002	0.5527	0.6254
C_7	−0.0004	0.0004	0.5637	0.5527
C_8	0.0002	−0.0004	0.4924	0.5637
C_9	0	0.0002	0.4667	0.4924
C_{10}	0	0	0	0.4667

Figure I.5.9 shows the cubic spline interpolated curve.

Splines are also used for *yield curve fitting* where the problem is to find the best fitting curve to interest rates on a variety of different liquid market instruments of similar maturities, including forward rate agreements and various money market rates. However, applying

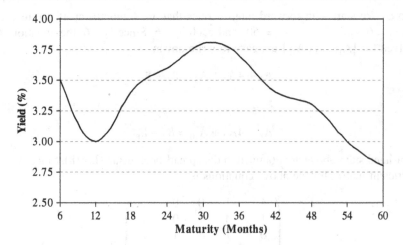

Figure I.5.9   A cubic spline interpolated yield curve

natural cubic splines to interest rates themselves is not necessarily the best approach. The best fit is often obtained by applying *basis splines* to the discount rates associated with each interest rate.[8]

Another common application of cubic splines is to the interpolation and extrapolation of an *implied volatility surface*. Liquid market prices are often available only for options that are within 10% of at-the-money and with a maturity no more than 1 year. However, hedging costs are factored into traders' options prices, and to assess these costs one has to consider many possible future values of delta. But delta depends on the implied volatility. Hence, from the relatively sparse market data available, one must interpolate and extrapolate the implied volatility surface at extreme strikes. Instead of natural cubic splines we could use basis splines or *Hermite polynomials*.[9] Naturally, if only a small amount of market data is available one could obtain quite different interpolated volatility surfaces, depending on the method used.

I.5.4   OPTIMIZATION

Optimization is the process of finding a maximum or minimum value of a function. In constrained optimization problems the possible optima are constrained to lie within a certain feasible set. One of the most famous optimization problems in finance has an analytic solution under standard assumptions. This is the *Markowitz problem* – to find a portfolio that is expected to deliver a minimum level of return whilst also minimizing risk – which is discussed in detail in Section I.6.3. But few other financial optimization problems have analytic solutions and in the vast majority of financial applications we need to use a numerical

---

[8] Basis splines – commonly called B *splines* – are splines where each spline function is not a cubic but is a weighted sum of certain pre-defined *basis functions*. Discount rates are defined in Section III.1.2.
[9] Wikipedia has a good entry on Hermite polynomials.

method, often a gradient algorithm, to find the maximum or minimum value of the function in the feasible domain.

Other financial applications of constrained optimization include the calibration of stochastic volatility option pricing models using a least squares algorithm and the estimation of the parameters of a statistical distribution. In the majority of cases no analytic solution exists and we must find a solution using a numerical method.

I.5.4.1 Least Squares Problems

Many statistical optimization problems involve changing the parameters of an objective function so that the function fits a given set of data as closely as possible. In other words, we want to find the *best fit* to our data. The least squares problem falls into this class, and the objective function is the *mean square error* (or the *root mean square error*) between the actual data and the fitted values of the data.

We have already encountered a least squares problem. In the previous chapter we applied the ordinary least squares algorithm to fit a linear regression model to historical data. We found an analytic solution to the problem in this case but in many other applications, such as calibrating an option pricing model, we need to fit much more complex functional forms than a linear model. And then only a numerical method will provide a solution.

Note that we tend to use the terminology *estimation* when we are finding the parameters of a discrete time model and *calibration* when we are finding the parameters of a continuous time model. For instance, by finding the best fit to historical time series data we 'estimate' the parameters of a GARCH model. On the other hand, we 'calibrate' the parameters of the Heston (1993) option pricing model by finding the best fit to a current 'snapshot' of market data, such as an implied volatility smile.

Let $\mathbf{y} = (y_1, \ldots, y_n)'$ denote the data that we want to fit;[10] $\boldsymbol{\theta}$ denote the parameters that we want to estimate/calibrate to the data; and $f(\boldsymbol{\theta}|\mathbf{x}) = (f_1, \ldots, f_n)'$ denote the function that we want to fit to $\mathbf{y}$, which depends on the parameters $\boldsymbol{\theta}$ and possibly other data $\mathbf{x}$.[11] The calibration (or estimation) problem is to find the parameters $\boldsymbol{\theta}$ so that each f_i is as close as possible to y_i, for $i = 1, 2, \ldots, n$. In other words, we want $f(\boldsymbol{\theta}|\mathbf{x})$ to be as close as possible to our data $\mathbf{y}$. The *error function* is defined as

$$\boldsymbol{\varepsilon}(\boldsymbol{\theta}|\mathbf{x}) = \mathbf{y} - f(\boldsymbol{\theta}|\mathbf{x}).$$

Now the general *least squares objective* for making $f(\boldsymbol{\theta}|\mathbf{x})$ as close as possible to $\mathbf{y}$ is

$$\min_{\boldsymbol{\theta}} \left[\boldsymbol{\varepsilon}(\boldsymbol{\theta}|\mathbf{x})' \boldsymbol{\varepsilon}(\boldsymbol{\theta}|\mathbf{x}) \right] \text{ such that } h(\boldsymbol{\theta}) \leq 0, \tag{I.5.21}$$

where $h(\boldsymbol{\theta})$ are the constraints on the values of the parameters, if these are necessary. In other words, (I.5.21) requires us to *minimize the sum of the squared errors* between the observed and fitted values.

An analytic solution to (I.5.21) rarely exists when f is not a linear function. In the general case we can minimize the sum of squared errors by applying an iterative scheme based on a

---

[10] This may be a time series such as daily returns on the FTSE100 index between 3 January 2005 and 31 December 2007, or a cross section such as prices or implied volatilities of all the options on the FTSE100 on 31 December 2007.
[11] For instance in simple linear regression $f(\boldsymbol{\theta}|\mathbf{x}) = (\alpha + \beta x_1, \ldots, \alpha + \beta x_n)'$ and $\boldsymbol{\theta} = (\alpha, \beta)'$. Note that f is a *vector*-valued function, which is why we denote it in bold.

gradient method. A popular algorithm in this class is the *Levenberg–Marquardt algorithm*.[12]
It has the form

$$\varepsilon\left(\theta_{k+1}\right) = \varepsilon\left(\theta_{k}\right) + \mathbf{J}(\theta_{k})\left(\theta_{k+1} - \theta_{k}\right),$$ (I.5.22)

where k denotes the number of the iteration and $\mathbf{J}$ is the *Jacobian matrix* of partial derivatives
of f with respect to θ, i.e.

$$\mathbf{J}(\theta) = \begin{pmatrix} \dfrac{\partial f_1}{\partial \theta_1} & \cdots & \dfrac{\partial f_1}{\partial \theta_m} \\ \vdots & \ddots & \vdots \\ \dfrac{\partial f_n}{\partial \theta_1} & \cdots & \dfrac{\partial f_n}{\partial \theta_m} \end{pmatrix}.$$ (I.5.23)

I.5.4.2   Likelihood Methods

Maximizing a likelihood function is a very flexible method for estimating the parameters
of any distribution and maximum likelihood estimation (MLE) is provided as a standard
procedure in the vast majority of statistical packages.[13] But algorithms for optimizing a
likelihood function are generally more complex than least squares algorithms, and gradient
methods do not always converge. If there are many parameters in the model then the
likelihood is a multi-dimensional surface that can be very flat indeed. In such circumstances
an iterative search algorithm can yield a local rather than a global optimum, or it may hit a
boundary if there are constraints on parameters.

Because differences in starting values and optimization methods, and even small differences in sample data, can lead to different results, a maximum likelihood procedure should
always be monitored more closely than its simple least squares relative. For instance, in
Example I.3.17 we used the Excel Solver to fit a Student t distribution to some financial
asset returns by maximizing the likelihood function. But readers may have noticed that the
Solver does not always converge to a solution in this problem; it depends on the starting
value. In fact we can only guarantee a sensible solution when the initial value for the gradient
algorithm is not too far away from the optimum.

To make inference on the estimated model we need to know the standard errors of the
parameter estimators; in fact for anything more than simple hypotheses we require their
entire covariance matrix. In Section I.3.6 we showed how to estimate the parameters of the
covariance matrix when the variables are assumed to be normally distributed. But when
MLE is applied to non-normal distributions the computation of the covariance matrix of the
estimators can be difficult.

In general the covariance matrix of the estimators can be calculated as -1 times the
inverse of the matrix of expected values of the second derivatives of the log likelihood
function:

$$\mathbf{V}(\theta) = -\mathbf{I}(\theta)^{-1}, \quad \text{where } \mathbf{I}(\theta) = E\left[\frac{\partial^2 \ln L}{\partial\theta\partial\theta'}\right],$$ (I.5.24)

---

[12] There is also a good entry in Wikipedia on this algorithm.
[13] MLE is introduced in Section I.3.6.

and $I(\theta)$ is called the *information matrix*. It is diagonal in the case of a normal density but otherwise it can be a complicated non-diagonal matrix. Often the expected values of the second derivatives of the log likelihood have to be approximated by taking their actual values, rather than expected values at the maximum likelihood estimates. But sometimes even the second derivatives may be impossible to compute, in which case we can use an alternative form for the information matrix that requires only first derivatives of the log likelihood:

$$I(\theta) \approx E\left[\frac{\partial \ln L}{\partial \theta} \frac{\partial \ln L}{\partial \theta'}\right].$$

I.5.4.3   The EM Algorithm

The *expectation–maximization* (EM) algorithm differs from standard MLE because it assumes there are some 'missing' or 'hidden' variables or parameters that cannot be observed directly in the data. For instance, suppose historical returns data $\mathbf{x}$ are generated by a mixture distribution with two components: one distribution has a high volatility and the other distribution has a low volatility. Given any single return in the data set $\mathbf{x}$, we cannot say for certain whether it was generated from the high volatility distribution or the low volatility distribution – we can only say that it was generated from the high volatility distribution with a certain probability, which we do not know. Indeed this probability is one of the parameters of the distribution that we want to estimate.

However, suppose that each return in our data set had an 'indicator' that specified which distribution it was drawn from. In other words, suppose we had a data set $(\mathbf{x}, \mathbf{y})$ where $\mathbf{y}$ is a variable that takes only values 0 or 1. For instance, let y_i take the value 0 when the high volatility density generated the associated return x_i and the value 1 when the low volatility density generated the return x_i. Then we would be in a complete information setting, where ordinary maximum likelihood can be applied to estimate the parameters. But we do not have such an indicator: the variable $\mathbf{y}$ cannot be observed, it is missing from our data. We call an unobservable or missing variable such as this indicator a *latent variable*.

The EM algorithm is designed to deal with these situations by making latent variables explicit in the maximization of the likelihood. Denote by θ the parameters of the function to be optimized and let $\mathbf{y}$ be a latent variable. The algorithm consists of iterating between two steps, the E-step and the M-step. The E-step is the calculation of the *expected log likelihood*, given the current estimates of θ and given some distribution $h(\mathbf{y})$ on the values of the latent variable. Then, in the M-step, an optimization method (typically, a gradient method) is applied to find a new value of θ that maximizes the expected log likelihood. The E-step is repeated, updated with the new value as the current value of θ and then the M-step again provides a further updated value for θ. Thus the algorithm proceeds, iterating between the E-step and the M-step until convergence is achieved.

I.5.4.4   Case Study: Applying the EM Algorithm to Normal Mixture Densities[14]

The EM algorithm is not a standard addition in statistical packages, but it is widely used to estimate the parameters of mixture distributions. Of particular relevance for our purposes is the use of the EM algorithm to estimate parameters of a *normal mixture distribution*.[15] The

---

[14] Many thanks to my PhD student Joydeep Lahiri for providing the results used in this section.
[15] Normal mixture distributions are introduced in Sections I.3.3.6 and I.3.4.7.

normal mixture case is relatively straightforward because the E- and M-steps in the iteration can be combined into a single iteration – see Bilmes (1998) for further details.

To illustrate the application of the EM algorithm, we apply it to fit a mixture of two normal distributions to the empirical daily returns distributions of two series. Figure I.5.10 shows daily FTSE 100 and S&P 500 index prices and Figure I.5.11 shows the daily $/£

Figure I.5.10   FTSE 100 (left-hand scale) and S&P 500 (right-hand scale) index prices, 1996–2007

Figure I.5.11   US Dollar–Sterling exchange rate, 1996–2007

exchange rate from 3 January 1996 to 2 March 2007. We take the daily log returns for the
stock indices and the exchange rate over the whole period.

Table I.5.1 reports the average annualized mean, volatility, skewness and excess kurtosis
of the daily log returns on the three series over the whole sample period. The annualized
means are all positive, though not much greater than the risk free return and the volatility
of the equity indices is far greater than that of the exchange rate. A significant negative
skewness is also apparent in the equity indices, especially in the FTSE 100, and all series
have significant positive excess kurtosis. Hence the daily log returns are far from being
normally distributed and a mixture of two log normal distributions will fit the data better
than a single normal distribution.

Table I.5.1 Mean and volatility of the FTSE 100 and S&P 500 indices and the
£/$ FX rate

	Annualized mean	Volatility	Skewness	Excess kurtosis
FTSE 100	4.62%	17.57%	−0.1514	2.6332
S&P 500	7.35%	17.73%	0.0205	3.2570
FX rate	2.04%	7.99%	−0.0803	1.0525

The EM algorithm fits a mixture of two normal densities to these data using free downloadable Matlab code.[16] The code normalizes the data to have zero mean and unit standard
deviation prior to fitting the parameters, just as we did when fitting the Student t distribution
by maximum likelihood in Example I.3.17. We present the results in Table I.5.2, in both
standardized and annualized form.

Table I.5.2 Estimated parameters of normal mixture distributions

	p	μ_1	μ_2	σ_1	σ_2
Standardized					
FTSE 100	0.3622	−0.08200	0.04657	1.461	0.5914
S&P 500	0.2752	−0.08361	0.03174	1.551	0.6796
FX rate	0.6150	−0.00104	0.00166	1.197	0.5547
Annualized					
FTSE 100	0.3622	−3.58%	9.28%	26.35%	5.48%
S&P 500	0.2752	−1.01%	10.52%	29.80%	7.84%
FX rate	0.6150	1.94%	2.21%	9.68%	4.01%

The results show that the equity indices have a 'normal' regime where returns volatility
is very low and the expected return is high and positive, but they also have a highly volatile
regime where expected returns are negative. The volatile regime occurs with a relatively low
probability: 0.3622 in the FTSE 100 and 0.2752 in the S&P 500. The $/£ exchange rate does
not exhibit such pronounced regime-specific behaviour. Of course we identify two regimes
because this is what has been assumed in our model, but there is less difference between

---

[16] The Fast EM_GM code is currently available from the Matlab code exchange site at http://www.mathworks.com/matlabcentral/
fileexchange/loadFile.do?objectId=9659&objectType=FILE.

the characteristics of the two regimes. The relative low excess kurtosis of the exchange rate returns indicates that a single normal distribution may be adequate for modelling returns, although a skewed Student t distribution would be much better, whereas for the equity indices a normal mixture distribution is able to capture the regime-specific market characteristics.

I.5.5   FINITE DIFFERENCE APPROXIMATIONS

This section focuses on the numerical methods that we apply to price and hedge options. Hence, it draws heavily on Chapter III.3 and readers are advised to gain at least some familiarity with the foundations of option pricing before reading this part of the chapter.

I.5.5.1   First and Second Order Finite Differences

Figure I.5.12 shows how the slope of the chord between two points approximates the first derivative of a function, i.e. the slope of the tangent:

$$f'(x) \approx \frac{f(x+h) - f(x-h)}{2h}. \qquad (I.5.25)$$

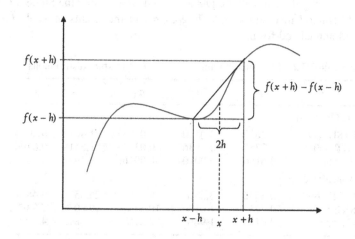

Figure I.5.12   Slope of chord about a point

Provided that h is small, this approximation is quite accurate. In fact, as $h \to 0$ the points converge to the point at $f(x)$, and hence we obtain the definition of the first derivative as

$$f'(x) = \lim_{h \to 0} \frac{f(x+h) - f(x-h)}{2h}.$$

We call (I.5.25) the *central finite difference* approximation to the first derivative of the function.

One-sided finite differences may also be used: for instance, the *forward* first order finite difference is

$$f'(x) \approx \frac{f(x+h) - f(x)}{h}, \tag{I.5.26}$$

and the *backward* first order finite difference is

$$f'(x) \approx \frac{f(x) - f(x-h)}{h}. \tag{I.5.27}$$

These are also valid only for a small value of h.

Applying a first order difference twice gives a central finite difference approximation to the second order derivative of the function, i.e.:

$$f''(x) \approx \frac{f(x+h) - 2f(x) + f(x-h)}{h^2}. \tag{I.5.28}$$

In exceptional circumstances, e.g. in a finite difference scheme for approximating the value of a partial differential equation (PDE) near a boundary, as in Section I.5.5.3 below, one might consider a one-sided approximation to the second derivative such as

$$f''(x) \approx \frac{f(x+2h) - 2f(x+h) + f(x)}{h^2}.$$

Repeated application of first order differences gives finite difference approximations to third, fourth and higher derivatives of a function.

I.5.5.2   Finite Difference Approximations for the Greeks

The Greeks of an option are the partial derivatives of an option price $g(S, \sigma, \dots)$ with respect to its risk factors – i.e. the underlying price S, the implied volatility σ, and so forth. The Greeks of an option depend on the formula used to price the option. The Black–Scholes–Merton Greeks have a simple analytic form given in Section III.3.7, but these only apply to standard European call and put options under the assumption that the underlying asset price follows a geometric Brownian motion. In general there are no analytic formulae for the Greeks of an option, or of a portfolio of options, and they are estimated using finite differences.

The first, second and higher order finite differences defined above are simply applied to the option price $g(S, \sigma, \dots)$. For instance, central finite difference approximations to the delta, gamma and vega are:

$$\delta \approx \frac{g(S+\varepsilon, \sigma, \dots) - g(S-\varepsilon, \sigma, \dots)}{2\varepsilon}, \tag{I.5.29}$$

$$\gamma \approx \frac{g(S+\varepsilon, \sigma, \dots) - 2g(S, \sigma, \dots) + g(S-\varepsilon, \sigma, \dots)}{\varepsilon^2}, \tag{I.5.30}$$

$$\nu \approx \frac{g(S, \sigma+\varepsilon, \dots) - g(S, \sigma-\varepsilon, \dots)}{2\varepsilon}. \tag{I.5.31}$$

The following example applies the finite difference method to estimate the delta, gamma and vega for a simple European option. Since in this case we have exact formulae for the Greeks we can quantify the error from the finite difference approximation.

EXAMPLE I.5.7: FINITE DIFFERENCE APPROXIMATION TO DELTA, GAMMA AND VEGA

Use finite differences to calculate the delta, gamma and vega for a European option with the following characteristics: $S = 1000$, $\sigma = 20\%$, $K = 1025$, time to expiry $= 30$ days, risk free rate $= 5\%$ and no dividends. In the case of delta calculate both the delta of the call option and the delta of the put option.

SOLUTION   The finite difference approximations for delta and gamma are achieved by perturbing the underlying price up by 1 and down by 1, each time revaluing the options, and then using (I.5.29) and (I.5.30). Similarly, we perturb the underlying volatility up and down by 0.01%, this time leaving the underlying price fixed, and again revalue the options to find the finite difference approximation to vega using (I.5.31). Then the finite difference approximations to the Greeks are compared with the analytic values based on the formulae given in Table III.3.4. In this case the errors induced by using the finite difference approximation are tiny: they are of the order of 0.01% or less.

Table I.5.3   Analytic vs finite difference Greeks

	Analytic	Finite difference
Delta (call)	0.370584	0.370585
Delta (put)	−0.629416	−0.629415
Gamma	0.006588	0.006588
Vega	1.083011	1.083007

I.5.5.3   Finite Difference Solutions to Partial Differential Equations

A partial differential equation is an equation involving partial derivatives of a function.[17] A very common PDE that is encountered in finance is the one that arises when we examine the price of an option. For instance, if we assume the volatility of the underlying price S over the life of the option is constant, and we can form a risk free portfolio consisting of the option and δ units of the underlying, this is called a *delta-hedged portfolio*. Then we can derive a PDE which describes the evolution of the option price.[18]

More specifically, if the underlying follows a geometric Brownian motion with constant drift μ and volatility σ, then the evolution of the option price f will follow the well-known *heat equation*,

$$f_t + (r-y)Sf_s + \tfrac{1}{2}\sigma^2 S^2 f_{ss} = (r-y)f. \tag{I.5.32}$$

Here r is the risk free rate of return, y is the dividend yield or carry cost and

$$f_t = \frac{\partial f}{\partial t}, \quad f_s = \frac{\partial f}{\partial S}, \quad f_{ss} = \frac{\partial^2 f}{\partial S^2}$$

are partial derivatives of the option price with respect to time and with respect to the underlying price.

---

[17] Partial derivatives are defined in Section I.1.5.1.
[18] See Section III.3.6 for the derivation.

When f is a standard European call or put this PDE has an analytic solution, the well-known Black–Scholes–Merton formula given in Section III.3.6.4. However, when the option is not a standard European call or put, or when volatility or the interest rate or the dividend yield or carry cost are not assumed to be constant, then there is no simple analytic solution to the PDE and usually a numerical method needs to be applied to solve the equation for the price of the option.

A common approach to finding the value of f that solves a PDE such as (I.5.32) is to approximate its partial derivatives using finite differences. The evolution of the option price f is represented in two-dimensional space (S, t) or $(\ln S, t)$. First the space is discretized, for instance using a *grid* such as that shown in Figure I.5.13.

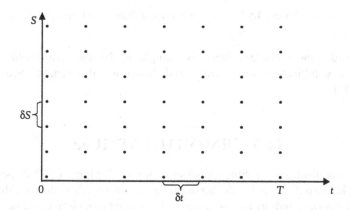

Figure I.5.13   Discretization of space for the finite difference scheme

Each point in the grid is called a *node*. There are two boundaries in the time dimension, corresponding to the current time $(t = 0)$ and the maturity of the option $(t = T)$. The possible values of the option at maturity, i.e. at the *terminal nodes*, are given by its pay-off function. For instance, the pay-off to a standard European call option with strike K is $[S - K]^+$, also written $\max(S - K, 0)$. Using the pay-off function, we fix the possible values of the option at the terminal nodes.[19]

We can now work backwards through the tree, as illustrated in Figure I.5.14. Starting at the terminal nodes we use finite differences to approximate the values of the partial derivatives in the PDE, and hence apply the PDE to find the possible values of the option at the nodes preceding the terminal nodes. Then we repeat this process, working backwards until we arrive at the initial nodes when $t = 0$. Finally, reading off the option value at the initial node corresponding to the current value of the underlying gives the option price.

A number of different finite difference schemes have been developed, depending on whether forward, backward or central differences are used to approximate the partial derivatives at each node. Some schemes suffer from *instability* in the following sense: a fine grid (i.e. with small steps δt and δS) should be best for approximating the option value accurately, but when the grid is made finer it also has more steps and so approximation errors can build

---

[19] There are also boundary conditions in the S dimension, at least at 0 and ∞, but there may also be finite positive boundaries; for instance, for an American option there is an *early exercise boundary*.

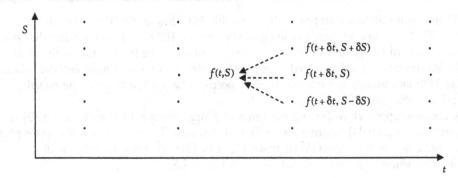

Figure I.5.14   A simple finite difference scheme

up. Currently the most stable scheme is thought to be the *Crank–Nicolson scheme*, which uses a combination of forward and backward differences. See Crank and Nicolson (1947).

I.5.6   BINOMIAL LATTICES

A lattice is a *discretization* of *n*-dimensional space for $n \geq 2$. Figure I.5.15 depicts a *binomial lattice*, which has two dimensions: the horizontal axis corresponds to the time dimension and the vertical axis corresponds to an asset price, *S*. Each point or *node* in the lattice corresponds to a possible price of the asset at a given time. No other times and no other values for the price at time *t* are considered possible. The more general term *tree* is used to describe a lattice where the nodes do not necessarily recombine at each point in time. Thus a lattice is also a *recombining* tree.

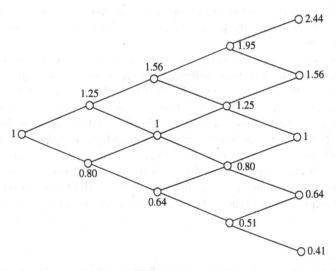

Figure I.5.15   A binomial lattice

I.5.6.1   Constructing the Lattice

The transition from a node A at time t to a node B at time $t + \Delta t$ is governed by a *transition probability*, which states the probability that during the time step Δt the asset price will change from its value at A to its value at B. In a binomial lattice we specify a transition probability p as the probability of an 'up' move in price (so $1 - p$ is the probability of a 'down' move) and a common simplifying assumption is that p is the same at every node.

It is typical to assume that the 'up' and 'down' moves in price are constant multiples of the current price. That is, if the current price is S then at the next node the price can be either uS or dS where $u > 1$ and $d < 1$. In order for the tree not to drift upward or downward, we require $u(dS) = d(uS) = S$, i.e. $u = d^{-1}$. For instance, Figure I.5.15 depicts a binomial tree with four steps where the price can move up by a factor of 1.25 or down by a factor of 0.8, starting at the initial price $S_0 = 1$.

Binomial lattices are commonly used to price path-dependent options and we shall consider such an application below.[20] To apply a lattice to option pricing we must specify some further structure: the length of the time step and the transition probability, both of which are typically assumed to be constant throughout the tree. For instance, if in the lattice depicted in Figure I.5.15 the time step is 3 months then we can apply this construction to price an option on S that expires 1 year from now. Also, the prices in Figure I.5.15 are expressed in current terms, but a value of 2.44 for instance, 1 year ahead is worth only $\exp(-r) \times 2.44$ today, where r is the risk free rate of interest.

I.5.6.2   Arbitrage Free Pricing and Risk Neutral Valuation

For 'no arbitrage' pricing of a standard European call option on S we buy or sell the option and then *delta hedge*. That is, if we buy the option we sell δ units of S, where the value of δ is chosen so that the portfolio's value is the *same* whether the price goes up or down, i.e. so that the portfolio is *risk free*.

Let the option price be f so that the portfolio's value is $f - \delta S$. Suppose the option value becomes f_u or f_d depending on whether the price moves up to uS or down to dS. Then if the portfolio is hedged against movements in the underlying price its value must be the same following an up move or a down move. That is

$$f_u - \delta(uS) = f_d - \delta(dS), \tag{I.5.33}$$

so that

$$\delta = \frac{f_u - f_d}{uS - dS}. \tag{I.5.34}$$

We can now apply the no arbitrage argument to derive a relationship between the discount rate r and the transition probability p. The initial value of the portfolio is $f - \delta S$ and after one time step its value is given by (I.5.33), which in present value terms may be written $\exp(-r\Delta t)(f_u - \delta(uS))$. Hence, for no arbitrage the following relationship must hold:

$$\exp(-r\Delta t)(f_u - \delta(uS)) = f - \delta S.$$

---

[20] In some cases more accurate prices can be obtained using a *trinomial lattice* where for instance the price can move up, or down, or stay the same, with certain transition probabilities.

Substituting in (I.5.34) and solving for f gives, after some calculations,

$$f = \exp(-r\Delta t)\,(pf_u + (1-p)f_d),$$ (I.5.35)

where

$$p = \frac{\exp(r\Delta t) - d}{u - d}.$$ (I.5.36)

For instance, suppose that in the binomial lattice depicted in Figure I.5.15 each time step is 3 months and the risk free interest rate is 5%. Then by (I.5.36) the transition probability would be

$$\frac{\exp(0.05 \times 0.25) - 0.8}{1.25 - 0.8} = 0.4724.$$

It can also be shown that the expression (I.5.36) for the transition probability is equivalent to the assumption that the underlying asset price S grows at the risk free rate.[21] In other words, we have a *risk neutral* setting where assets earn the risk free rate of return. The relationship (I.5.35) illustrates that arbitrage free pricing leads to the *risk neutral valuation principle*, i.e. that the option price at any time t is equal to the discounted value of its expected future price.

The expected value in (I.5.35) must refer to some probability distribution and we call this distribution the *risk neutral measure*.[22] The *fundamental theorem of arbitrage* states that there is no arbitrage if and only if there is a risk neutral measure that is equivalent to the measure defined by the price process (e.g. a lognormal measure when the price process is a standard geometric Brownian motion). Moreover, this measure is unique if the market is *complete*.[23]

I.5.6.3 Pricing European Options

The pay-off at expiry depends on the option characteristics, including the *strike* of the option K. A simple *call option* with strike K has pay-off $\max(S-K,\,0)$ and a *put option* with strike K has pay-off $\max(K-S,\,0)$. See Section III.3.9 for pay-offs to other options. Under risk neutral valuation, the price of an option is the discounted value of its expected future price. Therefore, the price of a European option is the discounted present value of its pay-off at expiry. However, this is not the case for path-dependent options – i.e. options whose values depend on the values that the underlying can take between now and expiry – such as American options or barrier options.

EXAMPLE I.5.8: PRICING EUROPEAN CALL AND PUT OPTIONS

Use a binomial lattice to approximate the price of a European put option with strike 105 and maturity 30 days when the current asset price is 100 and the risk free rate is 4%. Assume that the asset pays no dividends and that the lattice is discretized so that the time step Δt is 1 day and that the price can move up by a factor u or down by a factor d, where $u = 1.01 = d^{-1}$.

---

[21] This is easily seen by writing down the expected return on S over one period and substituting in (I.5.36).
[22] The general term *measure* is often used in finance to refer to a probability distribution.
[23] Full details are given in Section III.3.2.

SOLUTION   The transition probability is given by the relationship (I.5.36) as:

$$\frac{\exp\left(0.04/365\right) - 1.01^{-1}}{1.01 - 1.01^{-1}} = 0.5030.$$

We now compute the expected value of the pay-off, using the probabilities and outcomes of the *binomial distribution* with $N = 30$ and $p = 0.5030$. The binomial distribution gives the probability that the asset at the expiry date had x up moves and $N - x$ down moves, in other words that the expiry price is $u^x d^{(N-x)} S$.[24]

In the spreadsheet we use the Excel command BINOMDIST(x, N, p, false) to calculate this probability.[25] Adjacent to the probability we calculate the underlying price $u^x d^{(N-x)} S$, and adjacent to that is the corresponding pay-off for the put, i.e. $\max(K - u^x d^{(N-x)} S, 0)$. The expected pay-off is the sum of the products of the probabilities and the pay-offs. Finally, this is discounted to today's terms using the risk free interest rate, giving the option price as 5.294. This should be compared with the Black–Scholes–Merton price which is calculated in the spreadsheet as 5.285.

I.5.6.4   Lognormal Asset Price Distributions

The Black–Scholes–Merton pricing formula for European options is based on the assumption that the asset price process follows a geometric Brownian motion with constant volatility σ.[26] How should the binomial lattice be discretized to be consistent with this model?

Consider a risk neutral setting over a discrete time step Δt. No arbitrage pricing requires the underlying asset to return the risk free rate, r. Therefore, the log return $\ln\left(S_{t+\Delta t}/S_t\right)$ will have a normal distribution with mean $m = \mu \Delta t = (r - \frac{1}{2}\sigma^2)\Delta t$ and variance $\sigma^2 \Delta t$. Since $S_{t+\Delta t}/S_t$ has a lognormal distribution, we have:[27]

$$E\left(\frac{S_{t+\Delta t}}{S_t}\right) = \exp\left(\mu \Delta t + \tfrac{1}{2}\sigma^2 \Delta t\right) = \exp\left(r\Delta t\right),$$

$$V\left(\frac{S_{t+\Delta t}}{S_t}\right) = \exp 2\left(\mu \Delta t + \tfrac{1}{2}\sigma^2 \Delta t\right)\left[\exp\left(\sigma^2 \Delta t\right) - 1\right] = \exp\left(2r\Delta t\right)\left[\exp\left(\sigma^2 \Delta t\right) - 1\right].$$

Hence,

$$\begin{aligned} E(S_{t+\Delta t}) &= S_t \exp\left(r\Delta t\right), \\ V(S_{t+\Delta t}) &= S_t^2 \exp\left(2r\Delta t\right)\left[\exp\left(\sigma^2 \Delta t\right) - 1\right]. \end{aligned} \tag{I.5.37}$$

To answer our question, we seek p, u and d so that (I.5.37) holds. Taking the expectation and variance from the binomial lattice over a discrete time step Δt, we have

$$\begin{aligned} E(S_{t+\Delta t}) &= S_t\left[pu + (1-p)d\right], \\ V(S_{t+\Delta t}) &= S_t^2\left[pu^2 + (1-p)d^2 - (pu + (1-p)d)^2\right]. \end{aligned} \tag{I.5.38}$$

Equating expectations in (I.5.37) and (I.5.38) yields

$$\exp(r\Delta t) = pu + (1-p)d, \tag{I.5.39}$$

---

[24] See Section I.3.3.1 for further details on the binomial distribution.
[25] We have used full accuracy for p, so the difference between the binomial option price and the BSM option price has nothing to do with rounding errors.
[26] See Section III.3.6 for further details.
[27] The mean and variance of the lognormal distribution are given in Section I.3.3.5.

which is equivalent to the relationship (I.5.36). Equating the variances yields a new relationship between p, u, d and σ, i.e.

$$\exp(2r\Delta t + \sigma^2 \Delta t) = pu^2 + (1-p)d^2. \tag{I.5.40}$$

Hence, the discretization in a binomial lattice will be consistent with the assumption that the asset price process follows a geometric Brownian motion provided that conditions (I.5.39) and (I.5.40) hold. Since we have only two conditions on three parameters there are many ways in which conditions (I.5.39) and (I.5.40) can hold; in other words, there are many different parameterizations of a binomial tree that are consistent with an asset price following a geometric Brownian motion. We mention just two.

The discretization

$$p = \frac{\exp(r\Delta t) - d}{u - d}, \quad u = d^{-1} = \exp\left(\sigma\sqrt{\Delta t}\right), \tag{I.5.41}$$

due to Cox, Ross and Rubinstein (1979) provides a first order approximate solution to (I.5.39) and (I.5.40). Since $u = d^{-1}$ the centre of the lattice remains constant at the initial price of the underlying, as in Figure I.5.15. This is a useful property for pricing barrier options, because the level of the barrier can be easily represented in the tree. However, the discretization (I.5.41) loses accuracy at low levels of volatility. It has the disadvantage that as the volatility tends to 0 the lattice does not converge to an exponential trend, which is the case when the underlying asset price follows a geometric Brownian motion.

The discretization

$$p = \tfrac{1}{2}, \quad u = \exp\left(m + \sigma\sqrt{\Delta t}\right), \quad d = \exp\left(m - \sigma\sqrt{\Delta t}\right), \quad m = \left(r - \tfrac{1}{2}\sigma^2\right)\Delta t \tag{I.5.42}$$

(Jarrow and Rudd, 1982) provides a second order approximate solution to (I.5.39) and (I.5.40) which at the same time converges to an exponential trend as the volatility converges to 0. To see this, set

$$p = \tfrac{1}{2}, \quad u = \exp(m + \delta), \quad d = \exp(m - \delta)$$

and use the second order approximation

$$\exp(\delta) \approx 1 + \delta + \frac{\delta^2}{2}$$

in conditions (I.5.39) and (I.5.40) as follows. From (I.5.39) we have

$$\exp(r\Delta t) = \exp(m)\left(1 + \frac{\delta^2}{2}\right),$$

so that

$$r\Delta t = m + \ln\left(1 + \frac{\delta^2}{2}\right) \approx m + \frac{\delta^2}{2}. \tag{I.5.43}$$

From (I.5.40) we have

$$\exp(2r\Delta t + \sigma^2 \Delta t) = \tfrac{1}{2}\exp(2m)\left(2 + (2\delta)^2\right) = \exp(2m)\left(1 + 2\delta^2\right),$$

so that

$$2r\Delta t + \sigma^2 \Delta t = 2m + \ln(1 + 2\delta^2) \approx 2m + 2\delta^2.$$

Hence,

$$\left(r + \tfrac{1}{2}\sigma^2\right)\Delta t \approx m + \delta^2. \tag{I.5.44}$$

Then (I.5.42) is the solution to (I.5.43) and (I.5.44).

I.5.6.5 Pricing American Options

By discounting the expected value of its expiry pay-off at the risk free rate of return, as in Example I.5.8, we can obtain the price of any European style option at any time prior to expiry. However, American options may be exercised *before* the expiry date if it is profitable to do so. It can be shown that an American call on an asset paying no dividends is never profitable to exercise early, so their price is identical to the price of the corresponding European option. However, American puts may have early exercise even when no dividends are paid (see section III.3.3).

The *intrinsic value* of an option is what the option would be worth if it were exercised now. In Section I.5.5.3 we did not track the intrinsic value of the options at each node of the lattice, because this was not necessary for pricing a European option. Since a European option cannot be exercised before the expiry date we only needed to know the possible option values at the time of expiry. However, when pricing an American option we *do* need to fill in the intrinsic option values corresponding to each node of the tree.

In the next example a binomial lattice is used to price an American put by comparing, at each node in the lattice, the intrinsic value of the option (i.e. the value if it were exercised at that point in time) with the option value if it were exercised later. The maximum of the two values is taken as the option price at that node and then we move *backwards* through the lattice, computing the option price at each node. Then when we have worked back through the whole lattice we obtain the option price at the current time, i.e. its value at the initial node. We illustrate the method with a numerical example.

EXAMPLE I.5.9: PRICING AN AMERICAN OPTION WITH A BINOMIAL LATTICE

Use a four-step binomial tree to price (a) a European put an (b) an American put with strike 99 and maturity 200 days when the current price of the underlying is 100, the dividend yield is 0 and the risk free rate is 5%. Use the Cox–Ross–Rubinstein (CRR) parameterization with $u = 1.1$ and compare the binomial price of the European option with that obtained using the Black–Scholes–Merton formula.

SOLUTION   Figure I.5.16 displays the required four-step lattices. The first is the stock price lattice, which is computed by starting at 100 and working forward through the lattice, applying both upward and downward multiples to the previous stock price. Note that with the CRR parameterization, $d = 1.1^{-1} = 0.90909$.

The second is the lattice for the European put prices at each node in the tree, and these are computed by starting at the terminal nodes, where the prices are given by the pay-off max $\{K - S, \ 0\}$ based on the five different terminal values of S in the first lattice. Then working backwards through the tree, each time we apply (I.5.35) to obtain the option's intrinsic value at that node. Note that the risk neutral probability is determined from (I.5.41) by u, d, the risk free rate of 5% and the time step of 50 days, i.e. 0.13699 years. The price of the option, i.e. the value computed at the initial node, is 5.476. Note that the same value could be obtained without the tree, and using instead the binomial distribution as in Example I.5.8. This price is compared with the Black–Scholes–Merton price of 5.759. The Black–Scholes–Merton price is based on the volatility of 25.75%, which is calculated using (I.5.41). With only four steps in the tree there is a considerable difference between the two prices: as we use more steps in the tree the binomial price will converge to 5.759.

The third lattice is for the American put prices at each node in the tree. These are computed by again starting at the terminal nodes and working backwards through the tree. But now at each node we take the maximum of (I.5.35) and the value of the option if it were exercised at that point in time. That is, we use the intrinsic value

$$f = \max(\exp(-r\Delta t)(pf_u + (1-p)f_d), K - S). \tag{I.5.45}$$

For instance, the value of $99 - 90.9091 = 8.091$ replaces the European value of 7.924 at the equivalent node at step 3. Now applying (I.5.45) and working backwards through the tree gives the price of an American put as 5.771. As expected, since there is a premium for the possibility of early exercise, this is greater than the binomial price of the corresponding European option.

Stock Price:						146.410
					133.100	
				121.000		121.000
			110		110.000	
	100			100		100
			90.909		90.909	
				82.645		82.645
					75.131	
						68.301

European Put:						0.000
					0.000	
				0.000		0.000
			1.860		0.000	
	5.476			3.839		0.000
			9.350		7.924	
				15.267		16.355
					23.193	
						30.699

American Put:						0.000
					0.000	
				0.000		0.000
			1.899		0.000	
	5.771			3.920		0.000
			9.918		8.091	
				16.355		16.355
					23.869	
						30.699

Figure I.5.16   Computing the price of European and American puts

I.5.7   MONTE CARLO SIMULATION

The two preceding sections described numerical techniques that are commonly applied to price and hedge American and exotic options, i.e. binomial lattices and finite differences. But such methods do not always work well because they can become unstable, with approximation errors at each node propagating to produce sizeable inaccuracies for the option price. Simulation is a numerical technique that will always resolve a financial problem, even though it can take considerable time. Simulation may always be used to price and hedge options if other numerical methods fail. Simulation also forms the basis of one of the most commonly used value-at-risk approaches: the Monte Carlo VaR methodology that is described in Chapter IV.4.

In this section we begin by describing how random numbers are generated and then transformed to represent random draws from a given univariate distribution, i.e. the marginal distribution of a risk factor. Such random draws may then be used to simulate the evolution of a single financial asset price. But in many cases – e.g. for computing VaR or for pricing a multi-asset option – we need to simulate the evolution of several asset prices, and these simulations should reflect any co-dependencies that are observed between the returns. Here we restrict ourselves to simulating from multivariate normal or multivariate t distributed variables.[28] We explain how the Cholesky matrix of the returns covariance matrix is applied to transform a set of uncorrelated random draws to represent random draws from the multivariate distribution.

I.5.7.1   Random Numbers

The object of random number generation is to produce a sequence of numbers between 0 and 1 that are uniformly distributed and have no *periodicity*. That is, each number in the unit interval [0, 1] is equally likely to occur in the sequence and the sequence does not repeat itself however long it becomes. The only way to generate random numbers is to measure, without error, a physical phenomenon that is truly random. In practice computers generate *pseudo-random numbers*, which are almost impossible to distinguish from true random numbers. These pseudo-random numbers are generated by an initial seed, such as the time of the computer's clock, and thereafter follow a deterministic sequence.

A true sequence of random numbers can leave sizeable gaps in the unit interval unless a very long sequence of numbers is generated. *Low discrepancy sequences*, such as the Faure and Sobol sequences, are designed to generate *quasi-random numbers* which require fewer numbers in the series to cover the unit interval. Even though they will actually repeat themselves after a certain length of time, good random number generators have very high periodicity. The Excel command RAND() generates a pseudo-random number, but the generator has very low periodicity. By contrast, the *Mersenne twister* has a periodicity of $2^{19,937} - 1!$[29]

I.5.7.2   Simulations from an Empirical or a Given Distribution

To simulate a return from an *empirical* distribution using Excel it is easiest to place the empirical returns in a column, say column A, and use the command INDIRECT("A"& B1)

---

[28] See Section II.6.7 for an introduction to simulating from other multivariate distributions, using copulas.
[29] So called because this number is a Mersenne prime.

where cell B1 contains a random draw from the row number.[30] This generates a series of random draws from the empirical distribution. This type of sampling from an empirical distribution is commonly referred to as the *statistical bootstrap*.

Now suppose we want to generate a random draw x from a distribution with a given continuous distribution function $F(x)$. By definition $F(x)$ takes values between 0 and 1, and so, given any random number u in $[0, 1]$, we can set $u = F(x)$ and obtain the corresponding value for x using the inverse of F – that is, we set $x = F^{-1}(u)$. Figure I.5.17 illustrates the process in the case of a standard normal distribution when the random number generated is 0.3.[31] Note that given the sigmoid shape of the distribution function a uniform series of random numbers will be converted into simulations where more simulations occur around the expected value than in the tails of the distribution.

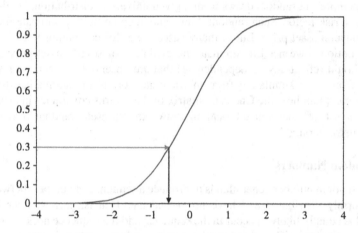

Figure I.5.17   Simulating from a standard normal distribution

A sequence of standard normal simulations can be translated into simulations from any other normal distribution using the inverse of the standard normal transformation.[32] That is, we translate a standard normal simulation z into a simulation on a normal variable with mean μ and standard deviation σ using

$$x = z\sigma + \mu.$$ (I.5.46)

I.5.7.3   Case Study: Generating Time Series of Lognormal Asset Prices

In this subsection we describe how to simulate a time series of asset prices that follow a geometric Brownian motion,

$$\frac{dS(t)}{S(t)} = \mu dt + \sigma dW(t).$$

---

[30] For instance, suppose the empirical returns are in cells A1:A1000. Use the command RANDBETWEEN(1,1000) in cell B1 and fill down column B. This creates a random draw from the row number in column B.
[31] This is the basis of the Excel command NORMSINV(RAND()), which generates a standard normal simulation.
[32] See Section I.3.3.4 for the specification of the standard normal distribution.

Geometric Brownian motion was introduced in Section I.1.4.5, and we derived the discrete time equivalent of geometric Brownian motion in Section I.3.7.3. Using Itô's lemma we showed that the log return, which is the first difference in the log prices, is normally and independently distributed with mean $\mu - \frac{1}{2}\sigma^2$ and variance σ^2.

Now suppose we fix μ and σ and simulate a sequence $\{x_1, x_2, \ldots, x_T\}$, where each x_i has mean $\alpha = \mu - \frac{1}{2}\sigma^2$ and variance σ^2 as described in the previous section. In a risk neutral world the drift μ is equal to the risk free rate r,[33] so (I.5.46) becomes

$$x_t = z_t \sigma + r - \tfrac{1}{2}\sigma^2, \tag{I.5.47}$$

where $\{z_1, z_2, \ldots, z_T\}$ are independent standard normal simulations. We suppose that the simulation $\{x_1, x_2, \ldots, x_T\}$ represents a set of log returns, i.e.

$$x_1 = \ln(S_1/S_0), \quad x_2 = \ln(S_2/S_1), \ldots.$$

for some sequence of asset prices $\{S_0, S_1, S_2, \ldots, S_T\}$ and for a fixed S_0 which is the current price of the asset. Given a simulation $\{x_1, x_2, \ldots, x_T\}$ and given S_0, we use x_1 to obtain the next price as $S_1 = \exp(x_1)S_0$. More generally the consecutive prices of the assets are given by

$$S_t = \exp(x_t)S_{t-1}. \tag{I.5.48}$$

So this is how we simulate prices that follow a geometric Brownian motion.

To illustrate (I.5.48) we generate some possible price paths for an asset that follows a geometric Brownian motion with drift 5% and volatility 20%. Suppose we generate the paths in daily increments over 1 year. Then we must use the daily drift $0.05/365 = 0.000137$ and the daily standard deviation $0.2/\sqrt{365} = 0.010468$ in the simulation.

For each price path we generate 365 standard normal simulations, using the Excel command NORMSINV(RAND()). Then we apply (I.5.46) to each standard normal simulation in turn with $\sigma = 0.010468$ and with

$$\alpha = 0.000137 - 0.5 \times 0.010468^2 = 8.2192 \times 10^{-5}.$$

This way we obtain the sequence $\{x_1, x_2, \ldots, x_{365}\}$ of independent normal log returns with the required daily mean and variance. Finally, we fill down the possible asset prices, starting with the current price $S_0 = 100$, say, using (I.5.48). The computations are done in the case study spreadsheet. Figure I.5.18 shows four possible paths for the asset price, but each time you press F9 a new set of random numbers is generated.

For pricing and hedging options it is common to simulate price paths of assets following alternative asset price diffusions, perhaps with mean reversion, stochastic volatility or jumps. Simulations are particularly useful when volatility is assumed to be stochastic.[34] Simulation is a crude but sure method to obtain option prices and hedge ratios. It allows one to consider a huge variety of processes and price and hedge virtually any type of path-dependent claim.

---

[33] Assuming, for simplicity, no dividend or carry cost on the asset; otherwise we would subtract this from the risk free rate to obtain the risk neutral drift.
[34] See Section III.4.5 for examples.

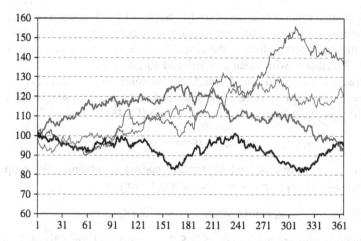

Figure I.5.18 Possible paths for an asset price following geometric Brownian motion

I.5.7.4 Simulations on a System of Two Correlated Normal Returns

Correlated simulations are necessary for computing the Monte Carlo VaR of a portfolio, and
we shall be drawing on the techniques described in this section very frequently in Volume IV.
Suppose we wish to generate two sequences of random draws that represent the returns on
correlated assets. For simplicity we shall again assume that each asset's returns are normally
distributed with means μ_1 and μ_2, standard deviations σ_1 and σ_2 and correlation ϱ. We first
write down the covariance matrix,

$$\mathbf{V} = \begin{pmatrix} \sigma_1^2 & \varrho\sigma_1\sigma_2 \\ \varrho\sigma_1\sigma_2 & \sigma_2^2 \end{pmatrix},$$

then we find its Cholesky matrix $\mathbf{C}$, i.e. the lower triangular matrix such that $\mathbf{V} = \mathbf{CC}'$.[35]
Now we take two independent standard normal simulations, z_1 and z_2, one for each asset
and set

$$\begin{pmatrix} x_1 \\ x_2 \end{pmatrix} = \mathbf{C}\begin{pmatrix} z_1 \\ z_2 \end{pmatrix}. \tag{I.5.49}$$

Then x_1 and x_2 will have the correct standard deviations and correlation, because taking
variance of the above gives

$$\mathbf{V}\begin{pmatrix} x_1 \\ x_2 \end{pmatrix} = \mathbf{C}\mathbf{V}\begin{pmatrix} z_1 \\ z_2 \end{pmatrix}\mathbf{C}' = \mathbf{CIC}' = \mathbf{V}.$$

Finally, adding μ_1 to x_1 and μ_2 to x_2 gives the required result.

I.5.7.5 Multivariate Normal and Student t Distributed Simulations

The argument above may be generalized to simulate sequences of returns on *many* correlated
assets. Suppose the asset returns have covariance matrix $\mathbf{V}$, which has the Cholesky matrix

---

[35] The calculation of the Cholesky matrix is explained in Section I.2.5.3.

C. Generate a matrix **Z**, with i.i.d. realizations that represent standard normal simulations. Then **ZC′** is a matrix that has columns which represent correlated normal variables with zero mean. Now take a row vector **μ** with elements equal to the means of each of the variables, and add this to each row of **ZC′** to obtain the matrix **X**. The columns of **X** will represent simulations on a set of correlated normal variables with the required means.

To illustrate this method we generate a set of simulations on a set of three correlated normal returns with the characteristics shown in Table I.5.4.

Table I.5.4 Characteristics of asset returns

	Asset 1	Asset 2	Asset 3
Mean	0.07	0.12	0.1
Standard deviation	0.2	0.3	0.25
Correlation matrix	1	0.5	0.75
	0.5	1	0.25
	0.75	0.25	1

The solution is implemented in the Excel spreadsheet for the case studies. Each time you press F9 three new sequences of 24 random numbers are generated. One such set of simulations **Z** is shown in Figure I.5.19. Not only are the simulations uncorrelated, the size of the simulated movements bears no relationship with the standard deviation of the assets.

We find the Cholesky matrix using the Excel Matrix add-in.[36] Then we apply this matrix to **Z**, as described above, adding on the mean returns to each row of **ZC′**. This way we obtain

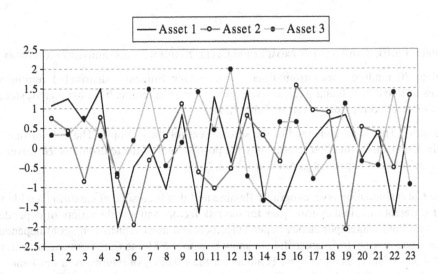

Figure I.5.19 A set of three independent standard normal simulations

---

[36] This is explained in Section I.2.5.3.

the matrix **X** of correlated simulations shown in Figure I.5.20. Clearly these simulations reflect the required covariance matrix.

It is simple enough to extend the example above so that the uncorrelated, zero-mean simulations are drawn from the standard Student t distribution. Then applying the expected return and the Cholesky matrix as we have for the standard normal simulations will transform the independent standard Student t distributed random draws into multivariate Student t distributed variables. The following example illustrates the method.

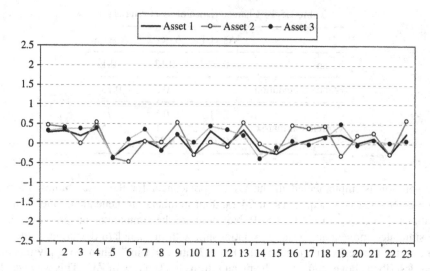

Figure I.5.20   A set of three correlated normal simulations

EXAMPLE I.5.10: SIMULATIONS FROM CORRELATED STUDENT t DISTRIBUTED VARIABLES

Simulate 20 random draws from three assets having Student t distributed returns with degrees of freedom 8, 6 and 9 respectively, when the asset returns have the means, standard deviations and correlations given in Table I.5.4.

SOLUTION   This is all contained in the spreadsheet for the example. The only difficulty is that the Excel TINV function returns only the positive half of the realizations. However, this can be adjusted as explained in Section I.3.5.3.

Monte Carlo simulation is an extremely flexible tool that is capable of capturing a wide variety of different marginal distributions for the risk factors and a wide variety of dependence structures, both contemporaneous dependence between asset returns and serial dependence of individual returns. In Chapter II.4 we show how to use Monte Carlo simulation with conditional dependence, using a GARCH model for the volatility of returns. And in Chapter II.6 we explain how to apply Monte Carlo simulation to returns that have different marginal distributions and to returns that have co-dependency that is captured by a *copula* function. And in Volume IV we make extensive use of Monte Carlo simulations to estimate portfolio value at risk.

I.5.8 SUMMARY AND CONCLUSIONS

This chapter has introduced the numerical methods that are commonly used to model financial risk. These include the following:

- *Iterative methods* for solving implicit equations, with applications that include the yield on a bond and the implied volatility of an option.
- Polynomial and spline techniques for *interpolation* and *extrapolation*, with applications to term structures of interest rates and implied volatility surfaces.
- Algorithms for finding the maximum or minimum value of a multivariate function, subject to certain constraints on the parameters. These *constrained optimization* techniques have many applications to portfolio optimization.
- Techniques for approximating a function's derivatives, based on *finite differences*. We have outlined how to use these techniques to compute the Greeks of an options portfolio and to solve partial differential equations for the evolution of options prices.
- *Binomial lattices* for pricing options based on the no arbitrage and risk neutral valuation principles. We have used lattices to price simple European and American options.
- Monte Carlo *simulations* of individual and correlated financial asset prices according to a given multivariate returns distribution. This technique will be used extensively in later volumes.

Computational finance is a very active area for research. Numerical methods that have been applied to many other disciplines are now finding applications to pricing and hedging the ever more complex products being sold in today's financial markets. But it is financial engineering rather than financial risk management that is the goal of computational finance. This chapter, which has merely provided a taster on the subject, only aims to equip a market risk manager with sufficient insight into the programs being developed by financial engineers and quants.

Introduction to Portfolio Theory

I.6.1 INTRODUCTION

This chapter examines the decisions made by investors, asset managers, risk managers and senior managers about their daily business. To utilize their resources efficiently they need to balance high return, higher risk activities with those that have low return but lower risk. But how should they choose the 'best' mix of activities? How can a fund manager choose his investments in different assets to optimize the performance of his portfolio? How should he measure the performance of his investments? And how can a senior manager allocate capital to different trading desks in an efficient manner? All the material presented in this chapter is motivated by these *optimal capital allocation* decisions.

There are two main applications of optimal capital allocation in finance:

- *Global asset management*. This is usually regarded as a multi-stage optimization process: first, select the optimal weights to be assigned to different asset classes (such as bonds, equities and cash); then, within each class, allocate funds optimally to various countries; finally, given the allocation to a specific asset class in a certain country, select the individual investments to maximize the investor's utility. Constraints on allocations may be needed, such as no short sales, or to restrict investments within a certain range such as 'no more than 10% of the fund is invested in US equities'.
- *Capital allocation in an investment bank*. First, the board selects optimal allocations to global product lines. Then, within each product line, the senior managers assign capital to different desks. Finally, the head of the desk will allocate limits to traders designed to maximize the (risk adjusted) return on capital. These allocations (e.g. the trading limits at the very end of the process) cannot be negative, which is the same in mathematical terms as the constraint that no short sales are allowed. And, just as a portfolio manager's attitude to risk will influence his choice of optimal portfolio, the degree of risk aversion of the head of desk will determine the trading limits that are optimal and the board's attitude to risk will determine their choice of allocation to global product lines. Even the performance of a trader, just like the performance of a portfolio or of a product line, can be compared in terms of risk-adjusted returns. In mathematical terms these problems are all equivalent.

In this chapter we consider the allocation problem from the perspective of an asset manager, but the same principles apply to capital allocation in an investment bank or in any other large financial institution.

The efficient allocation of sparse resources is the fundamental problem in microeconomics. Thus the mathematical concepts introduced here are those used in standard economic theory. The presentation of material in this chapter follows the chronological development. We begin with the theory of *utility functions* that was pioneered by Von Neumann and Morgenstern (1947). Section I.6.2 defines a decision maker's utility function and explains how to quantify his attitude to risk. We describe some standard utility functions that display different *risk aversion* characteristics and show how an investor's utility determines his optimal portfolio.

In the 1950s Harry Markowitz considered how to solve the *portfolio allocation* decision for a *risk averse* investor. In Section I.6.3 we consider the classical problem of portfolio selection that was introduced by Markowitz (1959). That is, how does an investor find the best mix of risky assets in his portfolio? We introduce the principle of *portfolio diversification* and the *minimum variance portfolio* allocation problem, with and without constraints on allocations. Then we extend this to consider the trade-off between risk and return and the *efficient frontier*.

Markowitz's work laid the foundation for the development of the *theory of asset pricing*, and we provide an overview of this in Section I.6.4. The theory is based on the principles of *single-agent optimization* and *market equilibrium*. We start by introducing the concept of the *market portfolio* which all rational investors in risky assets prefer to hold, and the *capital market line*. This leads on to the *capital asset pricing model* that was independently developed by Treynor (1965), Sharpe (1964) and Lintner (1965). Attempts to test the capital asset pricing model are surveyed and we outline its recent extensions. Section I.6.5 introduces the *risk adjusted performance measures* that are commonly used to rank investments. It is important to realize that we can always use a risk adjusted performance measure to *order* investments, but this ordering is not necessarily a *preference* ordering. Indeed, without a utility function it is not possible to state which investment is best for a particular investor. Section I.6.6 summarizes and concludes.

I.6.2   UTILITY THEORY

Among all the portfolios available to an investor, which one is regarded as optimal will depend on his attitude to risk and his perceived trade-off between risk and return. If an investor is very averse to taking risks he is more likely to choose a low return and low risk portfolio over a high risk and high return portfolio. To formulate the choice of optimal portfolio in a mathematical framework and hopefully to find a unique solution, it is convenient that the preferences of an investor be represented by a *utility function*. This section introduces the concept of a utility function, explains how it may be used to represent an investor's attitude to risk, introduces some standard utility functions and then derives the *mean–variance criterion* as the solution to an optimization problem that is relevant for investors that have a certain type of utility function.

I.6.2.1   Properties of Utility Functions

A utility function is a function $U: \Omega \to \Re$ from the space of all possible outcomes Ω to the real numbers $\Re$. For our purposes an outcome will be measured in terms of returns on an investment. Hence, our utility functions assign a real number to every possible allocation of capital and allocations may be ranked in order of preference by the size of their utility.

Risk preferences can be expressed rationally if decision makers accept a few elementary rules of behaviour that, to most, will appear quite natural. The four elementary rules are as follows:

(i) *Transitive preferences.* If an investor says he prefers outcome A to outcome B and he also prefers B to C, then he should prefer A to C.

(ii) *Independence.* If the investor is indifferent between outcomes A and B then for any outcome C he is also indifferent between the two gambles[1]

$$G_1 = \{A \text{ with probability } p \text{ and } C \text{ with probability } 1-p\}$$

and

$$G_2 = \{B \text{ with probability } p \text{ and } C \text{ with probability } 1-p\}.$$

(iii) *Certainty equivalence.* For any gamble there is a *certain equivalent* value such that the investor is indifferent between the gamble and the certain equivalent.

(iv) *Stochastic dominance.* Suppose G_1 and G_2 are two gambles over outcomes A and B, A is preferred to B and G_1 associates a higher probability with A than does G_2. Then we should prefer G_1 to G_2.

These four rules are sufficient to prove the existence of a utility function $U(W)$ that assigns a real number to any monetary amount W which we call the *wealth* of the investor.

An *investment* may be defined by a probability distribution over the possible outcomes, as illustrated in Example I.6.1 below. The *expected utility* of an investment P is defined as

$$E[U(P)] = \sum_{i=1}^{n} p_i U(W_i), \tag{I.6.1}$$

where $W_1, \ldots, W_n$ are the possible outcomes, in terms of the end of period wealth that can result from the investment, and these occur with probabilities $p_1, \ldots, p_n$.

EXAMPLE I.6.1: EXPECTED UTILITY

Consider two investments P and Q each with the same possible outcomes: they can return 0%, 10%, 20%, ..., 100%. The probabilities of these returns are different under each investment, otherwise they would be the same investment. Suppose P and Q have the distributions shown in Table I.6.1.

Table I.6.1 Two investments (outcomes as returns)

R	0%	10%	20%	30%	40%	50%	60%	70%	80%	90%	100%
$P_P(R)$	0.001	0.010	0.044	0.117	0.205	0.246	0.205	0.117	0.044	0.010	0.001
$P_Q(R)$	0.018	0.073	0.147	0.195	0.195	0.156	0.104	0.060	0.030	0.013	0.009

Now suppose that your utility function is

$$U(W) = W^2. \tag{I.6.2}$$

Calculate the expected utility of each investment.

SOLUTION   We replace the first row of Table I.6.1 by the utility associated with that return, leaving the probabilities of each outcome unchanged, and calculating the utility from (I.6.2). To calculate the utility associated with each return we must transform it into a figure that represents wealth. In Table I.6.2 we assume we have borrowed $10 with zero interest. So W is the return on $10. Although W is measured in dollars, $U(W)$ is not measured in dollars, it is simply a real number. For instance, if $R = 20\%$ then $W = \$2$ and $U(W) = 4$.

---

[1] A *gamble*, also called a *lottery*, is a probability distribution over possible outcomes Ω.

Table I.6.2   Two investments (utility of outcomes)

$U(W)$	0	1	4	9	16	25	36	49	64	81	100
$P_P(W)$	0.001	0.010	0.044	0.117	0.205	0.246	0.205	0.117	0.044	0.010	0.001
$P_Q(W)$	0.018	0.073	0.147	0.195	0.195	0.156	0.104	0.060	0.030	0.013	0.009

Taking the probability weighted sum of the utilities gives the expected utility of 27.51 for investment P and 19.99 for investment Q.

A utility function *orders* different investments so that if an investor has a choice between two risky investments P and Q he should always prefer the investment that has maximum expected utility. For instance, from Example I.6.1 we can deduce that the investor with utility function (I.6.2) prefers the investment P to the investment Q because P has the higher expected utility.

Notice that in the above example the outcomes were defined in terms of the percentage returns on an investment. This implied that our conclusion about which is the best investment is independent of the initial wealth of the investor. That is, he will prefer P to Q *whatever* his initial wealth, provided this is positive. So we could have assumed an initial wealth of $100 or $10 million instead of $10 and reached the same conclusion about our preference order between P and Q. But not all investments can be described by their possible percentage returns. For instance, the concept of a percentage return is very difficult to define for a long-short position, as we have seen in Section I.1.4.4. In that case we could define our investment as a distribution over profit and loss.

It can be shown that a utility function is only unique up to an *increasing affine transformation*. That is, choices resulting from the use of two utility functions, U_1 and U_2 will be identical if

$$U_1(W) = a + bU_2(W), \quad \text{with } b > 0. \tag{I.6.3}$$

For instance, we could replace our utility function $U(W) = W^2$ in the above example by the function $\tilde{U}(W) = 2W^2 - 1$ and our preference order over every possible investment would remain unchanged. In particular, since we prefers investment P to investment Q has higher expected utility $U(W) = W^2$ we also prefer P to Q under the utility $\tilde{U}(W) = 2W^2 - 1$.

Whilst expected utility can be used to order investment alternatives it is not on an intuitive measurement scale. It is just a real number which could be large or small, and positive or negative. The fact that we can rescale utility with an affine transformation (I.6.3) means that the actual number we see for a utility does not mean anything – it is only the *ordering* of the utilities that means something.

However, we can always translate the expected utility into a meaningful measure. We define the *certain equivalent* of an uncertain investment P as the monetary value $CE(P)$ that has the same utility as the expected utility as the investment. That is,

$$U[CE(P)] = E[U(P)]. \tag{I.6.4}$$

EXAMPLE I.6.2: CERTAIN EQUIVALENTS

Calculate and interpret the certain equivalents of the two investments in Example I.6.1, for an initial investment of $10.

Solution

$$CE(P)^2 = 27.75 \Rightarrow CE(P) = \$5.24,$$

$$CE(Q)^2 = 40.12 \Rightarrow CE(Q) = \$4.47.$$

Of course, $CE(Q) < CE(P)$ because we know from the expected utilities of the two alternatives that we prefer P to Q. The two certain equivalents tell us that we are indifferent between receiving \$5.24 for certain and investing \$10 in P, and that we are indifferent between receiving \$4.47 for certain and investing \$10 in Q. Since P has the higher certainty equivalent, it is the preferred investment.[2]

Both the certain equivalent and the expected utility are single numbers that can be used to rank investments. However, we prefer to use the certain equivalent because it has a more intuitive interpretation than expected utility. The advantage of the certain equivalent and expected utility is that the rankings they produce – which coincide if the utility function is strictly monotonic increasing – are a *preference ordering*. Thus we can make decisions based on these performance measures. Unfortunately, not all the risk adjusted performance measures introduced later in this chapter are associated with a utility function. Although we can rank investments using any measure, including any risk adjusted performance measure, we emphasize that it is theoretically meaningless to base an investment *decision* on a risk adjusted performance measure unless it can be associated with a preference order based on some utility function.

I.6.2.2   Risk Preference

We now consider the shape of the utility function. Usually we assume that 'more is better'. That is, the utility function is a strictly monotonic increasing function of wealth. Put another way, the *marginal utility* is always positive, i.e. $U'(W) > 0$ for every W. But $U''(W)$, which determines the curvature of the utility function, can take either sign. Figure I.6.1 depicts

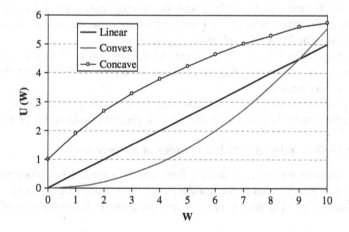

Figure I.6.1   Convex, concave and linear utility functions

---

[2] Note that the certain equivalents would be \$52.7 and \$63.3 respectively if our initial wealth was \$100 instead of \$10.

three utility functions. They all have positive marginal utility but one is convex, another is linear and the third is concave.

Using the curvature of the utility function, we can characterize the *risk preference* of an investor as follows:

- If $U''(W) > 0$, i.e. the utility is a convex function of W, there is an increasing marginal utility of wealth. In this case the investor is said to be *risk loving*.
- If $U''(W) < 0$, i.e. the utility is a concave function of W, there is diminishing marginal utility of wealth. In this case the investor is said to be *risk averse*.
- If $U''(W) = 0$, i.e. the utility is a linear function of W, the investor is said to be *risk neutral*.

An investment P may be described by a probability distribution over the utilities associated with all possible outcomes, as in Table I.6.2 above. Denote by μ_P and σ_P the expectation and standard deviation of wealth under this distribution. That is,

$$\mu_P = E[W] \text{ and } \sigma_P^2 = V[W]. \tag{I.6.5}$$

Using a second order Taylor series expansion of $U(W)$ around μ_P we have[3]

$$U(W) \approx U(\mu_P) + U'(\mu_P)(W - \mu_P) + \tfrac{1}{2}U''(\mu_P)(W - \mu_P)^2.$$

Now we take expectations of the above and use the tower law property, i.e.[4]

$$E[U(\mu_P)] = E[U(E[W])] = U(\mu_P),$$

and we also use the property that

$$E(W - \mu_P) = E(W) - \mu_P = 0.$$

This way we derive the following approximation to the expected utility of wealth resulting from an investment P:

$$E[U(W)] \approx U(\mu_P) + \tfrac{1}{2}\sigma_P^2 U''(\mu_P). \tag{I.6.6}$$

From (I.6.6) we may deduce that:

- If $U''(\mu_P) > 0$ then $CE(P) > U(\mu_P)$ and the investor puts a greater certain equivalent on an uncertain investment (i.e. a gamble) than its expected value. We conclude that the risk loving investor takes pleasure in gambling.
- If $U''(\mu_P) < 0$ then $CE(P) < U(\mu_P)$ and the investor puts a lower certain equivalent on an uncertain investment than its expected value. We conclude that the risk averse investor avoids gambling.
- If $U''(\mu_P) = 0$ then $CE(P) = U(\mu_P)$ and the investor has a certain equivalent equal to the expected return. We conclude that the risk neutral is willing to 'play the average'.

I.6.2.3 How to Determine the Risk Tolerance of an Investor

The utility function of an investor, or of a firm, can be encoded by recording the choices that the investor or the decision maker for the firm would make when presented with simple investment alternatives. The utility function can be used as a normative tool for making

---

[3] See Section I.1.6 for an introduction to Taylor expansion.
[4] This property is perhaps easier to understand when expressed in words, i.e. the expected utility of the expected utility is the expected utility.

choices among complex alternatives or as a risk policy statement to delegate the decision making authority.

To determine the *absolute risk tolerance* of a risk averse investor, which is the reciprocal of his absolute risk aversion coefficient,[5] we should present him with the following question. Suppose you can bet $X on a gamble where you receive either $2X or $\frac{1}{2}X$ with equal chances. That is, you have a 50:50 chance of doubling your money or halving it. What is the maximum amount that you are willing to bet? The answer is his absolute risk tolerance. For instance, suppose you are willing to bet $1 million on a gamble where you are returned either $2 million or $500,000 but you are not willing to bet more than this for a 'double-or-half' gamble. Then your coefficient of absolute risk tolerance is 10^6 (measured in $) and your absolute risk aversion coefficient is 10^{-6} (measured in $^{-1}$).

Similarly, to determine the *relative risk tolerance* of a risk averse investor, which is the reciprocal of his relative risk aversion coefficient, we should present him with the following question. Suppose you can gamble a certain proportion x of your wealth W on a lottery where you receive either $2(xW)$ or $\frac{1}{2}(xW)$ with equal chances. What is maximum proportion x that you are willing to bet? The answer is his relative risk tolerance. For instance, suppose you are willing to bet 20% of your total net wealth on a gamble where you are returned either double your net wealth or one half of it with equal chances, but you are not willing to bet more than this for a 'double-or-half' gamble. Then your coefficient of relative risk tolerance is 0.2 and your relative risk aversion coefficient is 5.

The quantification of risk attitude, through the assessment of risk tolerance and the construction of a utility function, is a very useful discipline. It allows decision makers to choose *consistently* between risky opportunities. For example, it is not uncommon to find investors showing risk aversion for a range of positive returns but a risk loving attitude for very positive or negative returns. This may be the result of cognitive biases or the consequence of conflict between the incentive of an individual and those of the firm for which he is acting. For example, it may not matter to an individual what losses he makes beyond a certain threshold because his career would have already been ruined;[6] or an individual may take a very small chance of winning a return that will change his life.

When examining a utility function and the different degrees of risk attitude expressed for different levels of returns, a decision maker has the opportunity to revise his preferences and perhaps choose to follow a more consistent pattern of behaviour. To illustrate, if a decision maker is risk averse for some levels of returns and risk loving for others, then a more consistent decision maker may take advantage of this pattern; she could make systematic gains at the expense of the first investor by offering a series of transactions that he will find attractive, even though they will result in a net loss for him. Most investors would want to avoid falling into this trap and should therefore adopt a utility function that is always convex. In other words, it is normally assumed that investors are risk averse.

I.6.2.4 Coefficients of Risk Aversion

We have seen above that diminishing marginal utility of wealth implies the investor is risk averse. The degree of risk aversion, i.e. the extent of the concavity of the utility function, is commonly measured by the *coefficient of absolute risk aversion*, which is defined as

---

[5] The *reciprocal* of a number x is $1/x$.

[6] A recent example of this is the rogue trader Jerome Kerviel who is blamed for losing over $7 billion for Société Générale.

$$A(W) = \frac{-U''(W)}{U'(W)}, \tag{I.6.7}$$

or by the *coefficient of relative risk aversion*, which is defined as

$$R(W) = \frac{-WU''(W)}{U'(W)}. \tag{I.6.8}$$

For instance, for the *logarithmic utility function*

$$U(W) = \ln(W), \ W > 0, \tag{I.6.9}$$

we have $U'(W) = W^{-1}$ and $U''(W) = -W^{-2}$. So by definition (I.6.7),

$$A(W) = W^{-1}. \tag{I.6.10}$$

Thus $A'(W) = -W^{-2} < 0$ and so the logarithmic utility has an absolute risk aversion that *decreases* with wealth. This means that the absolute value of his investment in risky assets will *increase* as he becomes more wealthy.

Likewise, by definition (I.6.8) the logarithmic utility function has coefficient of relative risk aversion given by:

$$R(W) = 1. \tag{I.6.11}$$

So the logarithmic utility has *constant* relative risk aversion. The interpretation of this is that an investor with a logarithmic utility will hold the same proportion of his wealth in risky assets however rich he becomes.

In general, investors with increasing absolute risk aversion, i.e. $A'(W) > 0$ will hold less in risky assets in *absolute* terms as their wealth increases. But investors with increasing relative risk aversion, i.e. $R'(W) > 0$, hold *proportionately* less in risky assets as their wealth increases. Investors may have increasing, constant or decreasing absolute or relative risk aversion depending on the functional form assumed for the utility function.

I.6.2.5 Some Standard Utility Functions

The Swiss mathematician Bernoulli, who was the first to promote the concept of utility functions,[7] argued that a man no matter how poor still has some positive net worth as long as he is alive. This attitude can be represented by the simple logarithmic utility function given by (I.6.9) above. We have just seen that the logarithmic utility has *constant relative risk aversion* (CRRA): indeed the coefficient of relative risk aversion is 1.

Another utility function that can be used to reflect CRRA is a simple form of the *power utility function* given by

$$U(W) = W^a, \ W > 0, a \neq 0.$$

In this form of power utility the coefficient of relative risk aversion is $R(W) = 1 - a$.

More generally a power utility has two parameters and takes the form

$$U(W) = (1 + bW)^a, W > 0, \ a < 1, \ b > 0 \tag{I.6.12}$$

Then the absolute risk aversion will always be linear and increasing with wealth.[8]

---

[7] See Bernoulli (1738).
[8] Further details on the properties of power utilities and of several other standard utility functions are given in the Appendix to Pézier (2008b).

Agents with CRRA want to hold the same *percentage* of their wealth in risky assets as their wealth increases. This may reflect the risk attitude of decision makers that are faced with extreme circumstances that could have a considerable effect on their state of wealth. However, it is more common that investment decisions will affect the wealth of the decision maker only marginally. If that is the case many decision makers prefer to adopt a *constant absolute risk aversion* (CARA) utility, where the absolute amount invested in risky assets is independent of their wealth.

There are only two types of utility functions with the CARA property. These are:

- the *linear utility function* given by

$$U(W) = a + bW, \ b > 0,$$ (I.6.13)

  which has CARA equal to 0; and
- the *exponential utility function* given by

$$U(W) = -\exp(-\gamma W), \ \gamma > 0,$$ (I.6.14)

  which has CARA equal to γ.

The exponential utility is an appropriate choice for an investor who wants to hold the same dollar amount in risky assets as his wealth increases. Hence the percentage of his wealth invested in risky assets will decrease as his wealth decreases, so the investor will have decreasing relative risk aversion but constant absolute risk aversion.

But the coefficient of absolute risk aversion is not very intuitive. It is measured in $\$^{-1}$ units if the initial wealth is measured in \$. For this reason it is usually easier to express the exponential utility in terms of the *coefficient of absolute risk tolerance*, which is measured in the same units as wealth. Risk tolerance also has an intuitive meaning, which risk aversion does not, as explained in Section I.6.2.3 above. If a problem that involves the exponential utility function *is* expressed in terms of a risk aversion coefficient the implicit assumption is that the initial wealth is 1 unit, for instance \$1 million. See Section I.6.2.7 for further discussion of this point.

If the percentage of wealth invested in risky assets increases with wealth, we may consider using the *quadratic utility function* which in its simplest form is given by

$$U(W) = W - aW^2, \ a > 0.$$ (I.6.15)

This only has increasing marginal utility when

$$U'(W) = 1 - 2aW > 0, \ \text{i.e.} \ W < (2a)^{-1}.$$

Hence the domain for a quadratic utility is restricted. By definition (I.6.8),

$$R(W) = \frac{2aW}{1 - 2aW}.$$ (I.6.16)

So we have

$$R'(W) = \frac{2a}{(1 - 2aW)^2} > 0.$$

Hence the quadratic utility function (I.6.15) has increasing relative aversion, which implies the absolute risk aversion must also be increasing. Hence a risk averse investor with a quadratic utility will decrease the percentage of his wealth (and therefore also the absolute amount) invested in risky assets as his wealth increases.

Finally, we mention that the certain equivalents of CRRA and CARA utility functions have different properties. Specifically the certain equivalent is multiplicative for a CRRA utility but additive for a CARA utility, in the following sense:

- **CRRA Property.** Let CE be the certain equivalent of an uncertain state of wealth W. Then for any $\lambda > 0$, λCE is the certain equivalent of the uncertain wealth λW. We sometimes refer to CRRA utility functions as having the *lambda property*.
- **CARA Property.** Let CE be the certain equivalent of an uncertain state of wealth W. Then for any δ, $CE + \delta$ is the certain equivalent of an uncertain state of wealth $W + \delta$. We sometimes refer to CARA utility functions as having the *delta property*.

I.6.2.6 Mean–Variance Criterion

Suppose an investor has an *exponential utility function* with coefficient of absolute risk aversion γ, i.e.

$$U(W) = -\exp(-\gamma W), \quad \gamma > 0.$$

Also suppose the returns on an investment portfolio are *normally* distributed with expectation μ and standard deviation σ. Then it is easy to show that the certain equivalent of the investment may be approximated as[9]

$$CE \approx \mu - \tfrac{1}{2}\gamma\sigma^2. \tag{I.6.17}$$

The best investment is the one that gives the maximum certain equivalent. But the expected portfolio return is[10]

$$\mu = \mathbf{w}'E(\mathbf{r}), \tag{I.6.18}$$

where $\mathbf{w}$ is the vector of portfolio weights and $\mathbf{r}$ is the vector of returns on the constituent assets. And the portfolio variance is

$$\sigma^2 = \mathbf{w}'\mathbf{V}\mathbf{w}, \tag{I.6.19}$$

where $\mathbf{V}$ is the covariance matrix of the asset returns. Hence, for an investor with an exponential utility function investing in risky assets with normally distributed returns, the optimal allocation problem may be approximated by the simple optimization

$$\max_{\mathbf{w}} \left\{ \mathbf{w}'E(\mathbf{r}) - \tfrac{1}{2}\gamma\mathbf{w}'\mathbf{V}\mathbf{w} \right\}. \tag{I.6.20}$$

This is the *mean–variance criterion*.

The next example illustrates the application of the mean–variance criterion to determine the optimal distribution of funds between two risky assets, for an investor with an exponential utility function. In this example, as in Example I.6.1, the utility is defined on the *returns* on the investment, and so we must multiply the utility function by the amount invested to find the utility of each investment. Similarly, to find the certain equivalent (I.6.17) of a risky investment we multiply by the amount invested. But here, as in the mean–variance criterion (I.6.20), we need to express the coefficient of risk aversion, γ, *as a proportion of the amount invested*. This is always the case when utilities are defined on returns. The example illustrates how to do this.

---

[9] This will be proved for a more general case in Section I.6.2.7.
[10] See Section I.2.4.2.

EXAMPLE I.6.3: PORTFOLIO ALLOCATIONS FOR AN EXPONENTIAL INVESTOR

An investor has \$1 million to invest in a portfolio with two risky assets with normally distributed returns. Asset 1 has an expected return of 10% with a volatility of 20% and asset 2 has an expected return of 15% with a volatility of 30%. The correlation between the two asset returns is -0.5. If the investor has an exponential utility function with an absolute risk tolerance coefficient of \$250,000, how much does he invest in each asset?

SOLUTION   The risk aversion coefficient, expressed as a proportion of the amount invested is the ratio of the amount invested to the risk tolerance of the investor, which in this case is

$$\gamma = \frac{\$1,000,000}{\$250,000} = 4.$$

So we need to maximize the objective function in (I.6.20) with $\gamma = 4$, i.e.

$$0.1w + 0.15(1-w) - 2 \times \left(0.2^2 w^2 + 0.3^2 (1-w)^2 - 2 \times 0.5 \times 0.2 \times 0.3 \times w \times (1-w)\right),$$

which may be rewritten as

$$-0.03 + 0.43w - 0.38w^2.$$

The first order condition is

$$0.43 - 0.76w = 0 \Rightarrow w = 0.565789.$$

This is a maximum because the second derivative of the objective function is negative. Hence \$565,789 is invested in asset 1 and \$434,211 is invested in asset 2.

We remark that if an exponential utility function is not appropriate, perhaps because an investor has constant relative risk aversion rather than constant absolute risk aversion, then there is no simple link between the expected utility of a portfolio and its mean–variance characteristics.

I.6.2.7   Extension of the Mean–Variance Criterion to Higher Moments

We have seen that it is convenient to assume that an investor borrows the funds used for investments at zero interest. This assumption allows one to consider the utility associated with an investment as being defined on the distribution of investment *returns* rather than on the distribution of the wealth arising from the investment. So we may write a utility function as $U(R)$, a function of the uncertain return R rather than as a function of the uncertain wealth W. In this case it is also convenient to express the coefficient of risk aversion that appears in the exponential utility and in the mean–variance criterion as a proportion of the amount invested, as in the example above.

Suppose the investment returns are non-normally distributed. Let μ and σ denote the expectation and standard deviation of the returns distribution (as in the previous subsection) and further denote by τ and $\varkappa$ the skewness and the excess kurtosis of the returns distribution. Apply the expectation operator to a Taylor expansion of $U(R)$ about $U(\mu)$, the utility associated with the mean return. This gives

$$E[U(R)] = U(\mu) + U'(R)\big|_{R=\mu} E[R-\mu] + \frac{1}{2}U''(R)\big|_{R=\mu} E\left[(R-\mu)^2\right]$$
$$+ \frac{1}{3!}U'''(R)\big|_{R=\mu} E\left[(R-\mu)^3\right] + \dots. \tag{I.6.21}$$

Since $E[U(R)] = E[U(P)] = U(CE(P))$, (I.6.21) provides a simple approximation to the certain equivalent associated with any utility function.

Now suppose the investor has an exponential utility function given by (I.6.14). Using (I.6.21) and taking the expansion to fourth order only, we have

$$\exp(-\gamma CE) \approx \exp(-\gamma\mu)\left(1 + \frac{1}{2}\gamma^2 E\left[(R-\mu)^2\right] - \frac{1}{6}\gamma^3 E\left[(R-\mu)^3\right] + \frac{1}{24}\gamma^4 E\left[(R-\mu)^4\right]\right),$$

or, since $\sigma^2 = E\left[(R-\mu)^2\right]$, $\tau = \sigma^{-3} E\left[(R-\mu)^3\right]$ and $\kappa = \sigma^{-4} E\left[(R-\mu)^4\right]$,

$$\exp(-\gamma CE) \approx \exp(-\gamma\mu)\left(1 + \frac{1}{2}(\gamma\sigma)^2 - \frac{\tau}{6}(\gamma\sigma)^3 + \frac{\kappa}{24}(\gamma\sigma)^4\right).$$

Take logs of the above and use the second order approximation[11]

$$\ln(1+x) \approx x - \frac{1}{2}x^2. \tag{I.6.22}$$

This gives, after some calculations, the following fourth order approximation to the certain equivalent associated with the exponential utility function:

$$CE \approx \mu - \frac{1}{2}\gamma\sigma^2 + \frac{\tau}{6}\gamma^2\sigma^3 - \frac{\varkappa}{24}\gamma^3\sigma^4. \tag{I.6.23}$$

where $\varkappa = \kappa - 3$. The mean–variance criterion (I.6.17) is a special case of (I.6.23) where the investment has zero skewness associated with its returns and we have ignored the fourth order term. In general, whenever a risk averse investor has an exponential utility, their aversion to risk is associated with negative skewness and increasing kurtosis as well as with increasing variance.

EXAMPLE I.6.4: HIGHER MOMENT CRITERION FOR AN EXPONENTIAL INVESTOR

Two portfolios have the returns characteristics shown in Table I.6.3. An investor with an exponential utility has $1 million to invest. Determine which portfolio he prefers when he invests:

(i) $1 million and his absolute risk tolerance coefficient is $200,000;
(ii) $1 million and his absolute risk tolerance coefficient is $400,000;
(iii) $1 million and his absolute risk tolerance coefficient is $100,000;
(iv) only $0.5 million and his absolute risk tolerance coefficient is $100,000.

---

[11] This approximation only holds when x is small. It follows from the expansion of $\ln(1+x)$ given in Section I.1.2.5.

Table I.6.3 Returns characteristics for two portfolios

Portfolio	Mean	Standard deviation	Skewness	Excess kurtosis
A	10%	12%	−0.5	2.5
B	15%	20%	−0.75	1.5

SOLUTION

(i)   The absolute risk aversion coefficient, as a proportion of the amount invested, is

$$\gamma = \frac{\$1,000,000}{\$200,000} = 5.$$

In the spreadsheet for this example the certain equivalent is calculated using the approximation (I.6.23) with this value for γ and with the moments for each portfolio shown in Table I.6.3. Portfolio A has a certain equivalent of $57,700 and portfolio B has a certain equivalent of $12,500, hence portfolio A is preferred.

(ii) If the risk tolerance were $400,000 instead of $200,000 then γ would be only 2.5 and portfolio B would be the preferred investment, with a certain equivalent of $92,188 compared with $80,763 for portfolio A. Hence, portfolio B is more attractive to a less risk averse investor.

(iii) When the risk tolerance is small, i.e. the investor is very risk averse, γ becomes very large and then both portfolios are considered too risky. In fact, if the risk tolerance is only $100,000 then $\gamma = 10$ and the approximation (I.6.23) gives a *negative* certain equivalent for both investments. Portfolio A has a certain equivalent of −$8,000 and portfolio B has a certain equivalent of −$250,000 relative to an investment of $1 million. But a negative *CE* implies that an investment is not attractive at all. We deduce that an exponential investor with $1 million of wealth should not invest all of it in either portfolio, if he is very risk averse.

(iv) Our answer to (iii) is based on an investment of $1 million, i.e. the entire wealth of the investor. With an absolute risk tolerance of $100,000 relative to a wealth of $1 million these two portfolios are not attractive as homes for *all* of the investor's wealth. But a smaller investment than $1 million *will* prove attractive: even if the amount invested is very small, the fact that the portfolios have positive returns guarantees that they will provide some attraction to the risk averse investor. For instance, the investor with a risk tolerance of $100,000 could invest only $500,000 in portfolio A. This gives him a positive certain equivalent of $28,850 which is greater than the certain equivalent of portfolio B. Note that his absolute risk aversion coefficient is 5 in this case, just as it was in part (i) and, since the amount invested has been halved, the certain equivalent is now one half of the certain equivalent in part (i).

I.6.3 PORTFOLIO ALLOCATION

This section concerns the classical problems in portfolio allocation – i.e. how to:

- allocate investments to minimize the variance of a portfolio;
- choose portfolio weights to achieve a required level for the expected return whilst minimizing the portfolio's variance; and
- minimize portfolio variance subject to several constraints on the portfolio weights.

We begin by focusing on the correlation between assets and how this influences the risk of the portfolio. The fundamental principle of portfolio diversification is explained, followed by the concept of *mean–variance analysis* that was introduced by Harry Markowitz in the 1950s.

The portfolio allocation problem assumes the assets have already been selected and asks how to make the best choice for the portfolio weights. The expected return on a linear portfolio is a weighted sum of the expected returns on its constituents. We shall use matrix notation in most of what follows, except in the simple case of two risky assets, so we denote the expected return by $w'E(r)$, where

$$E(\mathbf{r}) = (E(r_1), \ldots, E(r_n))' \text{ and } \mathbf{w} = (w_1, \ldots, w_n)'$$

are the vectors of expected returns on n risky assets and portfolio weights, i.e. the proportion of capital invested in each asset. In Section I.2.4.2 we explained how to express the variance of a linear portfolio as a *quadratic form* $\mathbf{w}'\mathbf{V}\mathbf{w}$ where $\mathbf{V}$ is the covariance matrix of asset returns.

We shall not be concerned here with the manner in which the forecasts of risk and return are constructed. For the purpose of the present chapter it does not matter whether the asset risk and returns forecasts are based on subjective beliefs, historical data with statistical models, or some combination of these.[12]

I.6.3.1 Portfolio Diversification

We illustrate the diversification principle using a simple example of a long-only portfolio with just two assets. We suppose that a proportion w of the nominal amount is invested in asset 1 and a proportion $1 - w$ is invested in asset 2 with $0 \leq w \leq 1$. We denote the volatilities of the assets' returns by σ_1 and σ_2 and the correlation of their returns by ϱ. Then the variance of the portfolio return R is given by[13]

$$V(R) = w^2\sigma_1^2 + (1-w)^2\sigma_2^2 + 2\varrho w(1-w)\sigma_1\sigma_2. \tag{I.6.24}$$

Suppose, for the moment, that asset 1 has been selected and we have fixed the portfolio weight w on that asset. But we have not yet selected asset 2, and we have several assets to choose from. All of these assets have the same returns volatilities but they have different correlations with the returns on asset 1. What is the effect of the correlation on the portfolio volatility? Which asset should we select (i.e. what should ϱ be) if we want to minimize the portfolio variance?

Figure I.6.2 shows the volatility of a portfolio with two risky assets, where the returns have volatilities 20% and 40% respectively and 75% of the funds are invested in the lower volatility asset. The portfolio volatility, plotted here as a function of the asset returns correlation, is a monotonic increasing function. The maximum portfolio volatility is 25%, which occurs when the asset returns have a correlation of $+1$, and the minimum volatility is 5%, which occurs when the asset returns have a correlation of -1.

We can derive general expressions for the upper bound and lower bound for the volatility of a long-only portfolio by writing the portfolio variance (I.6.24) as

$$V(R) = (w\sigma_1 + (1-w)\sigma_2)^2 - 2(1-\varrho)w(1-w)\sigma_1\sigma_2. \tag{I.6.25}$$

---

[12] Forecasting equity returns using factor models is covered in Chapter II.1, and covariance matrix forecasting is discussed in considerable detail in Chapters II.3 and II.4.

[13] This follows from the rules for variance operator given, for example, in Section I.3.2.6.

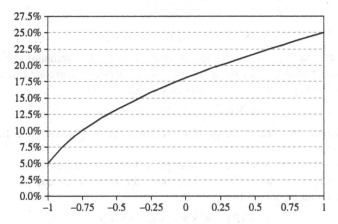

Figure I.6.2   The effect of correlation on portfolio volatility

This is a linear increasing function of correlation, so its minimum value will occur when $\varrho = -1$ and its maximum value will occur when $\varrho = 1$. We now prove that

$$|w\sigma_1 - (1-w)\sigma_2| \leq V(R) \leq w\sigma_1 + (1-w)\sigma_2, \text{ if } 0 \leq w \leq 1. \qquad (I.6.26)$$

Substituting $\varrho = -1$ into (I.6.25) produces the lower bound $|w\sigma_1 - (1-w)\sigma_2|$ for the portfolio volatility. For instance, in Figure I.6.2 the minimum portfolio volatility was $|0.25 \times 20\% - 0.75 \times 40\%| = 5\%$. Hence, to minimize the portfolio's volatility, we should choose the second asset to have the lowest possible correlation with asset 1, all else being equal. This observation also holds for a portfolio with more than two assets: the lower the correlations between all assets, the lower the portfolio volatility.

Now substituting $\varrho = 1$ into (I.6.25) shows that the weighted average of the asset volatilities $w\sigma_1 + (1-w)\sigma_2$ provides an upper bound for the portfolio volatility. For instance, the maximum portfolio volatility was $0.25 \times 20\% + 0.75 \times 40\% = 25\%$ in Figure I.6.2. The portfolio volatility is only equal to the weighted sum of the asset volatilities when the assets are perfectly correlated. This observation also holds for portfolios with several assets or components: when all components are perfectly correlated the portfolio risk is just the weighted sum of the component risks.

We now turn to the general problem of diversification in a portfolio of n risky assets. The $n \times 1$ vector of portfolio weights is denoted $\mathbf{w}$ and we assume these are all non-negative and that they sum to 1. The $n \times n$ matrix of variances and covariances of the asset returns is denoted $\mathbf{V}$. This may be written as $\mathbf{V} = \mathbf{DCD}$, where $\mathbf{D}$ is the $n \times n$ diagonal matrix of standard deviations and $\mathbf{C}$ is the correlation matrix of the asset returns.[14] We show that whenever asset returns are less than perfectly correlated then the risk from holding a long-only portfolio will be *less* than the weighted sum of the component risks.

To see this, write the variance of the portfolio return R as

$$V(R) = \mathbf{w'Vw} = \mathbf{w'DCDw} = \mathbf{x'Cx}, \qquad (I.6.27)$$

---

[14] If further explanation of this identity is required, see Section I.2.4.

where

$$\mathbf{x} = \mathbf{Dw} = (w_1\sigma_1, \ldots, w_n\sigma_n)'$$

is a vector where each portfolio weight is multiplied by the standard deviation of the corresponding asset return. If all the asset returns are perfectly correlated then $\mathbf{C} = \mathbf{1}_n$, the $n \times n$ matrix with every element 1.[15] In this case (I.6.27) yields

$$(\mathbf{w}'\mathbf{Vw})^{1/2} = w_1\sigma_1 + \ldots + w_n\sigma_n.$$

That is, the standard deviation of the portfolio return is the weighted sum of the asset return standard deviations.

But when some asset returns have less than perfect correlation then $\mathbf{C}$ has some elements that are less than 1. Since the portfolio is long-only, the vector $\mathbf{x}$ has non-negative elements, and in this case it can be shown that

$$V(R) = \mathbf{w}'\mathbf{Vw} = \mathbf{x}'\mathbf{Cx} \leq \mathbf{x}'\mathbf{1}_n\mathbf{x}. \tag{I.6.28}$$

The inequality (I.6.28) is the matrix generalization of the upper bound for the portfolio variance that was derived above for two assets.

We have thus proved the *principle of portfolio diversification*, i.e. that holding portfolios of assets reduces risk, relative to the sum of the risks of the individual positions in the assets. And the lower the correlation between the asset returns, the lower the portfolio risk will be. Maximum risk reduction for a long-only portfolio occurs when correlations are highly negative, but if the portfolio contains short positions we want these to have a high *positive* correlation with the long positions for the maximum diversification benefit.

In a long-only portfolio the weighted average of the asset volatilities provides an upper bound for the portfolio volatility, which is obtained only when the assets are all perfectly correlated. Hence, even when assets are highly correlated but not perfectly correlated, accounting for their correlations when measuring portfolio risk can lead to a substantial reduction compared with assessing the risks of each position separately.

Fund managers often seek to balance their funds by limiting exposure to *specific risk*, i.e. the risk on specific assets.[16] The principle of diversification implies that they can make their net specific risk very small by holding a large portfolio with many assets. But they are still left with an *irreducible risk* because of the exposure to a general market risk factor that is common to all assets.[17] The irreducible part of the assets returns will be highly correlated because of the common market factor, but the idiosyncratic parts of their returns are not usually highly correlated. Hence, the diversification effect over specific risks is strong. Empirical studies on US stock portfolios have demonstrated that holding about 30 stocks in a portfolio is usually enough for the net specific risk to become negligible.

I.6.3.2   Minimum Variance Portfolios

Again we begin by analysing a portfolio with two risky assets, and now we assume that the assets have been selected but we do not know the allocations. How should we choose the portfolio weight w on the first asset so that the variance (I.6.24) is minimized?

---

[15] Note that every column of $\mathbf{1}_n$ is the vector $\mathbf{1} = (1, 1, \ldots, 1)'$ and that $\mathbf{1}_n$ is not the identity matrix, $\mathbf{I}$.
[16] Also called *idiosyncratic risk*.
[17] Also called *systematic risk* or *undiversifiable risk*.

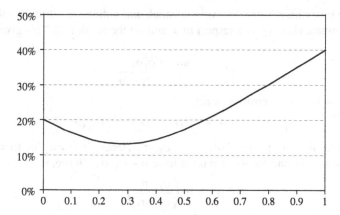

Figure I.6.3   Portfolio volatility as a function of portfolio weight

Figure I.6.3 takes the same two assets as those used to draw Figure I.6.2, but this time we fix the correlation to be −0.5 and draw the portfolio volatility as a function of the weight on asset 1.

The portfolio volatility is *not* a monotonic increasing function of the portfolio weight. It has a minimum value which in this example occurs when the weight on asset 1 is about 0.3. How can we find this *minimum variance portfolio weight* precisely? We write the portfolio variance as a function of the unknown weight w and differentiate, set the first derivative to 0 and solve for w. The following example illustrates the method.

EXAMPLE I.6.5: MINIMUM VARIANCE PORTFOLIO: TWO ASSETS

We have €1 million to invest in two risky assets: asset 1 has a returns volatility of 20% and asset 2 has a returns volatility of 30% and the returns have a correlation of −0.25. What allocations to each asset will minimize the variance of the portfolio? What is the volatility of the minimum variance portfolio?

SOLUTION   The portfolio's variance is

$$V(w) = 10^{-2} \times \left(4w^2 + 9\left(1 - w\right)^2 - 3w(1 - w) \right)$$

$$= 10^{-2} \times (16w^2 - 21w + 9).$$

Differentiating gives

$$\frac{dV(w)}{dw} = 32w - 21 = 0 \quad \text{when} \quad w = w^* = \frac{21}{32} = 0.65625.$$

This is a minimum since the second derivative is 32, which is positive. Hence, we should invest €656,250 in asset 1 and €343,750 in asset 2 to minimize the risk of the portfolio. Now substituting this optimal w^* in $V(w)$ and taking the square root shows that the volatility of the minimum variance portfolio is 14.52%, which is considerably less than either of the assets' volatilities.

In this example there was a non-trivial solution to the minimum variance problem, i.e. the optimal portfolio weight w was neither 0 nor 1. But if the correlation between the assets had been different this may not be the case. That is, not all values of ϱ admit a non-trivial solution to the risk minimization problem. For certain values of ϱ the optimal portfolio would allocate everything to the less volatile stock and nothing at all to the other stock. To see this, differentiate (I.6.24) with respect to w and set the result to 0. This gives the optimal portfolio weight

$$w^* = \frac{\sigma_2^2 - \varrho\sigma_1\sigma_2}{\sigma_1^2 + \sigma_2^2 - 2\varrho\sigma_1\sigma_2}. \tag{I.6.29}$$

The denominator is always positive, since

$$\sigma_1^2 + \sigma_2^2 - 2\varrho\sigma_1\sigma_2 = (\sigma_1 - \varrho\sigma_2)^2 + (1 - \varrho^2)\sigma_2^2.$$

But the numerator is only positive when $\varrho < \sigma_2/\sigma_1$. Hence, if $\varrho < \sigma_2/\sigma_1$ then $w^* > 0$. But we also require $w^* < 1$ and for this we must have $\varrho < \sigma_1/\sigma_2$. Hence, $0 < w^* < 1$ only when

$$\varrho < \min\left(\frac{\sigma_1}{\sigma_2}, \frac{\sigma_2}{\sigma_1}\right). \tag{I.6.30}$$

For instance, if $\varrho = 2/3$ in Example I.6.5 we would allocate everything to asset 1. And if $\varrho > 2/3$ and short sales are allowed we would invest *more* than €1 million in asset 1 and finance this by going short on asset 2. For instance, with a value $\varrho = 0.75$ we would invest €1.125 million in asset 1 and go short €125,000 on asset 2 to achieve the risk minimizing portfolio, which has a volatility of 19.84%.

EXAMPLE I.6.6: MINIMUM VARIANCE PORTFOLIO ON S&P 100 AND FTSE 100

How should we allocate funds between the S&P 100 index and in the FTSE 100 index? During 2006 the S&P index returned 5% with a volatility of 20% and the FTSE index returned 60% with a volatility of 20%. The returns on the two indices had a correlation of 0.55. Ignoring the exchange rate risk, and using only the historical risk and return in 2006, determine the proportion of capital we should invest in each index. How do the portfolio return and the portfolio volatility change as we change the portfolio weights? What is the volatility of the minimum variance portfolio?

SOLUTION   This problem is similar to that given in Example I.6.5, but in this case we present our solution graphically rather than algebraically. Figure I.6.4 depicts the portfolio's expected return on the left-hand scale and the portfolio volatility on the right-hand scale, as a function of the weight w on the S&P index along the horizontal axis. When all the funds are invested

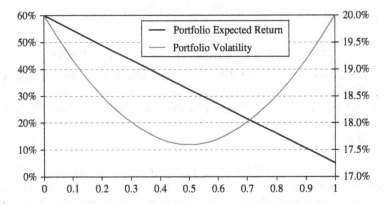

Figure I.6.4   Portfolio risk and return as a function of portfolio weight

in the FTSE index, the portfolio has an expected return of 60% and a volatility of 20%, and when all the funds are invested in the S&P index, the portfolio has an expected return of 5% and a volatility of 20%.

The expected return on the portfolio declines linearly with w but the portfolio volatility has a 'U' shape. The portfolio with minimum volatility occurs when we split our funds 50:50 between the two indices. This is because they have the same volatility, so the formula (I.6.29) gives $w^* = 0.5$. Whenever we have two risky assets with the same volatility, the minimum variance portfolio will allocate equal funds to each asset and their correlation has no effect on the minimum variance portfolio weight. The correlation only affects the variance of the minimum variance portfolio, and readers can verify this by changing the correlation in the spreadsheet for this example.

Figure I.6.5 represents the same data as in Figure I.6.4 in a different format. The horizontal axis is the portfolio volatility and the vertical axis is the expected return. The curve is drawn by varying the portfolio weight on the S&P 100 index. When $w = 0$ all the funds are invested in the FTSE 100 index, so the portfolio has volatility 20% with an expected return of 60%, and when $w = 1$ all the funds are invested in the S&P 100 index, so the portfolio has volatility 20% with an expected return of 5%. For intermediate values of w the set of points (x, y) with $x =$ portfolio volatility and $y =$ portfolio expected return describes a curve. When $w = \frac{1}{2}$ we have the minimum variance portfolio, which has volatility 17.6% and expected return $\frac{1}{2}(60\% + 5\%) = 32.5\%$.

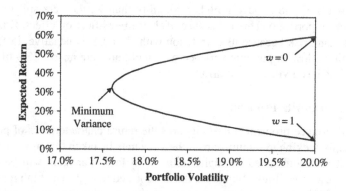

Figure I.6.5 Minimum variance portfolio

Next we state the general formulation of the minimum variance problem. The minimum variance portfolio of n assets is obtained when the portfolio weights are chosen so that the portfolio variance is as small as possible. We write the problem as

$$\underset{\mathbf{w}}{\text{Min}}\, \mathbf{w}' \mathbf{V} \mathbf{w}, \tag{I.6.31}$$

where $\mathbf{V}$ is the covariance matrix of asset returns and $\mathbf{w}$ is the vector of portfolio weights. Clearly the solution to (I.6.31) is $\mathbf{w} = \mathbf{0}$, i.e. if you make no investment you have zero risk. However, a non-zero allocation will place a constraint on the portfolio weights. The constraint is usually

$$\sum_{i=1}^{n} w_i = 1. \tag{I.6.32}$$

But in some cases, e.g. when the portfolio represents a spread trade, we would require the sum of the weights to be 0.

Any constraint on the portfolio weights restricts the feasible set of solutions to (I.6.31). It can be shown that the solution of (I.6.31) subject to the single constraint (I.6.32) is

$$\tilde{w}_i = \psi_i \left(\sum_{i=1}^{n} \psi_i \right)^{-1}, \tag{I.6.33}$$

where ψ_i is the sum of all the elements in the ith column of $\mathbf{V}^{-1}$. The portfolio with these weights is called the *global minimum variance portfolio* and it has variance

$$V^* = \left(\sum_{i=1}^{n} \psi_i \right)^{-1}. \tag{I.6.34}$$

EXAMPLE I.6.7: GENERAL FORMULA FOR MINIMUM VARIANCE PORTFOLIO

Three assets X, Y and Z have volatilities 15%, 20% and 40%, respectively. Their returns correlations are 0.5 for X and Y, -0.7 for X and Z and -0.4 for Y and Z. Find the minimum variance portfolio.

SOLUTION The spreadsheet for this example applies the formula (I.6.33) to obtain

$$\tilde{w}_1 = 66.07\%, \quad \tilde{w}_2 = 10.41\%, \quad \tilde{w}_3 = 23.52\%,$$

and the resulting minimum variance portfolio has a volatility of only 8.09%. Note that even though assets Y and Z have a higher volatility than X, they are still included in the minimum variance portfolio. This is because of their diversification effect. Z is particularly good at diversifying risk because its correlation with X and Y is negative. In fact, to obtain a portfolio with the lowest possible variance we should allocate nearly 25% of our funds to Z, even though Z has a volatility of 40%!

I.6.3.3 The Markowitz Problem

The minimum variance problem (I.6.31) ignores the return characteristics of portfolios. But rather than simply seeking to minimize risk, the view may be taken that more risk is perfectly acceptable if it is accompanied by higher returns. In fact, managers will be in danger of under-utilizing resources if insufficient capital is allocated to high risk, high return activities.

Markowitz (1959) places another constraint on the minimum variance problem, that the portfolio should be expected to meet or exceed a *target level of return* $\bar{R}$. Hence, the optimization problem becomes

$$\underset{\mathbf{w}}{\text{Min}}\, \mathbf{w}'\mathbf{V}\mathbf{w} \quad \text{such that} \quad \sum_{i=1}^{n} w_i = 1 \text{ and } \mathbf{w}'E(\mathbf{r}) = \bar{R}, \tag{I.6.35}$$

where $E(\mathbf{r})$ is the vector of expected returns on each asset and $\mathbf{w}'E(\mathbf{r}) = \bar{R}$ is a target level for the portfolio return. The Markowitz problem is easy to solve analytically. By writing down the first order conditions it is straightforward to show that the problem (I.6.35) has the solution

$$\begin{pmatrix} \mathbf{w}^* \\ \lambda_1 \\ \lambda_2 \end{pmatrix} = \begin{pmatrix} 2\mathbf{V} & 1 & E(\mathbf{r}) \\ \mathbf{1}' & 0 & 0 \\ E(\mathbf{r})' & 0 & 0 \end{pmatrix}^{-1} \begin{pmatrix} 0 \\ 1 \\ \bar{R} \end{pmatrix}, \tag{I.6.36}$$

where λ_1 and λ_2 are the *Lagrange multipliers* defined in Section I.1.5.4.

EXAMPLE I.6.8: THE MARKOWITZ PROBLEM

Suppose the three assets X, Y and Z of Example I.6.7 have expected returns 5%, 6% and 0%, respectively. Find a portfolio that is expected to return at least 6% with the minimum possible variance.

SOLUTION   The augmented matrix on the right-hand side of (I.6.36) is

$$\begin{pmatrix} 0.045 & 0.03 & -0.084 & 1 & 0.05 \\ 0.03 & 0.08 & -0.064 & 1 & 0.06 \\ -0.084 & -0.064 & 0.32 & 1 & 0 \\ 1 & 1 & 1 & 0 & 0 \\ 0.05 & 0.06 & 0 & 0 & 0 \end{pmatrix}$$

where the top left 3×3 block is twice the covariance matrix. Finding the inverse of this matrix and multiplying this by the vector $(0, 0, 0, 1, 0.06)'$ gives the solution

$$(w_1, w_2, w_3, \lambda_1, \lambda_2) = (0.3732, 0.6890, -0.0622, 0.095, -2.761).$$

Thus assigning weights of 37.32%, 68.90% and −6.22% of the nominal value of the portfolio to assets X, Y and Z, respectively, gives a portfolio that is expected to return 6%. This portfolio has smaller variance than any other portfolio of X, Y and Z that returns 6% and the spreadsheet for this example shows that the volatility of this minimum variance portfolio is 18.75%.

An alternative analytic expression for the solution to the Markowitz problem is

$$\tilde{w}_i = \frac{(a\psi_i - b\xi_i) - \bar{R}\left(b\psi_i - \tilde{V}\xi_i\right)}{b\tilde{V} - a^2} \tag{I.6.37}$$

where ψ_i is the sum of all the elements in the ith column of V^{-1}, ξ_i is the expected returns weighted sum of the ith column of V^{-1}, $\tilde{V}$ is the variance of the unconstrained minimum variance portfolio given by (I.6.34), and

$$a = \sum_{i=1}^{m} \psi_i E(r_i) \quad \text{and} \quad b = E(r)' V^{-1} E(r). \tag{I.6.38}$$

I.6.3.4   Minimum Variance Portfolios with Many Constraints

It is not usually possible to find an analytic solution for the minimum variance portfolio weights when more constraints are added to those in (I.6.35). For instance, suppose *no short sales* are allowed, i.e. the weights should never be negative. This time we add an *inequality constraint* and the problem becomes

$$\underset{w}{\text{Min}}\, w'Vw \quad \text{such that} \quad \sum_{i=1}^{n} w_i = 1, \quad w'E(r) = \bar{R}, \quad w_i \geq 0 \text{ for all } i. \tag{I.6.39}$$

The solution to (I.6.39) cannot be expressed analytically. In the following example we show how to use the Excel Solver to optimize a portfolio subject to no short sales and other constraints.

EXAMPLE I.6.9: MINIMUM VARIANCE PORTFOLIO WITH MANY CONSTRAINTS

Consider the same three assets as in the previous examples, but now we require the expected return on the portfolio to be at least 5%. If no short sales are allowed and we add the further constraint that no more than one half of the notional must be allocated to asset 2, what is the minimum variance portfolio?

SOLUTION   Figure I.6.6 illustrates the Solver settings for this problem. The solution is to allocate 51.2% of the notional to X, 40.7% to asset Y and 8.1% to Z, giving an expected return of 5% and a volatility of 11.92%.

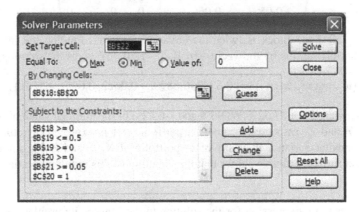

Figure I.6.6   Solver settings for Example I.6.9

I.6.3.5   Efficient Frontier

Consider a portfolio with n risky assets having portfolio weights $\mathbf{w}$. Denote the expected returns on the assets by the vector $E(\mathbf{r})$ and the returns covariance matrix by $\mathbf{V}$. Let $\mathbf{w}$ vary, and as it varies plot the expected portfolio return $\mu = \mathbf{w}'E(\mathbf{r})$ on the vertical axis and the portfolio standard deviation $\sigma = (\mathbf{w}'\mathbf{V}\mathbf{w})^{1/2}$ on the horizontal axis. Consider all possible allocations $\mathbf{w}$ such that the sum of the weights is 1. The set of all points $\left\{\mathbf{w}'E(\mathbf{r}),\ (\mathbf{w}'\mathbf{V}\mathbf{w})^{1/2}\right\}$ is called the *opportunity set* or the *feasible set* in $\{\mu, \sigma\}$ space.

Figure I.6.7 presents a stylized plot of the opportunity set. It is the set of all points in the shaded region. If a portfolio's risk and expected return lie on the bold line in Figure I.6.7 it is not possible to adjust allocations to gain higher expected return for the same level of risk, or less risk for the same level of expected return. For this reason we label the bold line in the figure the *efficient frontier*. The efficient frontier is the top and left boundary of the opportunity set. Marked on the figure are the global minimum variance portfolio and a minimum variance portfolio having a given level of return. The left-most point on the efficient frontier marks the risk and return of the global minimum variance portfolio which is given by (I.6.34).

If we take any two portfolios that lie on the efficient frontier, the curvature of the efficient frontier between them will depend on the correlation between the two portfolios' returns. The efficient frontier is just a straight line between them if the two portfolios have returns that are perfectly correlated. The boundary becomes more convex as their correlation decreases.

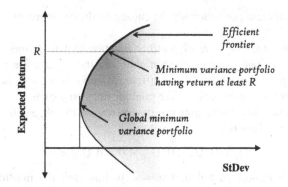

Figure I.6.7   The opportunity set and the efficient frontier

This is because the ability to reduce risk through portfolio diversification increases, even when no short sales are allowed. Other important properties of the efficient frontier are as follows:

- Any portfolio on the efficient frontier is a linear combination of any two other portfolios along the efficient frontier.
- Any portfolio along the efficient frontier is likely to contain all the assets in the opportunity set with either positive or negative weights, unless restricted to zero by constraints.
- If short sales are allowed there is no upper limit to the risk one can take and the opportunity set tends to infinity as increasing portfolio expected return is associated with increasing portfolio standard deviation.
- If the 'no short sales' constraint is imposed then the opportunity set cannot extend infinitely far along the direction of increasing risk. In this case the efficient frontier is the envelope of all portfolios lying between the global minimum variance portfolio and the maximum expected return portfolio.

The shape of the opportunity set is determined by the expected returns on each asset and the properties of the covariance matrix **V**. Two remarks about the expected returns and the asset returns covariance matrix are in order here:

- There is almost nothing one can learn about expected returns from past data. It is far better to look at the current economic situation and what we know about what is coming ahead. This is a key area where forward looking personal views are much better than extrapolations from historical returns.
- Generally speaking, the lower the correlations in **V** the more convex the boundary of the opportunity set. But the correlation estimates in **V** can vary considerably depending on the statistical model used to estimate them. Hence, the methods used to estimate **V** have a pronounced effect on the shape of the efficient frontier.

I.6.3.6   Optimal Allocations

The shape of the efficient frontier has a great influence on the optimal efficient portfolio, i.e. the portfolio on the efficient frontier that is regarded as being optimal by a certain investor. Different efficient portfolios will be chosen by different investors according to their preferences.

Indifference curves are *isoquants* of a utility function that is defined not on wealth but on other variables. For our purposes the variables are the expectation μ and the standard deviation σ of the portfolio returns. An indifference curve is a curve in $\{\mu, \sigma\}$ space that joins all points having the same utility, like contour lines on a map.

A risk averse investor has diminishing utility with respect to risk, and diminishing marginal utility of extra returns. That is

$$U_{\mu} > 0, \ U_{\sigma} < 0, \ U_{\mu\mu} < 0 \text{ and } U_{\sigma\sigma} < 0, \tag{I.6.40}$$

where the subscripts denote partial derivatives. In this case the indifference curves will be convex downwards, as illustrated in Figure I.6.8. The investor is indifferent between some high risk and high return and some low risk and low return portfolios. That is, he is willing to accept more risk only if it is accompanied by more return because he is risk averse.

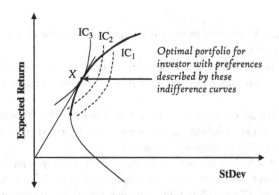

Figure I.6.8   Indifference curves of risk averse investor

Since the efficient frontier is convex upwards and the indifference curves of a risk averse investor are convex downwards there should be a unique optimal portfolio. Three curves are drawn on Figure I.6.8 representing increasing levels of utility. The maximum achievable utility is on the indifference curve IC_3 that is tangential to the efficient frontier, and the optimum portfolio X is at the point of tangency. Any other portfolio in the opportunity set will have a lower utility level.

Without the assumption of risk aversion, indifference curves will be either straight lines, for a risk neutral investor, or concave downwards, for a risk loving investor. Neither of these assumptions can guarantee a unique optimal portfolio. In fact risk loving indifference curves do not determine a finite solution, at least when short sales are allowed, as can be seen in Figure I.6.9. The risk loving investor would seek to go infinitely short the risk free asset and long the risky asset to achieve the highest possible risk and return.

Assuming an optimal portfolio can be found, it will require very frequent rebalancing. The shape of the efficient frontier changes very frequently, each time the investor changes his views about expected returns or revises his forecast of the covariance matrix. Hence optimal portfolios will not stay optimal for very long; they will require very frequent rebalancing,

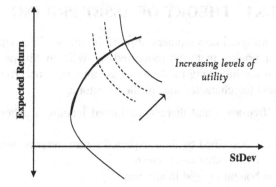

Increasing levels of utility

Figure I.6.9   Indifference curves of risk loving investor

which is very costly and is likely to erode any excess returns made by the portfolio. In that case the investor would be better off with a passive, index tracking portfolio.

Common methods for cutting rebalancing costs include the following:

- Using subjective forecasts for the covariance matrix and, especially, for the expected returns.
- Imposing extra constraints on allocations.
- Assigning current portfolio weights as a weighted average of currently recommended and past optimal allocations. This has the effect of smoothing allocations over time, but the resulting portfolio may be far from optimal and it may not respond enough to current market conditions.
- Setting rebalancing limits so that allocations are changed only if the weights recommended by the optimal portfolio exceed them. Depending on the range of these limits, which is an arbitrary choice, rebalancing cost can be substantially reduced but again portfolios may be far from optimal.
- Doing a limited amount of rebalancing in the direction indicated by the latest analysis.
- It is quite common that the shape of the efficient frontier is determined by just a few assets with unusually high expected returns. Hence, allocations to these assets may be constrained before the analysis and then excluding them from the feasible set used to determine the allocations to other assets.

The problems with efficient frontier analysis that are outlined above have a common root. This is that asset returns are stationary, *short term* processes that have no *long term* memory. It is asset *prices* and not asset returns that contain a memory of the past. By individually detrending each price to obtain the return we are actually throwing away our memory about comovements between asset prices. The optimal portfolios determined by this expected return and risk analysis which are crucially dependent, on the asset correlations, can only be optimal over the short term.[18]

---

[18] See Chapter III.5 on cointegration for further discussion of this important point.

I.6.4   THEORY OF ASSET PRICING

We continue our chronological development of portfolio mathematics with a brief overview of the theory of asset pricing that was pioneered by William Sharpe during the 1960s. The theory is based on the following fundamental assumptions concerning the assets in the investment universe and the characteristics of the investors:

1. There is a risk free asset and there is unlimited lending and borrowing at the risk free rate.
2. All assets are fully described by their expected return, returns standard deviation and returns correlation with other asset returns.
3. All assets can be bought or sold in any quantity.
4. All investors share the same information.
5. All investors are risk averse in the sense that they prefer the portfolio with the minimum variance corresponding to any given level of return.

In this section we first show that these assumptions lead us to a unique *market portfolio* of risky assets that all investors agree is the optimal basket of risky assets. In other words, all investors will hold portfolios that are a combination of the market portfolio and the risk free asset. This result is sometimes referred to as *Tobin's separation theorem*.[19] Then we follow the development of the capital asset pricing model, which introduces the concept of the *market beta* of an asset, also called its *systematic risk*. The model implies that assets with no systematic risk must earn the risk free rate, and any excess return over the risk free rate is proportional to the systematic risk. The market beta is derived from the covariance of the asset return and the market portfolio return. But the covariance is just the first moment of the joint distribution between the returns. We end this section by outlining some recent attempts to extend the concept of systematic risk so that it is based on higher moments than the covariance.

I.6.4.1   Capital Market Line

Given any portfolio P we can form another portfolio by placing a proportion w of our funds in P and a proportion $1 - w$ in the risk free asset.[20] The expected return on the new portfolio is given by

$$\mu = w\mu_P + (1 - w) R_f. \tag{I.6.41}$$

That is, the new expected return will lie on the line between P and R_f at a point that is determined by w. The standard deviation of returns on the new portfolio is given by

$$\sigma = w\sigma_P,$$

because the risk free rate has zero variance. Turning this around gives $w = \sigma_P^{-1}\sigma$ and substituting this into (I.6.41) gives

$$\mu = R_f + \sigma_P^{-1}\sigma \left(\mu_P - R_f\right), \tag{I.6.42}$$

i.e.

$$\mu = R_f + \lambda\sigma, \text{ where } \lambda = \frac{\mu_P - R_f}{\sigma_P}. \tag{I.6.43}$$

---

[19] See Tobin (1958).
[20] This w can be greater than 1, in which case we borrow at the risk free rate to invest more in P than we have in our funds.

The λ in (I.6.43) is called the *Sharpe ratio*. It follows that the expected return on any new portfolio that is a combination of the portfolio P and the risk free asset is on a line through P with slope λ that cuts the returns axis at R_f.

This is illustrated in Figure I.6.10. We also depict the opportunity set without risk free borrowing and lending (the dotted curve) and the efficient frontier when there is borrowing and lending at the risk free rate (the bold line). Under the five assumptions stated in the introduction to this section all investors will agree on the optimal allocation between all risky assets when there is no lending or borrowing. This allocation is called the *market portfolio*, and we denote it M.

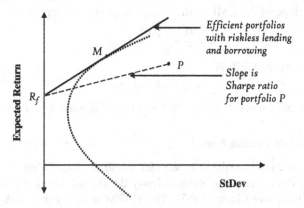

Figure I.6.10   Market portfolio

Some investors may choose to borrow at the risk free rate and others may choose to lend at the risk free rate depending on their preferences, but the net allocation over all investors to the risk free asset must be zero. Since all investors agree on the optimal portfolio containing only risky assets, the portfolio weights on each risky asset in the market portfolio must be proportional to its market capitalization.

By borrowing or lending at the risk free interest rate we can achieve any level of risk and return on the *capital market line* (CML), i.e. the line through the risk free interest rate R_f and the market portfolio M shown in Figure I.6.11. Portfolios to the left of M are combinations

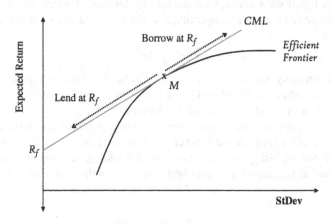

Figure I.6.11   Capital market line

of lending at rate R_f and holding M. Portfolios to the right are combinations of borrowing at rate R_f and holding M. The actual portfolio that will be chosen along this line depends on the risk preferences of the investor.

EXAMPLE I.6.10: THE CML EQUATION

Suppose the market portfolio has an expected return of 10% with a standard deviation of 20%. Find the equation for the capital market line if the risk free rate is 5%.

SOLUTION   The intercept of the CML is equal to the risk free rate of return, i.e. 0.05 in this example, and the slope of the CML is the Sharpe ratio (I.6.43) for the market portfolio, i.e.

$$\lambda = \frac{0.1 - 0.05}{0.2} = 0.25,$$

Hence the equation of the CML is

$$\mu = 0.05 + 0.25\sigma$$

where μ and σ are the expected return and the standard deviation of a portfolio.

I.6.4.2   Capital Asset Pricing Model

Markowitz's mean–variance analysis in the 1950s laid the foundations of the capital asset pricing model (CAPM) which was independently developed during the 1960s by Treynor (1965), Sharpe (1964) and Linter (1965). The CAPM assumes the existence of a market portfolio and the capital market line, but in themselves these do not tell us how to *price* risky assets. The purpose of the CAPM is to deduce how to price risky assets when the market is in equilibrium.

To derive the CAPM, we consider the conditions under which a risky asset may be added to an already well diversified portfolio. The conditions depend on the *systematic risk* of the asset, also called the *undiversifiable risk* of the asset since it cannot be diversified away by holding a large portfolio of different risky assets. We also need to know the risk free rate of return and the expected return on the market portfolio. Then we ask: given the systematic risk of an asset, what should its expected excess return be to justify its addition to our well diversified portfolio?[21]

The CAPM is based on a concept of *market equilibrium* in which the expected excess return on any single risky asset is proportional to the expected excess return on the market portfolio. That is,

$$E(R_i) - R_f = \beta_i(E(R_M) - R_f) \tag{I.6.44}$$

for all returns R_i on risky assets $i = 1, 2, \ldots, n$. On the left-hand side of (I.6.44) we have the expected excess return on the ith risky asset, and the CAPM equilibrium states that this must be proportional to the systematic risk of the asset, β_i.

The coefficient β_i represents the asset return's sensitivity to changes in the market return: if the expected excess return on the market portfolio increases by 1% then the expected excess return on the ith risky asset increases by β_i%. So β_i is a sensitivity risk measure relative to the market risk factor. For simplicity we refer to this risk measure as the *CAPM*

---

[21] The expected *excess return* on a risky asset (or portfolio) is the difference between the expected return on the asset (or portfolio) and the risk free rate of return.

beta of the asset. The term inside the bracket on the right-hand side is called the *market risk premium*: it is the additional return that investors can expect, above the risk free rate, to compensate them for the risk of holding the market portfolio.

If we know the asset's beta, the expected return on the market portfolio and the risk free rate of return then model (I.6.44) establishes the equilibrium value for the expected return on the asset, $E(R_i)$. Moreover, if we also know all future cash flows from holding the asset we could discount them using this expected return and thus obtain the current equilibrium price for the asset.

I.6.4.3 Security Market Line

The security market line (SML) depicted in Figure I.6.12 is the line derived from the CAPM equilibrium (I.6.44) where $E(R_i)$ is plotted as a function of the *CAPM beta*. It passes through the points $(0, R_f)$ and $(1, E(R_M))$ and has slope $E(R_M) - R_f$. In CAPM equilibrium the expected return and systematic risk of *all* risky assets lies along this line. And to determine how much return we require for a given level of systematic risk we simply read off the value from the SML corresponding to this level of beta.

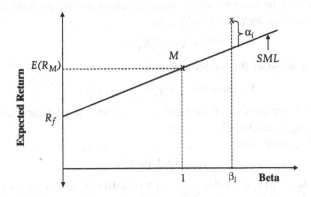

Figure I.6.12   Security market line

In the CAPM equilibrium no single asset may have an *abnormal return* where it earns a rate of return of *alpha* above (or below) the risk free rate without taking any market risk. The market is *not* in equilibrium if

$$E(R_i) - R_f = \alpha_i + \beta_i\big(E(R_M) - R_f\big), \quad \alpha_i \neq 0, \tag{I.6.45}$$

for any risky asset i. Then the asset will give a point that is above or below the SML according as its alpha is positive or negative. This is illustrated by the point X in Figure I.6.12.

If the market is not in equilibrium any asset with a positive alpha has an expected return that is in excess of its equilibrium return and so should be bought, and any asset with a negative alpha has an expected return that is below its equilibrium return and so should be sold. But abnormal returns will not continue indefinitely – over a period of time the price will rise as a result of buying pressure and the abnormal profits will vanish.

If we can observe a current market price for the asset then we can estimate a CAPM model for its equilibrium price and thus decide whether the asset is overpriced or underpriced relative to its equilibrium price. But we would not use this information to trade on the asset.

We need to be able to *forecast* the alpha of an asset, using a regression model based on the CAPM or some other factor model, in order to decide whether to add it to our portfolio. See Chapter II.1 for further details.

I.6.4.4 Testing the CAPM

The statistical test of the CAPM equilibrium is a test for the hypothesis

$$H_0 : \alpha_1 = \alpha_2 = \cdots = 0. \tag{I.6.46}$$

The CAPM is a cross-sectional model, but it is common to put the model into a time series context and to test the hypothesis (I.6.46) using historical data on the excess returns on the assets and the excess return on the market portfolio.

If the CAPM holds in every period and β_i is assumed to be constant over the whole sample of T observations, then the CAPM test may be based on a regression model of the form

$$E(R_{it}) - R_{ft} = \alpha_i + \beta_i \left(E(R_{Mt}) - R_{ft} \right) + \varepsilon_{it}, \tag{I.6.47}$$

for $i = 1, \ldots, n$ and $t = 1, \ldots, T$. Here ε_{it} is the stock's specific return and each intercept term α_i should be 0 if the CAPM model equilibrium holds.

This may be written in a more concise form, denoting the excess market returns by X_{Mt} and the excess returns on each stock by Y_{it}, as

$$Y_{it} = \alpha_i + \beta_i X_{Mt} + \varepsilon_{it}. \tag{I.6.48}$$

An equivalent expression of the model uses matrix notation:

$$\mathbf{y}_t = \boldsymbol{\alpha} + \boldsymbol{\beta} X_{Mt} + \boldsymbol{\varepsilon}_t, \quad t = 1, \ldots, T, \tag{I.6.49}$$

where $\mathbf{y}_t$ is an $n \times 1$ vector with ith element Y_{it}, $\boldsymbol{\varepsilon}_t$ is an $n \times 1$ vector with ith element ε_{it}, and $\boldsymbol{\alpha} = (\alpha_1, \ldots, \alpha_n)'$ and $\boldsymbol{\beta} = (\beta_1, \ldots, \beta_n)'$.

We may wish to assume that

$$\varepsilon_{it} \sim \text{ i.i.d. } (0, \sigma_i^2), \tag{I.6.50}$$

but we cannot assume that the error term on two different assets are contemporaneously uncorrelated. So, denoting by ϱ_{ij} the correlation between ith asset excess return and the jth asset excess return, and assuming this is constant over time, we have the covariance matrix

$$V(\varepsilon_t) = (\rho_{ij} \sigma_i \sigma_j) = \Sigma, \tag{I.6.51}$$

say. Now we can state the test statistic for the hypothesis (I.6.46) as

$$W = k_M \hat{\boldsymbol{\alpha}}' \Sigma^{-1} \hat{\boldsymbol{\alpha}}, \tag{I.6.52}$$

where

$$k_M = \left(1 + \left(\frac{\overline{X}}{s_X} \right)^2 \right)^{-1} \tag{I.6.53}$$

and $\overline{X}$ and s_X denote the sample mean and sample standard deviation of the excess return on the market portfolio. Under the null hypothesis W has a chi-squared distribution with n degrees of freedom.[22]

---

[22] See Chapter 5 of Campbell et al. (1997) for the derivation.

To test the hypothesis (I.6.46) we need to obtain historical data on the excess returns on the assets and the excess return on the market portfolio. For instance, monthly data over a 5-year period might be taken on each stock in the US, a broad market index such as the Wilshire 5000 may be taken as the market portfolio, and a risk free rate could be the US Treasury rate of a maturity equal to the investment horizon. A summary of the empirical evidence for and against the CAPM model is given in Campbell et al. (1997). The considerable evidence against the CAPM had led to the development of factor models that extend the basic assumptions of CAPM. Some of these models are reviewed in the next subsection.

I.6.4.5 Extensions to CAPM

The test for the CAPM described above assumes that the systematic risk of each risky asset is constant over time and that the error process in (I.6.49) is homoscedastic. Jagannathan and Wang (1996) and Bollerslev et al. (1988) propose time varying versions of the CAPM that allow the conditional variance of the errors to follow a GARCH process and the systematic risk to vary over time.

The CAPM also assumes that the returns on risky assets are fully characterized by their expected return and standard deviation, and tests of the CAPM equilibrium are based on the assumption that the joint distribution between the return on an asset and the return on the market portfolio is normal. But it is possible to extend this assumption to allow the joint distribution to be non-normal. In this case it is possible to derive an extension to the CAPM equilibrium where the systematic risk of a risky asset is related to the higher moments of the joint distribution.

In these *higher moment CAPM* equilibriums the skewness and kurtosis of the joint distribution between the returns on a risky asset and the return on the market portfolio are called the *coskewness* and the *cokurtosis* of the asset's excess return.[23] In Kraus and Litzenberger (1976) the coskewness captures the asymmetric nature of returns on risky assets and in Fang and Lai (1997) the returns leptokurtosis is captured by the cokurtosis.

The derivation of higher moment CAPM models is based on the higher moment extension of the investor's utility function that we derived in Section I.6.2.7. Maximizing the expected utility (I.6.21) leads to an equilibrium model of the form

$$E(R_i) - R_f = \theta_1\beta_i + \theta_2\gamma_i + \theta_3\eta_i, \tag{I.6.54}$$

where $\theta_1 + \theta_2 + \theta_3 = E(R_M) - R_f$ and

$$\beta_i = \frac{E(\tilde{R}_i\tilde{R}_M)}{E(\tilde{R}_M^2)}, \ \gamma_i = \frac{E(\tilde{R}_i\tilde{R}_M^2)}{E(\tilde{R}_M^3)}, \ \text{and} \ \eta_i = \frac{E(\tilde{R}_i\tilde{R}_M^3)}{E(\tilde{R}_M^4)} \tag{I.6.55}$$

are the covariance, coskewness and cokurtosis of the ith risky asset. Here $\sim$ denotes the mean deviation, i.e. $\tilde{R}_i = R_i - E(R_i)$ and $\tilde{R}_M = R_M - E(R_M)$.

Since Harvey and Siddique (2000) there have been numerous papers on empirical tests of the validity of higher moment CAPM equilibrium, and its application to asset pricing. Many of these are contained or reviewed in Jurczenko and Maillet (2006).

---

[23] These also called the *systematic skewness* and *systematic kurtosis* in some papers.

I.6.5 RISK ADJUSTED PERFORMANCE MEASURES

Asset managers and market risk managers tend to employ risk metrics for different purposes. The main concern of the risk manager is that the firm's capitalization is adequate to cover the risk of its positions in risky assets. The market risk manager needs to monitor risks on a frequent (e.g. daily) basis and to employ methods that focus on the proper aggregation of risks, taking into account the netting of positions and the correlations between assets and risk factors. Risk managers are not primarily concerned with the returns, although senior managers will use expected returns as well as risk to allocate capital across the different activities of the firm in an efficient manner.

By contrast, the main concern of an asset manager is to provide to his investors an accurate report of the fund's return as well as its risk. Both risk and return are usually measured relative to a benchmark, in which case we call them the *active return* and the *active risk*, respectively.[24] If fund managers consider only the active return then too much capital would be allocated to assets with a higher than average expected return but a commensurately higher risk. Similarly, if they consider only the active risk then too little capital would be allocated to the same assets. Most investors in actively managed funds have some degree of risk aversion and so require a limit on the active risk of the fund. By taking the ratio of active return to active risk in a *risk adjusted performance measure* (RAPM) it is possible for fund managers to rank different investment opportunities.

RAPMs are commonly used to rank portfolios in order of preference. That is, if the value of the RAPM is greater for investment A than it is for investment B then A is deemed to be preferred to B. But a preference ordering on RAPMs implies that preferences are already embodied in the measure. Unfortunately, only some RAPMs have a direct link to a utility function. Other RAPMs may still be used to *rank* investments but we cannot deduce anything about preferences from this ranking, so no decision should be based on the ranks. To make a decision we need a utility function.

There is a heated debate about which RAPM should be applied to different types of investments. Many RAPMs are based on downside risk metrics.[25] Unfortunately, downside RAPMs can rarely be linked to a utility function. Most are only concerned with returns that fall short of a benchmark or threshold return, so the utility function can be anything at all above that threshold. They have the strange property that investors are assumed to care nothing at all about the returns that are above the benchmark or threshold. Despite this obvious theoretical limitation, downside RAPMs are in common use. Clearly the theoretical foundation of the choice of RAPM is not of much concern to their clients.

This section begins with a review of the classical RAPMs that were introduced in conjunction with the capital asset pricing model during the 1960s. Then we ask whether they should be used to rank portfolios in order of preference. We explain how they are estimated and introduce some extensions that are designed to measure the performance of investments when a description of investors' preferences over higher moments of returns is important. Finally, we introduce the omega and kappa indices, which are currently very popular amongst practitioners, and discuss their properties.

---

[24] Readers should be aware of the pitfalls of using active risk, as measured by the *tracking error* of a portfolio. See the discussion in Section II.1.6.
[25] See Section IV.1.4.

I.6.5.1 CAPM RAPMs

This section describes the risk adjusted performance measures that are linked to the capital asset pricing model and its extensions. A fundamental RAPM is the *Sharpe ratio*, λ, which applies if the distributions to be compared have the same shape in the region of their expected values. For example, all the distributions that are being ranked should be normal, or they should all have a Student t distribution with the same degrees of freedom. The Sharpe ratio is relevant to a portfolio where there is the option to invest in a risk free asset. For instance, it can apply to the decision about allocations between cash and risky assets such as equities, commodities and bonds.

We assume that there is unlimited risk free lending and borrowing at the risk free rate R_f. In Section I.6.4.1 we introduced the *Sharpe ratio* as the slope of the capital market line. It is the excess of the expected return on an asset (or more generally on an investment portfolio) over the risk free rate divided by the standard deviation of the asset returns distribution, i.e.

$$\lambda = \frac{E(R) - R_f}{\sigma}, \tag{I.6.56}$$

where $E(R)$ and σ are the forecasted expected return and standard deviation of the asset or portfolio's returns.

Suppose we forecast an alpha for a risky asset in the CAPM framework (I.6.47) and that this alpha is positive. Then we may wish to add this asset to our well diversified portfolio, but the CAPM does not tell us how much of this asset we should buy. If our holding is too large this will affect the diversification of our portfolio. The asset has a non-zero specific risk σ, so if we add too much of the asset this will produce a specific risk of the portfolio that is also non-zero.

A risk adjusted performance measure associated with abnormal returns in the CAPM framework was proposed by Treynor (1965). The *Treynor ratio* is given by

$$TR = \frac{\alpha}{\beta}, \tag{I.6.57}$$

where α and β are the intercept and slope coefficients in (I.6.47). That is, β is the sensitivity of the asset's excess return to changes in the market portfolio excess return and α is the part of the asset's excess return that is not explained by the market excess return.

The optimal amount of a risky asset to add to our portfolio is given by another RAPM which is called the *information ratio* or the *appraisal ratio*. It is given by

$$IR = \frac{\alpha}{\sigma}. \tag{I.6.58}$$

The α alone is sometimes called *Jensen's alpha* after the paper by Jensen (1969) which argues that α is a more appropriate measure than TR or IR for ranking the performance of different portfolios. Thus if fund mangers make decisions according to this RAPM they would view the best investment as that with the largest α, irrespective of the risk. This can explain why some fund managers seem obsessed with finding 'alpha' and may not take so much care to measure their risks in an appropriate manner.

In the arbitrage pricing theory, introduced by Ross (1976), the CAPM is extended to multiple risk factors, leading to the multi-factor return models that are commonly used to identify 'alpha opportunities' in fund management today.[26] However, it is extremely

---

[26] Multi-factor models are introduced in Section II.1.3.

difficult to obtain a consistent ranking of potential portfolios using Jensen's alpha because the estimated alpha is so dependent on the multi-factor model used. For further details, and an application of Jensen's alpha to ranking hedge funds, see Alexander and Dimitriu (2005).

Although they are popular, the classical RAPMs have only a limited range of application. For instance, implicit in the use of the Sharpe ratio is the assumption that investors' preferences can be represented by the exponential utility and that returns are normally distributed. A logarithmic utility function satisfies the risk aversion condition but does not lead to the Sharpe ratio. And an exponential utility function applied to a non-normal probability distribution of returns does not lead to the Sharpe ratio either.

I.6.5.2 Making Decisions Using the Sharpe Ratio

The stochastic dominance axiom of utility was the fourth of the conditions stated in Section I.6.2.1 for the existence of a utility function. It implies that if exactly the same returns can be obtained with two different investments A and B, but the probability of a return exceeding any threshold τ is always greater with investment A, then A should be preferred to B. Formally, we say that an investment A *strictly dominates* another investment B if and only if

$$P_A(R > \tau) > P_B(R > \tau) \text{ for any } \tau, \tag{I.6.59}$$

and A *weakly dominates* B if and only if

$$P_A(R > \tau) \geq P_B(R > \tau) \text{ for any } \tau. \tag{I.6.60}$$

No rational investor should choose an investment that is weakly dominated by another. Yet we now show that the Sharpe ratio can fail to rank investments according to weak stochastic dominance.

EXAMPLE I.6.11: STOCHASTIC DOMINANCE AND THE SHARPE RATIO

Consider two portfolios A and B. The distributions of their returns in excess of the risk free rate are given in Table I.6.4. Which is the better portfolio? Does the ranking of the portfolios by the Sharpe ratio agree with this preference?

Table I.6.4   Two investments

Probability	Excess return A	Excess return B
0.1	20%	40%
0.8	10%	10%
0.1	−20%	−20%

SOLUTION   The only difference between the two portfolios is that the highest excess return from portfolio A is only 20%, whereas the highest excess return from B is 40%. Weak stochastic dominance therefore indicates that any rational investor should prefer B to A.

However, let us compare the Sharpe ratios of the two investments. We calculate the mean and standard deviation of the excess returns and divide the former by the latter. The results are shown in Table I.6.5. Hence, according to the Sharpe ratio, A should be preferred to B!

Table I.6.5 Sharpe ratio and weak stochastic dominance

Portfolio	A	B
Expected excess return	8.0%	10.0%
Standard deviation	9.80%	13.56%
Sharpe ratio	0.8165	0.7372

The Sharpe ratio does not respect even weak stochastic dominance, and the example given above can be extended to other RAPMs derived in the CAPM framework. For this reason they are not good metrics to use as a basis for decisions about uncertain investments.

I.6.5.3 Adjusting the Sharpe Ratio for Autocorrelation

The risk and return in an RAPM are forecast ex ante using a model for the risk and the expected return. Often both risk and return are forecast using the same model. They may also be estimated ex post using some historical data on returns, although ex post RAPM estimates are only useful in so far as investors may believe that historical information can tell us something about the future behaviour of financial assets.

An ex post estimate of the Sharpe ratio may be taken as

$$\hat{\lambda} = \frac{\overline{R}}{s}, \qquad (I.6.61)$$

where $\overline{R}$ is the sample mean and s is the sample standard deviation of the excess returns. And ex post estimates of the Treynor and information ratios may be given by

$$TR = \frac{\hat{\alpha}}{\hat{\beta}} \quad \text{and} \quad IR = \frac{\hat{\alpha}}{s}, \qquad (I.6.62)$$

where $\hat{\alpha}$ is the abnormal return, $\hat{\beta}$ is the systematic risk of the asset or portfolio that is estimated from the CAPM regression and s is the sample estimate of the specific risk of the asset or portfolio in this model.

The sample estimates are often based on monthly, weekly or daily data, but all quantities in (I.6.61) and (I.6.62) are usually quoted in annualized terms. Annualization is often performed on the sample estimates under the assumption that the returns are i.i.d. For instance, if the RAPM estimate is based on monthly data the mean monthly return would be multiplied by 12 and the standard deviation of the monthly return would be multiplied by $\sqrt{12}$ before applying the formulae above.

However, if portfolio returns are autocorrelated the standard deviation does not obey the square-root-of-time rule. If h denotes the number of returns per year the annualized mean (excess) return is still h times the mean return, but the standard deviation of the (excess) returns should be calculated using the scaling factor [27]

$$\sqrt{h + 2\frac{\varrho}{(1-\varrho)^2}\left[(h-1)(1-\varrho) - \varrho(1-\varrho^{h-1})\right]}, \qquad (I.6.63)$$

---

[27] We derive this adjustment to the annualization factor for a standard deviation based on the assumption that returns follow an autoregressive process of order 1. See Section II.3.2.4.

where ϱ is the first order autocorrelation of the (excess) returns. If the autocorrelation in excess returns is positive then (I.6.63) is greater than the square root of h, so the denominator in the Sharpe ratio will increase and the Sharpe ratio will be reduced. Conversely, if the autocorrelation is negative the Sharpe ratio will increase.

EXAMPLE I.6.12: ADJUSTING A SHARPE RATIO FOR AUTOCORRELATION

Ex post estimates of the mean and standard deviation of the excess returns on a portfolio, based on a historical sample of daily data, are 0.05% and 0.75%, respectively. Estimate the Sharpe ratio under the assumption that the daily excess returns are i.i.d. and that there are 250 trading days per year. Now suppose that daily returns have an autocorrelation of 0.2. What is the adjusted Sharpe ratio that accounts for this autocorrelation?

SOLUTION   We have the ordinary Sharpe ratio,

$$SR = \frac{0.05\% \times 250}{0.75\% \times \sqrt{250}} = \frac{12.5\%}{11.86\%} = 1.0541.$$

But calculating the adjustment (I.6.63) to account for a positive autocorrelation of 0.2 in the spreadsheet gives an annualizing factor of 19.35 instead of $\sqrt{250} = 15.81$ for the standard deviation. This gives an *autocorrelation adjusted Sharpe ratio*,

$$ASR_1 = \frac{0.05\% \times 250}{0.75\% \times 19.35} = \frac{12.5\%}{14.51\%} = 0.8612.$$

Clearly the adjustment to a Sharpe ratio for autocorrelation can be very significant. Hedge funds, for instance, tend to smooth their reported returns and in so doing can induce a strong positive autocorrelation in them. Taking this positive autocorrelation into account will have the effect of reducing the Sharpe ratio that is estimated from reported returns.

I.6.5.4 Adjusting the Sharpe Ratio for Higher Moments

The use of the Sharpe ratio is limited to investments where returns are normally distributed and investors have a minimal type of risk aversion to variance alone, as if their utility function is exponential. Extensions of the Sharpe ratio have successfully widened its application to non-normally distributed returns but its extension to different types of utility function is more problematic.

Another adjustment to the Sharpe ratio assumes investors are averse not only to a high volatility but also to negative skewness and to positive excess kurtosis. It is estimated as[28]

$$ASR_2 = \hat{\lambda} + \left(\frac{\hat{\tau}}{6}\right)\hat{\lambda}^2 - \left(\frac{\hat{\varkappa}}{24}\right)\hat{\lambda}^3, \tag{I.6.64}$$

where $\hat{\lambda}$ is the estimate of the ordinary Sharpe ratio, or of the Sharpe ratio that has been adjusted for autocorrelation as described above, and $\hat{\tau}$ and $\hat{\varkappa}$ are the estimated skewness and excess kurtosis of the returns. The adjustment will tend to lower the Sharpe ratio if there is negative skewness and positive excess kurtosis in the returns, which is often the case.

---

[28] The factors 1/6 and 1/24 are related to the coefficients in the Taylor series expansion (I.6.23). Pézier (2008a) derives this formula as an approximation to the generalized Sharpe ratio described in the next section.

EXAMPLE I.6.13: ADJUSTED SHARPE RATIO

The monthly returns and excess returns on an actively managed fund and its benchmark are given in Table I.6.6. Calculate the Sharpe ratios of both the fund and the benchmark and the adjustments for autocorrelation and higher moments described above.

Table I.6.6 Returns on an actively managed fund and its benchmark

Month	Return	Excess return	Benchmark return	Benchmark excess return
Jan-03	11.59%	11.29%	10.19%	9.84%
Feb-03	3.49%	3.14%	3.52%	3.17%
Mar-03	−14.76%	−15.11%	−13.76%	−14.11%
Apr-03	−2.88%	−3.23%	−3.26%	−3.61%
May-03	3.11%	2.73%	2.96%	2.59%
Jun-03	−4.61%	−4.98%	−2.95%	−3.32%
Jul-03	3.04%	2.66%	2.23%	1.85%
Aug-03	9.51%	9.13%	10.98%	10.60%
Sep-03	−3.15%	−3.52%	−2.56%	−2.94%
Oct-03	1.69%	1.29%	1.51%	1.11%
Nov-03	0.69%	0.29%	−0.60%	−1.00%
Dec-03	−1.87%	−2.27%	−2.34%	−2.74%
Jan-04	2.01%	1.61%	0.11%	−0.29%
Feb-04	2.72%	2.32%	2.84%	2.44%
Mar-04	−0.87%	−1.27%	−0.39%	−0.79%
Apr-04	4.71%	4.31%	4.39%	3.99%
May-04	1.22%	0.82%	0.16%	−0.24%
Jun-04	−3.78%	−4.18%	−4.26%	−4.66%
Jul-04	2.55%	2.15%	2.56%	2.16%
Aug-04	2.65%	2.22%	2.33%	1.91%
Sep-04	0.86%	0.43%	−0.43%	−0.85%
Oct-04	1.87%	1.44%	2.86%	2.44%
Nov-04	2.99%	2.56%	3.73%	3.30%
Dec-04	−5.79%	−6.21%	−5.76%	−6.18%
Jan-05	−0.72%	−1.12%	2.30%	1.90%
Feb-05	1.66%	1.26%	2.34%	1.94%
Mar-05	4.06%	3.66%	1.97%	1.57%
Apr-05	1.56%	1.16%	2.50%	2.10%
May-05	−3.82%	−4.22%	−3.34%	−3.74%
Jun-05	12.47%	12.02%	11.35%	10.90%
Jul-05	−4.82%	−5.27%	−4.56%	−5.01%
Aug-05	−3.63%	−4.08%	−2.89%	−3.34%
Sep-05	3.60%	3.15%	4.06%	3.61%
Oct-05	−1.81%	−2.26%	−1.36%	−1.81%
Nov-05	7.63%	7.18%	5.09%	4.64%
Dec-05	−3.97%	−4.42%	−4.36%	−4.81%

SOLUTION   Table I.6.7 summarizes the first four moments of the returns and their autocorrelations. The mean and standard deviation are quoted in annual terms and the annual volatility is calculated with and without the adjustment (I.6.63) for autocorrelation, in which $h = 12$ since the returns are monthly.

Table I.6.7   Statistics on excess returns

	Fund	Benchmark
Annual mean	4.89%	4.21%
Volatility (under i.i.d. assumption)	17.82%	16.76%
Skewness	−0.200	−0.176
Excess kurtosis	1.808	1.754
Autocorrelation	−0.220	−0.218
Volatility (autocorrelation adjusted)	14.53%	13.64%

Now we compute the ordinary Sharpe ratio and its two adjustments based on (I.6.63) and (I.6.64). The results are shown in Table I.6.8. There is a significant *negative* autocorrelation in the excess returns on the fund and on the benchmark. Adjusting for this autocorrelation leads to a large increase in the Sharpe ratio, so ASR_1 is greater than the ordinary SR.

Table I.6.8   Sharpe ratios and adjusted Sharpe ratios

	Fund	Benchmark
SR	0.2747	0.2510
ASR_1	0.3367	0.3083
ASR_2	0.3300	0.3034

Both the fund and the benchmark excess returns have negative skew and positive excess kurtosis. There are large downward jumps in price that are more frequent than upward jumps of the same magnitude, and both upward and downward jumps are more frequent than would be the case if the returns were normally distributed. Now we make a further adjustment to ASR_1. ASR_2 adjusts this ratio for aversion to negative skew and/or positive excess kurtosis, and since the fund and the benchmark exhibit both of these, ASR_2 is lower than ASR_1. However, in this example the most significant adjustment to the Sharpe ratios stems from the autocorrelation in excess returns.

I.6.5.5   Generalized Sharpe Ratio

Another extension of the Sharpe ratio to the case where returns are not normally distributed is the *generalized Sharpe ratio* introduced by Hodges (1997). This assumes investors have an exponential utility function and that they are able to find the maximum utility that can be associated with *any* portfolio.

Suppose only a small proportion of wealth is invested in a portfolio P that has a positive expected return and risk. Because P has positive expected return, the investor's utility is likely to be greater if he increased his proportion of wealth invested in P by a small amount. In fact, he may go on increasing his utility by investing a little more of his wealth in P until it becomes too risky to concentrate so much wealth in P. At this point increasing the investment in P would only serve to decrease his utility.

The utility gained at that point defines the maximum expected utility, EU^*, and we use this to define the generalized Sharpe ratio of the portfolio as

$$GSR = (-2\ln(-EU^*))^{1/2}. \tag{I.6.65}$$

Although this performance measure has nice properties it is more difficult to calculate than others, as it requires computation of the maximum expected utility. The exception is when the investor has an exponential utility function, since here we may use the fourth order Taylor approximation of the certain equivalent given in Section I.6.2.7 to approximate (I.6.65).

The mean μ, standard deviation σ, skewness τ and excess kurtosis $\varkappa$ correspond to the returns when there is a unit amount invested on the portfolio. Now suppose we increase the amount invested by a multiplicative factor $q > 1$. Then, using the approximation (I.6.23) to the certainty equivalent, we can express this approximately as a quartic function of q, i.e.

$$CE(q) \approx q\mu - \frac{1}{2}\gamma\sigma^2 q^2 + \frac{1}{6}\tau\gamma^2\sigma^3 q^3 - \frac{1}{24}\varkappa\gamma^3\sigma^4 q^4. \tag{I.6.66}$$

This can be maximized over q using the Excel Solver, and then we set the maximum CE equal to the maximum expected utility in (I.6.65) to find the generalized Sharpe ratio.

Pézier (2008a) approximates the value of q that maximizes (I.6.66) as

$$q* \approx \frac{\mu}{\gamma\sigma^2},$$

and shows for this choice of q that the maximum expected utility for the exponential investor is

$$EU^* \approx -\exp\left(-\frac{1}{2}\left(\frac{\mu}{\sigma}\right)^2 - \frac{1}{6}\tau\left(\frac{\mu}{\sigma}\right)^3 + \frac{1}{24}\varkappa\left(\frac{\mu}{\sigma}\right)^4\right). \tag{I.6.67}$$

But $\mu/\sigma = \lambda$, the ordinary Sharpe ratio. Hence,

$$-2\ln(-EU^*) \approx \lambda^2 + \frac{1}{3}\tau\lambda^3 - \frac{1}{12}\varkappa\lambda^4. \tag{I.6.68}$$

Note the generalized Sharpe ratio corresponding to the exponential utility is the square root of (I.6.68), i.e. for an exponential utility

$$GSR \approx \left(\lambda^2 + \frac{1}{3}\tau\lambda^3 - \frac{1}{12}\varkappa\lambda^4\right)^{1/2}. \tag{I.6.69}$$

Thus, when the utility function is exponential *and* the returns are normally distributed the generalized Sharpe ratio is identical to the ordinary Sharpe ratio. Otherwise a negative skewness and high positive kurtosis will have the effect of reducing the *GSR* relative to the ordinary *SR*.

EXAMPLE I.6.14: COMPUTING A GENERALIZED SHARPE RATIO

Assuming the investor has an exponential utility function, approximate the generalized Sharpe ratio for the fund and the benchmark of Example I.6.13.

SOLUTION   Continuing the previous example, the spreadsheet computes (I.6.69) with the annual mean, volatility, skewness and kurtosis given in Table I.6.7. The GSR for the fund is 0.3883 and for the benchmark it is 0.3560. Note that these are almost exactly the same as the results in Table I.6.8 for the Sharpe ratio adjusted for skewness and excess kurtosis. Indeed, Pézier (2008a) shows that (I.6.69) is approximately equal to (I.6.64).

I.6.5.6   Kappa Indices, Omega and Sortino Ratio

Kaplan and Knowles (2004) introduced a general form of RAPM that has lower partial moments in the denominator. These are the so-called *kappa indices*. The kappa index of order α is given by

$$K_\alpha(\tau) = \frac{(E(R) - \tau)}{LPM_{\alpha,\tau}(R)^{1/\alpha}} \tag{I.6.70}$$

where τ is some *threshold* return, $\alpha > 0$ but it need not be an integer, and $LPM_{\alpha,\tau}(R)$ is the *lower partial moment* defined by

$$LPM_{\alpha,\tau}(X) = E\left(|\min(0, X - \tau)|^{\alpha}\right)^{1/\alpha} = E\left(\max(0, \tau - X)^{\alpha}\right)^{1/\alpha}. \tag{I.6.71}$$

For instance the *first-order kappa index* is the excess return divided by the first order partial moment:

$$LPM_{1,\tau}(X) = E\left(\max(0, \tau - X)\right). \tag{I.6.72}$$

The first order kappa index is related to the *omega statistic* introduced by Keating and Shadwick (2002). Omega is the ratio of the expected return above the threshold to the expected return below the threshold, i.e.

$$\Omega(\tau) = \frac{E\left[\max(R - \tau, 0)\right]}{E\left[\max(\tau - R, 0)\right]}. \tag{I.6.73}$$

Kaplan and Knowles show that:

$$K_1(\tau) = \Omega(\tau) - 1. \tag{I.6.74}$$

The second order Kappa index with threshold equal to the risk free rate of return is also called the *Sortino ratio* and was introduced by Sortino and van der Meer (1991).

All kappa indices increase as the threshold decreases. They are negative when $\tau > E(R)$, zero when $\tau = E(R)$, and positive when $\tau > E(R)$. But how do they increase? Higher order kappa indices are more sensitive to the choice of the threshold. They are also more sensitive to skewness and excess kurtosis because the higher order lower partial moments are more sensitive to extreme returns.

EXAMPLE I.6.15: OMEGA, SORTINO AND KAPPA INDICES

For the fund in Example I.6.13 with threshold equal to (a) the benchmark return and (b) the risk free rate, calculate the kappa indices of order α, for $\alpha = 1, 2, 3, 4$. Hence, find an estimate for the Sortino ratio and for the omega statistic with respect to the two different thresholds.

SOLUTION   With an ex post estimate the same sample of returns should be used to estimate the lower partial moment and the expected return, the latter being the sample mean return $\overline{R}$. When the threshold return is the benchmark we base the calculations of omega and kappa indices on the monthly *active* returns from the fund. When the threshold return is the risk free rate we base the calculations on the monthly *excess* returns. In both cases we annualize the numerator and the denominator of the kappa statistic, to present results in annual terms. These are calculated in the spreadsheet and summarized in Table I.6.9.

Table I.6.9   Kappa indices

Kappa index	Threshold return	
	Benchmark	Risk free
K_1	0.1186	0.2362
K_2	0.2194	0.4102
K_3	0.2392	0.4318
K_4	0.2369	0.4175

The Sortino ratio is 0.4102, i.e. the second order kappa index relative to the risk free return. The omega statistic is found by adding 1 to the first order kappa index value, i.e. 1.1186 relative to the benchmark and 1.2362 relative to the risk free rate. The kappa indices of order 2 and order 3 are higher than those of order 1 due to the negative skewness and positive excess kurtosis in the returns.

Currently there is much debate among fund managers and academics about the appropriate choice of kappa index and threshold. Which kappa index should we use to rank portfolios? We cannot answer this question by linking the kappa index to a standard utility function. Any utility associated with a kappa index will be a strange type of utility, because it can be anything at all for 'upside' returns that are above the threshold. In other words, it must be assumed that the investor could not care less about gains made above a certain threshold.

All we can say about the utility associated with a kappa index is that as the investor becomes more risk averse he starts caring more about the skewness and excess kurtosis of downside returns. Thus very risk averse investors could rank portfolios using a high order kappa index ($\alpha = 3$ or 4), and investors who are less risk averse could rank portfolios using lower order kappa indices. How to choose the threshold remains an open question. Some might argue that there is a theoretical advantage to setting the threshold as the risk free rate. Others argue that since the investor must be indifferent to returns above the threshold, the threshold should be very high and certainly much higher than the risk free rate. Some even make an *ad hoc* choice of threshold which may not be the same in the numerator and the denominator of (I.6.70).

I.6.6 SUMMARY AND CONCLUSIONS

The first major aim of portfolio theory is to model the behaviour of investors and, in particular, the portfolios that they hold under certain assumptions about their *preferences*. The second major aim is to derive the prices of financial assets under certain assumptions about their returns distributions and the behaviour of investors. Portfolio theory is built on the concept of a *utility function* that was introduced by Von Neumann and Morgenstern in 1947. Then, in the 1950s Harry Markowitz introduced a simple framework to model the trade-off between risk and return, and this framework has allowed us to investigate the way that investors allocate funds to risky assets under certain idealized assumptions. Still, the Markowitz theory said nothing about how the prices of assets would be formed in an *equilibrium market*. It was not until the 1960s that Treynor, Sharpe and Lintner independently sowed the seeds for the modern theory of asset pricing.

We began the chapter with a concise introduction to utility theory and an understanding of the properties of utility functions. A *utility function* embodies the preferences of an investor concerning the risky assets that are available in his investment universe. By choosing an appropriate utility function we can represent an investor who is risk loving, risk neutral or risk averse. In the theory of asset pricing, as opposed to option pricing, it is standard to assume that an investor is risk averse, and in this case there is a simple method to assess his coefficient of absolute risk aversion and his coefficient of relative risk aversion. In fact we find it easier to assess the *coefficient of risk tolerance*, which is the reciprocal of the *coefficient of risk aversion*, since the former is easy to interpret as the maximum the investor is willing to bet on a 'double-or-half' gamble, with equally likely outcomes.

The *exponential utility function* is particularly tractable to work with. An investor with an exponential utility can form optimal portfolios by maximizing a mean–variance criterion, since this is equivalent to maximizing his expected utility of an investment. The exponential utility also allows the mean–variance criterion to be extended to higher moments where investors have aversion to negative skewness and positive excess kurtosis as well as the variance of portfolio returns.

The next part of the chapter opened with the *portfolio optimization* problem, of minimizing portfolio risk subject to possible constraints on portfolio weights and/or on target returns. This led to the classical *portfolio allocation* problem, i.e. how a rational investor should allocate his funds between the different risky assets in his universe and how much borrowing (or lending) at the risk free rate of return he should do to leverage his returns. We have explained what is meant by an *efficient portfolio* and have introduced the concept of a *market portfolio*, which all investors prefer as the optimal bundle of risky assets. The market portfolio weights are determined by the *market capitalization* of each asset. It is this theory that led to the introduction of capitalization weighted broad market equity indices, such as the Standard & Poor's indices in the US.

Finally, we provided an overview of the classical theories of asset pricing and portfolio selection. The *capital asset pricing model* that was introduced in the 1960s provided the first theory of the formation of asset prices in market equilibrium. Under this theory, assuming we know the returns on the market portfolio and the risk free asset, we can deduce the equilibrium expected return on the asset by using an estimate of its systematic risk.

Most fund managers admit there is a possibility for deviations from the market equilibrium. That is, they expect that some assets have *abnormal returns*. The skill of a fund manager relies on accurate forecasts of the expected returns and systematic risk on all risky assets, and on the market portfolio. These forecasts are made in the context of the capital asset pricing model (or its extension to a multi-factor, time varying or higher moment asset pricing model) and they provide the fund manager with a solution to the portfolio selection problem. That is, conditional on the returns on the market portfolio and the risk free asset, and given forecasts of the systematic risks of risky assets, the fund manager can identify those assets that present promising investment opportunities.

The problem is that too many assets seem to provide promising investment opportunities. Investors need some way to rank possible portfolios in order of preference. The utility function of an investor always endows him with a preference order but, whilst the standard *risk adjusted performance measures* do indeed provide a ranking of different investment opportunities, they usually say nothing at all about preferences! Thus fund managers should not use risk adjusted performance measures to recommend allocations to investors.

The classical risk adjusted performance measure is the *Sharpe ratio*. This measure is only appropriate under restrictive assumptions about portfolio returns characteristics and the investor's preferences. However, the Sharpe ratio has a number of simple and approximate extensions: for instance, to accommodate autocorrelation, skewness and positive excess kurtosis in portfolio returns. Other classical risk adjusted performance measures include *Jensen's alpha*, the *information ratio* and the *Traynor ratio*. These are very difficult to measure, being dependent on the specification and estimation of a multi-factor regression model, and very different results are obtained from different multi-factor models of portfolio returns. Moreover, it is difficult to find any utility function that provides a foundation for the use of the Treynor ratio or Jensen's alpha.

Other types of performance measures have recently become popular. The kappa indices are downside risk adjusted performance measures. The *kappa index* of order 2 goes by the more popular name of the *Sortino ratio* and the kappa index of order 1 is related to the *omega statistic*, which is the ratio of the expected return above some threshold to the expected return below this threshold. The omega statistic is simply a transformation of the portfolio's return distribution. So it does not contain any more information than the distribution itself. But of course, this is true for all risk adjusted performance measures.

Many risk adjusted performance measures that are commonly used today are either not linked to a utility function at all, or if they are associated with a utility function we assume the investor cares nothing at all about the gains he makes above a certain threshold. Kappa indices can be loosely tailored to the degree of risk aversion of the investor, but otherwise the rankings produced by the risk adjusted performance measure may not be ranking in the order of an investor's preference! The only universal risk adjusted performance metric, i.e. one that can rank investments having any returns distributions for investors having any type of utility function, is the *certain equivalent*. The certain equivalent of an uncertain investment is the amount of money, received for certain, that gives the same utility to the investor as the uncertain investment.

References

Adjaouté, K. and Danthine, J.P. (2004) Equity returns and integration: Is Europe changing? *Oxford Review of Economic Policy* 20, 555–570.

Alexander, C. (2001) *Market Models: A Guide to Financial Data Analysis*. John Wiley & Sons, Ltd, Chichester.

Alexander, C. and Barbosa, A. (2007) Effectiveness of minimum variance hedging. *Journal of Portfolio Management* 33, 46–59.

Alexander, C. and Dimitriu, A. (2005) Rank alpha funds of hedge funds. *Journal of Alternative Investments* 8, 48–61.

Alexander, C. and Kaeck, A. (2008) Regime dependent determinants of credit default swap spreads. *Journal of Banking and Finance* 32. In press. http://dx.doi.org/10.1016/j.jbankfin.2007.08.002.

Baele, L., Ferrando, A., Hördahl, P., Krylova, E. and Monnet, C. (2004) Measuring European financial integration. *Oxford Review of Economic Policy* 20, 509–530.

Berben, R.P. and Jansen, W.J. (2005) Comovement in international equity markets: A sectoral view. *Journal of International Money and Finance* 24, 832–857.

Bernoulli, D. (1738) Specimen theoria novae de mensura sortis. *Commentarii Academiae Scientarum Imperialis Petropolitnae* 5(2), 175–192. Translated into English by L. Sommer (1954): Exposition of a new theory on the measurement of risk, *Econometrica*, 22, 23–26.

Biais, B.R., Glosten, L. and Spatt, C. (2005) Market microstructure: A survey of micro-foundations, empirical results, and policy implications. *Journal of Financial Markets* 8, 217–264.

Bilmes, J.A. (1998) A gentle tutorial of the EM algorithm and its application to parameter estimation for Gaussian mixture and hidden Markov models. http://crow.ee.washington.edu/people/bulyko/papers/em.pdf (accessed October 2007).

Black, F. and Scholes, M. (1973) The pricing of options and corporate liabilities. *Journal of Political Economy* 81, 637–654.

Bollerslev, T., Engle, R. and Wooldridge, J. (1988) A capital asset pricing model with time-varying covariances. *Journal of Political Economy* 96, 116–131.

Campbell, J.Y., Lo, A.W. and Mackinley, A.C. (1997) *The Econometrics of Financial Markets*. Princeton University Press, Princeton, NJ.

Castagna, A. and Mercurio, F. (2007) The vanna-volga method for implied volatilities. *Risk* 20(1), 106–111.

Chen, S., Lee, C. and Shrestha, K. (2003) Futures hedge ratios: A review. *Quarterly Review of Economics and Finance* 43, 433–465.

Cox, J.C., Ross, S.A. and Rubinstein, M. (1979) Option pricing: A simplified approach. *Journal of Financial Economics* 7, 229–263.

Crank, J. and Nicolson, P. (1947) A practical method for numerical evaluation of solutions of partial differential equations of the heat conduction type. *Proceedings of the Cambridge Philosophical Society* 43, 50–64.

Fama, E.F. (1970) Efficient capital markets: A review of theory and empirical work. *Journal of Finance* 25, 383–417

Fang, H. and Lai, T. (1997) Cokurtosis and capital asset pricing. *Financial Review* 32, 293–307.

Goetzmann, W.N., Li, L. and Rouwenhorst, K.G. (2005) Long-term global market correlations. *Journal of Business* 78, 1–38.

Greene, W. (2007) *Econometric Analysis*, 6th edition. Prentice Hall, Upper Saddle River, NJ.

Harvey, C. and Siddique, S. (2000) Conditional skewness in asset pricing tests. *Journal of Finance* 54, 1263–1296.

Heston, S. (1993) A closed-form solution for options with stochastic volatility with applications to bond and currency options. *Review of Financial Studies* 6(2), 327–343.

Hodges, S.D. (1997) A generalisation of the Sharpe ratio and its applications to valuation bounds and risk measures. Financial Options Research Centre Working Paper, University of Warwick.

Jagannathan, R. and Wang, Z. (1996) The conditional CAPM and the cross-section of expected returns. *Journal of Finance* 51, 3–53.

Jarrow, R. and Rudd, A. (1982) Approximate option valuation for arbitrary stochastic processes. *Journal of Financial Economics* 10, 347–369.

Jensen, M., (1969) Risk, the pricing of capital assets, and the evaluation of investment portfolios. *Journal of Business*, 42, 167–247.

Joanes, D.N. and Gill, C.A. (1998) Comparing measures of sample skewness and kurtosis. *The Statistician* 47, 183–189.

Jurczenko, E. and Maillet, B. (2006) *Multi-moment Asset Allocation and Pricing Models*. John Wiley & Sons, Ltd, Chichester.

Kaplan, P. and Knowles, J. (2004) Kappa: A generalised downside-risk performance measure. *Journal of Performance Measurement* 8, 42–54.

Keating, C. and Shadwick, F. (2002) A universal performance measure. *Journal of Performance Measurement*, 6, 59–84.

Kim, S.J., Moshirian, F. and Wu, E. (2005) Dynamic stock market integration driven by the European Monetary Union: An empirical analysis. *Journal of Banking and Finance* 29, 2475–2502.

Kraus, A. and Litzenberger, R. (1976) Skewness preference and the valuation of risky assets. *Journal of Finance* 31, 1085–1100.

Lintner, J. (1965) The valuation of risk assets and the selection of risky investments in stock portfolios and capital budgets. *Review of Economics and Statistics* 47, 13–37.

Lo, A.W. (ed.) (2007) *The International Library of Financial Econometrics*. Edward Elgar, Cheltenham.

Lumsdaine, R.L. and Prasad, E.S. (2003) Identifying the common component of international economic fluctuations: A new approach. *Economic Journal* 113, 101–127.

Maclachlan, D. and Peel, A. (2000). *Finite Mixture Models*. John Wiley & Sons, Inc., New York.

Malevergne, Y. and Sornette, D. (2003) Testing the Gaussian copula hypothesis for financial assets dependences. *Quantitative Finance*, 3, 231–250.

Mandelbrot, B. (1963) The variation of certain speculative prices. *Journal of Business* 36, 394–419.

Markowitz, H. (1959) *Portfolio Selection*. John Wiley & Sons, Inc., New York.

Merton, R. (1973) Theory of rational option pricing. *Bell Journal of Economics and Management Science* 4(1), 141–183.

Merton, R.C. (1974) On the pricing of corporate debt: The risk structure of interest rates. *Journal of Finance* 29, 449–479.

Miller, I. and Miller, M. (1999) *John E. Freund's Mathematical Statistics*, 6th edition. Prentice Hall, New Delhi.

Newey, W.K. and West, K.D. (1987) A simple, positive semi-definite, heteroskedasticity and autocorrelation consistent covariance matrix. *Econometrica* 55, 703–708.

Pézier, J. (2008a) Maximum certain equivalent returns and equivalent performance criteria. ICMA Centre Discussion Papers in Finance.

Pézier, J. (2008b) Risk and risk aversion. In C. Alexander and E. Sheedy (eds), *The Professional Risk Manager's Guide to Finance Theory and Application*. McGraw-Hill, New York.

Phillips, P.C.B. and Xiao, Z. (1998) A primer on unit root testing. *Journal of Economic Surveys* 12, 423–69.

Ross, S. (1976) The arbitrage theory of capital asset pricing. *Journal of Economic Theory* 8, 343–362.

Sharpe, W.F. (1964) Capital asset prices: A theory of market equilibrium under conditions of risk. *Journal of Finance* 19, 425–442.

Sortino, F. and Van Der Meer, R. (1991) Downside risk. *Journal of Portfolio Management* 17, 27–31.

Stephens, M.A. (1976) Asymptotic results for goodness-of-fit statistics with unknown parameters. *Annals of Statistics* 4, 357–369.

Teall, J.L. and Hasan, I. (2002) *Quantitative Methods for Finance and Investments*. Blackwell, Oxford.

Tobin, J. (1958) Liquidity preferences as behaviour towards risk. *Review of Economic Studies* 25, 65–86.

Treynor, J. (1965) How to rate management of investment funds. *Harvard Business Review* 43, 63–75.

Vidyamurthy, G. (2004) *Pairs Trading: Quantitative Methods and Analysis*. John Wiley & Sons, Ltd, Chichester.

Von Neumann, J. and Morgenstern, O. (1947) *The Theory of Games and Economic Behaviour*. Princeton University Press, Princeton, NJ.

Watsham, T. and Parramore, K. (1996) *Quantitative Methods in Finance*. Thomson Learning, London.

Wessa, P. (2006) Kernel Density Estimation (V1.0.3) in Free Statistics Software (V1.1.21). Office For Research Development and Education. http://www.wessa.net/rwasp_density.wasp/ (accessed December 2007).

White, H. (1980) A heteroscedasticity consistent covariance matrix estimator and a direct test for heteroscedasticity. *Econometrica* 48, 817–838.

Wilmott, P. (2006). *Paul Wilmott on Quantitative Finance*, 3 volumes. John Wiley & Sons, Ltd, Chichester.

Wilmott, P. (2007). *Paul Wilmott Introduces Quantitative Finance*. John Wiley & Sons, Ltd, Chichester.

Statistical Tables

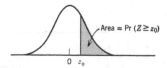

1 Standard Normal, Cumulative Probability in Right-Hand Tail
(For Negative Values of z, Areas are Found by Symmetry)

z_0	NEXT DECIMAL PLACE OF z_0									
	0	1	2	3	4	5	6	7	8	9
0.0	.500	.496	.492	.488	.484	.480	.476	.472	.468	.464
0.1	.460	.456	.452	.448	.444	.440	.436	.433	.429	.425
0.2	.421	.417	.413	.409	.405	.401	.397	.394	.390	.386
0.3	.382	.378	.374	.371	.367	.363	.359	.356	.352	.348
0.4	.345	.341	.337	.334	.330	.326	.323	.319	.316	.312
0.5	.309	.305	.302	.298	.295	.291	.288	.284	.281	.278
0.6	.274	.271	.268	.264	.261	.258	.255	.251	.248	.245
0.7	.242	.239	.236	.233	.230	.227	.224	.221	.218	.215
0.8	.212	.209	.206	.203	.200	.198	.195	.192	.189	.187
0.9	.184	.181	.179	.176	.174	.171	.169	.166	.164	.161
1.0	.159	.156	.154	.152	.149	.147	.145	.142	.140	.138
1.1	.136	.133	.131	.129	.127	.125	.123	.121	.119	.117
1.2	.115	.113	.111	.109	.107	.106	.104	.102	.100	.099
1.3	.097	.095	.093	.092	.090	.089	.087	.085	.084	.082
1.4	.081	.079	.078	.076	.075	.074	.072	.071	.069	.068
1.5	.067	.066	.064	.063	.062	.061	.059	.058	.057	.056
1.6	.055	.054	.053	.052	.051	.049	.048	.047	.046	.046
1.7	.045	.044	.043	.042	.041	.040	.039	.038	.038	.037
1.8	.036	.035	.034	.034	.033	.032	.031	.031	.030	.029
1.9	.029	.028	.027	.027	.026	.026	.025	.024	.024	.023
2.0	.023	.022	.022	.021	.021	.020	.020	.019	.019	.018
2.1	.018	.017	.017	.017	.016	.016	.015	.015	.015	.014
2.2	.014	.014	.013	.013	.013	.012	.012	.012	.011	.011
2.3	.011	.010	.010	.010	.010	.009	.009	.009	.009	.008
2.4	.008	.008	.008	.008	.007	.007	.007	.007	.007	.006
2.5	.006	.006	.006	.006	.006	.005	.005	.005	.005	.005
2.6	.005	.005	.004	.004	.004	.004	.004	.004	.004	.004
2.7	.003	.003	.003	.003	.003	.003	.003	.003	.003	.003
2.8	.003	.002	.002	.002	.002	.002	.002	.002	.002	.002
2.9	.002	.002	.002	.002	.002	.002	.002	.001	.001	.001

z_0	DETAIL OF TAIL ($._2135$, FOR EXAMPLE, MEANS .00135)									
2.	$._2228$	$._1179$	$._1139$	$._1107$	$._2820$	$._2621$	$._2466$	$._2347$	$._2256$	$._2187$
3.	$._2135$	$._3968$	$._3687$	$._3483$	$._3337$	$._3233$	$._3159$	$._3108$	$._4723$	$._4481$
4.	$._4317$	$._4207$	$._4133$	$._5854$	$._5541$	$._5340$	$._5211$	$._5130$	$._6793$	$._6479$
5.	$._6287$	$._6170$	$._7996$	$._7579$	$._7333$	$._7190$	$._7107$	$._8599$	$._8332$	$._8182$
	0	1	2	3	4	5	6	7	8	9

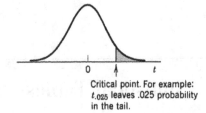

Critical point. For example:
$t_{.025}$ leaves .025 probability
in the tail.

2 t Critical Points

d.f.	$t_{.25}$	$t_{.10}$	$t_{.05}$	$t_{.025}$	$t_{.010}$	$t_{.005}$	$t_{.0025}$	$t_{.0010}$	$t_{.0005}$
1	1.00	3.08	6.31	12.7	31.8	63.7	127	318	637
2	.82	1.89	2.92	4.30	6.96	9.92	14.1	22.3	31.6
3	.76	1.64	2.35	3.18	4.54	5.84	7.45	10.2	12.9
4	.74	1.53	2.13	2.78	3.75	4.60	5.60	7.17	8.61
5	.73	1.48	2.02	2.57	3.36	4.03	4.77	5.89	6.87
6	.72	1.44	1.94	2.45	3.14	3.71	4.32	5.21	5.96
7	.71	1.41	1.89	2.36	3.00	3.50	4.03	4.79	5.41
8	.71	1.40	1.86	2.31	2.90	3.36	3.83	4.50	5.04
9	.70	1.38	1.83	2.26	2.82	3.25	3.69	4.30	4.78
10	.70	1.37	1.81	2.23	2.76	3.17	3.58	4.14	4.59
11	.70	1.36	1.80	2.20	2.72	3.11	3.50	4.02	4.44
12	.70	1.36	1.78	2.18	2.68	3.05	3.43	3.93	4.32
13	.69	1.35	1.77	2.16	2.65	3.01	3.37	3.85	4.22
14	.69	1.35	1.76	2.14	2.62	2.98	3.33	3.79	4.14
15	.69	1.34	1.75	2.13	2.60	2.95	3.29	3.73	4.07
16	.69	1.34	1.75	2.12	2.58	2.92	3.25	3.69	4.01
17	.69	1.33	1.74	2.11	2.57	2.90	3.22	3.65	3.97
18	.69	1.33	1.73	2.10	2.55	2.88	3.20	3.61	3.92
19	.69	1.33	1.73	2.09	2.54	2.86	3.17	3.58	3.88
20	.69	1.33	1.72	2.09	2.53	2.85	3.15	3.55	3.85
21	.69	1.32	1.72	2.08	2.52	2.83	3.14	3.53	3.82
22	.69	1.32	1.72	2.07	2.51	2.82	3.12	3.50	3.79
23	.69	1.32	1.71	2.07	2.50	2.81	3.10	3.48	3.77
24	.68	1.32	1.71	2.06	2.49	2.80	3.09	3.47	3.75
25	.68	1.32	1.71	2.06	2.49	2.79	3.08	3.45	3.73
26	.68	1.31	1.71	2.06	2.48	2.78	3.07	3.43	3.71
27	.68	1.31	1.70	2.05	2.47	2.77	3.06	3.42	3.69
28	.68	1.31	1.70	2.05	2.47	2.76	3.05	3.41	3.67
29	.68	1.31	1.70	2.05	2.46	2.76	3.04	3.40	3.66
30	.68	1.31	1.70	2.04	2.46	2.75	3.03	3.39	3.65
40	.68	1.30	1.68	2.02	2.42	2.70	2.97	3.31	3.55
60	.68	1.30	1.67	2.00	2.39	2.66	2.92	3.23	3.46
120	.68	1.29	1.66	1.98	2.36	2.62	2.86	3.16	3.37
∞	.67	1.28	1.64	1.96	2.33	2.58	2.81	3.09	3.29
	$= z_{.25}$	$= z_{.10}$	$= z_{.05}$	$= z_{.025}$	$= z_{.010}$	$= z_{.005}$	$= z_{.0025}$	$= z_{.0010}$	$= z_{.0005}$

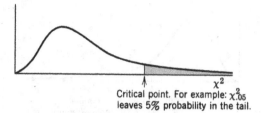

Critical point. For example: $\chi^2_{.05}$
leaves 5% probability in the tail.

3 χ^2 Critical Points

d.f.	$\chi^2_{.25}$	$\chi^2_{.10}$	$\chi^2_{.05}$	$\chi^2_{.025}$	$\chi^2_{.010}$	$\chi^2_{.005}$	$\chi^2_{.001}$
1	1.32	2.71	3.84	5.02	6.63	7.88	10.8
2	2.77	4.61	5.99	7.38	9.21	10.6	13.8
3	4.11	6.25	7.81	9.35	11.3	12.8	16.3
4	5.39	7.78	9.49	11.1	13.3	14.9	18.5
5	6.63	9.24	11.1	12.8	15.1	16.7	20.5
6	7.84	10.6	12.6	14.4	16.8	18.5	22.5
7	9.04	12.0	14.1	16.0	18.5	20.3	24.3
8	10.2	13.4	15.5	17.5	20.1	22.0	26.1
9	11.4	14.7	16.9	19.0	21.7	23.6	27.9
10	12.5	16.0	18.3	20.5	23.2	25.2	29.6
11	13.7	17.3	19.7	21.9	24.7	26.8	31.3
12	14.8	18.5	21.0	23.3	26.2	28.3	32.9
13	16.0	19.8	22.4	24.7	27.7	29.8	34.5
14	17.1	21.1	23.7	26.1	29.1	31.3	36.1
15	18.2	22.3	25.0	27.5	30.6	32.8	37.7
16	19.4	23.5	26.3	28.8	32.0	34.3	39.3
17	20.5	24.8	27.6	30.2	33.4	35.7	40.8
18	21.6	26.0	28.9	31.5	34.8	37.2	42.3
19	22.7	27.2	30.1	32.9	36.2	38.6	32.8
20	23.8	28.4	31.4	34.2	37.6	40.0	45.3
21	24.9	29.6	32.7	35.5	38.9	41.4	46.8
22	26.0	30.8	33.9	36.8	40.3	42.8	48.3
23	27.1	32.0	35.2	38.1	41.6	44.2	49.7
24	28.2	33.2	36.4	39.4	32.0	45.6	51.2
25	29.3	34.4	37.7	40.6	44.3	46.9	52.6
26	30.4	35.6	38.9	41.9	45.6	48.3	54.1
27	31.5	36.7	40.1	43.2	47.0	49.6	55.5
28	32.6	37.9	41.3	44.5	48.3	51.0	56.9
29	33.7	39.1	42.6	45.7	49.6	52.3	58.3
30	34.8	40.3	43.8	47.0	50.9	53.7	59.7
40	45.6	51.8	55.8	59.3	63.7	66.8	73.4
50	56.3	63.2	67.5	71.4	76.2	79.5	86.7
60	67.0	74.4	79.1	83.3	88.4	92.0	99.6
70	77.6	85.5	90.5	95.0	100	104	112
80	88.1	96.6	102	107	112	116	125
90	98.6	108	113	118	124	128	137
100	109	118	124	130	136	140	149

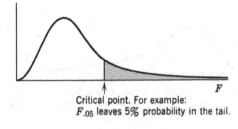

Critical point. For example:
$F_{.05}$ leaves 5% probability in the tail.

4 *F* Critical Points

		DEGREES OF FREEDOM FOR NUMERATOR									
		1	2	3	4	5	6	8	10	20	40	∞
1	$F_{.25}$	5.83	7.50	8.20	8.58	8.82	8.98	9.19	9.32	9.58	9.71	9.85
	$F_{.10}$	39.9	49.5	53.6	55.8	57.2	58.2	59.4	60.2	61.7	62.5	63.3
	$F_{.05}$	161	200	216	225	230	234	239	242	248	251	254
2	$F_{.25}$	2.57	3.00	3.15	3.23	3.28	3.31	3.35	3.38	3.43	3.45	3.48
	$F_{.10}$	8.53	9.00	9.16	9.24	9.29	9.33	9.37	9.39	9.44	9.47	9.49
	$F_{.05}$	18.5	19.0	19.2	19.2	19.3	19.3	19.4	19.4	19.4	19.5	19.5
	$F_{.01}$	98.5	99.0	99.2	99.2	99.3	99.3	99.4	99.4	99.4	99.5	99.5
	$F_{.001}$	998	999	999	999	999	999	999	999	999	999	999
3	$F_{.25}$	2.02	2.28	2.36	2.39	2.41	2.42	2.44	2.44	2.46	2.47	2.47
	$F_{.10}$	5.54	5.46	5.39	5.34	5.31	5.28	5.25	5.23	5.18	5.16	5.13
	$F_{.05}$	10.1	9.55	9.28	9.12	9.10	8.94	8.85	8.79	8.66	8.59	8.53
	$F_{.01}$	34.1	30.8	29.5	28.7	28.2	27.9	27.5	27.2	26.7	26.4	26.1
	$F_{.001}$	167	149	141	137	135	133	131	129	126	125	124
4	$F_{.25}$	1.81	2.00	2.05	2.06	2.07	2.08	2.08	2.08	2.08	2.08	2.08
	$F_{.10}$	4.54	4.32	4.19	4.11	4.05	4.01	3.95	3.92	3.84	3.80	3.76
	$F_{.05}$	7.71	6.94	6.59	6.39	6.26	6.16	6.04	5.96	5.80	5.72	5.63
	$F_{.01}$	21.2	18.0	16.7	16.0	15.5	15.2	14.8	14.5	14.0	13.7	13.5
	$F_{.001}$	74.1	61.3	56.2	53.4	51.7	50.5	49.0	48.1	46.1	45.1	44.1
5	$F_{.25}$	1.69	1.85	1.88	1.89	1.89	1.89	1.89	1.89	1.88	1.88	1.87
	$F_{.10}$	4.06	3.78	3.62	3.52	3.45	3.40	3.34	3.30	3.21	3.16	3.10
	$F_{.05}$	6.61	5.79	5.41	5.19	5.05	4.95	4.82	4.74	4.56	4.46	4.36
	$F_{.01}$	16.3	13.3	12.1	11.4	11.0	10.7	10.3	10.1	9.55	9.29	9.02
	$F_{.001}$	47.2	37.1	33.2	31.1	29.8	28.8	27.6	26.9	25.4	24.6	23.8
6	$F_{.25}$	1.62	1.76	1.78	1.79	1.79	1.78	1.77	1.77	1.76	1.75	1.74
	$F_{.10}$	3.78	3.46	3.29	3.18	3.11	3.05	2.98	2.94	2.84	2.78	2.72
	$F_{.05}$	5.99	5.14	4.76	4.53	4.39	4.28	4.15	4.06	3.87	3.77	3.67
	$F_{.01}$	13.7	10.9	9.78	9.15	8.75	8.47	8.10	7.87	7.40	7.14	6.88
	$F_{.001}$	35.5	27.0	23.7	21.9	20.8	20.0	19.0	18.4	17.1	16.4	15.8
7	$F_{.25}$	1.57	1.70	1.72	1.72	1.71	1.71	1.70	1.69	1.67	1.66	1.65
	$F_{.10}$	3.59	3.26	3.07	2.96	2.88	2.83	2.75	2.70	2.59	2.54	2.47
	$F_{.05}$	5.59	4.74	4.35	4.12	3.97	3.87	3.73	3.64	3.44	3.34	3.23
	$F_{.01}$	12.2	9.55	8.45	7.85	7.46	7.19	6.84	6.62	6.16	5.91	5.65
	$F_{.001}$	29.3	21.7	18.8	17.2	16.2	15.5	14.6	14.1	12.9	12.3	11.7
8	$F_{.25}$	1.54	1.66	1.69	1.66	1.66	1.65	1.64	1.63	1.61	1.59	1.58
	$F_{.10}$	3.46	3.11	2.92	2.81	2.73	2.67	2.59	2.54	2.42	2.36	2.29
	$F_{.05}$	5.32	4.46	4.07	3.84	3.69	3.58	3.44	3.35	3.15	3.04	2.93
	$F_{.01}$	11.3	8.65	7.59	7.01	6.63	6.37	6.03	5.81	5.36	5.12	4.86
	$F_{.001}$	25.4	18.5	15.8	14.4	13.5	12.9	12.0	11.5	10.5	9.92	9.33
9	$F_{.25}$	1.51	1.62	1.63	1.63	1.62	1.61	1.60	1.59	1.56	1.55	1.53
	$F_{.10}$	3.36	3.01	2.81	2.69	2.61	2.55	2.47	2.42	2.30	2.23	2.16

DEGREES OF FREEDOM FOR DENOMINATOR

		DEGREES OF FREEDOM FOR NUMERATOR										
		1	2	3	4	5	6	8	10	20	40	∞
	$F_{.05}$	5.12	4.26	3.86	3.63	3.48	3.37	3.23	3.14	2.94	2.83	2.71
	$F_{.01}$	10.6	8.02	6.99	6.42	6.06	5.80	5.47	5.26	4.81	4.57	4.31
	$F_{.001}$	22.9	16.4	13.9	12.6	11.7	11.1	10.4	9.89	8.90	8.37	7.81
10	$F_{.25}$	1.49	1.60	1.60	1.59	1.59	1.58	1.56	1.55	1.52	1.51	1.48
	$F_{.10}$	3.28	2.92	2.73	2.61	2.52	2.46	2.38	2.32	2.20	2.13	2.06
	$F_{.05}$	4.96	4.10	3.71	3.48	3.33	3.22	3.07	2.98	2.77	2.66	2.54
	$F_{.01}$	10.0	7.56	6.55	5.99	5.64	5.39	5.06	4.85	4.41	4.17	3.91
	$F_{.001}$	21.0	14.9	12.6	11.3	10.5	9.92	9.20	8.75	7.80	7.30	6.76
12	$F_{.25}$	1.56	1.56	1.56	1.55	1.54	1.53	1.51	1.50	1.47	1.45	1.42
	$F_{.10}$	3.18	2.81	2.61	2.48	2.39	2.33	2.24	2.19	2.06	1.99	1.90
	$F_{.05}$	4.75	3.89	3.49	3.26	3.11	3.00	2.85	2.75	2.54	2.43	2.30
	$F_{.01}$	9.33	6.93	5.95	5.41	5.06	4.82	4.50	4.30	3.86	3.62	3.36
	$F_{.001}$	18.6	13.0	10.8	9.63	8.89	8.38	7.71	7.29	6.40	5.93	5.42
14	$F_{.25}$	1.44	1.53	1.53	1.52	1.51	1.50	1.48	1.46	1.43	1.41	1.38
	$F_{.10}$	3.10	2.73	2.52	2.39	2.31	2.24	2.15	2.10	1.96	1.89	1.80
	$F_{.05}$	4.60	3.74	3.34	3.11	2.96	2.85	2.70	2.60	2.39	2.27	2.13
	$F_{.01}$	8.86	5.51	5.56	5.04	4.69	4.46	4.14	3.94	3.51	3.27	3.00
	$F_{.001}$	17.1	11.8	9.73	8.62	7.92	7.43	6.80	6.40	5.56	5.10	4.60
16	$F_{.25}$	1.42	1.51	1.51	1.50	1.48	1.48	1.46	1.45	1.40	1.37	1.34
	$F_{.10}$	3.05	2.67	2.46	2.33	2.24	2.18	2.09	2.03	1.89	1.81	1.72
	$F_{.05}$	4.49	3.63	3.24	3.01	2.85	2.74	2.59	2.49	2.28	2.15	2.01
	$F_{.01}$	8.53	6.23	5.29	4.77	4.44	4.20	3.89	3.69	3.26	3.02	2.75
	$F_{.001}$	16.1	11.0	9.00	7.94	7.27	6.81	6.19	5.81	4.99	4.54	4.06
20	$F_{.25}$	1.40	1.49	1.48	1.46	1.45	1.44	1.42	1.40	1.36	1.33	1.29
	$F_{.10}$	2.97	2.59	2.38	2.25	2.16	2.09	2.00	1.94	1.79	1.71	1.61
	$F_{.05}$	4.35	3.49	3.10	2.87	2.71	2.60	2.45	2.35	2.12	1.99	1.84
	$F_{.01}$	8.10	5.85	4.94	4.43	4.10	3.87	3.56	3.37	2.94	2.69	2.42
	$F_{.001}$	14.8	9.95	8.10	7.10	6.46	6.02	5.44	5.08	4.29	3.86	3.38
30	$F_{.25}$	1.38	1.45	1.44	1.42	1.41	1.39	1.37	1.35	1.30	1.27	1.23
	$F_{.10}$	2.88	2.49	2.28	2.14	2.05	1.98	1.88	1.82	1.67	1.57	1.46
	$F_{.05}$	4.17	3.32	2.92	2.69	2.53	2.42	2.27	2.16	1.93	1.79	1.62
	$F_{.01}$	7.56	5.39	4.51	4.02	3.70	3.47	3.17	2.98	2.55	2.30	2.01
	$F_{.001}$	13.3	8.77	7.05	6.12	5.53	5.12	4.58	4.24	3.49	3.07	2.59
40	$F_{.25}$	1.36	1.44	1.42	1.40	1.39	1.37	1.35	1.33	1.28	1.24	1.19
	$F_{.10}$	2.84	2.44	2.23	2.09	2.00	1.93	1.83	1.76	1.61	1.51	1.38
	$F_{.05}$	4.08	3.23	2.84	2.61	2.45	2.34	2.18	2.08	1.84	1.69	1.51
	$F_{.01}$	7.31	5.18	4.31	3.83	3.51	3.29	2.99	2.80	2.37	2.11	1.80
	$F_{.001}$	12.6	8.25	6.60	5.70	5.13	4.73	4.21	3.87	3.15	2.73	2.23
60	$F_{.25}$	1.35	1.42	1.41	1.38	1.37	1.35	1.32	1.30	1.25	1.21	1.15
	$F_{.10}$	2.79	2.39	2.18	2.04	1.95	1.87	1.77	1.71	1.54	1.44	1.29
	$F_{.05}$	4.00	3.15	2.76	2.53	2.37	2.25	2.10	1.99	1.75	1.59	1.39
	$F_{.01}$	7.08	4.98	4.13	3.65	3.34	3.12	2.82	2.63	2.20	1.94	1.60
	$F_{.001}$	12.0	7.76	6.17	5.31	4.76	4.37	3.87	3.54	2.83	2.41	1.89
120	$F_{.25}$	1.34	1.40	1.39	1.37	1.35	1.33	1.30	1.28	1.22	1.18	1.10
	$F_{.10}$	2.75	2.35	2.13	1.99	1.90	1.82	1.72	1.65	1.48	1.37	1.19
	$F_{.05}$	3.92	3.07	2.68	2.45	2.29	2.17	2.02	1.91	1.66	1.50	1.25
	$F_{.01}$	6.85	4.79	3.95	3.48	3.17	2.96	2.66	2.47	2.03	1.76	1.38
	$F_{.001}$	11.4	7.32	5.79	4.95	4.42	4.04	3.55	3.24	2.53	2.11	1.54
∞	$F_{.25}$	1.32	1.39	1.37	1.35	1.33	1.31	1.28	1.25	1.19	1.14	1.00
	$F_{.10}$	2.71	2.30	2.08	1.94	1.85	1.77	1.67	1.60	1.42	1.30	1.00
	$F_{.05}$	3.84	3.00	2.60	2.37	2.21	2.10	1.94	1.83	1.57	1.39	1.00
	$F_{.01}$	6.63	4.61	3.78	3.32	3.02	2.80	2.51	2.32	1.88	1.59	1.00
	$F_{.001}$	10.8	6.91	5.42	4.62	4.10	3.74	3.27	2.96	2.27	1.84	1.00

DEGREES OF FREEDOM FOR DENOMINATOR

Index